BURNING HORIZON

BURNING HORIZON

British Veteran Accounts of the Iraq War 2003

JULIAN WHIPPY

CASEMATE

Oxford & Philadelphia

Published in Great Britain and the United States of America in 2023 by
CASEMATE PUBLISHERS
The Old Music Hall, 106–108 Cowley Road, Oxford OX4 1JE, UK
and
1950 Lawrence Road, Havertown, PA 19083, USA

Hardback Edition: ISBN 978-1-63624-297-2
Digital Edition: ISBN 978-1-63624-298-9

A CIP record for this book is available from the British Library

Printed and bound in the United Kingdom by CPI Group (UK) Ltd, Croydon, CR0 4YY

Typeset in India by Lapiz Digital Services, Chennai.

For a complete list of Casemate titles, please contact:

CASEMATE PUBLISHERS (UK)
Telephone (0)1226 734350
Email: casemate-uk@casematepublishers.co.uk
www.casematepublishers.co.uk

CASEMATE PUBLISHERS (US)
Telephone (610) 853-9131
Fax (610) 853-9146
Email: casemate@casematepublishers.com
www.casematepublishers.com

The views and opinions expressed are those of the author alone and should not be taken to represent those of His Majesty's Government, MOD, HM Armed Forces or any government agency.

Front cover image by Neil Wraith, Royal Marines; back cover image from Shutterstock.

Contents

Foreword

'The scent, and smoke, and sweat … are nauseating at three in the morning.' So wrote Ian Fleming in the opening sentence of his first novel, *Casino Royale*. Although the setting was an upmarket gambling den, when Fleming bashed out these words on his Triumph typewriter in 1952, he was thinking of the Second World War, which had finished only seven years earlier. He was then Commander Fleming, chief of staff to the Director of Naval Intelligence, and knew a thing or two about all-night stints in military operations rooms. *Casino Royale* was all about Fleming transferring his memories of military risk-taking to the roulette wheel.

What you are about to read here is Julian Whippy's oral history of a more modern military adventure. Study of the Iraq War, which began in 2003, is today clouded with strongly held opinions about the national leadership of the era, and suspicion of true geopolitical agendas. *Burning Horizon* concerns itself only with the March–April invasion phase from a UK military perspective. It also evokes exactly that unglamorous, Fleming-esque atmosphere of stale socks, cigarettes, perspiration, and anxiety, associated with military endeavour.

On a cautionary note, this volume is not about the politics of the decision to invade Iraq, nor about the subsequent occupation. Using lessons from the administration of Germany and Japan in 1945, it had been explained to British military personnel that a Coalition Provisional Authority (CPA) would be established as soon as the invasion phase was over. Its purpose, with the US-led Office for Reconstruction and Humanitarian Assistance (ORHA), was to act as a caretaker administration in Baghdad until a democratically elected government was in place. The CPA/ORHA would employ Iraqis and retrain their institutions, such as the police and the army, to swiftly put the country back on its feet. Thus, those taking part did so in good faith.

The business of donning a military cloak and shouldering a weapon requires a literal and metaphorical contract. The latter involves the state undertaking to pay, clothe, equip, and feed you and see you will come to no harm, and if you do, to mend you for as long as it takes. In return, your country can send you where it wishes, on whatever duties, that it has set out in justification to its people and the wider world. In effect, by serving your country, you are signing a blank cheque, of unlimited service that might result in your death. Those who went to Iraq, or the wider theatre, did so having discussed the matter with their consciences, their families, their commanders, and their mates.

No one foresaw a lingering presence in the region, least of all Her Majesty's Government. Due to the Coalition's failure to re-employ the disbanded local army and police forces, tens of thousands of angry, unemployed young men, guided by outside actors with their own agendas, took to the streets that summer and fomented an insurgency. This is when the bulk of the Coalition casualties incurred in Iraq happened, and is outside the scope of this book. The descent into domestic violence was never preordained, as some have argued, and need not have happened.

Technically, this is the story of Operation *Telic 1*, the invasion of Iraq, conducted during a few weeks of March-April 2003. Unlike the Pentagon outside Washington DC, which labels military deployments to reflect their strategic purposes, the Ministry of Defence in London uses a computer to generate random names which betray no obvious objectives. Thus, the US-named Operation *Iraqi Freedom* was codenamed *Telic* to the British and *Falconer* to the Australians. In jest, the meaningless *Telic* was soon understood as an acronym for Tell Everyone Leave Is Cancelled. As invasion morphed into occupation, the unexpected counterinsurgency that fell on the Coalition ensured there would be thirteen *Telics* in all, lasting from January 2003 until 30 April 2009, with a protracted presence of training missions for two years after that.

With 46,000 personnel deployed in early 2003, the UK-Australian force matched that assembled for Suez in 1956 and neared the 53,000 present in the first Gulf War of 1991. It dwarfed the British contribution in Korea (1950–53) and the Falklands (1982). What we have here, therefore, is an important record of one of the largest military undertakings since the Second World War. Due to its size and influence, it is vital that we have both official and unofficial records of the hopes, fears, and achievements of those who were there.

It was a major feat to position the huge force with their 15,000 vehicles and 9,100 shipping containers in the Gulf within 10 weeks. They were commanded by a three-star UK National Contingent headquarters led by Air Marshal Brian Burridge, with Peter Wall (a future CGS) as his chief of staff. This independent organisation was blistered onto the American Central Command (CENTCOM) base, outside Doha in Qatar. With a light hand on the tiller explaining the historical context, Julian Whippy wisely lets the service personnel speak for themselves. By interweaving their recollections, he provides us with a continuous narrative thread of what life was like, across all the services, in those surreal days of March and April 2003.

Due to the controversial nature of the process of deciding to go to war, and the frustrations felt – some voiced here – by those serving during their deployments, the official UK record of the events of 2003 includes the results of two government investigations: the National Audit Office report of December the same year, and the lengthy *Chilcot Enquiry*, announced in 2009 and published in 2016, as well as several unit-level lessons learned pamphlets, essays and articles. Much is available online, but the official narrative is remarkably sparse. At the 20-year mark there is no official account of the invasion or occupation. As the UK generally discourages its military and civil servants from writing memoirs and profiting from them whilst in receipt of government pay, there are lamentably few British personal accounts in circulation. The Ministry of Defence has retreated into itself to become book-shy. Most of what is available is penned from an American point of view.

Burning Horizon goes a long way to redress this balance, for here we have a spread of voices, spread between the navy, marines, army, and air force. Among them are also some of the 9,500 reservists who deployed on *Telic 1* and in its aftermath. Here I must declare an interest, for I was amongst those mobilised at the beginning of 2003. Within days, I found myself in Qatar, in the Air Marshal's lair, acting as his historian and later moving into the UK divisional operations room at Basra airport. Julian Whippy's assemblage of recollections instantly brought back to me the Ian Fleming-like atmosphere of a headquarters at war. The bird table maps with their unit symbols depicting life-and-death encounters, no longer a wargame. The Star Wars 'blue force tracker' electronic screens showing the real-time positions of Coalition assets. Hollywood-like drone footage of dramatic encounters with the opposition, common these days, but then a novelty.

The author evokes those mad, masked rushes to sandbagged air raid shelters and trenches. To calm his nerves, I recall a corporal teaching himself to juggle, using field dressings. Here we have the frustrations of kit shortages played out alongside Scud alerts, the humour of tumbling out of armoured vehicles ensconced in sleeping bags, and the incredulity of militants arriving by taxi to fire at armoured vehicles and departing in the same manner. By contrast, we read of friends wounded and killed. I vividly remember the stomach-churning impact on us all of the loss in the opening hours of a US-crewed Sea Knight helicopter carrying Royal Marines, followed by an RAF Tornado brought down by a Patriot battery's 'friendly' fire. Colleagues, with whom we had bantered days earlier.

Secure by time and distance, wrapped in our strategists' armchairs, it is easy to forget that the persistence of war is a reality of our history. It is our stubborn companion as we travel forward through the years. Twenty years after the Iraq invasion, *Burning Horizon* reminds us of the cost, not just of waging war, but of keeping personnel and equipment trained and ready. After decades of wars of choice for the West, ongoing Russian aggression in Ukraine reminds us that we do not always have the luxury of opting for combat or peace. For all these reasons, I commend to you Julian Whippy's important tale of ordinary men and women who did extraordinary things when that choice was made in March 2003.

Peter Caddick-Adams
January 2023

Acknowledgements

Strangely enough I can thank the Covid-19 pandemic as the instigator for this book. While it throttled my business of battlefield tours close to death, it kick-started a need for us, as a company, to keep talking to our clients about military history while we could not actually travel together. Hosting Zoom calls on military themes, one day we were asked to present on various amphibious operations through the ages. My business partner, Clive Harris, loves all things Roman and also talks frequently about the Gallipoli campaign, so those were two areas he wanted to cover. I avoided the obvious D-Day landings of 1944 and concentrated on another favourite of mine, Dieppe 1942. I then wanted to find recent operations to bring the Zoom call up to date. I knew the Royal Marines were involved in the second Iraq war in 2003 but when I started to research it, I found very little. There are long shelves full of books and articles about the politics, Tony Blair, Hans Blix and the weapons of mass destruction (WMD) but little about the fighting soldier with their boots on the ground. Having been a battlefield guide for over 20 years I have met a lot of World War 2 veterans and their families. The statement I hear most is 'I wish I had asked my dad what he did in the war, it's too late now.'

Operation *Telic* in 2003 was the largest deployment of British armed forces since 1945. The war in Iraq, although short and often described as unpopular, was a war nevertheless and those that did their duty, some of whom died for their Queen and country, deserve to have their story told and their voices heard. This book is my attempt in a small way to reach out to those veterans and record them for the future before it's too late and another generation has gone taking its stories to the grave.

Much of the content of the book comes from my interviews with over 50 veterans – literally hundreds of hours of audio recordings.

I would like to thank a number of people who have helped with this book. First and foremost a big thank you to all the veterans who helped me with their input. Many of them gave up afternoons or evenings to be interviewed in person, on Zoom calls or on the phone. Most offered up diaries and sketches, maps and photographs, all of which have been gratefully received. This is a book for you all and, as they say, you know who you are. (But they are listed at the back too!)

Friend, former army officer and *Telic* veteran Mike Peters gave me encouragement for the project from day one, constantly fed me snippets and also introduced me to the publishers, Casemate. Mike also provided me with valuable unpublished material on the Army Air Corps (AAC) during the war which has been very useful. The Guild of Battlefield Guides has been a rich vein to tap into as far as *Telic* veterans are concerned, so I thank the guild for its assistance when I have tried to reach out to its membership. My business partner, Clive Harris, has been a great sounding board and always keen to hear me waffle on about Iraq. He also identified some veterans who have given valuable input. Clive was also agreeable to me taking time off from the work of running Battle Honours for which I am grateful.

Dr John Greenacre helped me find some great information on the AAC and introduced me to Bertie Banfield DFC. Ex-Irish Guardsman Frankie Howell, now one of the Captain of Invalids at the Royal Hospital Chelsea, helped me connect with his old regiment and with the Chelsea Pensioners themselves. Captain Nathan Morley at the Tower of London was Regimental Adjutant of the Royal Regiment of Fusiliers (RRF) and proved most helpful and proactive in reaching veterans from that fine regiment.

Many others helped along the way. Gareth Davies gave me advice on all things armour as he sat gazing out of his kitchen window at a passing Challenger on Salisbury Plain. Sappers Rey Fadil and Andy Abbott provided me with fascinating matter about the work of Explosive Ordnance Disposal (EOD) and shared their stories of a most dangerous of worlds. Lt Col Neil Wraith, RM provided lunch in the most glorious of settings at HMS *Drake*, and allowed me use of his maps of Operation *Houghton*. Likewise, Ben Farrell of the Micks opened up his memory and files of maps from Iraq – and I must not forget Bob Giles for showing me 'his bullet' that took half his lung out.

I also would like to express thanks to my great friend, ex-detective Ian Trantum, for his suggestions about interview procedures and the questionnaire process, and the advice from his friend Prof Becky Milne of Portsmouth University also on interview procedures. My friend Peter Caddick-Adams has had a rough year with an unexpected cardiac incident yet still found time to offer words of advice and write the foreword. Thanks, too, to Ruth Sheppard, the publisher at Casemate, for her considered opinions, advice and guidance. Paul Hewitt at Battlefield Design has been helping me with maps for more than 10 years and is a solid reliable designer and illustrator of all things military.

My last and greatest thanks, of course, go to my long-suffering wife, Angie, who has put up with my endless ramblings and total absorption in writing this book. I hope this goes on to explain my vacant days.

PROLOGUE

Kuwait border, March 2003

Thousands of tired eyes stared out into the dark desert night. Clouds of dust and grit were being thrown up by hundreds of vehicles hampering the view of the drivers. At the same time, an almost impenetrable sandstorm swirled across the flat plain depleting situational awareness yet further.

In the rear of the vehicles sat thousands of soldiers. Some were quietly caught up in their own thoughts. Others, lit only by the eerie shielded glow of internal red night lights, swapped stories and talked rubbish to break the tension. Many expected to die soon and, like millions of soldiers throughout history, needed distraction.

At multiple points across many miles, similar convoys faced north. They were all made up of British military vehicles, and they were about to roll into a sovereign country in an invasion codenamed Operation *Telic*.* As well as the ground convoys massed on the Kuwait–Iraq border were air assets circling high above, helicopter squadrons sweeping low overhead and an amphibious task force anchored offshore in the Persian Gulf. Also heading north, tearing across the night sky were dozens of Tomahawk cruise missiles. It was 20 March 2003 and the second Gulf War, the second invasion of Iraq in 12 years, was under way.

Sweltering in the back of his tin box – an FV432 armoured carrier, a vehicle from the 1960s, – Maj John Cotterill acted as watchkeeper on the radio net. With his radio earphones on and the FV432 rear doors closed, he was no longer able to hear the boom of the Royal Artillery firing 155mm shells in salvos towards Iraq, nor could he hear the clattering helicopters of the USMC Cobra gunships as they flew above the British column. As he travelled north through the border from the forward assembly area (FAA), the unforgiving suspension and the rocky nature of the desert made noting down radio messages very difficult. Attached to the Irish Guards, Maj

---

* Op *Telic* was the codename under which all the United Kingdom's military operations in Iraq were conducted between the invasion in 2003 and the final withdrawal in 2011. After the initial invasion phase concluded troops from the UK rotated through Iraq on six-month deployments, still under the banner of Operation *Telic* but with subsequent numberings. For example, *Telic 2* ran from July 2003 to November 2003. The last phase was *Telic 13* in 2009.

Cotterill was in one of the follow-on units in 7 Armoured Brigade trailing behind the Royal Fusiliers, Royal Scots Dragoon Guards (RSDG) and Black Watch.

Cotterill noted that the Fusiliers crossed into Iraq and immediately came under fire from Americans to their west. Fortunately, someone passed a message promptly and put paid to the friendly fire. It was an ominous start to the operation and one which would sadly be repeated at a high price.

To the east of the breach in the border US Navy SEAL Team Three was landing on the Al-Faw peninsula, having inserted via Blackhawk helicopters. Close behind the SEALs, British Royal Marines were also heading via Sea King helicopters to secure the oil-pumping stations that fed waiting tankers in the Persian Gulf. West of the breach, paratroopers from 16 Air Assault Brigade (16 AAB) advanced from Kuwait into the desert west of Basra in a fleet of trucks, as their supporting Lynx helicopters flew screening patrols 80km ahead of them over the Rumaila oilfields.

Far above the armoured column as it slowly moved north, way out of view to the naked eye, an RAF Boeing E-3D Sentry AWACS aircraft orbited the battlefield co-ordinating the vast on-call fast-jet fleet. RAF Flt Lt Andy Johnson was the tactical director aboard the Sentry and was already busy setting up a close air support (CAS) mission for Special Forces on a Scud hunt.

'Hello Bondo, this is Cobra 24. Troops in contact requesting close air support.'

Flt Lt Johnson selected a suitable asset, a pair of US F-16s, and returned the call, 'Cobra 24, this is Bondo. Flesh One Three, F-16s are en route your position over.'

Those few words across the airspace had vectored in two fighter-bombers to help the US ground troops in action.

Back on the desert floor, after 40km hunched over the map table with his earphones on, Maj Cotterill uncurled himself from the rear of his FV432 when it bounced to a stop at Shaiba Air Base near Basra. As soon as the rear door opened, he heard gunfire again. Once the Brigade command post (CP) had been set up – this time surrounded by shell scrapes and defensive trenches – he continued the routine of four hours on each of the two radio nets and four hours off. His sleeping location was less than 100m from a battery of AS-90 155mm Royal Horse Artillery guns which seemed to be firing incessantly, but he was so tired he still went to sleep for his four hours.

When he woke up, he went over to the gunnery team and asked what they were firing at. They replied that the guns were so accurate they could target and hit individual buildings in the middle of Basra 15km away. His abiding memory of that battlefield is the noise of those guns and the vista of great, great columns and clouds of thick black smoke from burning oil installations everywhere he looked. He could also see huge flames of burning gas on the horizon and smoke so vast and dense that it blocked the sun.

CHAPTER I

Shock and Awe 2001

Today, our fellow citizens, our way of life, our very freedom came under attack in a series of deliberate and deadly terrorist acts. The victims were in airplanes, or in their offices; secretaries, businessmen and women, military and federal workers; moms and dads, friends and neighbors. Thousands of lives were suddenly ended by evil, despicable acts of terror.

The pictures of airplanes flying into buildings, fires burning, huge structures collapsing, have filled us with disbelief, terrible sadness, and a quiet, unyielding anger. These acts of mass murder were intended to frighten our nation into chaos and retreat. But they have failed; our country is strong.

A great people have been moved to defend a great nation. Terrorist attacks can shake the foundations of our biggest buildings, but they cannot touch the foundation of America. These acts shattered steel, but they cannot dent the steel of American resolve. ... America and our friends and allies join with all those who want peace and security in the world, and we stand together to win the war against terrorism.

PRESIDENT GEORGE W. BUSH
11 SEPTEMBER 2001

From today forward the main effort of the US Army must be to prepare for war with Iraq.
GENERAL ERIC SHINSEKI
CHIEF OF STAFF OF THE US ARMY
9 OCTOBER 2002

If there were any question about the commitment of the British armed forces to being involved in 21st-century security affairs, it was answered on 11 September 2001 when four jetliners were transformed into weapons of mass destruction directed against the United States' homeland. The world sat in shock watching the news as events unfolded in New York and Washington, DC. Though not explicit at that time, the British military had already had its marching orders delivered that morning.

American intelligence experts were circulating the names Osama Bin Laden, Saudi Arabia and Iraq on the day the twin towers fell in New York. There was to be no knee-jerk reaction and each source and threat would be analysed and dealt with in turn. Afghanistan and the Taliban, it appeared, would be first. As to Iraq's possible complicity, there was no compelling evidence and, indeed, strong scepticism on the British side.

In the weeks and months that followed 9/11 Prime Minister Tony Blair and President George Bush spent a lot of time side-by-side. At the Labour Party Conference in October Blair's speech focussed on the Americans: 'We were with you at the first. We will stay with you to the last.' As if that wasn't enough to show the Americans that Britain was with them, the Band of the Coldstream Guards marched out at Buckingham Palace for the Changing of the Guard to the 'Star-Spangled Banner' – a small but unprecedented event that initiated thousands of messages of gratitude and thanks from across the pond.

At a dinner in the White House on 20 September 2001 the two leaders agreed on dealing with the Taliban first. At that stage there was no agreement to follow that by invading Iraq. After the dinner, the party travelled together to Capitol Hill where Bush addressed a packed Congress and dispelled any doubts about his ability to lead the country in a crisis. His speech was a roaring success, every sentence drawing applause from senators and congressmen of both parties. Blair was described as 'our truest friend' which also drew thunderous applause.

Christopher Meyer, Her Majesty's Ambassador to the United States of America, said in his memoirs, *DC Confidential*, 'Afghanistan and Iraq were different. In both the issue was regime change. The goal was to remove the governments of both countries and to replace them with something better, in Afghanistan this was done with the blessing of the United Nations and International law; in Iraq it was not.'[1]

The Westphalian principle of the sanctity of national sovereignty stems from a 17th century treaty and is part of the United Nations' Charter. However, US elder statesman Henry Kissinger, who was appointed chairman of the newly established National Commission on Terrorist Attacks Upon the United States, delivered a speech in California in 2002 saying that – in certain circumstances – action violating a national frontier could be justified. It was his way of saying, on behalf of President G. W. Bush, that war in Iraq could be justified as pre-emptive action. He did list three conditions which must be met: military action must be brought to a rapid and successful conclusion; the diplomacy had to be got right; and it had to have a clear plan for the succession to Saddam and not to leave dealing with the question until after he had been deposed. In the event, none of Kissinger's conditions were met in 2003.[2]

Working towards an overthrow of Saddam Hussein from the inside was an Iraqi rebel, Ahmed Chalabi. He had been lobbying in Washington for years asking for funds to arm his party, the Iraqi National Congress (INC). His stock in trade was to present plans to overthrow Saddam and back them up by saying conditions were ripe in Baghdad to perform the overthrow; all it needed was a little pressure from the West.

Bill Clinton fell for it in 1995 and the CIA helped Chalabi with a rebellion. It failed but the INC and Chalabi did not go away. He suggested to Washington that if Iraq was taken and Saddam deposed, he and his INC would be waiting in the wings to ensure political stability and, vitally, ensure the West would be seen as liberators. It feels like these were big seeds being sown and in 2003, the flowers bloomed.

The Axis of Evil

Having toppled the Al Qaeda-backed Taliban Government of Afghanistan in just a few months, heads began to turn towards other 'rogue states'. First used by the Clinton administration, which listed Cuba, Iran, Iraq, Libya and North Korea, in 2000 'rogue states' became 'states of concern'; in 2002 they would become President Bush's 'axis of evil'.

The 9/11 attacks were not the first on United States interests. Since the first Gulf War in 1991 there had been attacks in 1996, when a US Army barracks in Saudi Arabia had been blown up, in 1998 on US embassies in Kenya and Tanzania, and in 2000 when Al Qaeda had attacked the destroyer USS *Cole* while it was in Aden harbour. Cruise missiles launched against Sudan and Afghanistan had been the only retaliation thus far.

On 29 January 2002 President George W. Bush delivered the annual State of the Union speech. Clearly, the responsibility of the security of 300 million Americans fell heavily upon his shoulders, and the cataclysmic shock of 9/11 woke him up to the threat of further atrocities from state-sponsored terrorists. He put Iraq, Iran and North Korea on notice as marked regimes. They were the axis of evil, each with the capability and willingness to help Al Qaeda. It was a danger that could no longer be ignored. If necessary, they should be destroyed by pre-emptive action. The United States could not afford to wait and see if weapons of mass destruction (WMD) were being developed in Iraq for imminent use in 'dirty bomb attacks' on the US mainland as was being suggested in CIA reports.

The scene was set for the second invasion of Iraq in 12 years. American strategists foresaw, after the invasion, a new Iraq with a stable democracy offering a haven for US military bases. It would also reduce dependency on the Saudis and their oil. A close ally, Saudi Arabia was a country not without problems, least of which was that Osama Bin Laden was born there as were most of the 9/11 hijackers. Despite the enormous economic and military power of the United States, it still prefers to act with allies rather than without. After all, the sheriff and his posse are the American way.

The September Dossier (2002)

In a 55-page document authored by British Intelligence sources, allegations were made that Iraq had developed WMD and could deliver chemical and biological agents. One chapter said Saddam Hussein's military could deliver the weapon after only a 45-minute preparation phase. This led to *The Sun* headline 'BRITS 45 MINS

FROM DOOM'; the *Daily Star* said, 'MAD SADDAM READY TO ATTACK: 45 MINUTES FROM CHEMICAL ATTACK'.

Without exception, all of the allegations within the document that became known as the September Dossier have since been proven to be false. Gen Michael Laurie, one author of the dossier, gave evidence to Sir John Chilcot's subsequent enquiry saying, 'the purpose of the dossier was precisely to make a case for war, rather than set out available intelligence'.[3]

Welsh scientist and weapons expert David Kelly gave evidence at the Foreign Affairs select committee hearing in July 2003, where he spoke about the September Dossier and associated leaks to BBC journalist Andrew Gilligan. On BBC Radio 4's *Today* programme Gilligan stated the 45-minute claim was inserted by Alistair Campbell, a claim for which Kelly denied being the source. However, he did admit to the MOD that he had spoken to Gilligan and leaked information about his work with UN weapons inspection programmes. He further admitted to having off the record chats with other journalists where he discredited the suggestion made by US Secretary of State Colin Powell that Saddam had a mobile fleet of lorries producing biological weapons, 'They are not mobile germ warfare laboratories. They are lorries producing hydrogen to fill balloons, just like the Iraqis say they are'.[4]

The intense scrutiny and growing media attention was too much for Kelly and he committed suicide in woodland near his home in Oxfordshire two days after the inquiry. Prime Minister Tony Blair set up a government inquiry into Kelly's death. Lord Hutton's inquiry concluded that no other parties had been involved in his suicide, although some still have their doubts.

There are many that suggest the Blair and Bush 20 September 2001 White House meeting decided on the invasion of Iraq, while others suggest the UN mandates and Saddam's failure to co-operate fully were the final straw in early 2003. For the soldiers, sailors and air force personnel of the United Kingdom the politics mattered not: they were being mobilised into the largest UK deployed force since World War 2 and would be heading to Iraq as part of Operation *Telic*.

Iraq – A Brief Summary

Virtually landlocked and surrounded by six countries, Iraq is bordered to the north-west by Syria and Turkey, to the east by Iran, to the south Kuwait and Saudi Arabia and to the west Jordan. It has only 50km of coastline on the Persian Gulf in the south.

With a hot arid climate, daytime summer temperatures can often reach a blistering 50°C. Surprisingly, at night in winter temperatures often drop to freezing. Apart from the more mountainous north, rainfall is rare and much of the country is desert and scrubland. Iraq is dominated by two vast rivers, the Tigris and the Euphrates, which run north to south merging into the Shatt al-Arab near the Persian Gulf.

Along the rivers are rich fertile lands and around the mouth of the Shatt al-Arab flooded marshlands pervade. The area is known as the Garden of Eden.

At the end of World War 1 the three provinces that made up the country were amalgamated into one kingdom – State of Iraq – under a League of Nations mandate administered by Britain. On the urging of King Faisal, Britain granted Iraq independence in 1932. Britain later withdrew completely in 1947.

Throughout the late 1950s and up until 1979 Iraq was deeply troubled with coups, uprisings and political unrest which led to many thousands being killed including the king. Eventually a political group – the Ba'ath Party – emerged in control with Saddam Hussein acceding as president in 1979, although he had been in charge for some years.

Neighbouring Iran suffered a revolution in 1979 when Mohammad Reza Shah Pahlavi, the Shah of Iran, was overthrown and Ayatollah Khomeini returned for exile to rule, replacing a prosperous pro-western attitude with an anti-Western theocracy. Taking advantage of the turbulent conditions within Iran, Saddam Hussein invaded in 1980.

The Iran–Iraq war was a costly and bloody affair which raged back and forward for nearly eight years at a cost around one million dead, a tenth of that number civilians. Iraq used chemical weapons – mustard and sarin gas – against Iranian troops and civilians. In 1988, in the face of crippling losses in materiel and spiralling economic problems Iran grudgingly accepted a ceasefire. It's difficult to work out the international support for either of the countries. Henry Kissinger is known to have said 'it's a pity they both can't lose'. According to recently released CIA files, the United States had clear knowledge of the Iraqi use of chemical weapons, and had provided satellite imagery maps and intelligence prior to their attacks.[5]

In August 1990 Iraq invaded Kuwait and within two days had annexed the country. Saddam declared Kuwait the nineteenth state of Iraq and installed a puppet government. There are several suggested reasons for the invasion: the vast debt Iraq had with Kuwait – an estimated $14 billion to cover loans during the Iran border wars being the most obvious. Iraq also suggested Kuwait's surge in oil production was keeping Iraqi oil prices low. Also significant, Saddam Hussein's government was struggling with popularity at home and has been seen with many countries (Argentina and the United Kingdom in the Falklands come to mind), a foreign war is often a good way to boost national pride and popularity for the party in power, if successfully undertaken.

A seven-month-long period of occupation followed before the UN-sanctioned and US-led Gulf War – codenamed Operation *Desert Storm* – began in January 1991. In one of the most intense air bombardments ever known, 100,000 air sorties dropped over 88,000 tons of bombs during a 42-night campaign. The entire Iraqi Air Force, the military command structure and most of its ground forces were annihilated.

One Iraqi soldier is said to have remarked 'our Brigade suffered more from Allied air power in 30 minutes than it did in eight years against Iran'.[6]

In what some say was a 100-hour ground war, the coalition forces swept the so-called 'elite' Republican Guard aside and routed Iraqi resistance. The retreating Iraqi forces began a scorched-earth operation setting alight over 700 oil wells. Their forces were also burnt, pounded continually by Coalition air power, with the main road north out of Kuwait City being christened the highway of death. The British contingent operated under Operation *Granby* at a cost of £2.5 billion, most of which was paid by Saudi Arabia. During the fighting 47 British personnel were killed.

Winning the 1991 war gave great pleasure to the winners but the pleasure was short lived, as Saddam sought ways to evade terms of the ceasefire. Much of the Republican Guard had been left intact and many Iraqi helicopters continued to fly. To this day there are many who believe the United States brought the 1991 war to a premature conclusion.

Iraq had a population of 24 million in 2003, 80% of which was Arab in ethnicity with two million Kurds populating the north. 65% of the population was Shia Muslim and the remainder largely Sunni Muslim. The population in the south is largely Sunni because the regime preferred Sunnis for jobs in the oilfields. The Shia-Sunni divide proved to be a fault line and a great driver of the conflict following the toppling of Saddam in 2003.[7]

Prior to the invasion, British military, political and diplomatic leaders appear to have had a confused understanding of the situation in southern Iraq. Ten years of isolation, crushed beneath UN sanctions with no diplomatic presence or trade, meant a fragmented and distorted view of the situation and one which even today can easily lead to divergent Western views of the Iraqis as wicked henchmen of Saddam Hussein or downtrodden, oppressed tomato farmers. This lack of physical contact with Iraqis led to real intelligence failures and left numerous voids on US/UK knowledge of the Iraqi Army's willingness to fight. Crystal-clear digital photography and satellite imagery showed where every airfield, dockyard, barrack block and tank park were but none of that could say how well the ships and tanks were maintained or whether the soldiers and sailors manning them had the slightest inclination to fight or not.

Reminiscent of Germany under Hitler in 1945, the military leadership of Iraq in 2003 was paralyzed by fear of its own president. His delusional paranoia fatally handicapped his generals and diplomatic staff alike. Hussein's main preoccupation was the brutal policing of his own people and uncovering and destroying any internal threat to his presidency. The Iraqi secret police would have given Stasi, the Gestapo and the KGB a run for their money in creating a paranoid population that spied on its neighbours, tortured prisoners and buried them in shallow, unmarked graves. The structure of his military was such that it was impossible for a unit to launch a coup without knowledge of another, thus exposing the plot and risks. The

Republican Guard was also kept in check by regular executions of the officer class to discourage disloyalty. Soldiers who even reported bad news or discontent in the ranks faced arrest and expulsion. There was no truth given to the commanders.

Iraq was divided into four regional command zones, each headed by a Ba'ath Party official, fiercely loyal to the president, who all sat outside the military chain of command. All army units within the region could be directed by the regional controller. In the south this was Ali Hassan al-Majid, known as Chemical Ali, who had no formal military training at all. During January 2003, the threat of US invasion grew more likely and the plans inside Iraq stepped up. Rather than build defences, however, the main efforts of Chemical Ali were in beefing up preparations to subdue any uprising in the Shia-dominated south. Units of the ultra-loyal Fedayeen* moved south to Basra in readiness to put down a revolt.

Conventional forces did make some efforts to prepare, with Seersucker, FROG-7 and ABABIL-100 missile crews moving to new hidden launch pads and several ammunition depots being emptied and relocated in schools and hospitals to avoid being bombed. The 51st Infantry Division moved south to the Kuwait borders including bases at Az Zubayr and Basra. Iraqi naval infantry moved into the Al-Faw peninsula and Umm Qasr port, while 704th Infantry Brigade spread itself across the Rumaila oilfields west of Basra. Taking up positions beneath the date palms along the Euphrates River near Al-Qurnah was the Iraqi 6th Armoured Division with its vintage 1970s T-55 tanks and BMP APCs. After the 2003 war, captured Iraqi officers admitted that most of their vehicle fleets had not been supplied with spare parts since the first Gulf War and were crippled with lack of parts, allowing, at best, 50% of strength to be put on the road.

The lack of available vehicles, shortage of money and no spare parts meant that meaningful large-scale exercises were a rarity. The subsequent boredom and demotivation lead to new lows of despondency in the military. Badly paid, they sat in barracks with nothing to do facing rising levels of absenteeism. The same Iraqi officers also added that many of them hoped the war, when it came, would be very short so they did not see the wholesale destruction of their country once again and their men did not get killed fighting for a cause they no longer supported. However, it should also be noted that there were some well-trained units still loyal to the cause and in no mood to roll over at the first sign of a British soldier climbing over the border fence.

---

* The Fedayeen Saddam were a paramilitary organisation loyal to the Ba'ath Party who operated outside of the army structure. The name in Arabic was chosen to mean 'Saddam's men of sacrifice'. They were fiercely loyal and often brave but usually poorly trained and equipped mainly with small arms. The commander of the Fedayeen, Uday Hussein, son of Saddam, was reportedly an avid fan of *Star Wars* and designed the helmet in the style of Darth Vader.

Britain, December 2002

Capt Mike Peters was Regimental Signals Officer (RSO) for 3 Regiment, Army Air Corps (AAC), and had his own office in the command troop hangar at RAF Wattisham alongside the RAF Search and Rescue unit and its bright yellow Sea King helicopter. AAC helicopters had taken over the base from Cold War RAF jets in 1993.

In mid-December 2002, as the traditional morning coffee brew spluttered and dripped in the corner, Peters busied himself with a plethora of tasks relating to upcoming training on the base when the phone rang. It was the 3 Regiment adjutant at RHQ (regimental headquarters). The call confirmed that, after several months of anticipation, he was going to be involved in the invasion of Iraq and he needed to go up the road to RHQ for a briefing. He remembers:

> The briefing finally put an end to the sham of the previous months' cloak and dagger activity. All of us within HQ 3 Regiment with the non-sexy jobs – like the RSO, logisticians and planners – had been told in November 2002 we were likely to invade Iraq, but we were not allowed to tell anyone, even in our squadrons and especially not the paratroopers of 16 AAB with whom we worked so closely. We were not allowed to ask for maps or any desert-related campaign equipment because officially the government had not announced nor committed to any campaign against Saddam Hussein's Iraq. As a veteran of Operation *Granby* in 1991, I fully understood what was going to be needed for another war and I knew full well just how long it takes the army to move from a peacetime footing to mobilized war readiness. The stagnant pause caused by Tony Blair and the government's indecisiveness crippled us in our preparedness and led to some unforgiveable cock ups and shortages.

This faltering start to proceedings is somewhat at odds with the previous few years under the Labour Party leadership, during which Britain had stood shoulder to shoulder so often with its close US ally and took part in decisive operations in Kosovo in 1999, and in 2001 in Sierra Leone and the toppling of the Taliban regime in Afghanistan. Tony Blair's rousing speech at the COBRA meeting following the 9/11 attacks in New York and Washington, DC declared that the United States was under attack by enemies of civilisation and Britain would stand side-by-side with their ally. The direction of travel was clear, Britain would maintain a seat at the top table with President Bush but to do so meant it had to keep up with the Americans come what may.

Alistair Campbell, Blair's head of communications recounts in his diary that in October 2002 a delegation from the Ministry of Defence, led by Secretary of Defence Geoff Hoon and Chief of the Defence Staff, Admiral Sir Michael Boyce, went to present their options to the Prime Minister on British military involvement in a US-led invasion plan for Iraq. Laying out pros and cons of various options, Campbell comments that Blair could not make up his mind.

'Blair said it was not no, but it was not yes.' At the end of the meeting no one knew what was needed or what should happen next. This was a 'Sofa Government' in action.[8]

In reality, military preparations were already underway as Col James ('Jim') Tanner of the Staffordshire Regiment had found out some time earlier:

> On 7 July 2002 I was summoned to HQ 1 (UK) Armoured Division (1 UKDIV) in Herford, Germany. The briefing was with the division's Chief of Staff [Col, 1 UK] Patrick Marriot, the Commander of Royal Artillery and Commander Royal Engineers and a staff officer – very few people at all. We were not allowed to take notes. I wrote in my diary after the meeting 'Is this the road to war?'

The Coalition's mission against Iraq was, in the words of 1 (UK) Armoured Division's commander, Major General Robin Brims, 'to defeat the enemy, and it was agreed among British forces that defeat meant to "render his [Saddam's] armed forces incapable of interfering with our [Coalition] activities". It was not necessary to destroy the enemy forces, simply to render them ineffective.' Originally intended to invade Iraq from the north, the British component of the invasion in fact invaded from Kuwait. Its main job was to secure the flank of US forces advancing towards Baghdad, to take the oil infrastructure in south Iraq – particularly on the Al-Faw peninsula, the Rumaila oilfields and the pumping station at Az Zubayr – before it could be destroyed by the Saddam regime, and to isolate significant urban areas, notably the city of Basra.

1 UKDIV was embedded with the US 1st Marine Expeditionary Force and worked closely with the 15th Marine Expeditionary Unit (MEU). The division's tasks were divided between; 7 Armoured Brigade (the Desert Rats), which attacked north from Kuwait towards Basra paralleling the advance of US 1st Marine Division which advanced towards Baghdad. By capturing and holding the bridges over the Shatt-al-Basra, 1 UKDIV ensured that that no enemy forces could advance south and cut the Coalition's lines of communication. The 16th Air Assault Brigade followed the US 1st Marine Division and took hold of the Rumaila oilfields. 3 Commando Brigade, Royal Marines (RM) took and held the Al-Faw peninsula. In total some 22,000 personnel of 1 UKDIV took part in Operation *Telic* exceeding, as Brims put it, 'all expected defence-planning assumptions, both in terms of volume and in the length of time to deploy.' Militarily, British forces did exactly what they were asked to do.

CHAPTER 2

Brown Envelopes

I was mobilised by receipt of a letter, which I still have, on 21 February 2003. It was headed Notice of Compulsory Call Out and signed by Colonel Gibson, Royal Army Medical Corps (RAMC). I was in the second tranche of reserves being called up, some of my colleagues got called up the month before to join 34 Field Hospital, and they went ahead. 202 Field Hospital is a Territorial Army (TA) unit, normally run with around 600–650 reservist staff. For Op *Telic* it comprised of around one-third of its usual staff from 202 but the other two-thirds, like me, were drawn from a host of other TA and regular units to bring it fully up to strength. The hospital had around 200 beds and the staff split into three eight-hour shifts: mornings, afternoons and nights.

I had a lot of experience as an A&E nurse, but I was placed in charge of the infectious diseases ward in Kuwait. We expected to be dealing with chemical weapon injuries but of course that didn't happen, and most of our admissions were suffering from D&V (diarrhoea and vomiting). ...

At Chilwell, Nottingham we were processed for deployment and issued a bit of extra kit, but not enough. All the NBC [nuclear, biological and chemical] stock was out of date and the wrong colour for a desert. It was all rather amateur and rushed. The best part of this process was the Royal Green Jackets who gave us some good, relevant and current training. We learned how to safely handle a host of Iraqi weapons, had an input on mines and unexploded bombs, reminders of the Geneva conventions and, interestingly, we had combat first aid refreshers. Despite the fact they were the infantry and we were the doctors and nurses, they handled that well. Many of us held positions that are not in A&E, so it was good to get back to basic first aid for soldiers.

The final lecture had us held in silence, we were absolutely shitting our pants. It was called conduct on camp. We all knew we were going to war and were OK with that but the idea that we could be subjected to long-range missile strikes and possibly be captured by enemy forces really brought it home to us that the intensity of full-on war was going to be different to a deployment in Bosnia or Belfast. It was capped off by the instruction to make a will.

MAJ DAVID GREEN, RAMC

The call up, mobilisation or deployment of different military units uses different terminology and is undergone in different ways according to separate laws, traditions and processes. In the Regular Army word filters down through the chain of command so troops that are in their normal place of work, barracks or on exercise will hear very quickly, with this news being formalised in orders posted prominently on walls. For the reservists in the TA things are done differently due to the very nature of their sporadic gatherings at perhaps weekly drill nights. Many specialist reserve units like field hospitals have so many reserve staff in extremely specialist roles – dentists, haematologists and operating theatre assistants – that upon mobilisation they gather their staff from across the country. Most of these TA soldiers were mobilised for Operation *Telic* by means of an MOD letter delivered in a brown HM Government envelope. It transpires that a great many of the TA already knew they were likely to be going by the means of the army rumour service.

Sgt Rey Fadil, RE, an explosive ordnance disposal (EOD) expert, had been a regular soldier for eight years when he started a family, so left the regulars and kept up his army contact by joining the TA. He was also still a reservist because he had signed on originally for 22 years, and if you leave before the 22 years you remain as reservist for the balance. He remembers:

> Just after breakfast, the postman had been, and my eight-year-old daughter came into the kitchen with a mundane-looking brown envelope. I opened it up and straightaway I saw the MOD letterhead, I knew I was going to war. My daughter burst into tears and my wife followed suit.
>
> When I was mobilised for *Telic* it was because I was a still an ex-regular reservist, not as a member of the TA. This caused a few logistical issues, not least because my TA CO didn't know anything about me being mobilised under a reservist banner.
>
> I was working for Gravesend local council at that time and my boss tried to stop me going to Iraq by claiming an exemption. I am glad that he failed as I really wanted to go. In fact, it was my duty to go. A few weeks later at Chilwell Camp we were being processed for mobilisation and we underwent medical, eyesight and hearing tests. I had a problem in one eye and the optician said that I didn't need to go, she could have downgraded me. I said that I wanted to go and when she asked why I said, 'I have to get up each morning and look at my own face in the mirror'.

Not long before *Telic*, there was some feeling that if the TA infantry was not used for mobilisation soon, it may well fall foul of the saying 'use it or lose it!' The relationship between the Regular Army and TA has always been somewhat strained and on occasion downright hostile. Looking at one case, that of 16 Air Assault Brigade (AAB), we can see how the call-up process on Operation *Telic* worked for both regulars and their reserve counterparts. 2 PARA was already deployed on Operation *Banner* in South Armagh, so was missing from the available order of battle for the brigade. This meant that the other remaining battalions, 1 PARA, 3 PARA and 1 Royal Irish, needed to be up to strength. This meant 4 PARA (TA) was going to get the call to fill in the shortages.

Lt Col Giles Orpen-Smellie, CO of 4 PARA, took a phone call from brigade warning him of this likelihood on 2 January 2003. 4 PARA held a good degree of credibility with its Regular Army brothers and so this process was both expected and soundly delivered. The regulars normally ran on full strength at 645 all ranks, but with *Telic* they were authorised to raise that to 687. 4 PARA was asked to provide 118 soldiers.[1]

There was then a pause of two vital weeks before the final authority was released for the TA soldiers to augment the regulars. This was valuable lost time when the TA soldiers could have got ahead with their integration into the battalions. The British Army delivered 6,540 call-out notices. 4,870 soldiers reported for duty and 3,787 were accepted into active service.

Mobilisation rules direct that individual soldiers are not to be consulted prior to receipt of their 'brown envelopes.' With a TA soldier his first loyalty is to his family, his second to his civilian employer and his third to the army. Yet the army seemed content to give them only 14 days' notice, or less, to set their life in order before being torn away, and put in harm's way, for an unknown period. Political indecision meant that the brown envelopes did not get posted until 29 January, wasting yet more valuable time. Yet despite this 4 PARA achieved 57% of the declarations of willingness to go abroad in just 24 hours.

Cpl Paul Burton, 104 Battalion, Royal Electrical and Mechanical Engineers (REME) remembers receiving his call-up and the effect it had on his home life:

In early February 2003 I was at home watching the TV with my wife when the home phone rang around 7pm. It was my CO. I said, 'Hello Sir, is it on?' Before I even had the answer my wife started to cry. She knew I would be going. My wife had been very opinionated about the military and didn't really want me to carry on in the Reserves. I spent years placating her, but I think the call-up for *Telic* was probably a final straw. I think I may have fought on some more years to stay together but *Telic* was a big turning point in our marriage.

Before my time in the army, I had spent time in the Royal Navy on board HMS *Brave* in the Arctic Circle, but I was always seasick, so I left the navy. I knew I wanted to somehow stay involved so I joined the TA. I have ended up doing 30 years' reserve service in the TA REME alongside my civilian day work.

When the brown envelope came through, I was advised to put my financial affairs in order and to give my wife power of attorney. When I saw that advice in black and white it brought me back down to earth. However, I was so excited, there was no way I was going to miss it. When I look back on it, like now, I realise what a large undertaking this was but when you are in your 20s, you're a lot easier going.

I was then mobilised to Chilwell for all the admin with about 100 other REME guys. One pleasant surprise was the pay clerk adding up what my pay would be. They matched my lorry driving job first, then added on hardship allowances and later overseas allowances. I was getting far more than just working for Wincanton, who had stopped paying me while I was mobilised, which was fair enough. The dental assessment made me nervous; I didn't have great teeth and I saw that people were being sent home with any signs of dental issues. Fortunately, I passed that and the medical.

My Mum and Dad came to my house to say goodbye and my wife and two young boys waved me off on the train. When I boarded the train, they gave me what was like an autograph book. It had been passed around my family, extended family and friends and contained a lot of good luck messages. I sat on my kit in the area between two carriages on the train and read the book. It brought a tear to my eye and was the first time that I felt some apprehension and being honest, I was worried that there might be a chance I would not return.

The two biggest hurdles for call-ups historically are dentistry and medical checks. Regulars get all their medical health care included but TA soldiers are not covered which can lead to soldiers falling at these hurdles. In total, only one failed his dentist check but five failed medicals. Three soldiers asked for second opinions but there was no changing of minds, and they were not getting on the bus. The remaining healthy soldiers joined their new host units after 17 days, having spent some of that time at Chetwynd Barracks, Chilwell, Notts – the army's main mobilisation centre.

The final aspect that caused most angst in TA mobilisation was that of agreed pay scales around means testing of the TA soldiers through the Reserve Standards Award (RSA) and Reserve Hardship Award (RHA). RSA lifted a TA soldier's salary to £22,000 if he could show that he was earning at least that in civilian life. RHA lifted his army salary above that to match that of his civilian pay if he could prove he had liabilities to match. One private in 4 PARA was a city banker earning £70,000. He was awarded both the RSA and RHA, so his army pay fully made up for his lost earnings in the city. However, a lance corporal who was an engineer earned £100,000 in his day job but was unable to prove his outgoings (probably through frugal and wise planning). He was left on the baseline £25,000 for a lance corporal. None of these affected pensions. In the event of death in service, a soldier's wife would only get the standard army pension for the rank; for example, that of a private, would have been around £8,000 per annum.

Another EOD Royal Engineer, WO2 Andy Abbott, a one-time regular in 22 Field Squadron, had been in the TA for 25 years and was based at Rochester:

> Early in 2003 my CO, Steve Squibb, called me and said, 'We need volunteers for Kuwait to mobilise.' I was desperate to do the job I had trained to do, so on 20 February we got the group together in the TA Centre bar in Rochester. The CO gave a briefing to the guys and their partners. It was the first time we had been mobilised since WW2. Because the intel was EOD heavy with a threat of NBC, he wanted to let us all know what he thought it would look like. I had one minute before the briefing to finally confirm to my Mrs that I was going. My Mrs was fine, but one guy's wife completely lost it: he wasn't even going overseas, he was going to Wimbish, Essex!
>
> We moved to Chilwell barracks where our training team from the Royal Green Jackets obviously had the hump with us and overloaded the CS tablets so much, we threw up. We also received about 7 injections! Not sure what they all were – Anthrax, Tetanus etc. 4 in one arm and 3 in the other – I was so ill. It wasn't right, there should be gaps between them and all that. My wife, Sue, came up for a weekend and had a big medical boot on her foot as she had just had a bunion removed. We had a nice weekend in hotel off camp, but when she dropped me off, I knew it would be a while before I saw her again. It was actually 6 months! It was emotional and I felt bad for leaving her and the four kids. It felt new and unknown as she left. I didn't sleep in a proper bed for the next 5 months.

There were numerous women in the ranks of Operation *Telic* personnel in many of the combat service and combat service support roles and lots more in the ranks of the Royal Artillery. In the ranks in 2003 the progress of the last decade was still a way off, but despite the forward steps for equality and diversity, there are still issues, as Lt Zoe Ferry, RLC identifies:

I served for 20 years in the army and at my leaving speech in 2020 which was attended by brigade, and divisional commanders I said, 'I've been coming to work for 20 years dressed as a man, with room for a penis I don't have and no room for breasts which I do! Isn't it time this was sorted out?'

In 2003, 17 years before, Zoe was a lieutenant in Iraq, in command of the evacuation squadron, a transport unit with 5 General Support Medical Regiment (GSMR). Her troops would drive battlefield ambulances (BFAs) and supply trucks for the medical unit. Her commanding officer had just been sacked as a drunk in the UK and had not yet been replaced, meaning a somewhat shortened chain of command, which was made worse:

> To cap that little problem off, just as we went to depart UK my sergeant came to my office in tears and begged me not to send him to war. He broke down and couldn't be taken. Fortunately, his replacement, Sgt Walker, was a great guy and we got on very well.

Zoe's twin sister Gayle, older by eight minutes, worked as an A&E nurse at Reading Hospital and was also a TA nursing officer who had been mobilised with 202 Field Hospital, to which Zoe's ambulances from 5 GSMR would deliver the wounded. The hospital was on the Kuwait border once war started. Due to the perceived high threat of chemical weapons, medical units and field hospitals in Kuwait would have decontamination units attached to them. The units would be staffed by men and women of the Royal School of Army Music and the various army bands from stations all over the country. The band of the 1st Queen's Dragoon Guards, based at Swanton Morley near Dereham in Norfolk, was chosen in 2003 to accompany the Operation *Telic* medical forces going to Iraq. Band Sergeant Major (BSM) Leigh Sharpe commanded the unit in Norfolk and it was 25 years since he had walked into the Army Careers office in Blackpool aged just 15. He remembers:

> At Woolwich they trained young Army musicians for the Royal Engineers, Royal Signals and Royal Artillery. I was badged Royal Artillery and after juniors went into the 80-piece band for the Royal Artillery, still based at Woolwich. In the early 1980s there were nearly 70 Regimental Bands. They are nearly all gone now.
> I was posted to the Paras in 1992 as Bandmaster and the first thing I was told was that the band had a poor reputation with the battalions. Apparently when they deployed to the Falklands in 1982, the Bandmaster said the band could not go because it had some musical appointments. I was shocked but also determined to try and mend that relationship. Musicians were trained medics who would have been sorely needed on Mount Longdon and Goose Green; it was unfathomable that they had not gone south to the Falklands. So, in January 2003 when we were adventure training – I call it a holiday – skiing in Italy, I got a phone call from the CO who told me that we were being deployed to Iraq as a decontamination unit attached to a medical dressing station. I was determined we would all go and do our bit.

In 2003, the British Army still had a sizeable force based in Germany and several of the units slated for *Telic* were pulled from Celle, Herford, Bad Fallingbostel (the Bad meaning Spa was added to the name in 2002 but is usually dropped by British servicemen) and Hohne. 1 Royal Regiment of Fusiliers (1 RRF) was at Celle, 30km north-west of Hannover. An armoured infantry regiment, it was equipped with Warrior infantry fighting vehicles and the reconnaissance platoon used little Scimitar light tanks which were already 25 years old, or more. The Scimitar grew out of an original design to supply the army fighting in Malaya with a light tank small enough to fit through the trees on rubber plantations. By 2003 it equipped many armoured recce units and was armed with a reliable but old-fashioned, non-stabilised, three-round clip-fed 30mm Rarden cannon. The 1 RRF Recce Platoon commander, Capt Ed Pugh, had taken a few days' leave in London:

> I was waiting for a tube train at Earl's Court underground station when my mobile phone rang. It was my platoon second in command who simply said, 'You'd better get back here boss; I think it's on.' I knew that the Fusiliers were considered a strong battlegroup and we had just got back from Canada so were right up to speed with our training. It would very likely therefore be falling to me as the lead reconnaissance unit of a leading battlegroup to head up the invasion of Iraq. Gulp!

The German city of Munster, also the home of British Army units since 1945, lies 160km north of Celle and in January 2003 was naturally still in the grips of mid-winter. L/Sgt Robert Giles of 1 Irish Guards (1 IG) was based there:

> The temperatures in Munster had been so low that the hatches had frozen on our vehicles and the radios had suffered as a result of conditions reminiscent of Stalingrad, not Baghdad. Previously in Germany, as we tried to warm our feet, we'd taken ironic comfort in the fact that Rommel's troops had trained in the same area, some 65 years before us. The Desert Fox had gone on to enjoy varying degrees of success in the deserts of Libya, Algeria and Tunisia. Well, we'd just have to go one better than him, and it had been the Desert Rats, 7 Armoured Division, the division we now found ourselves in, which had helped Rommel's demise in the North African desert. Well, it wasn't a division as such, it was a brigade, but it carried the name and symbols of its predecessors who were commanded by Monty, and the press hadn't been slow to pick up on it.
>
> I was sad as I left Germany. In fact, I was depressed right throughout the flight, and for the first week in Kuwait. The reason lay with the age-old story of just meeting a girl about four weeks before I left for war. She was a stunning, Teutonic six-foot blonde, the better-looking younger sister of Claudia Schiffer type of girl. As it turned out she proved to be as reliable as an Austin Rover Allegro rather than a Volkswagen Golf.

The regular soldiers like BSM Sharpe, Capt Pugh, L/Sgt Giles and Lt Ferry were deployed directly with their units. Many other regulars who wanted to be deployed found themselves in units not slated to travel or in posts that were involved in UK training or staff work. They started their own journey by trying to get permission to deploy on *Telic*. The training teams at Warminster's School of Infantry started to see a rise in non-attendees on courses in late 2002. People were being posted to Kuwait and cancelling their courses. At the start of January, the decision was made to cancel all the courses because so many students were away. The staff at Warminster found themselves looking at rather empty diaries. Staring at one such empty page was Maj John Cotterill. With 26 years' regular service, he was the chief instructor of the five-week Combined Arms School Course at Warminster. Cotterill had been commissioned in the Worcester and Sherwood Foresters in 1977 and spent two years on attachment to the Sultan of Oman's Parachute Regiment in the 1980s. Being the only English speaker for miles, he quickly learned to speak Arabic. He also served on operations in the Balkans, Cyprus, Germany and Belize but it was undoubtedly his five years' service in Northern Ireland that taught him how to survive:

> Five years in Northern Ireland really taught me how to stay alive. The art for us was to be totally unpredictable. Patterns could be learned by the IRA and that's what killed soldiers, so we were unpredictable and made sure we would change tactics, timings, routes and methods all the time.
>
> In 2003 my plan was that I wanted to spend another two years at Warminster, but to have any credibility as the Chief Instructor of the Combined Arms courses I needed to go to Iraq to get that experience of a real shooting war. That motivated me to go and find a way out to Iraq. I went and saw my boss and asked if I could go and he said, 'No, not under any circumstances.' I then pulled together what I called my 'War CV' listing my skills and attributes, not least of which was my ability to speak Arabic. I then circulated the CV to everyone I thought relevant on my distribution list. My boss, of course, got to hear about this and I was warned that if I did it again, I would be sacked from Warminster.
>
> Fortunately, I didn't need to send it out again, as the CV had landed on a desk in 7 Brigade HQ, and I was invited by email to join the operations desk as a watchkeeper. It was below my 'pay grade' as a senior major, but I didn't care, I wanted to go and so hurriedly set off to Hannover on a flight from Birmingham Airport. My father-in-law had served in the Desert Rats in World War 2, and we still had one of his patches, so before I flew out, I sewed his old patch onto my sleeve.
>
> I was a staff officer and so my personal weapon was a 9mm Browning pistol which caused the BA check in staff at Birmingham some excitement. I was in civvies but when they asked if I had packed my bags and was there any prohibited articles in the luggage I said yes! After some explanations and proof of Army ID, I was allowed aboard as was the Browning, in the hold. I left my wife and two daughters aged 15 and 11 behind. A few days later, on February 20 I flew to Kuwait.

Also bound for the HQ of the Desert Rats was Col Jim Tanner. An officer with a slightly unusual background, Tanner was brought up on a council estate in Catford, south London. His father had hated the Royal Navy when he was conscripted in World War 2, which tarnished his view of the military. However, his uncle made it to RSM in Hong Kong and Kenya and in his Number One dress uniform it all looked rather glamourous compared to grimy south London. With the pomp, shine and glamour of the Royal Tournament ringing in his ears, young Tanner joined the army and to the amazement of his family was commissioned as an infantry subaltern in 1976.

> I was on Operation *Granby* in 1991. The knowledge of wars is lost by most and if you have read a history book about war with Arabs you know that they don't end well, and they are at your heels continually. Sadly, most senior soldiers appear not to have read those books and even fewer of the politicians have. For instance, A.J Barker's *A Neglected War* and Russell Brunt's *The Siege* tell how utterly wet, cold and miserable it can be in Mesopotamia (Iraq) during winter. Because of that I made sure I took my big sleeping bag. Others did not and got very cold.

In 2001, as a colonel, I was in command of a collective all-arms training group and set up Exercise 'Saif Sareea II' in Oman. It was a huge exercise, involving three brigades: two British – 4 Armoured and 3 Commando – and one Omani. It culminated with one of the largest firepower demonstrations on the planet. The GOC was General Robin Brims who I got on well with and he had really let me get on with it. Many lessons learned on 'Saif Sareea II' proved of value on Telic. We saw plainly how utterly poor some of our formations were at living in the field because they were out of practice.

Movements of large units practicing timetabled routes of march and mitigating against air, chemical and ground threats was woeful by many. It was clear that the army's own corporate memory had been forgotten since Granby and the Cold War exercises in Poland with British Army of the Rhine (BAOR). Severe budget cuts were to blame as well. There simply was not the money to pay for such huge exercises for the army and so larger formation training that tests such things became purely tabletop exercises. One other problem highlighted was that for a period, movements had been put in under G4 Logistics.* But it is not an administrative task, it should be G3 Operations. If it is treated as a logistics exercise that is how people approach it – just look at the mess Putin got into with Ukraine and the 40-kilometre column stranded at Kiev.

Lieutenant Colonel Tanner's uncle, like many others, had been stationed in Hong Kong. British postings there were common in the 1950s–90s with the army maintaining a unit from the Brigade of Gurkhas on the territory until 1997 when sovereignty was handed back to China. One such officer posted to Hong Kong for several years was Regimental Medical Officer Jeremy Tuck, working with the Gurkhas. During his time in the subtropics Tuck developed an interest in tropical medicine and gained further qualifications in that field which were utilised on deployments to East Timor and the African Congo. Lt Col Jeremy Tuck, RAMC commanded 5 GSMR:

I left my house to go to Kuwait on Operation *Telic* at 08:30. I was in my full army combats complete with Bergen and a sports bag. It probably wasn't my best plan, because to leave the house I had to walk across a children's playground and, of course, at that time all the kids were turning up at the playground with mums and dads. They were all looking at me and whispering about who I was and where I might be going. My wife and children were at my family home in London, but I was stationed in Preston and working at Fulwood Barracks, commanding the regiment and had been given the primary schoolhouse in Broughton village as my billet.

Alongside chemical weapons the invasion of Iraq posed many other specific theatre threats. The proliferation of land mines in the 1980s' Iran–Iraq war had left the region scattered with a plethora of unexploded mine threats. Millions of mines were reported to have been scattered in southern Iraq and along the Iranian border, most of which were lost in unmarked or forgotten minefields, posing a huge risk to the Coalition forces in 2003. Land mines have a nasty habit of moving. It's natural to assume that a mine, once dug into the subsurface, will stay put. In fact, the opposite can be true. Movements of subsoil levels, heavy rain and interference by construction machines can all cause mines to move from their original location.

---

*   G1 is Personnel, G2 Intel, G3 Ops, G4 Logistics.

In Iraq, shifting sands blown by sandstorms will simply carry minefields away and deposit them elsewhere. In the Falklands, Argentinian anti-personnel mines laid in hillside peat bogs in 1982 have slowly shifted downhill, still hidden by grasses, and fall out into stream beds and even onto the beaches. To counter this threat – and also to deal with the Iraqi penchant for leaving dangerous explosive hardware simply lying around – the British forces were to see the deployment of the newly formed Joint Forces Explosive Ordnance Disposal team. The MOD saw fit to pool all the bomb disposal experience of the British Army, RN and RAF in one combined team. Such comings together often appear good on paper but the friction that can arise from three distinctly different organisations, their history, rank structure, equipment and approach to tasks, can be counterproductive. The job of getting this new dysfunctional family ready for deployment fell at the feet of RSM Nick Pettit, QGM. North London-born Pettit had been awarded the Queen's Gallantry Medal and Joint Commander's Commendation for gallantry in Bosnia so was a well-respected and capable senior NCO in 33 Regiment, RE:

> In the meetings when they finally all turned up, there were so many bunfights, I thought to myself, 'Oh my God we are going to be fighting ourselves more than anyone else'. It got confusing because we would have to have our bags packed at 24 hours' notice to move, then it went up to 72 hours, then dropped back to 36 hours. So, we planned the schedule accordingly and straight away got told we only had a week.
>
> As a new tri-service group, I think we were going to be the only unit going to war that had not properly trained together. It became apparent very early on that we needed to teach the RAF basic fieldcraft, from erecting camouflage nets to basic formations and what actions to take upon certain incidents taking place. They lacked the cut and thrust; it was all very laid back and easy-going with the RAF. There was no get up and go. We had to show them how to live in an armoured vehicle, how to react if you lose a vehicle in a night convoy and what to do if a vehicle gets caught in a minefield.[2]

Ironically, as it is clear he had a dislike for the RAF, RSM Pettit ended up having to go into Iraq as 2IC of the RAF-led EOD team that would accompany the Joint Helicopter Force (Iraq) – JHF(I). It gave great amusement to everyone in the engineers and was, no doubt, a great source of banter. The RAF were not keen on Nick being with them either. Pettit says in his memoir, *Modern Day Hero*: 'We were just lining up for a briefing at JHFC when the RAF squadron leader came up to me and said, 'I don't want you, I don't want you as part of this group. I don't want you crossing the border with us, I don't know who you think you are, but you are not coming with the Joint Helicopter Force.'

Fortunately, that sort of friction in most British units was rare and the opposite is far more common. Working in the close confines of tanks in an armoured regiment there is no room for such animosity and the tight cohesion needed to operate and fight a Challenger tank is evident in the ranks of the Royal Tank Regiment (RTR). The RTR was created from the Royal Tank Corps in 1939, 23 years after the tank was first used in the battle of Flers-Courcelette in September 1916. After World War 2, year after year witnessed round after round of cutbacks and amalgamations. The RTR in 2003 had shrunk to just two regiments, both of which were deployed on *Telic*. First specialised in NBC detection and Second was a traditional armoured regiment with Challenger tanks. Lt Ian Cross served with the latter:

> It may not be unique, but it certainly is very unusual that I went with the same tank crew, my first and only brand-new troop, in a brand-new tank, just after my initial training in 2001, through exercises in Canada and deployments in Kosovo through to war fighting in Iraq with Falcon Squadron. We took each other from basic new guys to the finishing line in Iraq.
>
> My nine-month troop leaders course taught me about all the roles within the Challenger tank. We could drive it, load and operate the gun and even do some basic maintenance. The final part at Warminster also teaches you about working with armoured infantry and the Warrior IFV, all of which completely shaped me in time for Iraq. However, the climb down from the years spent together in our tank to the finish of the war and returning to Germany in a peacetime mood left us all feeling extremely dejected and asking ourselves 'what now?'

Unusually, 2 RTR used names rather than numbers for its four squadrons. So, there was Badger, Cyclops, Egypt and Falcon. RHQ was named Nero.* Each squadron had four troops of three tanks. The troops were numbered, and Falcon contained 14, 15, 16 and 17 Troops. Callsigns for each troop followed a pattern with the Troop Leader in 14 Troop answering as One Zero, the Troop Sergeant as One One and the Troop Corporal as One Two. The squadron commander, usually a major, was callsign Zero Bravo and his 2IC was Zero Charlie. With 14 main battle tanks (MBTs) per squadron, the regiment fielded 56 tanks at full strength, as well as many other lighter armoured vehicles for supply, command, medics and recovery. Lt Cross again:

> Our build-up exercises for *Telic* were in the sleet and snow on the Fallingbostel ranges in Germany, so not useful nor realistic for the desert heat of Iraq. We then painted the tanks desert yellow, running out of paint halfway through. The tanks were loaded on flatbeds on the German railway with much of our personal kit. I waved goodbye to 'Three Zero' and just hoped we would reunite in Kuwait.
>
> I bought my own desert uniform including boots because the army never issued it. My sergeant went online with my sizes and grabbed a load for me. The QM did try and palm us off with some faded beige tatty-looking kit, but it turned out it was all 15 years old from Op Granby and was rather moth-eaten. My driver went to Iraq in full Northern European green DPM uniform as he never got any proper kit. Having been issued body armour with plates for Iraq, we were told to give it up for the infantry who hadn't received theirs and weren't going to be sat inside an armoured box. The lack of body armour is completely unforgiveable. In tank units, we accept that if the tank is hit, we are unlikely to survive, but the body armour at least keeps you intact and makes body recovery and burial easier. Tanks attract fire and are loaded with high explosive shells and hundreds of gallons of fuel, but if you dwell on that too long, you'd go mad.

---

*   During *Telic 1*, Badger was not in theatre. Small black insignia of a falcon's head, a sphinx and a single eye can be seen on 2 RTR Challengers' turrets, denoting their squadron identification. After the war, HM the Queen awarded the regiment an additional Battle Honour for Iraq – Al Basrah 2003 – the first new honour for 50 years.

I made a note in my diary 'Our bus to the aircraft at Hannover to fly us to Kuwait was at 23:00, it was then delayed until at least 01:00 so we went to the mess and got drunk and watched soft porn. We came back at 01:30 when it was delayed again until 05:30 so we went to bed. At 05:30 off we went, it was nice to get going.' We flew on an unpainted chartered 'Atlantic Air' 747 aircraft and sat in what would be business class although there was no business class cabin service!

One of the threads that runs through a great many army accounts of their journey to Kuwait in 2003 is their clear displeasure with the RAF and how they carried out their role of getting the soldiers out to the Gulf. The RAF are often referred to by the army and marines as 'Crab Air' which is a derogatory term from the light blue uniforms worn by the RAF which was the same colour as a greasy ointment known as 'crab fat' which was used to treat pubic lice a long time ago. Crab Air appears not to have showered itself in glory at Brize Norton according to Maj Mike Peters, AAC and his recollections of his journey to Kuwait in February 2003:

What I remember most about this phase of the war was the messing around we were given at Brize Norton. We were in transit accommodation at South Cerney near Cirencester and seemed to get lost in a Bermuda Triangle between there and Brize which was only 25km away. I was part of an advance party from 3 AAC consisting of the CO, the Ops Officer, me as Regimental Signals Officer and a couple of others. Our party of six was replicated across the whole of 16 AAB's other units, so six officers and senior NCOs from 1 PARA, six more from 3 PARA, six from the Royal Irish including the CO, Lt Col Tim Collins, plus several officers from the Royal Engineers' advance party and the Royal Artillery recce party. Each group had radios and personal weapons as well as individual kit.

When we arrived at South Cerney it was like the RAF didn't know there was a war coming and had never moved anyone around the world before. We were moved from one room to another by a corporal who appeared to know nothing and care less. We found out that there was no RAF aircraft to take us, and we would be going, at some point, on a chartered 747 by Iceland Air. After a few hours we were taken on a coach to Brize Norton, and we could see an Iceland Air 747 parked on the dispersal. We waited for about 12 hours with no one telling us anything, sat in a bare waiting area. The coach came back then, and we were told to go back to South Cerney and we would fly tomorrow. I found out after that much of the delays were caused by diplomatic failures in securing the air routes to Kuwait. Some Arab countries did not want to allow 'military' flights through their airspace if they were going to invade another Arab state. The next morning, we were got up really early, had breakfast and got herded on to the freezing-cold chartered double-decker school bus and taken to Brize, where we could see the 747 sat in total darkness, no power, lights or stairways connected. We knew it was a waste of time. We waited around in the empty buildings with no news or updates from anyone. Then late in the afternoon the coach took us back to the accommodation. This went on repeating itself for four days.

Just to maximise our pain, we had checked in our luggage (Bergens) on day one and had not been allowed to get them back since 'due to security'. So, we literally had no toiletries, changes of clothing or anything to make life more bearable. The other crowning glory was that RAF Brize Norton was run by contractors who did not work at weekends. So, on the Friday afternoon the little WH Smith kiosk and the coffee shop closed, so there was even less to drink, read or pass the time. It was incredible that the RAF knew we were travelling to go war fighting and yet they continued to run it like it was a part-time civilian airport. Their check-in security approach was laughable – they were telling soldiers they couldn't take bayonets as they were sharp objects. They took away our little camping gas burners as they were dangerous. One Gurkha soldier went to the war with his grandfather's Kukri knife that he had carried on active service in Burma, the RAF Police tried to take it off him and it was only because the whole aircraft of soldiers stood by him that they relented.

We were all travelling early, ahead of our brigade for a good reason and every day we sat twiddling our thumbs was going to reduce our effectiveness. We needed to get out to identify camps, training areas, supply chains, liaise with our allies, sort out communications, arrange delivery of ammo and recce the ground. The RAF flew all their own aircraft out, but the army had no choice but to put its aircraft (Lynx and Gazelle) onto ships for the long voyage to Kuwait. There was even doubt that the ships would make it to Kuwait in time for the invasion day. They did, with only days to spare, but you need a day or two minimum to reassemble the aircraft, oil the parts, fold out rotor blades, test the aircraft on the ground then in the air before even moving it to the squadron. The radio kit we had checked in also went missing on the flight and was never delivered to the regiment.

Eventually, we cracked and Lt Col Collins insisted that the RAF duty officer was called to see us to tell us what the hell was going on and to arrange better facilities. The RAF's primary role in combined-arms operations is to get the army to where it needs to be. They had singly failed us by a combination of sleep deprivation, losing our kit and lowering our morale. Crab Air had been like an effective Fifth Columnist movement against us.

News of the deployment to the desert travelled across the Royal Navy in a similar fashion to the army; however, for some sailors the message, although unofficial, had come earlier because of the need to reposition them around the globe including sailing from one ocean to another rather than flying. Nineteen ships of the Royal Navy and a further six of the Royal Fleet Auxiliary sailed for the Persian Gulf for Operation *Telic*. The more obvious vessels were the aircraft carrier HMS *Ark Royal* and HMS *Ocean*, the amphibious helicopter landing ship. Vital little minehunters were also included in the form of HMSs *Sandown, Grimsby, Bangor, Blyth, Ledbury* and *Brocklesby*. Supporting these ships would be the traditional fleet of Type 42 destroyers such as HMSs *Cardiff, Liverpool, Edinburgh* and *York*. HMSs *Chatham, Richmond* and *Marlborough* were Type 23 frigates providing escort to the fleet. Often tasked with fleet protection, deep beneath the waves was the submarine fleet. As well as sinking enemy submarines and shipping with traditional torpedoes, they can also launch from hidden positions offshore cruise missiles that provide shock and surprise to any distant enemy. HMS *Splendid* of the 'Swiftsure' class and HMS *Turbulent*, a 'Trafalgar' class, were chosen for duty in the Gulf.*

Turbulent had passed through the Suez Canal and the Red Sea and just before Christmas 2002 docked in the Indian Ocean, south of the Maldives at Diego Garcia. Some of the crew took on provisions and others went on leave, like Welsh Marine

---

* Submarine S87 HMS *Turbulent*, known to most as 'Turbs', had left UK waters in May 2002, long before Operation *Telic* was sanctioned but being nuclear-powered could spend a great deal of time at sea. Displacing around 5,000 tons, 85m long, second in the seven-ship 'Trafalgar' class, *Turbulent* could travel at 30kts submerged with unlimited range thanks to its Rolls-Royce nuclear powerplant. It had a complement of 130 and was equipped with five torpedo tubes that could fire up to 30 Spearfish torpedoes or Tomahawk cruise missiles.

Engineer Mechanic Anthony Williams, who was on his first patrol with *Turbulent* having trained at HMS *Raleigh* in Devon and earned his specialist Golden Dolphin badge as a submariner engineer by doing six more months training:

> I took the bus into Peterborough Armed Forces Careers Centre in April 1999 to sign on for the Navy and was told it was quicker to join if you went in as a submariner than wait 12 weeks more to join the surface fleet. I hadn't previously thought about a career in the military but as a 19-year-old with no direction, one morning my dad gave me a brochure and said, 'I've made you an appointment for 10 o'clock, get the bus into town.' It was the best thing that ever happened to me.
>
> After qualification my main job was engineering the ship systems, other than the nuclear reactor, so our team of 12 fixed the heating, cooling, water systems and toilets. We also had another job which I found the most interesting – helping maintain and operate the periscope systems on the command deck. I had been involved in a 'Perisher' course on *Turbulent* where new submarine commanders are tested. I enjoyed the role as it allowed me to see and hear what was going on with command of the vessel and what was going on above us. I also had a small digital camera and the lens fitted nicely over the eyepiece of the periscope, and even the officers would ask me to take some still photos for them so they could look at what was viewed as a still image.
>
> The submarine has two periscopes: one is for search, the other for attack. The latter is much thinner and smaller, so it leaves less wake and is harder for an enemy to see in the water. The search periscope, or hoist as we called it, was larger and had the infrared camera and satellite comms attached to it. On the officer's command we would operate the hoist and then adjust it so they could scan the horizon. If it was dark outside, they would rig the deck for darkness and dim all the lights and then draw a big black velvet curtain around the hoist, so the officer was in total darkness, a bit like a photographer's dark room. This meant that his eyes could adjust to darkness on the surface.

Williams enjoyed his 10 days' leave pass and managed to get back for five days with his family in South Wales before returning to the Indian Ocean atoll. He continues:

> As my crew mate and I got back to the boat after Christmas, still alongside at Diego Garcia, we could see a convoy of trucks on the quayside and what we recognised as Tomahawk cruise missiles being loaded into *Turbulent*. Fortunately for us the last of the missiles were being loaded as we boarded. It sounds like a simple task but it's far from easy and can take all day, so it was a right result to get back as they finished. We all knew that a full load of Tomahawk missiles was very likely to only mean one thing. We slipped our moorings at 03:00 the next morning and headed north towards the Persian Gulf, diving deep to avoid detection.

3 Commando Brigade, under Brig James Dutton, although often used as a standalone Royal Marine brigade, was chosen for Operation *Telic* as an integral part of 1 UKDIV. The fighting commando elements would be 40 and 42 Commando backed by 29 (Commando) Field Artillery and 539 Assault Squadron, RM and two squadrons of Commando-badged Royal Engineers. A lesser-known unit that is only platoon-sized, as a brigade asset is the Royal Marine Police Troop. The unit provided close protection for the brigadier, liaised with the Intelligence Corps and Military Police regarding prisoners and interrogations and also acted as guides for route planning and some convoy escort duties. All ranks are lance corporal or

above for the necessary role sometimes called for in internal policing. Ex-Grenadier Guardsman with nine years' service, Steve Penney joined the Royal Marines as a mature soldier in 1999, earning the merit of King's Badge as best recruit. After a year with 45 Commando, he became a dog handler and joined the Police Troop:

> If you are a professional athlete, you do not train for ever and then never go to a competition. The same applies to soldiers; having done years of training we want to go on operations. I like the freedom and excitement of operations. I enjoyed soldiering so volunteered to go on *Telic* with the Police Troop. I always knew I would join the military – I tried at 16 for the marines but they thought I was too young and immature, so went to join the Grenadier Guards at Munster. I did nine years as a Guardsman, but the endless public duties became too much. Tower of London, St James's Palace, Windsor Castle and Buckingham Palace: working 24 hours on duty and 24 hours off, relentlessly for three years. Counting bricks and pacing up and down was monotonous, I prefer soldiering to parades. I then did two tours, back-to-back, in Ireland one attached to the Irish Guards as a medic, then as a GPMG [general-purpose machine gun] gunner on the second tour. I was also on Op *Granby* in '91 as a medic so by the time *Telic* came around I had plenty of experience and was raring to go when the troop was deployed with 3 Commando Brigade HQ.

Also within 3 Commando Brigade HQ sat the Media Ops team. The main effort of Media Ops in any military operation is to communicate the principal themes and messages to the appropriate audiences in pursuit of the desired effect whilst remaining sensitive to media interests. Media Ops focus on the need to maintain public and political support and hence freedom of action and manoeuvre. The media have an influence on adversaries, allies and neutrals, so it is essential that Media Ops works closely together to ensure that the right message is put across to the right audiences. It must avoid giving the impression that the media are being manipulated in any way and at the same time the Media Ops team needs to manage operational security and, where possible, the safety of embedded press corps. Effective media handling helps shows accountability, improves morale, sustains public support and helps rebut untrue or inaccurate stories. One only needs to see the impact of Ukrainian farmers towing Russian tanks to understand how effective the media can be. The SO1 lieutenant colonel in charge of the Media Ops team for *Telic* was 39-year-old Ben Curry, RM who had served in 42 Commando on Operations *Banner* (Northern Ireland) and *Herrick* in Afghanistan in 2002:

> I found out I was going to Iraq when I was at Northwood Headquarters – also known as HMS *Warrior* – which is near Watford, Hertfordshire. I understood I would again be performing the role of SO1 Media Ops. I had not long come back from Op *Jacana*, the British actions in Afghanistan after 9/11, and was familiar with what would be needed. In fact, many of the journalists and camera crews had also been in Afghanistan with us, so we already knew each other. I didn't like nor trust most of them further than I could throw them, but we had, on the most part, professional working relationships. After a little revision on first aid and my NBC drills I said goodbye to my wife and three sons in Somerset and joined a big grey ship that took us to Kuwait. I can't accurately remember which one I was on; they are all so similar, but it may have been HMS *Ocean* or HMS *Albion*.

Sailing on board *Ocean* was one half of the fighting teeth of 3 Commando Brigade. 40 (on *Ocean*) and 42 Commandos, pronounced *Forty* and *Four Two* respectively, were the fighting units. Manpower-wise they are a little smaller than a typical army battalion and each has around 700 men. 42 largely travelled by air to Kuwait and waited in the desert with the rest of the army. Captain Stuart Taylor was with 42 Commando:

> I walked into the living room at my mum's house in Broadstairs just before Christmas 2002 with a big smile on my face. I had just had a call from my commanding officer. My mum and girlfriend asked why I was smiling, and I said, 'We are going to war.' My mum just nodded sanguinely but my girlfriend burst into tears. Looking back, I could have handled it better!
>
> I come from a family of military, so it was no surprise when I felt that I wanted to join myself. My grandfather was in the RAF and went to France with the British Expeditionary Force (BEF) in 1940. He was an RAF signaller attached to an artillery unit in 1939 until he came off the Dunkirk mole onto one of the little ships and was evacuated back to England.
>
> The blokes in my company in 2003 had been drawn from all over and were both tough and capable. Historically, guys always go on about how tough it was back in the 1940s or 1980s and how it's easier today: well, that is utter rubbish. The standards, training and ethos in the corps have not changed and blokes on *Telic* were as good as any that had gone before them.

The Royal Marines were undergoing yet another restructure, meaning J Company, commanded by Maj Oliver with Capt Taylor as 2IC, was a new unit. Having served in Bosnia, South Armagh and Kosovo, Taylor had plenty of experience as a troop commander and as a captain. The new formation called *Commando 21* was designed around four rifle companies (J, K, L and M), two equipped with wheeled transport and two with tracked Hägglunds Bv206S all-terrain vehicles.

J Company was a close-combat company, with a few Land Rovers but mainly on foot. It would work with K, which was a manoeuvre-support company using wheeled Steyr-Puch Pinzgauers. L and M companies mirrored that arrangement but all used Bv206Ss. The manoeuvre companies were heavily armed with MILAN wire-guided anti-tank weapons and machine guns. *Commando 21* didn't work due to mobility issues. It effectively meant a two-tiered structure where one would outstrip the other for speed. Capt Taylor continues:

> Helicopters were heavily relied upon but if that was not an option, we used 4-tonners (Bedford lorries) to get us into battle. We always joked on exercises 'Don't worry lads, you won't ever go into battle on a Bedford!' When we approached Basra in 2003 it was exactly like that, we were lorried to the start line in a column of Bedfords! 40 Commando even had to use commandeered Iraqi trucks when it moved up the Al-Faw on Op *James*.

A key component in the delivery and sustainment of 3 Commando Brigade was to be the integral helicopter force of the Fleet Air Arm (FAA) and the attached squadrons from the RAF. With 19 years of Royal Navy experience, by the time of Operation *Telic* Jon Pentreath, from Dorset, was a lieutenant commander in charge of 845 Naval Air Squadron, FAA. He had qualified as a pilot on the Sea

King Mk 4 helicopter in which he accumulated most of his flying hours but had also qualified on the Lynx.

In 1982 his father, David, on board HMS *Plymouth*, took the surrender of Argentinian forces on the island of South Georgia before the main Falkland Islands battles. HMS *Plymouth* also engaged the enemy at Falkland Sound and was hit by several bombs dropped by Mirage fighter-bombers, all of which failed to explode. The Pentreath ancestors also include an able seaman who fought at Trafalgar, so it is fair to say they have the Royal Navy in their blood. Lt Cdr Pentreath:

> Whilst we were not officially told until January 2003 that we would be deployed to Iraq, we had already brought most personnel back to the UK in autumn 2002 in anticipation of the event. In the Navy we have what is known as 'Nelson's blind eye'. This meant we often ignore what we are told officially and do what we believe will be best! By the time we went on Christmas leave, end of 2002, given the constraints the government put us under, we were as well prepared as we could be.
>
> We trained to operate with the Royal Marines in the Arctic. If you can survive, operate and fight in that environment, you can pretty much do it anywhere in the world, more easily. In the early 2000s we would often operate at remote, forward bases with just one or two aircraft, close to the front lines with engineers and supply specialists at each Forward Arming and Refuelling Point (FARP). It can be risky due to the proximity of the enemy and may be less likely a tactic today.
>
> Since 9/11 detachments from 845 had been in the Gulf for Exercise 'Saif Sareea II' and aboard ships patrolling off Dubai and Bahrain.

Training continued at a pace for the squadron in the new year, especially on all aspects of low-level night flying and operating with the AR5. The AR5 was an aircrew respirator which had a large rubber hood and neck seal with a transparent visor, microphone and drinks inlets. It was outdated even in the 1990s but was all the RN had at the time. Pilots found it very difficult to fly in, and even more so when combined with night vision goggles (NVGs).

Flying for the RAF in the deserts of the Gulf had also been a constant for 10 years as Operation *Southern Watch* had been in operation since the summer of 1992. The stated purpose was ensuring the Iraqi compliance with United Nations Security Council Resolution 688. The resolution demanded that Iraq ended its repression of human and political rights for all citizens in Iraq. It was adopted at the end of the 1991 Gulf War that had left Saddam Hussein in power. He had brutally bombed his own people, mainly in the south, as punishment for what he perceived as weakness in their support of his position. From 1992 until 2003 US, UK and a few French warplanes flew from Saudi Arabia and Kuwait to patrol the southern Iraqi airspace below the 32nd parallel and ensure they were not being aggressive to their own people. Numerous incursions and violations led to several aircraft being shot down in the first years of the programme. A MiG-25 Foxbat was shot down by an F-16 in 1992 in what was the first ever air-to-air kill by an USAF F-16 fighter and a first kill by the Hughes AIM-120 AMRAAM.

One of the most effective and potent aircraft in the RAF fleet operating over Kuwait and Iraq (under the RAF Operation *Jural*) was the Boeing E-3D Sentry AWACS. The E-3D offered better radar and longer-distance radio coverage than any ground-based equipment. Based on the Boeing 707, it is easily recognisable by the rotating circular radar dome on top of the fuselage. By the late 1990s the AWACS had evolved into an airborne co-ordinating centre for both defensive and offensive operations. So, rather than simply look for an approaching enemy aircraft, the RAF and USAF could speak to and co-ordinate a variety of missions such as air-to-air refuelling, assistance to army units on the ground with CAS, combat search and rescue (CSAR) missions and medical evacuation flights away from the battlefields.

One of the crew operating at 34,000ft in the E-3D Boeing aircraft was Flt Lt Andy Johnson. With eyesight poor enough to stop him joining the forces initially, after six years as a Merseyside police officer Andy tried again for the RAF and got in:

I became a fighter controller in 1982 after training at Cranwell. I spent much of my first 10 years moving between RAF Buchan in Scotland, Saxa Vord in the Shetlands and Mount Kent in the Falklands. This is not air traffic control, but you do spend time on radar and radios talking to fighter aircraft, trying to intercept enemy aircraft or deconflicting others.

In 1991 I went on Operation *Granby* to Dharan to support the British Tornado force providing operational support and intelligence. In 1992 I was accepted to train as crew for the new AWACS E-3D Sentry, a new aircraft to join the RAF fleet. The flightdeck crew is normally four: there is a crew of 15–18 personnel. I trained to be a fighter allocator but eventually became a tactical director in charge of those 18 people.

As well as other technical training, I needed to undergo another stringent medical. All was OK, but my eyesight was still borderline, so they issued me some 'defence spectacles'. They were hideous, almost like comedy store thick-rimmed glasses, so I invested in contact lenses. Despite this I was over the moon to finally be flying. I flew more than 200 flights over Bosnia and in that time saw how effective the Sentry was but I was also part of the programme changing how it operated for the future.

After 9/11 it got very busy over Afghanistan. It was enormously busy during Operation *Anaconda* with the US forces in the mountains, and our learning curve was steep. We had a good crew there and it remained broadly the same team into Operation *Telic* in 2003.

Combined with our Afghan experience, we trained in Nevada on Exercise 'Red Flag', and this really helped us understand the USAF systems, procedures and even callsigns, so when *Telic* came around we were well switched on to working with them. Bearing in mind that most of the assets we could call upon were American, that level of understanding was key. One thing 'Red Flag' tried to do was allow new pilots to get as close to war as was possible in a peacetime exercise. American research showed that most US pilots shot down in Vietnam were shot down within their first 10 missions. So, if pilots could fly their first 10 on 'Red Flag' exercises, it might mean fewer of them would be shot down in future wars.

We practised our own emergencies too: onboard fires, with everyone going through drills to do with smoke and fumes and cabin decompression. If that happened, you could connect direct to the aircraft system if you were seated; however, if you had to walk around, as you would in an emergency, small portable oxygen bottles used by the tech guys had only lasted 15 minutes, so we all trained in how to fill their spare bottles for them. If we were really in the shit over Afghanistan and Iraq, there was nowhere to land so I am pretty sure we would all have died, and the RAF did take DNA samples in case of a catastrophe.

We were all issued combat survival waistcoats (CSW) also known as SERE vests (survive, evade, resist and extract) that had various gadgets to help if we found ourselves behind enemy lines: radio beacon, compass, knife and water. We were also issued a 9mm Browning pistol which I felt was hopeless.

There are nine mission crew consoles on an AWACS in three rows of three desks. The front row, facing backwards, are the aircraft controllers; the middle row faces forwards with the tactical director, surveillance chief and data chief; then the last row of three do the tracking and radar tasks. However, just before *Telic* a tenth console was fitted to all the RAF AWACS, which I believe proves as a country we were preparing for another war despite what Tony Blair said at that stage.

After three or four postponements in deploying to Iraq I was eventually rung at home just before 07:00 on Friday, 28 February 2003. I was told we were to take off at 10:00 so needed to be in for a briefing at 08:15. My wife Jo and my two daughters were expecting me to take the call, but after all the delays had started to think it maybe wouldn't happen. The goodbye was hard, mainly because I could not say when I would be back.

After the briefing, complete with Bergen, CSW, respirator haversack and a sleeping bag, I went out to the aircraft. It was totally rammed with extra non-crew personnel who were hitching a ride out to Saudi Arabia. We took off on time at 10:30 and turned to the east, climbing as we did so.

The role of aerial intelligence begun with aerial photography way back in World War 1 but evolved with improved technology and the growing number of ground-to-air threats, especially after the first Gulf War. On Operation *Granby* in 1991 the RAF had little experience of war and had prepared for a role over Northern Europe – very different to the conditions found over Iraq with the proliferation of AA guns and SAMs (surface-to-air missiles). Holes in RAF expertise, intelligence, planning and briefing were contributory factors to losing eight Tornados (one was a training incident), four in the first week of operations. During the 2,000+ missions of the air offensive, four fell to SAMs. Sqn Ldr Andy White, RAF had 18 years' service and was in command of the Tactical Imagery and Intelligence Wing (TIIW) when *Telic* started:

TIIW was born to help pilots survive their missions by providing them with expert threat analysis, including avoidance and awareness. It took the RAF several years to produce a training package for the newly formed role but in the meantime, we had already started in post! Fortunately for me, my first posting as RAF Intelligence was to No 41 Squadron full of Jaguar pilots who had flown over Iraq, and they shared with me many of the things they experienced with copious suggestions of just what would help them next time around. Later in 2005 I went on to command the RAF Intelligence School which was great because I was able to train youngsters before they were posted, unlike the scenario I had had to deal with.

In 2003, RAF imagery analysis was performed for the reconnaissance squadrons by their own internal reconnaissance intelligence centre (RIC). It had become clear, however, that it was a bit wasteful to have specialist staff on each squadron who were not necessarily carrying out daily tasks. Centralisation of this skilled resource was deemed the way forward and we had just carried that out in time for deployment to *Telic*. I left my young son and wife at home, went to Brize Norton where I heard that we were being flown to Ali Al Salem Air Base in northern Kuwait. I was happy about this because I had been based there a few times in the 1990s and it would feel a bit more familiar.

The aircraft that carried out photo-reconnaissance (PR) for the RAF at this time were mainly the GR4 Tornado and the aged but much-loved Canberra. Some additional work was undertaken by Jaguars and Harriers. By 2003, the Canberra was 50 years old. It was the RAF's first jet-powered bomber and had been developed by English Electric to replace the wartime de Havilland Mosquito. It could fly to an incredible 60,000ft and with its stable airframe and comparative high speed, its starring role in photographic work was uncovered. Over 900 Canberras were built in the UK and a further 451 in the United States (403) and Australia (48) under licence. It was used across the world from Chile to Sweden.

No 39 Squadron, RAF is a dedicated PR unit based at RAF Marham in Norfolk. Today, it remotely flies General Atomics MQ-9 Reaper drones but in 2003 flew the Canberra for the role. What topped off the Canberra for its photographic role was the mounting of an American camera system that was way ahead of its time. This allowed the Canberra to work in a stand-off mode – meaning it was totally out of sight from the target, probably at 50,000ft and virtually invisible. It was a phenomenal strategic reconnaissance aircraft, the British equivalent of the U2 spy plane without quite the edge of space capability.

The Tornado on the other hand was a tactical reconnaissance option. It had a similar camera system that also allowed stand-off capabilities when equipped with the RAPTOR (Reconnaissance Airborne Pod Tornado) which saw its first operational use whilst on Operation *Telic*. The canoe-shaped pod is mounted underslung on the Tornado fuselage and contains sensors, an image recorder and an air-ground data link. The camera lens is gyro-stabilised and can fix on a target while the plane is moving. It has since been used on Polish F-16s and Japanese maritime patrol aircraft.

Far from the role of photo-reconnaissance is that of close air support to ground troops. Dozens of fighter and fighter-bomber aircraft flew in support of the UK forces providing both CAS and precision strikes well in advance of the ground troops. The UK air strike capability was largely built around the Tornado and Harrier squadrons. The RAF CAS phase became known as the KI/CAS phase – standing for kill-box interdiction/close air support. KI/CAS was a USMC concept adopted for the operation. The whole of Iraq was divided into kill boxes. Boxes were either 'open' or 'closed'. If closed, aircraft could only attack under positive direction from an FAC. If 'open' and beyond the forward line of own troops then aircraft were weapons free on targets they identified themselves.

Kill-boxes were automatically closed unless opened with the agreement of the Combined Forces Land Component Commander. In the absence of such agreement, they were subject to three types of close air support, all of which necessitated positive direct control of the aircraft. Type 1 required the terminal controller to have sight of both the aircraft and the target – a rare occurrence during the campaign; Type 2 required the terminal controller to have sight of either the aircraft or the target; Type 3 enabled air strikes to take place when the terminal controller could see neither aircraft nor target. Ultimately, KI/CAS accounted for 75% of RAF Tornado and Harrier tasking.

Neither aircraft is well suited to close air support. The Tornado is designed as a point attack aircraft and the Harrier had been a low-level attack aircraft until the mid-90s when it then flew at medium altitude to best use its laser designator. For close air support, coming in fast and low meant the thermal-imaging airborne laser designator could not cope with small tactical target being called for and positive identification was problematic.

There had been no requirement for air support from the British Army since the 1982 Falklands War. None of the aircrew had any real experience of close air support and were all entrenched in extensive mission planning and briefings on single known targets, backed up with mission folders of photographs and threat analysis on planned in and out routes. By contrast in the KI/CAS role, aircraft were simply dispatched to a specific kill-box to await tasking. This was like stepping back in time to Normandy 1944 when whole squadrons of Typhoons, Mustangs and Spitfires would loiter over the battlefields in what became known as the cab rank system and would be called upon when required, just as a hotel porter calls on a waiting taxi at a hotel cab rank.

Complicating matters further was the requirement to operate in kill-boxes of urban environments. The chance of collateral damage in a city was high, the chance of seeing the target was low. Consequently, a high proportion of taskings returned without releasing weapons. An added factor influencing offensive operations was the ability for the fast jets to loiter over the target areas. For the RAF this ability was being diminished by the residual threat from anti-air missile systems near Basra. This threat meant that high value, slow-moving assets like air-to-air refuelling tankers had to stay south of the border, thus pulling the fighters to the south, off station, to refuel.

This snapshot of stories begins to tell the tale of how Britain mobilised its forces in 2003. From brown envelopes on the doormat at breakfast time, to phone calls in the ops room and 'quiet words' transmitted across the waves to 'Turbs' in the Indian Ocean: no matter how they were called, they answered and were on their way, willingly.

CHAPTER 3

Kuwait: Planning and Waiting

Every day in Kuwait was spent training. I was a corporal on paper but acting as sergeant in the Assault Engineer Platoon, so we spent our time checking our equipment, practicing locating and clearing mines and plenty of medical training. We had already done some live firing in Oman on our way to Kuwait. In the evenings we improved our accommodation which was only basic 12 x 12 tents surrounded by a sand berm. The portaloos were terrible. Sitting in a sweaty box smelling of poo is hardly appealing at any time but in 40°C desert heat with hundreds of flies it's downright grim. Before the portaloos arrived, we had the Sappers make long drops dug in the sand. One soldier went to a long drop latrine and had a cigarette. He dropped the butt down the long drop, and it promptly burst into flames, scorching a certain part of his anatomy between his legs. A few moments earlier another soldier had poured fuel down there to burn off the waste but had to go and look for a lighter. Medic!

When we cleaned our kit, one guy wanted to sharpen his bayonet to perfection. He was at it for hours. He said it was so sharp it would slice paper. To demonstrate his handy work, he proceeded to draw the bayonet across a sheet of paper and looked surprised as it turned red. He had cut through it and the leg he had it rested on. Medic!

We were in our final harbour area before the invasion when a storm occurred. I couldn't believe it. Here we were in the desert in a massive downpour. In the morning the flood water was up to the doors of the vehicles, and we had a guest in ours. A huge lizard that must have sought sanctuary from the water had climbed in our vehicle. It was not grateful and it bit anyone trying to get it out. Medic!

Cpl Chris 'Freddie' Kruyer, 3 Para

While thousands of British personnel streamed across the skies and oceans on their way to the deserts of Kuwait, a far smaller number were beavering away at the plans for the likely invasion. It was far from concrete that Britain would invade, especially while Tony Blair gave out caveats that Britain was not committed to any specific action. Delicate negotiations still trundled on at the United Nations involving American, French, British and Russian diplomats trying to find a way to get a more joined-up approach to the UN Security Council resolutions. American planners, meanwhile, were forging ahead with various options, some of which included British troops.

The chain of command had at least been agreed, should invasion be called for. AM Brian Burridge was the designated UK national contingent leader to work alongside the US head of CENTCOM (Central Command), Gen Tommy Franks. UK Land

Forces were led by Maj Gen Robin Brims. The RAF contingent was headed up by AVM Glenn Torpy and the maritime force by Rear Adm David Snelson. UK Special Forces had an increasingly bigger role to play in the coming events and were led by Brig Graeme Lamb.

In the 1991 Iraq war CENTCOM commander US Gen 'Storming' Norman Schwarzkopf had little time for special forces (SF) and saw the invasion as a purely conventional affair. SF teams were only assigned the most limited of roles. Schwarzkopf, like many senior soldiers in 1991, was a product of the Cold War, where huge, static, heavy forces faced off against each other in Germany, a million miles away from the vast open desert, facing asymmetric threats from a technically inferior yet capable enemy in Iraq. The launching of Scud missiles from the open plains of western Iraq into Israel prompted action in 1991, and SAS and US Joint Special Operations were hurriedly assigned a role of interdicting the mobile Scud launchers. After-action analysis of the 1991 anti-Scud campaign suggested little success was achieved. However, 12 years on and with the successes of SF teams in Afghanistan, General Franks was far more open to their widespread use – so much so that they were to be given the task again of denying the Iraqis the use of western Iraq to launch Scud missiles. The force allocated was called Joint Special Operations Task Force-West (JSOTF-W). Its nucleus was the US Army's 5th Special Forces Group together with British SAS and SBS units and a team from the Australian SAS. Exercises were held in the desert of the western United States with all the JSOTF components being tested in their potential role of Scud hunting. A secondary role was also built in: to harass and pin down Iraqi conventional forces and interdict supply columns.

The main conventional US ground troops were also on their way to the Gulf. The US Army's V Corps was to launch its forces from Kuwait and strike deep into the Iraqi countryside and forge north for Baghdad. The US 3rd Infantry Division was the principal striking force for the Americans. The term 'infantry' is a misnomer, as it was had a substantial armoured component with hundreds of M1 Abrams tanks and M2 Bradley infantry fighting vehicles (IFVs). The Americans also had a sizeable formation from the US Marine Corps (USMC) on its way to the Gulf. The USMC's 1 Marine Expeditionary Force (1 MEF) would be embedded with the British in the Basra area during the initial invasion stage.

Once British troops arrived in Kuwait for the build-up phase, experiences vary but on the whole veterans are critical of the conditions they lived in and the poor level of planning that was due to the political indecision and the tardy arrival of kit and supplies. Many veterans express their displeasure that the army could not fulfil or supply its own mission. It laid down what was to happen but was unable to provide people and equipment at the right time and location to ensure it was possible. Examples of the unpreparedness and poor kit are numerous. Here are the thoughts of WO2 Andy Abbott, RE EOD:

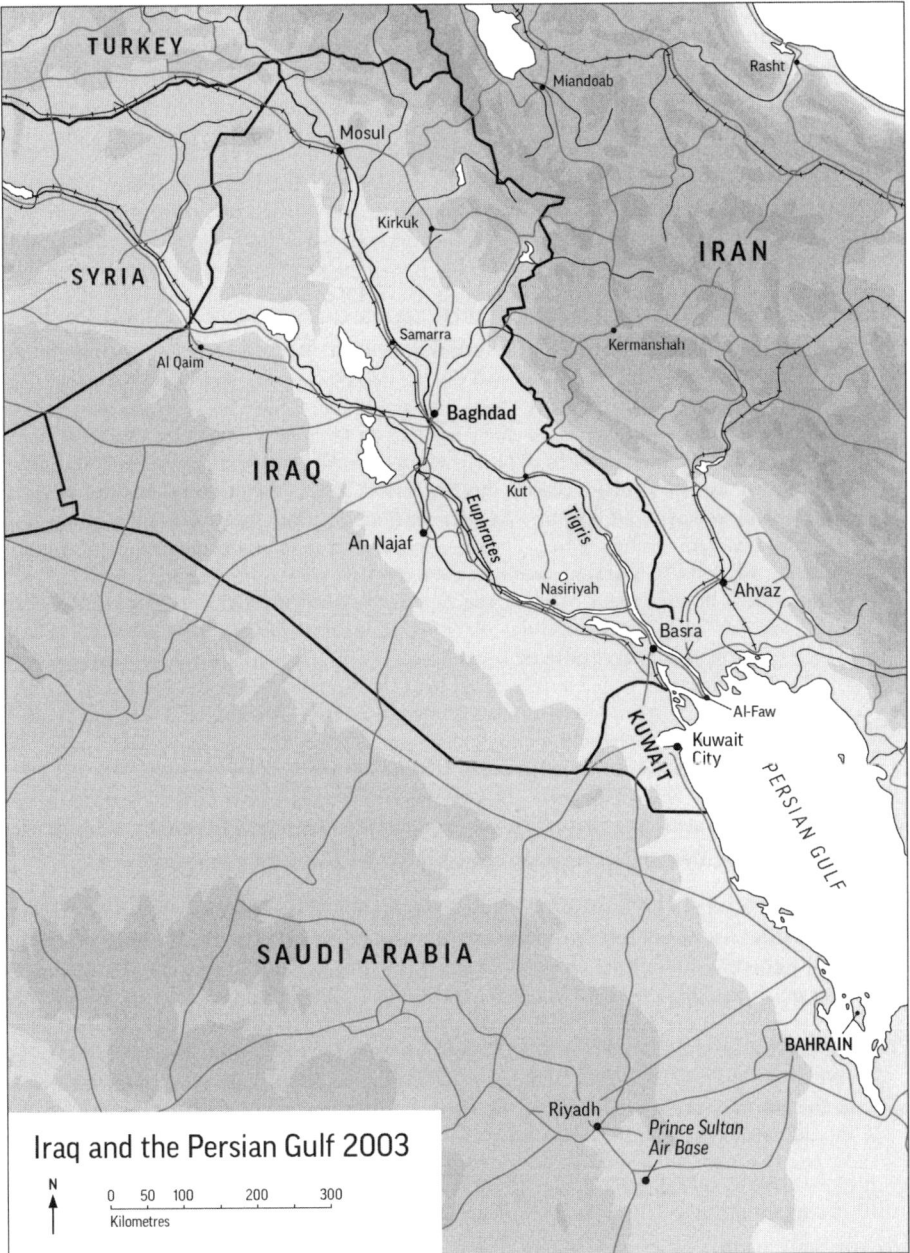

Iraq and the Persian Gulf 2003

N

0   50   100   200   300

Kilometres

We flew from Brize Norton to Kuwait on a hired French 747. We were housed in giant tents in Kuwait – contractors helped us put them up. We still had no desert kit and were still in greens. I had to purchase a new Bergen and was given a blue holdall bag for kit and a duffel bag which looked even less military. I didn't think it at the time but now I realise there wasn't enough kit, there was bugger all, but you just get on with it. I had purchased my own inflatable kip mat from Costco, it was brilliant. It felt like the guys at the base camps back in Kuwait had all the desert kit.

We swapped a lot of kit and food with the Americans. Their MREs were better than ours. I even got a nice US Army sun hat which the guy had worn in 1991 on the first Gulf War. I loved that hat, a relic of '91 and then 2003, it went with me everywhere. I kept it for years and when I lost it in India on holiday, I was gutted.

They couldn't believe we were still in Dark Green/Brown DPM when they were all head to toe in Desert DPM. They think of EOD as like special forces, so it was easy swapping a shoulder patch badge or two for a good bit of uniform or boots. Of course, when the war started, as EOD we had to de-badge and the only thing that identified us was a small red-coloured plastic sticker in the shape of a bomb that was in the windscreen of the Rover. In fact, we surrendered our rank sliders, ID cards and everything – all that we had was our dog tags. It was a bit daunting.

The 'augmentees' – the 11 of us – were seen as add-ons! Augmentees was the term used to describe reinforcements that arrived singly from a host of different UK units. Others from the unit were radio operators and drivers. I took over as sergeant major in the regular HQ Squadron, 22 Regiment as theirs had gone home due to personal issues. The threat of chemical weapons was big, and we had to set up a new decontamination unit with showers. I felt the threat was very worst case and was frightening. I had seen lots of stuff about it, the blister and nerve agents including VR and VX, and wondered how good our kit – smock, trousers and overshoes – was going to be if he used them. We also had fuel suits – giant inflated suits and helmets – we had them to do an EOD task over the top of everything else with breathing apparatus as well. Naked strips! With a bucket of water in the face.

The Press came and visited but we were briefed by our own press team. No TV, so the feed from the big picture started to fade. Sue knew more than me. We had 10–15 minutes a week on a Sat phone, but I only used it two or three times. We had to sign it out and it was quite strict. Blueys [forces free air letters] came from home and friends. Our phones were confiscated.

As the run-up to action continued, tempers began to fray and mistakes were made. Col Jim Tanner remembers one that could have had serious consequences:

> While we were all still warming up and preparing before the invasion, there was a minor incursion which caused a stir that went all the way up to the UN HQ in Washington, DC. A small section of Royal Scots Dragoon Guards Recce Platoon and a company of Irish Guards went north, crossing the DMZ at the 5km berm line – a ditch and berm constructed in 1991 as part of the Kuwait defences. The British armoured convoy headed into the DMZ and up to the Iraq border and was spotted by a UN lookout post who called it in. The report flowed up and up the chain of command all the way to Washington, whereupon the message then came all the way back down to HQ 1 UKDIV. By then the incursion mistake had been realised and the column was back in Kuwait, no harm done.
>
> Next morning at the morning briefing Brig Graham Binns made rather light of the incursion but the US Army colonel attached to HQ went berserk saying that it could have started the war. We all just shrugged and said, 'You need to lighten up, pal.'

At sea, Dr Sarah Chapman-Trim was serving with the Royal Australian Navy and had a range of problems to deal with:

I was part of the medical team on HMAS *Kanimbla* so as well as being a psychologist, I could help with the ward functions. We did some battle damage and firefighting training aboard *Kanimbla* but after only 10 days sailed from Sydney under a bright blue January sky with a band playing. We were all in whites lined up on deck waving. I was single then and no one waved me off, which I was glad about as it allowed me to focus on the job in hand. We refuelled off Darwin on the northern tip of Australia and then turned to the north. I was on the bridge wing, looking at the beautiful blue ocean and the Australian coast as it slowly disappeared as we went to war. There was another Australian Navy ship close by and they were headed elsewhere, and some waves were exchanged with crew from her bridge. I did not know it then, but one officer on the other ship who was waving at us was the navigator. He and I met years later, and he is now my husband.

I remember more about our homecoming in May 2003 – as we came around the headland, I saw Sydney Harbour Bridge and dozens of small ships and thousands of people waving on the dockside. It brought a lump to my throat.

We joined a task group of two frigates, HMASs *Anzac* and *Darwin*, and sailed up into the Gulf. My role was as the first point of contact for any critical incident or trauma suffered by the crew: to restore functionality and make assessments on repatriations after any incidents. We provided a service to command on the temperature of the ship's company. I helped people who were having difficulty sleeping, others who felt a bit overwhelmed or out of their depth – so I did some empowerment and assertiveness training – and one or two who were struggling with the philosophical aspects of going to war. Later, some crew members struggled with issues around the body recovery tasks we undertook after our smaller vessels had fished out bodies in the waterways near Basra.

The ship was old and a bit leaky, so a bit past its best. We had our respirators with us as the chemical threat was considered real, but it didn't keep me awake at night!

In Bahrain I had to fly ashore to pick up a member of the crew who had got himself arrested for being drunk outside a hotel whilst on leave. It had taken a week or so to get the authorities to release him and it was then decided that I should conduct a debrief of the sailor to assess him and the treatment he had experienced in the jail.

One member of the ship's crew threatened to kill the captain one night and went to the small-arms locker to get a firearm. He really was in a dark place and needed some serious talking to before the medical team could take care of him. I also had to deal with a crew member who was found to be injecting controlled drugs and stealing drugs on board. After he was admitted to the ship's hospital, he self-declared as a user and discharged himself from the navy, accepting all the consequences. I often wonder where he is now.

Flt Lt Andy Johnson had left home on 28 February 2003 and was immediately involved in briefings:

We took off on time at 10:30, landing in the dark at Prince Sultan Air Base (PSAB) in Saudi at 17:45. PSAB is a vast air base with mile upon mile of runways and taxiways, hangars, maintenance depots and crew buildings. Dozens of aircraft were parked up, E-3s, E-8 JSTARS, tankers, RC-135W Rivet Joints and Hercules C-130s. On every corner were concrete barriers and MP teams. After a few minutes we offloaded and were put on a crew bus which somehow was led down a dead end by an airfield 'follow me' vehicle, something that, of course, made us all laugh. After a local briefing about the threat level and instructions on air raid warnings, we were allocated to four-man rooms and got our heads down just after midnight.

Over the next few days, we had countless briefings and meetings with American teams over rules of engagement (ROE), no-fly zones and CSAR. We were allocated our new callsign – Brutus. We had been callsign Spartan in Afghanistan. At the meeting, on hearing our new callsign, one of the crew shouted, 'Great, we go from being one oiled up Mediterranean poofter to another.'

All the while, more and more personnel and assets were arriving in country. On one day alone we were astonished to see the US contractors erect 72 huge tents. Their work rate was phenomenal.

I was also issued 'goolie chits' and gold. Since the 1920s the RAF has issued pilots and aircrew a small card that boasts the Union Flag on one side and vital messages in several languages on the other, promising to pay rewards for keeping the airman safe, thus preserving his most personal of items! Essentially it is a safe passage card for downed aircrew, intended to bribe local civilians not to harm the holder of the card. They got the nickname 'goolie chits' after eye-watering stories on the Northwest Frontier emerged in the 1920s of prisoners being castrated.

I was also given several gold coins – South African Rands – another last-ditch measure to help us if we went down behind the lines. Thankfully, I never needed the gold or the chits.

On Tuesday, 4 March we flew our first Operation *Southern Watch* mission. Our role was to provide a presence, monitor Iraq's compliance with the UN Security Council resolutions and to enforce the Southern No-Fly Zone. We were bound by Britain's ROE which were more restrictive than US rules. We were not, however, prohibited from acting as a conduit to US aircraft who flew with their own rules, and I stressed this to my team. If we encountered enemy air, we planned on *sliding* to the south-west away from the enemy threat. If it continued to close, we would *retrograde* – i.e. run away – at maximum speed and call for friendly assistance. If we also dropped below 20,000ft that would help get below the level of Iraqi radar. The Iraqis had MiG-25 Foxbats at Al Asad Air Base only 300km from Kuwait and it wouldn't take long for a MiG to reach us.

We went into an orbit – we call them 'Oriole' orbits – to check radar and found we had comms problems. We tried to call the US E-3, but their radio discipline was so poor we couldn't get a word in edgeways. After a few minutes most of the comms problems were sorted and we moved toward the patrol pattern. I then noticed we were in a left turn, facing south-west, which puzzled me somewhat.

I called the flight deck, 'Flight deck, TD [Tactical Director].' No response.

Again, louder, 'Fight deck, TD.' No response.

We were now turning toward the Iraq border, which we had explicit orders not to cross.

Eventually the flight deck replied in a tetchy voice 'We are dealing with a nav problem.' The pictorial display on our screens could have been a great help for nav but the navigator seemed reluctant to ask for or accept our help. Our tight turn increased, and I felt the aircraft pitch up and buffet, then ease off and then buffet again. We were now inside Iraq. I called out angrily to the flight deck 'Can you sort this out.' Our orbit had taken us briefly into Iraq, back into Kuwait and was turning once again back toward Iraq. There was no immediate response, I called again, 'We are now no more than 15km from the border again, I suggest we reverse right!' We rolled out to the south and remained on that heading for 10 minutes while they sorted out their problems. We had been put in a dangerous position because the navigator was too proud to accept help. It was a long post-flight debrief and we had to work harder on crew coordination.

News of our little excursion into Iraq had spread and, of course, the resulting banter was furious!

On 5 March Col Rob Green, USAF explained during a five-hour briefing the outline of our upcoming mission. We were to be part of a team operating in and over western Iraq against ground-based time-sensitive targets (TST), mainly in the shape of Scud missile systems. The 410th Air Expeditionary Wing (AEW) was made up of US Air National Guard squadrons operating some 30 F-16C fighters. They were squadrons from Alabama, Utah and Colorado. The British contingent numbered eight RAF GR7 Harriers and two Canberra PR9 PR aircraft. There were four British AWACS E-3Ds, two US AWACS and several electronic surveillance (Rivet Joint) aircraft as well as an RC-135S Cobra Ball which tracks ballistic missiles.

Ground-based teams were from the US 5th Special Forces Group (Task Force – TF – 20), British SAS and SBS squadrons (TF7) and an Australian SAS team (TF14). The aim with this potent and mobile force was primarily to prevent Saddam Hussein from launching Scud missiles, mainly against Israel. The second objective was to find, fix and destroy the estimated 6,000 hide sites and any associated launch equipment. While the SF ground teams inserted into the desert of western and north-west Iraq, the 410th AEW patrolled and deterred by its presence, especially along the main roads which were known to be used by the Scud launch teams.

Further input was given from 'Bloodhound', the tobacco-chewing AWACS veteran Maj Woody Pietz, USAF and then by a guy known only as 'Caveman' who was UK SF who finished his input by saying, 'When you see a target, use as much force as you need. But please, only use as much as you need. We will be very close.'

The F-16C had been chosen for this task along with the GR7 as they were fitted with Litening, a targeting pod mounted externally on the aircraft. The pod contains a high-resolution, forward-looking, infrared sensor that displayed an infrared image of the target to the pilot. It had a wide field of view for search capability and narrow field of view for target attack. The pod also housed a laser designator to support the delivery of laser-guided bombs.

Sunday, 9 March. After a very frustrating morning trying to contact my family via the internet, and failing, I went to church. There was a gospel service with the American forces, most of the congregation was black, and I loved it. The Chaplain, Effson Bryant, led the service, and it was the epitome of what I imagined such services would be like. Lively, uplifting worship and an excellent choir. It lasted well over an hour, and I was very glad I had gone along. Elsewhere, the tension of the crew was evident with lots of arguments and surly comments creeping in. Issues over phoning home and laundry assumed unreasonable proportions. Frustration at the lack of action was building and this was further fuelled by the pure speculation from the BBC and Sky News.

I sought solitude, as time for quiet reflection was difficult at the base, but in the evening, I attended the other Christian church service; this time it was predominantly white. It was amusing to see how restrained white worshippers were compared with the earlier service.

As I walked slowly back to the accommodation block, I noted how PSAB had continued to grow. Tent City was bigger and large numbers of ISO containers were stacked everywhere. More aircraft had arrived, including six more KC-10 Extender tankers. I think there were close to 100 air-to-air tankers now on base. The evident surge in equipment at PSAB coupled with the news that Hans Blix and the UN Monitoring team were not getting total cooperation from the Saddam Hussein regime told me that we were close to D-Day.

Callsign Brutus flew several more training flights over Jordan in mid-March, during which the crew practised some of the procedures for operating with Caveman SF ground teams. There were numerous technical breakdowns and minor snags which illustrated that the coming operation would not be as easy as hoped. It was also noted how busy the airspace was becoming and that activities such as refuelling, effectively in a cab rank of aircraft with combined closing speeds over 950mph, could be described as hazardous.

The congested airspace was divided up into layers, for rotary aircraft this generally meant operating sub-200ft above the ground. The Army Air Corps Gazelles and Lynx were arriving a great deal closer to the Iraq border than the RAF at PSAB and found themselves in tented camps just like the armour and infantry units. S/Sgt 'Bertie' Banfield, AAC had made himself as comfortable in his cot space as he could, and with three months of working in Oman just behind him, he did not find it too difficult. As a forward air controller (FAC), he had been flown to

Kuwait in February as part of an advance party so that he had plenty of time to meet and practise with his USMC counterparts. With 19 years' service, including his initial eight in the Royal Artillery, he was a very experienced soldier and capable Gazelle pilot. Bertie was normally in 4 Regiment but like most units that go to war, 3 Regiment was short-staffed and he was sent across to the sister regiment as an augmentee. He recalls:

> When acting as an FAC and airborne in the Gazelle my callsign was Spindle, which is a rubbish callsign, but I didn't get to choose it. The job of the Gazelle is to spot the enemy and then bring assets to bear on them. That can be artillery, other armed helicopters like Lynx or Cobra or fast jets like the US F-18 Hornet. We had a lot of practice with the US ANGLICO [Air Naval Gunfire Liaison Company] teams so we could understand the US systems, processes and nuances as well as jargon and terminology. We practised for days with the US Marine teams out on the ranges, which were just areas of desert. The team we worked with was led by US Marine GySgt Bunker, known as 'Gunny.' He was a squat Latino reserve Marine, with years of regular service too, who told me that just before Iraq he had been working as a mercenary in Columbia and returned to Texas when he heard the call up was on for Iraq. One day out on the range we were joined by a USMC captain who was a cross between John Wayne and Clint Eastwood. He was one of the ANGLICO officers and he loved what he did and enjoyed seeing fast air and gunships come in dropping bombs or rockets. He also liked to make the most of the day and see that the system was working almost like a cab rank system, meaning aircraft were orbiting close by ready to act on our calls as the FACs. We had a bit of a break in aircraft availability which he was grumbling about and clearly not happy with. He stomped off in front of us all, stood with his hands on his hips and shouted out 'someone has to have something to bring to the goddamn party.' At that point a young artillery officer from the RHA piped up in a very reedy, squeaky voice and said rather nervously, 'I have, sir, callsign Hardman.' John Wayne turned around and said laughing, 'You have gotta be shitting me!'

The Aerospatiale Westland Gazelle flew into army service in 1974, so by 2003 was already nearly 30 years old yet remains today in limited service even at 50 years of age. Designed for reconnaissance, battlefield liaison and casualty evacuation, the Gazelle normally has a crew of two and can take two or three passengers. They have no armour plating but the pilots do sit in armoured seats. Gazelles rely on their speed and manoeuvrability rather than weaponry to survive and can cruise at 165mph. The Gazelle was the first helicopter to feature a Fenestron tail instead of a conventional rotor. It is this enclosed rear rotor that gives the iconic whistling sound. Much to the annoyance of army pilots like Bertie Banfield, just before *Telic* a vital piece of kit was removed from the roof of the Gazelles. Laser target designators were still somewhat new but added so much capability to the Gazelle as an FAC platform. The pilot could point his roof-mounted laser at a target, and 'paint' it, making it visible to friendly aircraft looking for the target who could then drop bombs and missiles that could also 'see' the laser-painted target. Inexplicably, prior to the war, these bits of superb equipment were removed and sent to the Fleet Air Arm. This left the army Gazelle pilots feeling exasperated. They knew that their radio systems were often faulty and lacked range so coupled with the removal of the laser designators meant they may be finding the enemy once inside Iraq but wouldn't be able to tell anyone where they were!

The role of the RSO was to try and get all the radios in 3 AAC to work across an area the size of Wales. The encrypted radios held by 3 AAC were nearly the same in number as the whole of 16 AAB, meaning it was a very radio and data-heavy environment to operate in. The RSO, Maj Mike Peters, pushed some of his best men way out into the desert to act as 're-bro' – re-broadcast stations. These three- or four-man teams in a Land Rover with trailer were expert signallers who would erect the 8m mast to help 'bounce' radio messages from the Gazelle and Lynx patrols, who were often over enemy lines, back to Regimental or Brigade HQ. Each day, the ops plans may mean pulling the re-bro teams from one area and sending them 50km in another direction to achieve the coverage. Maj Peters remembers:

On *Granby* back in 1991 we had weeks of desert training before we attacked but for Telic, because of the political delays in getting us to theatre, we only had a few days and it really meant that a lot of scheduled 'work ups' were never done. We discovered that this had one advantage. The granules of dust wore out the leading edge of the rotors far quicker than we expected and may have caused shortages or failures had we had extended work-up flights, but the shortened exercise time helped us slightly on that matter.

We were deploying with a Cold War armoury (Lynx and Gazelle) and Cold War comms equipment (BATCO and Clansman radios) so we hoped to be able to fight well enough alongside the other component parts of 1 UKDIV. In fact, there was a briefing from each of the brigades at HQ one day in Kuwait, explaining their capabilities and expected roles. There was much 'willy waving' by the maroon berets of the Paras and the green 'cabbage hats' of 3 Commando Brigade. Very cleverly, 7 Brigade had a female briefing officer give a superb briefing with a very calm and efficient manner – it put the others in the shade. I only wanted to ask one question at the end, and it was based on my own *Granby* experience, from when the division was much more cohesive and used to working with each other, than the sort of cobbled together division we had on *Telic*. Standard operating procedures (SOPs) were dying out, so I asked, 'At night when troops basher up (sleep), what side of the vehicle is the division sleeping on?' It sounds like a really daft question but if the driver of a Challenger tank, at night, comes across a unit sleeping near their vehicles they will want to know which side to pass, to avoid crushing those sleeping. SOPs exist to tell people that, but they were almost a thing of the past as each brigade did its own thing. They didn't have the answer. It was a worrying time, it felt like a lot of units had started to think they were special and therefore no one was normal or standard.

There was a poor understanding at 16 AAB about what aviation could and would do in the forthcoming battles. The three infantry battalion commanders (1 PARA, 3 PARA and 1 Royal Irish) and our CO went to a big briefing where a set of orders was given out and each infantry CO was given product consisting of maps, overlays, aerial photographs and a briefing pack. Our boss of 3 AAC came back with nothing. The four planning teams all stood around the bird table and only three of them had been given intelligence to work with. It was clear then that 16 Brigade had no idea how to use us or what we may need. When it started, they straight away asked us to do lots of tasks for which we needed all that product to assist us, just like everyone else. It was almost like they had forgotten what had been learned on *Granby* and they were setting up to fight a war from the 1980s. It was not a happy headquarters. Several people had just been sacked and the commander, Brig Jonathan 'Jacko' Page, had previously been in armour and didn't really like the Army Air Corps. It was like the old cavalry who didn't like the newfangled tank in 1916.

Mostly, however, the British military forces were still massing inside Kuwait. BSM Leigh Sharpe was there:

I flew into Kuwait from Brize Norton and landed on 3 March 2003. The camp was close to the Iraq border, and I remember we got several Scud warnings, but none landed close to us. We trained with the medical units to understand how we could help them and demonstrated our own kit and methods for them. We also fixed up ColPro (collective protection) tents. These provided a forced-air environment in which pressurised air was pushed in to keep contaminants outside. If they were wounded, personnel would be stripped off and decontaminated at the doorway before they continued into the medical facility. It sounds good but I was not confident that it was good enough to keep out a single pinhead-sized poison droplet.

In fact, when I was told to go and pick up the incoming vehicles and supplies for our team, I was expecting to take delivery of a special mobile shower system like the Fire Brigade have at chemical incidents, that firemen walk into and get blasted by the big multi-jets. How wrong I was. I got given a bucket, some bleach and a bog brush.

Can you honestly imagine going up to a wounded hairy-arsed Para who already thinks you are gay because you are in the band and then saying to him, 'It'll be all right,' as you slip your marigold gloves on and say through your rubber mask, 'I just need to rub you down with this bog brush!' He is going to shoot you.

I wasn't confident about any of it. We were in a desert with truly little water and yet our key role relied heavily on a water supply to wash people and kit off.

Cpl Paul Burton, REME was attached to the Black Watch Battlegroup (BG):

I got off the bus in Kuwait after flying in via Frankfurt at a big, tented city run by the Americans. We played endless games of hurry up and wait and each time we moved, some people were detailed off to join a unit. It felt a bit like being on the airport transfer coach going on holiday between resorts and every time it stopped, we looked to see where they were being dropped.

I still wasn't sure which unit I was going to be posted to apart from it being the Black Watch Battlegroup. Then there was literally a dozen or so of us left and I was told that I (Cpl Burton) would be going to 'B Workshops' in the rear area. One of the others was L/Cpl Barton. He was to go up to the front lines with B Company as a fitter. I was not happy about his, I wanted to be up front with the lead elements. We then did some more quality sitting about waiting. Later that afternoon a Land Rover pulled up and the guy leaned out and said, 'Corporal Barton.' I looked over and saw Barton was asleep. Seizing the moment, I said, 'I am Corporal Burton.' The driver waved and said, 'Jump in mate.' I picked up my Bergen and tool kit which I had been issued at Chilwell. The driver said, 'You can't bring that we ain't got room,' so I dumped my tool kit. When I left Iraq the CQMS asked for it and I said I could give him a grid reference as to where I last saw it. He laughed but said I would get charged for losing it. I never did though!

I later found out that L/Cpl Barton stayed in Kuwait in the rear area and got so fed up he went home early. I was not proud of what I did to get on the forward position but at least I had an interesting time. You snooze you lose!

As the REME Light Aid Detachment for B Company, The Black Watch, we had two FV430s and a Warrior recovery vehicle. There were nine of us.

On two occasions we were given a grid reference to attend. It was about 3km away so we could easily walk to it. The first time it was for a church parade and the second a briefing from some American two-star general.

The church parade was well attended. Three of us walked on a bearing to the grid and found the padre with his altar. I found it quite enlightening and although I had never been remotely religious, I found myself taking it very seriously and having a quiet word with the good man above to keep me safe. It was on the way back that we encountered a big issue: our first sandstorm. As we were only walking 3km in one direction, it was amazing to see how disorientated you could become. Swirling sand and grit blew about and there was a fine dust that covered everything and made vision more than arm's length impossible. We got hopelessly disorientated, agreed we were lost and decided that the best thing was to go firm and sit it out. About an hour later once the storm had passed, vision started improving and slowly revealing itself in front of us was our camp, only 200 yards away!

Around 10 March I was told that the CO of the Black Watch needed more NCOs to back fill some of his sections. They understood that I had recently qualified to sergeant. I pointed out that the REME sergeants' course is nothing like the infantry course in Brecon! However, they did agree that I would make a good 2IC of a section. The corporal had been a sergeant before and had been busted down. So, I now found myself in a B Company section and having to bring myself up to speed on some infantry drills very rapidly.

Initially the Jocks clearly didn't like me. First, I was English and second, I was from a REME unit. I didn't dare tell them I was also TA and not regular – that would have been too much for them! I feel that gradually I settled in and because I was helping repair and maintain their Warriors that helped me get accepted, a little.

Around 18 March we were told that the invasion was imminent and we moved forward to a position codenamed Barnsley. This was just short of the Iraq border. I believe the CO was from Barnsley in Yorkshire. We spent about 24 hours in Barnsley at 30 minutes' notice to move. I spent much of this time reflecting on what I had left behind at home and what invading Iraq meant. It suddenly became very real and serious. During this short period, we were watching the RAF and USAF going over the border to carry out the initial bombing campaign. This added to the realism. I found it quite hard to believe that those pilots were going onto Iraq to KILL the enemy, to soften them up for us to carry out the initial invasion. It was like living in a story told by my grandparents about World War 2 and the Battle of Britain.

I learned to shut away home and the family and tried to forget that they even existed. Many of the others spent a lot of time writing to their families but I decided not to. I had already written a letter to my wife, one to my parents and one to my two sons. These letters were to be opened in the event of my death. That was an extremely hard thing to do and it took me ages to write them, but once the letters were finished, I was able to park the family away and crack on with the job. On reflection, I might have given up worrying about my possible death by assuming I would not make it back, and thus I no longer had anything to worry about. This is a feeling that I still struggle to accept today and feel bad about.

Even with the training schedule we had time to write home. We were able to write blueys. I sent them to my mum and dad, wife and kids, and brother and sisters but it was difficult to not keep repeating myself. After about six weeks my wife became exceedingly difficult to write to. It quickly became apparent that there was a rift growing between her and my family. She distanced herself from them and soon the communication was all about her. After a while we received 20-minute tokens to use on a Sat phone. Each phone call with my wife ended in arguments which started to affect me. By the middle of May I took the difficult decision not to communicate with home at all. I did not want to go home to face the situation and at one point I tried unsuccessfully to get a second back-to-back tour.

Five years after returning from Iraq my marriage was over. The root cause, I believe, was my going to Iraq.

Maj Gareth Davies, RTR of the Joint NBC (JNBC) Regiment felt that *Telic* was cobbled together compared to *Granby* in 1991:

I was heavily involved in chemical, biological, radiological and nuclear (CBRN) training, technology and capability between 1999 and 2002. I saw lots of intelligence flowing that showed Iraq had chemical weapons, some of which it admitted to having while for others there was less or no proof. We know he used it against the Kurds at Halabja in 1988 so I didn't feel there was any conspiracy by the UK government spin doctors. The evidence came from elsewhere at the UN.

I went to the Middle East on a C-17 Globemaster, initially attached to the RAF, based at PSAB in Saudi Arabia. PSAB is so large there is a dual carriageway to help you get around the expanse of buildings, hangars and runways. I spent quite some time in the CAOC (Combined Air Operations Centre). Having never been in such a place before, I was really impressed. It was more like a sci-fi command centre than I ever imagined. A large, raised dais sat in the middle for the command team and all around were hubs of desks and huge computers and streaming TVs. 24-hour news channels would show in one corner, rolling tactical maps in another and live stream 'Predator porn' on another showing UAV [unmanned aerial vehicle] camera footage. The British RAF commander kindly introduced himself and spent 20 minutes showing me around – a very nice thing to do for a subordinate officer. I found my role within the support cell which had elements such as force protection, medical, environmental health and NBC.

Everyone strolled around the CAOC in flight suits displaying badges on their arms '2000 hours Tornado' or '1500 hours F-16'. There was this one female US Marine staff officer who had a similar badge but it had the Microsoft symbol on it and read '2000 hours PowerPoint'.

After about a week I realised there was not a full-time role for me at PSAB and I flew to Ali Al Salem Air Base in Kuwait to join the JNBC Regiment.

Oddly, I was put on a tiny Royal Flight that was being used by the RAF in theatre to haul people about between the bases. Even though there was no royalty on board, the crew treated us like we were royals with the full-on welcome at the top of the steps, cucumber sandwiches and comfortable seats.

The JNBC Regiment had people in two main roles: biological detection and chemical recce and survey. The biological detection involved using 4-ton lorries with a rigid box body which contained a three-stage detection system. It sampled the air, examining it for particles. These were then processed to identify what the particles contained – such as anthrax or pneumonic plague. These vehicles were operated by G Squadron, 2 RTR.

Chemical recce and survey are two separate functions, but both can be done by the Fuchs six-wheeled APC – a vehicle developed in Germany in the 1970s which has gone on to provide the base vehicle for many specialist functions in NATO countries. It's the survey function that makes the vehicle valuable. It can identify exactly where a threat is and mark it. The JNBC Regiment on *Telic* had eight or nine Fuchs operated by D Squadron, 1 RTR and the RAF Regiment.

The last core function, performed by H Squadron, was decontamination. This was handled by powered Kärcher pressure washers mounted on big 8x8 Foden trucks with giant water tanks. It wasn't very technical but worked well.

Detached from the unit for *Telic* was a small group of RTR NBC specialists who went to work for American Maj Gen Keith Dayton. He was head of the Sensitive Site Exploitation (SSE) Team. This team went to any reported finds of WMD. They would search, seize, analyse and package anything for inspection by the UN or back at The Hague. This team went all the way to Baghdad.

Individual soldiers at the rank of corporal were issued three-coloured detector papers to help them detect and identify chemical agents. We could work out whether it was H-mustard.

G-non-persistent nerve agents or V-nerve agent. Lower ranks were only given one-colour paper to detect nerve agents.

The commanding general of the US 1st Marine Division (1 MARDIV) was Maj Gen 'Mad Dog' Mattis who served for 40 years and rose to be a four-star general and later became Secretary of State for Defence under President Trump. General Mattis requested that the JNBC Fuchs be attached to his division. This was agreed to by 1 UKDIV and I was appointed as the liaison officer embedded at the 1 MARDIV HQ with a USMC warrant officer and British staff sergeant.

Initially relationships were very good, but tensions rose over whether we would be crossing the border with them due to the indecision in Westminster. The Marines even had to have a contingency plan for going without us and our valuable Fuchs vehicles. Of course, we eventually did go with the Americans and the Fuchs crews went forward at regimental level and so their RTR crews were amongst the first British (other than SF) to go over the border. I went across shortly after in my Land Rover with 7 RCT (Regimental Combat Team), 1 MARDIV and crossed the border just west of Safwan.

Dressed in desert combats that I had left over from my first invasion of Iraq in 1991, I had a 9mm Browning pistol and I scrounged 10 rounds of ammo from the Marines. The British Army provided me with neither current desert DPM clothing nor any ammunition. I had three sets of the '91 desert combats and I sent one off to get cleaned at the mobile laundry unit. I never saw these again so washed them myself after that in a bowl of cold water.

Capt Ed Pugh, Recce Platoon, 1 RRF felt let down by the planners, the government and, consequently, the logistics chain:

My abiding memory of my time in Kuwait is one of utter frustration. Key kit was either missing, in short supply or didn't work. Our platoon had been fortunate enough in only recently taking delivery of eight new recce cars. (The army has a tradition of referring to any vehicle used in reconnaissance as a 'car'.) We had eight Scimitars in the platoon, and even though their design was 30 years old, they were now equipped with some kit that really elevated their usefulness. We had a tactical navigation and targeting system (TNTLS) that helped us identify both exactly where we were and, importantly, where something else we could see was. The other kit which complemented TNTLS was ESPIRE. This system combined a thermal imager, a laser rangefinder and GPS positioning. Coupling these two pieces of equipment together on the top of our turret enhanced our capability tenfold. You can imagine our frustration then, when in Kuwait we needed some spares to repair the kit and there was no sign of any such spares.

After chasing my tail with the QM and the REME supply teams, we got nowhere and I actually got hold of the office number for the manufacturer, the Thales Group, in England and rang them. After some laborious explanation as to who I was and where I was making my call from, I got put through to a chap in their supply chain who was adamant that boxes full of the spare part we needed had already been despatched in a blue half-size ISO container that should by now be in port at Kuwait. The army was not using any trackable logistic system, to my knowledge, so we drove to the port and started breaking open every blue half-size ISO container in the vain hope of finding the Thales boxes. We returned empty-handed and even more downhearted. It sounds funny now, but at the time it really wasn't. We knew this kit was vital and it might keep us alive. Tony, my quartermaster, was a mature soldier, an ex-Royal Anglian senior NCO, and he was actually in tears with frustration at not being able to supply the kit. When we crossed the border, we only had half the ESPIRE systems functioning.

Tony even had to say to me, 'Boss, that 30mm ammunition you have is our entire stock, so you either use it now in Kuwait training, or you keep it for crossing the border into Iraq.' On top of those lamentable issues was the niggling doubt that our NBC supplies were adequate. Personal issue NBC suits were down to just two each, with none held in reserve, and the NBC filters on the Scimitar were nowhere to be found, meaning that we had a vehicle which should be capable of protecting its crew from the outside NBC threat, so we wouldn't have to wear respirators inside, but due to the lack of filters it was useless.

The saving grace for me was the quality of my men. To get into Recce Platoon you have to be a very good soldier, willing to try hard and put the effort in with motivation and intelligence. They were an experienced bunch, at least five or six had seen action in 1991.

For Cpl Scott Blaney, REME *Telic* was his second Gulf war:

The CRARRV, pronounced *Krarv*, is 60 tons of power and it's a beautiful machine. I have been known to kiss it, I loved it so much.*

By the time of *Telic* in 2003 I had been in the REME for 15 years and, even if I say so myself, I was a good mechanic and recovery specialist. I had also been on numerous active operations including Bosnia, Afghanistan and the 1991 Gulf War. When I went to Kuwait in '91 I lied about my physical fitness to serve. My unit was not chosen to go but the unit that was going needed a few reinforcements and augmentees, so I volunteered. However, I still had a plastic cast on my ankle from an injury picked up in training. I knew they wouldn't pass me fit to go overseas so before I limped up to the office at Fallingbostel, I took the pliers from the Part 3A kit on the truck we used and cut the cast off my ankle. It was enough to keep under the radar and off I went on Op *Granby*.

In 2003 I went back to Iraq as a full screw on the CRARRV. The sergeant in charge was a huge great bloke we called *Kaffir* James because he was from South Africa. He was about 6ft 3in tall with ginger hair and all smiles. The lance jack was a mate I had known for a long while, Steve Marshall. He was also a recovery mechanic. We were attached to 7 Armoured Brigade in 2003, so I was with the Warrior-mounted Royal Fusiliers, Black Watch and the Challengers of the Queen's Royal Lancers.

Before we rolled into Iraq, I was working at the Udairi ranges in Kuwait for a while. That was in a FV434 recovery vehicle which I hated. It was an old piece of worn-out 1970s crap. In fact, much of the equipment we and the Royal Engineers had was known as *Jurassic Park*, it was that old.

On the 434 I was crewed with a guy nicknamed Butch who was a big fat bloke. He and I didn't get on at all, especially after I told him I was putting him on a diet. Every day I screened his ration pack or MRE and took out all the sweet things and desserts. He really was fat. Fortunately, that wasn't for long, and I was soon back with Kaffir and Stevie on the CRARRV, in time for G-day [the start of ground operations].

For Maj Stu Taylor, RM of 42 Commando remembers the training before the operation:

---

*   CRARRV – the Challenger Armoured Repair and Recovery Vehicle – is based on the Challenger tank chassis. It is one of the most powerful recovery vehicles in the world with a Rolls-Royce 12-cylinder 1,200hp Condor engine. Its main 'armament' is a large dozer blade on the front and a powerful winch which can pull 68 tons. A small crane on the top of the superstructure can lift 6 tons for load-handling operations. Typical tasks for the CRARRV include recovery of damaged, ditched or overturned armoured vehicles on the battlefield. The dozer blade can also breach obstacles, earth move, prepare firing positions and fill in ditches. With its three-man, highly trained crew, equipped with power tools, welding and cutting equipment all of which is carried on the vehicle, an armoured unit with a CRARRV really does have an extremely capable multi-function giant Swiss Army Knife.

After we had been notified we were going to Iraq, we had a month of focussed training at Caerwent and Sennybridge and upon arrival in theatre we spent seven more weeks training in Kuwait – so by mid-March 2003 we were very well prepared and itching to get going. Just before the invasion I wrote to my then girlfriend and said, 'If we are to go to war, and I think we are, then there is not a better bunch of blokes to go with.'

Blueys were exchanged with some of my friends and family whilst in Kuwait, but the best thing was a 20-minute phone call we were allowed each week on a Sat phone. I made my final call about five days before we went into Iraq and after that we had no comms at all.

We did have BBC and Sky News teams with us, and I was interviewed by both – my family subsequently saw these on the news. By the time they were broadcast, we were already over the border and fighting. Surprisingly, when we fought our way into Basra and took the palace on the river, we met up with the news teams again and they very kindly allowed us to use their own mobile phones to call our loved ones. I also wrote another bluey while I sat in Saddam's palace, asking my girlfriend to send me some new underpants.

As well as NBC refresher training with our out-of-date respirators, we did a lot of live firing in the desert on all the weapons. We also did rehearsals with the USMC aviation wing. They used CH-46 Sea Knights and MH-53 Sea Stallions helicopters, which all seemed quite old. The plan was that we would be lifted in by the US Marines, but as it transpired, due to the crash with the first wave that carried our Royal Marine Brigade Recce Force [a USMC Sea Knight crashed around midnight on 21 March killing the eight Royal Marines and four US aircrew], the Americans refused to fly. Hasty plans were quickly redrawn, and the RAF stepped up and flew us in later using Chinooks and Pumas. There was a lot of friction between the US Marine Aviation Commander and the British Commandos due to this refusal to fly and it took a long time to mend that rift.

The outline plan was that we would be securing the northern flank of 40 Commando on the Al-Faw peninsula, so we practised the loading and unloading drills and then did a full rehearsal at night complete with a 30-minute flight phase. We were crammed into the MH-53 Sea Stallion, all with full kit and Bergens. That was a scary trip. We did final approach to the landing site, and we could feel it was very bumpy with turbulence. The pilot went to touch down, but it really grounded out hard, jerking and jolting us all, then immediately lurched upwards. It was one of the scarier moments in my life. We thought he was losing control. Three times he went around and each time he just bumped then lifted off, not easy with a helicopter weighing about 22 tons. We weren't the only ones; another helicopter broke its undercarriage on the rehearsal. Anecdotally we heard that the American pilots were not well-practised at flying in the dark on instruments, whether that was a factor in the invasion day crash of the CH-46, I don't know.

Lt Col Ben Curry, RM, SO1 Media Ops for 3 Commando Brigade, reached the Gulf by sea:

We disembarked at Kuwait City and were bussed to an American-built and run tented camp, north of the city, in the desert. The food was ropey and there was a lot of boredom. For some of my meetings I had to go to the Hilton Hotel in the city, so I always went to the buffet and ate as much as I could. On one occasion we ate so much fresh fish and fruit I walked out with stomach cramps thinking I wouldn't need to eat for a week.

The constant Scud alerts were really draining. Everyone carried their respirator everywhere. On one occasion in the mess hall an alert had us all masking up, but one chap had obviously forgotten his and went sprinting out to get it: a lot of people were laughing at him.

When you check your S10 respirator, you are always told to check that the canister was in date. If it wasn't, then you had to see the quartermaster for a fresh one. In Kuwait we took delivery of a ton of war supplies from UK storage including S10 canisters. They were all out of date. This was swiftly followed by a message from some civil servant sitting in Whitehall which said that the date was only advisory and that they would be fine for another two years! We all thought that it was bullshit and that they were lying.

The NBC suits come shrink-wrapped in plastic and held with rubber bands. I went to open my new suit and the rubber band just cracked into pieces; it was completely perished. The hood of the suit has a drawstring around the face of the hood so you can pull it tight against the respirator. The drawstring on mine had fallen apart and wouldn't work. The charcoal lining was crumbling away at my feet. It was evidence of MOD failings. Because the Cold War was cold, and they didn't think the threat was real any longer, they had left all this stuff to rot. It didn't give us a warm and fuzzy feeling! Many of us already felt let down, but I especially, in Media Ops, had to tow the party line.

Even before the war started, I had felt my own misgivings about the reasons for the war. We knew Saddam Hussein was a very unsavoury character with chemical weapons, but I am not sure he had the ability to project mass destruction.

During the pregnant-pause phase, to keep the media occupied we went up to see 42 Commando to do a piece to camera about what the marines had by way of personal equipment. This marine had been briefed obviously so the press gathered around him, and he started showing them his laid-out kit, his SA80 rifle, his ammunition and so forth. Then he showed them his metal mess tins and in one of his tins he had some ladies' knickers and a pair of stockings and suspenders. He said, 'This is my lingerie and I always make sure I wear it when going into battle.' I think some of the media put it out!

Maj David Green, RAMC was carried to the Gulf by a civilian airline:

We went to Kuwait on a chartered aircraft, I think it was a 747 from Iceland or somewhere. The seats were so cramped and hard we couldn't wait to get off. I remember the aircraft banking on approach and being able to see the airfield we were turning towards. The sight was simply staggering. What looked like hundreds of warplanes were lined up in never-ending deep rows, alongside similar numbers of stores in piles and green containers. The combined military power was so impressive. It freaked the air hostesses out a bit, and they couldn't get us offloaded quick enough.

Our tented base for 202 Field Hospital was within Camp Coyote in northern Kuwait. Our tents were like big white marquee things that had been hired from the Saudi Arabian government. Most of the time the tents are in storage but are used for the Mecca Hajj pilgrimage. Inside, we had metal bunk beds for about 60 people and each person had a small amount of space. It was cramped and hot, with no air-conditioning. Getting to sleep was a challenge sometimes, with all the 60 people coming and going at different times with their shift patterns throughout 24 hours. Privacy was non-existent, and there really was nowhere else to go if you were not on shift. In fact, with the wards being air-conditioned, it was far more pleasant on duty than off! Some people took to trying to sleep outside. With the heat being so intense, they searched for the slightest breeze. Centralised feeding took place in another tent, with contractors providing the so-called meals. It was bloody awful! One day an ex-Para sergeant major who was with us totally flipped and stormed into the kitchens shouting at the staff and telling them how ruddy awful it was.

One day I had reason to take some blood samples for analysis in Kuwait Military Hospital in the city and when the business was finished, they invited the two of us to stay for dinner. We obviously looked famished and ate loads. They also put piles of lovely leftover food into boxes which we took back for the night shift at the field hospital. Samosas, kebabs, fresh green salads, diced fruits – it all went down very well.

Our base was built just south of HQ 1 UKDIV, north of Kuwait City on the side of the main supply route (MSR) toward Iraq. The hospital was built up mainly by a series of large connecting green canvas tents. The main entrance led straight to A&E and then running off that were seven operating theatres. These were rigid modular kits that came delivered on a lorry or aircraft. They were like a mini-operating theatre with lights, power, AC, oxygen and suction machines etc. Then there was a series of wards: a normal medical ward, orthopaedic ward, intensive care, pathology unit, infectious diseases ward, physio unit, X-ray and a pharmacy. There were little admin units bolted on as well and a tent for the two army chaplains we had. They did a marvellous job, visiting each ward every day offering pastoral care and encouraging words as well as lots of practical help around welfare and family liaison. They obviously held church parade and dealt with the dead too.

It was pretty much like a district general hospital in any British town or city. Close by was a helicopter landing site but it was far enough away that the rotor downdraft would not blow the tents down or shower us in sand and grit. Ambulances brought most casualties in by road, so there was a place for them near A&E. The roads that led to the hospital were named Holloway Road and The Mall. The area right outside the main entrance, of course, was nicknamed Harley Street, and naturally the row of operating theatres was named Broadway.

We also had the wonderful mobile bath and laundry unit next door. It may not be the most glamourous of units, but they were such a good bunch. They were mainly there to deal with hospital bed linen and our scrubs, but they always found time to help us get our dobie (washing) done and have a much-needed shower.

The other unit I must mention is the band that was attached to us as stretcher bearers and decontamination teams. I can't remember their title, but they were certainly from Scotland. There was not too much for them to do, as no chemical weapons were encountered and the flow of casualties was light. They did, however, provide armed guards for the wards when we were dealing with Iraqi prisoners of war. They also had brought their instruments with them, not only just the traditional pipes and drums but their guitars and keyboards too. They acted like a concert party and performed a few times; it was a real morale booster.

Our ward saw a lot of dehydrated soldiers on the tail end of their D&V infection. We would get them rehydrated with supportive therapy, give them some anti-vomiting medicine and they wouldn't need to stay for that long, so we had a high admission rate and high discharge rate. We also had cases of chicken pox, impetigo and salmonella.

Sqn Ldr Andy White, RAF had been posted to Ali Al Salem Air Base in northern Kuwait several times in the late 1990s, so it felt familiar to be back in 2003:

On Op *Telic* we operated the TIIW, with around 35 staff, from a clutch of purpose-made pods that were delivered via aircraft to Kuwait and moved then by truck. The pods were like a portacabin and had been designed with our workstations built in. They were winched down off the truck and connected in the shape that suited us, depending on the deployment needs. The Tornado RAPTOR kit and our cabins were all brand new and not officially adopted. There were different designs for the cabins: one was for image analysis, another for admin and ops planning. We quickly found that the design had not been signed off with operating in a desert in mind. With the computers, screens and radios all turned on the heat became unbearable and kit started to malfunction. The first thing we did to mitigate this was erect Arctic camouflage scrim netting over the cabins. It lowered the temperature by a whole degree! One of our flight engineers then cobbled together a tube of connected plastic water bottles with the tops and bottoms cut off. He gaffer-taped them all together and ran the tubing from the air-conditioning unit direct to the rear of the computers. It really worked well and kept us going.

Attached to the TIIW were two US Marines, and we had sent two of our NCOs on attachment to them. They were blown away by RAPTOR and the end-product we disseminated to the pilots.

With the Americans included I had enough staff, but we didn't have enough equipment – there were more photographs being taken than we could analyse on the machinery.

Tasks were dictated from Riyadh for the next day, and we would help brief the squadrons with threat analysis and then also examine the imagery after their flight. The RAPTOR contained an air-ground digital data link that was meant to allow the Tornado crew to transmit the imagery direct to us while it was still in the air flying back to base. It didn't work. We had to wait until it landed. Then a digital data cassette was removed from RAPTOR and plugged direct to our workstation for analysis.

The sales pitch for RAPTOR was that it could image the whole of Cyprus in just two passes of the aircraft, and you wouldn't see it doing it either – which is impressive, but only if you have enough computers and staff to look at the product! The RAPTOR-equipped Tornados flew 120 reconnaissance sorties between 20 March and 15 April.

Such an asset as TIIW was in demand from all quarters. British Army staff officers had previously been told about it and had been on exercises and training with the unit, so naturally when *Telic* gathered pace, 1 UKDIV requests for imagery flooded into Andy's office:

We had to remind them that on this operation we were classed as a theatre asset and for the time being we reported to the USMC, so were undertaking reconnaissance for 1 MEF. This was a cause of friction that I could do nothing about. To underline the importance of 3 Commando Brigade's assault on the Al-Faw, securing the oil and gas infrastructure, we were ordered to provide them with imagery for the planning of Operation *Houghton*. The later attacks on Basra by UK 7 Armoured were for a large part unsupported by us, which I know hampered their planning, but my orders were to prioritise the US advance on Baghdad.

One other aspect of the work undertaken by TIIW was on TSTs. This was often when UK SF or US SF put in urgent requests for a fly-by of something they had eyes on. This was usually in western Iraq where the SF teams were hunting Scud missile launchers. The Iraqis had learned not to leave the launchers parked in the open back in 1991, so in 2003 they would be widely dispersed and parked hidden underneath bridges and flyovers or even inside large garages and warehouses. If the SF teams could not get close enough to confirm, they could ask for an aerial fly-by at an oblique angle to offer confirmation on what was deemed such a TST. The RAF kept 32 aircraft assigned to the TST role. Sqn Ldr White recalls:

On one TST we were requested to fly and analyse something one of the US Marine units was reporting off to their flank on the Baghdad MSR. They were observing at a distance something which looked unusual way off in the sand. As soon as the GR4 landed, the data was downloaded. My two analysts quickly identified a well-camouflaged and dug-in Iraqi Battalion HQ, with radio antennas, trenches, and bunkers under cam netting. I phoned PSAB to confirm no friendly forces at that grid and having had that confirmed, I was told two F-15 Strike Eagles had been quickly diverted onto the target. 10 minutes later we were told, 'Target destroyed.' It was one of the most satisfying fast-time tasks we helped action.

On the first night of air operations (21–22 March) the RAF launched dozens of raids on Iraq. The original air plan suggested 16 nights of bombing and strikes prior to the ground invasion. These preparatory air strikes were to include targeting known as 'shock and awe'. The start of air operations was known as A-day, while the start of ground invasions 16 days after would be known as G-day.[1]

Once ground operations started it was anticipated that offensive air power would fulfil a variety of roles, encompassing attack, interdiction and CAS. Plans in December 2002 reduced the bombardment phase to only five days and squadrons altered plans accordingly. However, later changes by Combined Forces Commander General Franks merged A and G days together.

The merger was due to concerns that air attacks would warn Iraqis of the imminent invasion, thus tactical surprise would be lost and they may well start setting fire to their oil wells. Of greater concern was that Iraqi missiles would target Coalition ground forces mustering in Kuwaiti assembly areas.

The final fly in the ointment was a CIA intelligence feed into President George W. Bush the day before the invasion was due to begin. A trusted source had told a CIA agent the expected whereabouts of Saddam Hussein and some key subordinates. The chance of eliminating Hussein in one swoop was too tempting for GWB to pass up and he authorised a surprise strike on the Dora Farms complex south of Baghdad, allegedly housing Hussein. F-117 stealth fighters and a Tomahawk cruise missile struck the target. The agent had been wrong, however, and Saddam was still at large.

With the cat potentially out of the bag, General Franks then called forward the ground plan to begin on the evening of 21 March. The air plan was too complicated to alter at this late stage so would finally begin after the ground plan but on the day it had been set by the planners, 21 March.

The RAF contribution would be 88 fast jets and 38 support platforms – more aircraft than the RAF had deployed on a single operation since the first Gulf War and more, in all probability, than it will ever deploy again. Original plans had the assets split between the north and south. The northern option was quashed when the Turkish Government vetoed using its air bases, so all operations swung south to be based in Kuwait, Saudi Arabia, Qatar, Bahrain and Cyprus. This was a huge undertaking and involved 6,000 RAF personnel over four weeks under command of Air Vice Marshal (AVM) Glenn Torpy.

Right up to G-day a few RAF aircraft were flying over Iraq under the rules of engagement for Operation *Jural/Southern Watch*. At 18:00 (Iraq) on 19 March the rules changed whilst these aircrews were in the air, allowing them to begin offensive operations across Iraq. SAS units had already inserted via Jordan the previous day, moments after the vote in the House of Commons to authorise military action had been passed.

Without the 'shock and awe' phase, air commanders pointed out that their forces would not be able to degrade the Iraqi Integrated Air Defence System (IADS) which could mean more likelihood of anti-aircraft guns and SAMs being used against Coalition raiders. As it transpired, the liberal use of Tomahawk cruise missiles from submarines and surface vessels in the Gulf, combined with numerous air-launched

Storm Shadow cruise missiles,* meant that the vast majority of the Iraqi IADS had already been destroyed or severely degraded.

The 7 Brigade HQ set-up was 48 vehicles and around 300 people working out of a pattern of tents. The main HQ tent was in the centre, and then running off this at angles were smaller sub-tents housing the various command branches: G1 Personnel and discipline, G2 Intelligence, G3 Operations, G4 Logistics, G5 Planning, G6 Signals and IT, G9 Civil and media affairs. In comparison, on Operation *Granby* in 1991, the Brigade HQ was only 105 staff and 30 vehicles. For Operation *Telic* there were additional roles that did not exist on *Granby* – such as the JNBC Regiment, Phoenix Battery (UAV) and media liaison teams. Even so this rise in staff numbers was noted after the war as being top heavy and cumbersome. The HQ was described as providing orders 'too large and too late'.[2] For instance, HQ 1 UKDIV produced a 'base plan' in which the given mission and concept of operations ran to 13 pages for subordinates. Many say that such complex orders lead to mental inflexibility and were too big to digest. In one order the mission ran over 20 lines; on another battlegroup order the eight sub-units were given eight tasks each but with no stated purpose or priority.

British HQs were now four times larger than they were in 1945 and this growth seems to be rather inexplicable. Evidence shows British HQs in 2003 were too large with overlapping functions and had officers of inappropriately high rank.

The British Army's analyses of previous wars show common shortcomings. Formation reports, with commendable loyalty, show a tendency to avoid criticism of superiors. Weaknesses are glossed over and reports tend to lean heavily on positive outcomes and lack, perhaps, a balanced view. For example, the Kirke report into lessons of World War 1 was not published until after the death of Field Marshal Earl Haig in the 1930s.

Conclusions in the 2003 report state, 'Much of the work and orders produced at HQ was nugatory. Subordinates can and did work well without them. Much of the observed work in HQ did not lead to effective output, with staffs being too large and doctrinal purpose and mission statements needing further work in future.'[3] The report did also finish by saying this in context of what was clearly overwhelming professionalism and a high level of performance by the troops involved.

Camp Rhino sat next to Route 80, which is a six-lane highway that runs north–south from Kuwait City to Safwan then Basra in Iraq. The camp was not far from

---

*   RAF Tornados launched the 1,900kg Storm Shadow missile from as far as 400km from target. The missile would accelerate to 800kph while dropping to only 25m above the ground. With a 3m wingspan and 6m long, it would fly nap of the earth with terrain-avoidance technology until close to the target, then climb to altitude for a final view of the target. It is a fire-and-forget weapon, meaning it cannot be called back or alter course. The 450kg warhead has a delay fuse allowing it to penetrate deep buried concrete bunkers before detonating. RAF No 617 Squadron fired the missiles for the first time on Operation *Telic*.

the outskirts of Al Jahra and slightly overlooked by the Mutla Ridge. In 1991 this was the same spot that got the nickname 'Highway of Death' when retreating Iraqi forces fleeing Kuwait were attacked by American, British and Canadian aircraft as they attempted to get back to Iraq. In scenes reminiscent of the closing of the Falaise Gap in Normandy 1944, hundreds of vehicles in a giant traffic jam got pounded by rockets and bombs. Around 1,500 vehicles were destroyed or abandoned in the graveyard-like setting. The air attack had begun on 26 February when USMC Intruder aircraft struck the head and tail of the column with cluster bomblets. Dozens of US Navy aircraft from USS *Ranger*, British Tornados and Canadian strike aircraft then flew numerous sorties against the stranded vehicles over the next 10 hours. As some determined Iraqis in pick-ups, commandeered buses and even motorbikes, tried to flee across country, they then ran into Coalition ground troops who had set up blocking forces. One by one they were picked off.

The death toll remains unknown. One journalist said he 'lost count of the Iraqi corpses crammed into smouldering wreckage or slumped faced down in the bloody sand'. The scenes of the utter devastation transmitted on TV are thought to have been a factor in President Bush's decision to declare a cessation to hostilities the next day.

Maj John Cotterill remembers Camp Rhino:

> Having slept under a cam net in my bivvy bag, which I did for most of the campaign, I walked across towards the main command post. Looking out at the area, it was a dry stony desert with zero trees. Apart from the nearby infamous Mutla Ridge, it was featureless. It was my first day in the tented Brigade HQ and Graham Binns, the commander of 7 Brigade, came up to me and asked me who I was. He then said, 'What do you do?' I told him I was the duty watchkeeper, but he asked what I did in my day job. When I told him I was in command of the Combined Arms School Course at Warminster, he just laughed. It obviously tickled him that I had got away out to Kuwait.
>
> In my month at Rhino I was teamed up with two Irish Guards officers to be the watchkeepers. We rotated, operating four hours on the brigade net, four hours on the divisional net then four hours off duty, to eat and sleep. This went on and on and on. Even when I was asleep under the cam net, against the side of the FV432 which housed the radios, I could still hear the radio traffic. It was incredibly busy on the radio net, with people waiting to get on the entire time. No sooner had one person finished transmitting, another person called up with a message. We had to log the call and try and obtain answers for units or inform the CO or other commanders. It was a treadmill, really hard work to do this day after day with so little sleep.
>
> It probably didn't help that we were also on such a limited diet. For 36 days I ate nothing but ration pack, Menu D 'Pork Stew'. I had no fresh fruit, vegetables or bread in that month. In fact, once I crossed to Iraq, I only drank hot sweat tea in the daytime and ate one meal of Menu D after the heat of the day started to drop. I lost 1.5 stone [9.5kg] in that time.
>
> Every evening we had a G2 Intelligence brief from all the intelligence gurus, including the location of every single Iraqi unit and formation, talking about SAM missiles, armour positions and so forth, in tremendous detail. Threat is the combination of capability and intent. The G2 went on and on just about location and capability. At the end of every brief, Brig Graham Binns, who was a gruff Yorkshireman, would say, 'Thank you for that, but just one question. Will they fight?' Not once in all the briefings could they answer him.

Marine Engineer Mechanic Anthony Williams, RN was aboard HMS *Turbulent* when it left Diego Garcia for the Gulf:

> We slipped our moorings at 03:00 the next morning and headed north towards the Persian Gulf. I worked six hours on, six hours off, for the entire time we were at sea. When I was off duty I could eat, shower, sleep or relax. My rack (bunk bed) was in a stack of three beds, and there were about 9 or 10 stacks in a room. When you lie flat in your bed which is exactly six foot long, there is another bunk only a few inches above your nose. 30 guys sleeping, snoring and farting and all coming and going at different times. Some guys had to hot bunk, that is share a rack with someone on an opposite shift to you, leaving their sleeping bags on the rack. Privacy doesn't really exist. To get a bit more personal space, I volunteered to run the washing machines which were tucked in a space like under your stairs. There was one washer and two driers and me in there, but I had my personal CD player and earphones in and I could get away from it all for an hour. The bonus was I got paid £4 per day extra for doing it!
>
> Food was pretty good, and the enlisted men ate with the officers which is not the normal tradition. When at sea, under the water, time becomes less relevant, as do days of the week because you just have no idea of time, day or weather when so deeply submerged. It was the meals that told you what day it was. Fish and Chip Friday, Steak Saturday, Roast Dinner on Sundays, Curry on a Monday and so on.
>
> The most dangerous activity for a submarine is to be on or close to the surface. Coming back to periscope level, say 20–30m below the surface, the submarine is blind and deaf as it comes up and it can be dangerous to other shipping, of course. All men are out of their racks at harbour stations, compartments are secured and hatches manned. When we did get close to the surface, if it was rough weather, the boat could really get tossed about but once we submerged deep it would be calm again.
>
> Having arrived in the Persian Gulf in January we moved a little closer to Iraq and then started to circle endlessly at periscope depth, just waiting for the word to fire. We waited for about 10 weeks doing these patterns only about 30m under the surface.

845 Naval Air Squadron landed aboard HMS *Ocean* after the helicopter assault ship had departed Plymouth and sailed away from the Devon coast in January 2003. With around 40 helicopters aboard, *Ocean* was transporting a vital component of the British Expeditionary Force's capability. For many in the navy, the memories of the disaster in 1982, when the MV *Atlantic Conveyor* was sunk sailing to the Falklands carrying most of the task force helicopters, would not have been far away as *Ocean* sailed into the Atlantic. Lt Cdr John Pentreath, RN was aboard:

> I hate saying goodbye, but on 16 January 2003, a crisp winter day, Laura and the children waved goodbye to us from Ham Hill as we flew off to join HMS *Ocean*. I did not see my family again until 28 May. Our 10 aircraft flew in formation from RNAS Yeovilton down to the south-west where *Ocean* had just set sail from Plymouth to rendezvous with us. 845 was then joined by 847 Squadron which was equipped with six Lynx and six Gazelle helicopters rather like the Army Air Corps. HMS *Illustrious* was embarked with five Chinooks and four Sea King Mk 7s for airborne surveillance and control. 820 Squadron also had Sea Kings for ship-to-shore lift. The whole grouping was under command of Commander Amphibious Task Group (COMATG), at that point Cdre Jamie Miller. I am glad to say we did not lose any aircraft or crew from our squadron on the deployment.

The Sea King was a fabulous aircraft, but it was primarily designed to operate in northern Europe, over the sea where it rarely gets over 25°C. The engines struggle to perform when over hot arid ground and lose the power of lift. When this is combined with modifications and additional equipment being fitted over the years, you get to see a marked reduction in lift capacity, from 25 troops down to maybe eight by the time of *Telic*. Halfway through the deployment in 2003, 845 Squadron had new engines fitted to their aircraft which improved this somewhat.

Rather like the Sea King, HMS *Ocean* had been designed around a different set of needs. She was all set to embark a marine task force and an air group, transit to Norway over six days, disembark and return over a further six days. Her inboard systems – like heating, sewage treatment and, of course, personal space – had in mind a three-week tour, not four months at 40°C. Consequently, most aboard found it less than ideal with systems failing frequently. Lt Cdr Pentreath continues:

> I was very fortunate as squadron commander to have my own cabin on six deck, quite a way down under the hangar deck. The 'chain gang' made endless noise shackling down the aircraft above me. My bunk was narrow and had a desk underneath it with a tiny bit of storage. Most officers shared cabins. Senior ratings usually had cabins for four or six men and the enlisted men were on mess decks for 30 men with bunks for three men.
>
> *Ocean* was like a hot tin box, with a thousand sailors and marines all trying to get some space and a breath of fresh air on deck. Friction was commonplace as units vied for space to exercise or practise on the limited deck space. The entire flight deck was out of bounds if only one aircraft was flying – something that led to very inconvenient time windows being allocated for its use. Fortunately, common sense and operational necessity meant more flexibility was needed and very soon the vast flight deck space saw marines test-firing machine guns off the aft while a Sea King took off from the bow and a fitness training class occupied the centre.

Navy Task Group 03 transited the Suez Canal and into UAE waters on 1 February 2003. There it rehearsed some landing exercises with helicopters along similar lines to that which would ultimately represent the landings on the Al-Faw peninsula. Lt Cdr Pentreath was initially not very confident of the outline plan laid before him and joked in his diary that it should be renamed 'Operation Certain Death' after the TV Show *Blackadder*. Subsequent changes and the introduction of the US Navy SEALs improved his impression. However, he noted in his diary on 4 February:

> A very close call tonight. One of our Sea Kings nearly collided with a Lynx from 847. A combination of factors seems likely; funnelled, congested airspace, *Ocean's* radar is U/S, a very dark night with Lynx crew not wearing NVGs and the Sea King pilot wearing AR5 kit. We are very lucky.

HMS *Ocean* docked in Dubai on 15 February to have her radar fixed and while there for three days the crew and embarked troops were allowed downtime but not a run ashore. Televised aboard was the Six Nations England v France Rugby International, dubbed Le Crunch. England won 25–17 and a few tins of beer and some rousing Royal Marine Band tunes rang out on the hangar deck. There were a few sore heads the next morning.

Work was by now, 24 February, at full steam to develop the combined SEAL team and 3 Commando Brigade plan for seizing the Al-Faw. Planning meetings were held in Kuwait and Lt Cdr Pentreath noted his concern with the status of the plan in his diary.

> It appears that this operation is being planned by lots of separate people in isolation. We must have a more co-ordinated approach, there are just too many moving parts for it to work otherwise. Our flight back to HMS *Ocean* from Kuwait was most unpleasant, visibility down to less than a mile with a dust storm and then finding ourselves flying through a radio station with masts up to 500ft high. Back aboard I voiced my concern about the lack of co-operation and was immediately made Air Mission Commander! I must now provide the co-ordination that I wanted. Bugger! I should take it as a compliment, but it will be a difficult task that will divorce me from daily squadron life for a time.

Most of the British planners found the American system of briefing very tedious and in far too much detail with 'death by power point' a popular summary. What did raise morale was the presence of the US AC-130H Spectre gunship and A-10 Warthog crews, who would be providing much of the close air support. The need to avoid friendly fire was a key element in the now maturing plan. Imagery showed that running down the middle of the Monitoring and Metering Station (MMS) central road, the secondary landing site, was a line of telecoms pylons which could create a real hazard to the helicopters in the assault, so it was planned to include demolitions experts in the first wave, equipped to destroy the pylons. Echoing strongly of the D-Day 1944 coup de main operation at Pegasus bridge in Normandy, when Royal Engineers were included in the glider teams to blow up strong wooden poles planted by the Nazis as an anti-invasion device. Operation *Houghton* in 2003 would similarly see demolition teams needing to run around the battlefield and blow things up!

A further and unexpected welcome source of intelligence came from the Sea King Mk 7 with its search radar. It was found that it could track and identify vehicles like cars and even motorbikes at up to 100km away. This allowed planners to stand off and establish patterns of life and routes to and from likely enemy locations. It could also track other air assets and provide the UK commanders with an integral radar picture, separate to that provided by US assets.

Beyond planning were rehearsals. These were a practical exercise to see if plans and estimates were going to work when, literally, you can get 'grit in the gearbox'. One element that showed up as an issue early was the time it took for US helicopters to refuel compared with British counterparts. US MH-53s took off from Kuwait, flew out to a designated simulated drop-off point, then returned to the base to refuel and take a second load forwards. British pilots would come in and do a tactical refuel, all landing close by a fleet of fuel bowsers, refuel and then be off again fairly quickly. Lt Cdr Pentreath saw the MH-53s returning:

> We saw the squadron coming back at about 300 feet and do an orbit over the FARP. Then the lead aircraft broke away and very slowly approached the landing position near the bowser. Only when the dust had cleared, literally, did the second aircraft start its approach, and so on. It took about an hour to do all eight aircraft, by which time the leading aircraft needed another

refuel as it had been idling on the ground for 60 minutes. Just after this the five RAF Chinooks came in, and landed altogether and were all down, refuelled and gone in a fraction of the time. It was clearly the issue about collisions and dust clouds from their disaster in 1980 in Iran.

To improve their performance the Americans adapted their plan and adopted a piece of tarmac highway which they closed to traffic and essentially made it into a landing site, with a lot less dust flying about. Even the Chinooks followed suit, as it was so much better for the pilots and ground crew. It shows the value of rehearsals.

Saturday, 1 March saw the visit of Adm Sir Michael Boyce to HMS *Ocean*. He was the Chief of Defence Staff and addressed the embarked troops and crew on the cleared deck. Lt Cdr Pentreath noted in his diary:

> He was friendly and spoke clearly but didn't really have much to say! He indicated that he thought war was now inevitable and that it would be around 19–23 March if diplomatic avenues are exhausted.

Present at a more intimate dinner after the admiral's address was Rear Adm Adrian Johns, captain of HMS *Ocean,* Captain Alan Massey of HMS *Ark Royal*, Cdre Adrian Miller COMATG, the captains of HMS *Liverpool* (Cdr Martin Ewence) and HMS *Edinburgh* (Cdr Guy A. Robinson), and Col Gordon Messenger, CO of 40 Commando. On the menu was sautéed mushrooms in a filo parcel drizzled with white wine fusion and pimento oil followed by roast supreme of chicken filled with salmon and tiger prawns with a balsamic reduction, wilted ribbon of zucchini and carrots and crushed new potatoes. Dessert was a chocolate and vanilla bavarois with mango and rum syrup. The maître d' poured Misty Peak Chardonnay and port. Jon Pentreath and Maj Bill O'Donnell, RM the COs of 845 and 847 Squadrons respectively, also ate with the admiral and celebrated Pentreath turning 37 the next day, although he says he would have rather been at home with his wife and kids enjoying half term on holiday.

On Monday, 17 March Lt Cdr Pentreath held what was known as a 'clear lower deck' on HMS *Ocean,* where he addressed the entire gathered team of 845 Squadron and wrote in his diary:

> I spoke about professional satisfaction, pride, trust, honour and courage. The overwhelming feeling is that everyone just wants to get started, everyone is up for it. But in my heart of hearts, I do not think it is worth dying for and I will not have achieved success for 845 unless everyone comes home. Later we held a very poignant church service on the flight deck just as the sun set and the moon rose. There were about 120 present for the address by Reverend Andy Phillips, RN. I read a lesson from Isaiah and Maj Bill O'Donnell (847) said the Royal Marine Prayer.

Maj Neil Wraith had joined the Royal Marines in 1989 serving in the Commaccio Group (protecting nuclear assets), 45 Commando and as a landing craft officer on HMS *Fearless*. He then became an anti-tank officer before promotion to major as a staff officer at HMS *Warrior* in Northwood. In 2003 he was serving in 40 Commando and sailed from Plymouth for the Gulf in HMS *Ark Royal* on 15 January. He was with COMATG, in 3 Commando Brigade HQ:

At the time of leaving, officially we were going on a pre-planned exercise to Cyprus and the Persian Gulf. We were made aware that we would divert to support any operations against Iraq should the need arise. Our first stop was Scotland to take on ammunition stocks. One of the big advantages of the brigade is that it travels together complete with its required logistics. I heard many stories of army units scrabbling around for kit and ammo, but the opposite was true with us. I had QMs coming to my cabin asking if I needed anything and offering me new bits of shiny kit.

On arrival in Cypriot waters, we began some amphibious training with the embarked 40 Commando marines. It was at this stage that the ops officer for 40, Maj Simon Hickman, was returned to the UK due to an emergent and sadly terminal medical condition. Lt Col Gordon Messenger, in charge of 40 Commando, came to me and asked if I would be their new ops officer. The last thing my wife, who was in the RAF, had said to me as she waved me off was 'don't volunteer for anything and don't do anything stupid'. With that phrase ringing in my ear, I of course said yes in a few seconds flat. I transferred across to HMS *Ocean* to join the bulk of 40 Commando. Funnily enough my wife, Jules, was with the RAF as part of 16 AAB and ended up in Kuwait before me. I did manage to meet up with her in Kuwait at a planning brief and we had our picture taken together. She was doing air intelligence work for 16 Brigade HQ.

The words MMS and Al-Faw peninsula first came onto my radar in late 2002 when I was still with COMATG. The potential environmental disasters that could unfold if the MMS and pumping nodes were sabotaged were enormous. The peninsula became a key objective for the British to secure. I became involved in the lower level of planning for the assault and helped plan the rehearsals on the full-size mock-up of the MMS that had been built, in secret, in the desert of Kuwait. The rehearsals were dubbed MOAR 1 and MOAR 2 (mother of all rehearsals). We spent a lot of time with the US Navy SEALs and ensured we could operate and fully understand each other. Live firing, PT, NBC and first aid were being taught in every corner of the ship (HMS *Ocean*). During one lesson a combat medic talked about the use of tampons in gunshot wounds to stem the flow of bleeding. The marines then all went to the NAAFI and cleared out the stocks of tampons and there had to be an announcement asking for a 'tampon amnesty'. The ship's female population got rather concerned when faced with being at sea for a considerable voyage with no sanitary arrangements. Marines were asked to return their newfound first aid kits.

NBC training is not known as a marine sport and many were very out of practice with drills and NBC kit, so naturally this changed en route to Kuwait and became a focus for many hours below decks. They perceived the threat as real, and this threat was reinforced when they arrived in Iraqi positions later and found all sorts of chemical weapon warning and protection kit piled up and discarded. Maj Neil Wraith continues:

> As we waited at TAA [Tactical Assembly Area] VIKING on the final day, there was yet another Scud alert. Several missiles had gone overhead, and others impacted further afield, which forced us to take cover and mask up again. After the all-clear sounded the sight of one unfortunate marine's head, still with respirator on, came poking up out of the shit trench, which had been the closest available cover to him, was greeted with cheers all around.

The vehicles of 3 Commando Brigade were largely wheeled lightweight types but the mailed fist of 7 Armoured Brigade was led by the Challenger 2 tanks of the RSDG and 2 RTR. The Challengers of 2 RTR left Germany on trains that took

KUWAIT: PLANNING AND WAITING • 59

them to the port of Emden where they were loaded on to the roll-on roll-off ship MV *Eddystone*.

Eddystone weighed anchor on 19 February bound for Kuwait. The troops themselves flew to the Middle East on 4 March, arriving just a few days ahead of the tanks. The tanks and crews only had two weeks to make final preparations including weapon calibration, uparmouring and 'desertisation'. The latter included the attachment of skirts and extended mud flaps to cut down the giveaway dust clouds tanks make when moving. A modified air-filtration system was also added.

With a great deal of effort, the regiment was reported ready but the CO, Lt Col Piers Hankinson, noted there were a considerable number of shortages as the logistics chain creaked under the strain. Desert-themed combat dress, NBC detection spares and, most notably, 300 sets of body armour were all missing. Hankinson felt forced to give priority to the dismounted infantry in his battlegroup and some of his own men who were not crews of the well-armoured Challengers. The lack of body armour would have tragic consequences.

Lt Ian Cross of Falcon Squadron, 2 RTR remembered the build-up:

> The camp in Kuwait was not ready for us and we spent the first few nights under the stars sleeping on a roll mat, longing for our comfy kit to arrive on the tanks coming from Germany. It was bloody cold at night. The food was totally awful, so we were quick to use the boiling vessel (BV) inside the turret next to the operator to cook our rations and brew tea in.
>
> When the vehicles arrived, we got into full swing of training and work up exercises. For a Tankie, the Challenger is home, and you can be very self-contained and self-reliant for a long time. We knew how to live on the tank: we had little tents, solar showers, paperback books to read, storage bins for luxuries the infantry cannot carry, the BV to heat water for tea and ration packs. We made it as comfortable as we possibly could. We even tweaked the interior, so it worked for us. The commander's gun scope is a rubber face guard that you lean into to see the gunsight picture, but is difficult to use wearing glasses, which I did. I cut two grooves in the rubber so I could still wear my glasses. I also adapted my commander's seat. I never wore the seatbelt as it felt horribly constrained, and it worried me that I would not be able to get out quickly if we got hit. For the best situational awareness tank commanders have always ridden with their heads out the hatch but been ready to drop back inside if fired at. I found that by wedging a spare seat back behind the top of my own seat, I could sit down on the wedge with my head out but instantly drop inside onto my proper seat if I needed to. I also wedged my kneecap into the rubber eyepiece of the gunsight, which stopped me banging my knee on every road bump.
>
> My gunner, Tpr 'Vinny' Wienand, was older than me and had come to Britain from South Africa where he had been a police officer. He was an excellent gunner and was utterly fearless. He would sit below and in front of me, so all I ever saw of him was the back of his head. He was sandwiched in, with his left shoulder against the gun and his right side against the turret wall. He had nothing to look at and his only view of the outside world was through his gunsight. He had terrible motion sickness and would often use his helmet to be sick in, which he passed back to me to throw out the hatch. I have this abiding memory of working on the tank and bailing out smelly puke.
>
> Cpl 'Verge' Maguire was my operator. He was a senior corporal in the squadron. His job was to load the gun, operate the radio, observe with me and operate the GPMG on the roof pintle mount. He rarely sat down in the tank as he had to stand to load and worked

on the other side of the breach to Wienand. He was such a good guy and would always look after me when it came to mealtimes. If we were on the move or in action, 'Verge' was always covered in sweat and sand which seemed to get inside the tank through every corner, he was always heaving the main gun rounds into a new position, so he knew what type of ammunition was where when needed in a hurry. The other masterpiece from 'Verge' was his home-made cool box. He drilled two holes in either end of a 5.56 ammo box and ran one of the air-conditioning tubes through it. The box got quite cold and was just big enough for two small bottles of water to sit in. That was nectar! To have chilled water – even just a few sips – in the heat of the day was a godsend.

Lastly, down in the front, alone in his solitary confinement, was our driver, Tpr 'Strawberry' Field. The driver sits almost recumbent in a very comfortable seat centrally in the middle of the tank. His entry/exit hatch is above his head and, of course, can be obstructed by the main gun if it is in position above him. To alleviate this problem, the driver's seat is on rails and if needed can be pulled back toward the turret where he can then twist out of the seat and escape through another hatch. 'Strawberry' and I often went for a couple of days without seeing each other. Once he had got into his driving compartment, I could not see him. The operator could pass food or water to him over his left shoulder and we could all talk on the intercom.

The intercom was just for us within our own tank, but we also had two Clansman radio sets. We called them A and B sets. A set was tuned to allow me to speak to the other two tanks in 16 Troop. Set B was on the squadron net. This arrangement could easily get you very wound up trying to do so many things at once.

Scud and gas alerts were a constant and were the greatest threat to any of us. We did feel, however, that we were as well prepared as we could be, and the NBC kit was in good order. The final new piece of kit we took was the short-barrelled SA80 carbine. It was just the job for taking on and off the tank and made storage easier too. Only the driver and loader have the SA80. It was the first time we saw it in Kuwait, so we went for a day on the Udairi ranges to get used to it. Its barrel is 20cm shorter than the standard SA80. I only had a silly Browning pistol with 13 rounds, which just got in the way. The only thing I ever used it for was trying to shoot out streetlights when we were near Basra, and we were trying to hide the tank in the shadows. We laughed when the 9mm rounds pinged off the thick glass and didn't break it!

I customised my own kit to suit me. I got hold of some old canvas '58 pattern webbing and just had the Browning pistol on one side and the S6 respirator haversack on the left. I wore nothing else in the turret that would hinder my rapid exit. My pockets were usually bulging with personal kit too. Stuffed behind my seat I kept a grab bag which had my sleeping bag, my diary, some food and water and another 13 rounds of 9mm ammo. I had scrounged an infantry helmet which I preferred to the standard tank crew helmet. Firstly, I found it more comfortable; second, the radio headset was not integral, meaning you could leave the helmet but still stay in touch on the headset which was worn straight on the head. Lastly, it was my belief that it was better designed and in the event of a bullet strike was more likely to save me than the cheap tanker helmet. Fortunately, I never put that to the test. When we met the Americans on the ranges, they were astonished at our ragtag appearance. They didn't actually even know we used a different tank to theirs. Some had never seen a Challenger, which, of course, was very worrying. We invited the US crews to come and eat with us so they could get used to us, and hopefully then not shoot us.

Special panels were installed on our vehicles that show up cold when seen in thermal imagery to help with friendly vehicle recognition. That was in addition to the usual placing of an orange flag on the roof for aircraft to see, as they scream down at 500mph from 10,000ft! A digital transponder called blue force tracker was also meant to help with a digital picture of where the friendly fleet was but there were never enough, and they were not 100% reliable.

Our Challengers changed in appearance while we were in the Kuwait build-up. Vickers, the manufacturers, came out and specially fitted these huge slabs of extra armour on each side and a sort of nose cone on the front. The existing Dorchester armour is already very thick and incredibly strong, but this was now called 'uparmouring'. Vickers took one tank at a time into a sealed-off, secure tent to carry out the works. It was all hush-hush how they did it. The extra weight was noticeable in performance and the engine had to work harder to lug it all around. They took it off when we went back to Germany as the strain on the suspension and engine was too much.

The Fusiliers of 1 RRF had rearranged the battalion organisation to match the upcoming mission in Iraq, which they knew would involve working with tank squadrons. To that end, they took their normal three rifle company arrangement and merged it into two heavy companies, Y and Z. X company drew the short straw and was chopped to bolster the others. The battalion then consisted of the two rifle companies, a manoeuvre support group with MILAN, recce, mortars and an HQ group. The companies each had three rifle platoons and a manoeuvre support section in another Warrior with snipers and machine guns.

The two companies had three platoons each, and each platoon had four Warriors – three containing a rifle section each with the fourth an HQ vehicle. The Warrior has its own integral two- or three-man crew and can carry a section of eight men in the rear. The armoured infantry employed an extra sergeant per platoon to be the mounted commander whenever the officer dismounted and was away from the vehicles. The senior sergeant would stay with and command the four vehicles until the officer returned. Lt Chris Rees-Gay, 1 RRF kept a diary:

> 3 March 2003 The longest day ever just trying to get my Warrior painted. It's done now and it took three minutes, and it really shows. It's got big boot footprints across the deck and lots of sand and grit mixed in making it rather lumpy. We are now on the longest night march. It's meant to have been 70km and taken five hours, but it has already taken seven. No thanks to Seamus (platoon commander) making us turn around about five times and look like a Benny Hill sketch.
>
> 6 March 2003 Today, we were given our most likely tasks. We were tasked with securing the border crossing point and then the lateral main road, codenamed Sioux-falls, before blocking the exits from Basra, relieving the USMC, defeating the remaining Iraqi 51 Division and preparing to secure Basra International Airport. At the end of the O-group it began to rain, can you believe it? In the desert and now it's raining.
>
> 7 March We had a big day on the ranges, but no one can give us a solution to the stoppages on the A2 (SA80A2). It is now very worrying.

With Sky News playing 24 hours a day on the TV in the mess tent, it came as no surprise that the men of the Fusiliers got more than an inkling that the day was getting closer. The Operations Warrant Officer, WO2 Dave Satchell, had created a football pitch-sized sand-table model of the assembly and border-crossing area. Each berm, trench, fence and bridge were shown in model form, and thus allowed soldiers to walk about on it to understand the moving parts of the plan. This level of preparation proved invaluable and not one vehicle crew could have been left uncertain of exactly what they would find once they met the Recce Platoon at FAA Barnsley. Capt Ed Pugh explains:

> One of the less glamorous roles of Recce Platoon is to mark routes and assembly areas. So it was that we trundled off to mark out FAA Barnsley where the vast majority of 7 Brigade would muster from their desert camps, before crossing into Iraq. My main issue, of course, was a complete lack of kit to mark the area with. I had been given orders to mark Barnsley and when I asked for the stores needed to complete the vast task I was met with a shrug of the shoulders. I briefed my guys the night before and said to them, 'I know I am always reminding you not to steal stuff, but tonight is an exception. I want you to go out and find, beg, borrow and steal the kit we need to mark Barnsley. My advice will be to start by looking at the Military Police camps, they do route marking and I bet will have stacks of the stuff, go on.'
>
> The boys didn't disappoint. As we moved up to FAA Barnsley early on the 19 March we were weighed down with pickets, tape, sign boards and route direction arrows.

The rest of the RRF BG was put on alert with notice to move reduced to 12 hours. The Brigade HQ group was in a tent at 10:00 on 19 March, wargaming the breakthrough of the breach, when Brig Binns was called away suddenly, only to reappear two minutes later. 'How soon before you can move?' The wargame was cancelled and the men broke away to prepare their units for the move up to FAA Barnsley. There was, of course, still time for a splendid luncheon for the officers of the battlegroup complete with tablecloths. The enlisted men had their own tasks and went about their business in their own way. L/Cpl Smith, Y Company, 1 RRF remembers:

> It was only after our orders that it really hit home. We were going to war, and this was not another exercise. I was apprehensive about the reality of my job in looking after the section. I always knew what was expected of me but the realisation that I would now be doing it in war made me more conscientious and meticulous in my duties. I felt that if I didn't do what was expected of me, I would be letting the soldiers down.
>
> The commanding officer's speech just before deployment made me feel good and righteous with a great purpose. After the speech we went back to the Platoon, wished each other luck, shook hands, and had pictures taken. We also went and looked for friends in other sections and wished them good warfighting and good luck.[4]

Lt Rees-Gay noted in his diary:

> Orders now arrived for us to move up and secure Objective Golf (Bridge 4) on Basra Canal. Even maybe a move onto Basra International Airport. We had a surreal O-group with the OC on the turret reading out 12 Platoon's mission. This is for real. Started taking our NAPS tablets but not sure if I will carry on as the Doc is not taking his! Looking forward to tomorrow, a big day doing the real job! We are now on one hour notice to move.
>
> I have written my last 'If I do not make it letters'. I have a pit in my stomach.

The British Army medical evacuation chain in 2003 looked much like it would have done in 1945 and even as far back as 1918. Lifesaving technology and medicine had come a long way but the overall set up and terminology would be recognisable across the century.

The primary aid for any soldier who is wounded on the front line will come from himself, if capable, or his section or troop. If serious, the battalion's own stretcher bearers and the regimental medical officer (doctor) will administer care at the regimental aid post where a triage system will assess who needs further care and how promptly they need it. If needed, the wounded soldier will then be taken from the aid post, usually housed near battalion HQ, to the next stage back by the close-support medical regiment. This will be to the casualty clearing station which runs a damage limitation and early intervention system of medical aid designed to stabilise patients for onward journey to hospital. For this next portion of the wounded soldier's journey, he would be transported by 5 General Support Medical Regiment around 40km rearward to 202 Field Hospital.

5 GSMR also provided primary care across the whole of the division rear area at a series of primary care nodes where soldiers falling ill or suffering with D&V could report on sick parade. They could also see a dentist and have minor walk-in surgery. Interestingly, after the invasion the dentist was one of the busiest people as the captured Iraqis had terrible oral health. Lt Col Tuck of 5 GSMR:

> On the last night before we crossed the border, we had a briefing with the assembled teams and the Deputy Chief of Staff, Col Andy Cowling, addressed us, and I made a note of what he said in my diary (which is now in the IWM).
> 'For us in this room, this is the chance of a lifetime. Tomorrow, for some of our soldiers this will be their last chance of life so get it right!'

RSM Nick Pettit, RE went to Iraq as part of an advance party to look at the camps in Kuwait and the ground they would train in. One of the main tasks the Joint Forces EOD Group (JFEOD) anticipated was preventing Iraqi saboteurs from destroying the infrastructure in the oilfields. The 1991 invasion of Kuwait by Iraq had shown just how devastating attacks on the oilfields can be to both a country's economy and the environment.

Nick spent days learning about oilfields and GOSPs, pumping stations, pipelines, inlet valves, the port of Umm Qasr and all manner of data to do with the Rumaila oilfields' infrastructure. He knew how best to blow one up and, therefore, where best to look for devices placed by the enemy. To help him in his search for intelligence on the oilfields he would ask UK intelligence services for satellite or aerial imagery and could generally get it within a week or so. He found that if he asked the Americans next door, they would get it for him almost instantly:

> Walking into their HQ was like walking into NASA. There were computer screens on the roof, four of them, and they must have been 20ft square, plotting the country. It was just like a modern sci-fi movie. When I walked back into the British building it was like being back on set for *Zulu*, in comparison.
> The Americans helped us cope on every front, every day. As usual the British soldier overcomes and adapts to every situation, making him the best, but we were not supported from the moment we arrived, when it came to food, toilet paper and even ammunition. We

had to share the ammunition, we had to sign for five rounds of 9mm pistol ammo if we left camp then give it to someone else if they went out.[5]

The Americans next door were the 52nd Ordnance Battalion. They continued to help RSM Pettit when it came to training aids. They had dummy 'safe' copies of just about every bomb, mortar, rocket and mine that they might ever come across – vital learning tools for British EOD teams arriving in country. In the final few hours before British troops crossed into Iraq there were numerous Scud and gas alarms which led to false alarms and much running to shelters. In the confusion one senior NCO thought he had been attacked with a nerve agent and injected himself with the Combo pen carried in his respirator haversack. The auto-injector pen acts against chemical weapons but if used when not suffering from such a weapon it has severe consequences that lead to hospitalisation. With his heart rate going through the roof and suffering from psychedelic hallucinations, the NCO was loaded onto an ambulance and taken back to hospital in Kuwait. No one laughed at all.

Building up their stocks of ammunition in the desert were the three main artillery units fighting with the division: 3 Regiment, Royal Horse Artillery (3 RHA), 7 RHA and 29 (Commando) RA. 3 RHA was equipped with 32 155mm AS-90 armoured SP guns. The two other RA units were equipped with the older but still effective 105mm Light Gun that can be towed by another vehicle or slung beneath a helicopter. 12 Regt RA was the division's air defence unit, equipped with 32 Starstreak high-velocity missile launchers which were to see very little action due to the degradation of Saddam's air force prior to the invasion. 3 RHA when fully augmented numbered just shy of 1,000 troops with 32 guns. Together, they became one of the largest – and certainly the most powerful – British artillery units ever fielded. There were problems, however, as Brig Andrew Gregory was CRA (Commander Royal Artillery) 1 UKDIV outlines:

> The structure of available assets for Operation Telic was severely hampered by striking firemen in the UK, which drew away nearly 19,000 personnel. This meant that numerous highly capable individuals and whole units were omitted from the Order of Battle. One organisation that illustrates this best was the Royal Artillery. The three deployed field artillery regiments needed to be augmented by other units to bring them to a war footing as so many gunners were driving the Green Goddess fire engines across England and Wales.[6]

Deep fires – the very long-range capability – was traditionally the role of the Royal Artillery's Multi-Launch Rocket System (MLRS) that had performed so well in 1991 and which has a devastating effect out to 40km. However, for *Telic* it was decided that the MLRS would not be deployed. USMC air power was chosen as the weapon to replace it. One reason for this was that the Basra area was criss-crossed with oil pipelines and pumping stations, so the possibility of collateral damage with what was considered an area weapon discounted its use.

12 Regiment's 325 troops were the new boys. This state-of-the-art surveillance, tracking and acquisition unit was equipped with UAVs (Phoenix drones) and weapon-locating radar (WLR). *Telic* was to be the first true test for Phoenix. Introduced in the 1990s, it was a twin-boom, catapult-launched, piston-engined drone capable of loitering for four hours. Developed by BAE in Stevenage, with a wingspan of 5m, it had a sensor pod under its belly that beamed live-stream video imagery to the ground control station. Phoenix was operated in pairs from the back of trucks, so it did not need a runway – unlike the US drones – meaning it could stay closer to the front and provide that immediacy of support on the forward edge of battle. The regiment provided a forward tactical party for each of the division's three brigades to help integrate the platform to each battlegroup. 1 UKDIV's commander, Maj Gen Robin Brims, later commented, 'Phoenix was one of the division's battle-winning equipments'. There was still much to learn, not least of which was a lack of understanding by battlegroup commanders of exactly what the UAV was for. Some less suitable tasks reported included: looking for underwater defences in the Shatt al-Arab, looking at suspicious tarmac squares and monitoring Fedayeen pick-up trucks. Much to the dismay of the RAF was the prospect of army Phoenix teams controlling close air support, which was a long way from the accepted doctrine in 2003. The gunners of 32 Regiment, however, saw the writing on the wall and did begin cueing US Predator drone strikes and US F-18s and A-10s onto Iraqi targets with some considerable success. By the end of the short campaign, Phoenix was in demand and had truly proven itself.

Combat support included, as always, the Royal Engineers in the order of battle for Operation *Telic*. The engineer units included, 28 Regiment, 32 Armoured Regiment, 39 Regiment, 9 (PARA) Squadron, 9 Assault Squadron and 59 Squadron (both 3 Commando Brigade).

S/Sgt Mark Goldsmith had joined the army in Norwich aged 22. He had been a bricklayer for three years, so the careers sergeant signed him up for the Royal Engineers. By 2003, Mark was a staff sergeant with 65 Field Support Squadron, 28 Engineer Regiment, RE. The squadron arrived from Hameln, Germany in February with its huge fleet of vehicles and stacks of equipment. Its three troops consisted of bridging specialists, plant operators (diggers and cranes) and a resources troop using vehicles mounting the Demountable Rack Offload and Pick Up System (DROPS). These 15-ton lorries could drop a 20ft ISO container or other palletised equipment off the back of the chassis.

> We moved three or four times in Kuwait, each time getting gradually closer to the border. The last harbour we had was just west of the main road from Iraq into Kuwait south of Safwan. We were set up in an old quarry that was deep into the ground on three sides. It worked well to be hidden from view and fire, but we felt vulnerable to the enemy had they somehow broken through and got onto the edge overlooking the quarry. I remember organising patrols at dusk to go out and secure the rim. It was ridiculous though, as we each only 10 rounds of ammunition

for our SA80s. What we did was surrender our ammo to those going on patrol. I went up on the rim later and could see across the borders to the north and I saw several of the big oil wells burning, lighting up the night sky.

As a resource specialist I was responsible for running the field park where all the stores were positioned ready to be issued out. I remember an officer coming to me and saying how he wanted all the kit and stores lined up in nice, neat lines, with all the bridging in one corner, assault boats and rafts next to that, and so on. I politely told him that it was not good practice to keep all equipment of one type together in case of an air raid or artillery strike when one shell could destroy everything of one type in one go. He scuttled off and left me to it.

With all the units that were due now in place in Kuwait, most of them moved to their respective assembly areas, Gryphon (the 16 AAB FAA), Barnsley or Viking, and the final few hours slipped past before the invasion began. L/Sgt Bob Giles, 1 IG, had to change his plans unexpectedly:

> Hours before we got the go ahead to drive north into Iraq, my own skills of adaptability would be tested. Due to one of our lads breaking a leg during a training exercise, I was shifted out of the turret of the vehicle I was commanding into another platoon and placed in charge of a section of six men in the back of callsign 2-3 Alpha. Although this change of appointment meant the last three months of training in my vehicle with the same crew and the same lads had all been for nothing, I was quietly pleased. It had seemed to me that it was the lads in the back of the vehicles who would truly be at the coalface when the shit hit the fan. They would be the ones fighting at close quarters, with bayonet and hand-to-hand. It would turn out that the new section I inherited would become very close to me, and I would develop a sense of responsibility to the six lads that lasted well after the war and continues today. I would sleep, eat and drink with them for the next six weeks, as well as laugh with them, shout at them, fight alongside them and have my life saved by them.

The marking out of FAA Barnsley had taken the RRF Recce Platoon all day and hours later they were still acting as glorified parking wardens moving and directing people. Capt Ed Pugh was there:

> I even missed my biggest O-group of my service because latecomers and other units needed shifting around the assembly area. I ended up having just a ten-minute 'turret' brief about me leading the invasion into Iraq!
>
> With everything in place, we finally grabbed a few minutes to ourselves with a brew when miraculously the post arrived. Just like most deliveries, it was for me, and my crew ribbed me about it. I had been with the crew for about 18 months, and they were great. L/Cpl 'Sandy' Sanderson was the driver and my gunner was Cpl Alan 'Jonna' Johnson, an unflappable, humorous Geordie. On the eve of the invasion, I received an e-bluey (printed email) from my Dad. On other days I got numerous letters, parcels and gifts, the most useless of which was a foot-high plastic masturbating soldier, which caused much amusement but had to be buried in the sand as there was no room for such niceties in the tiny Scimitar.
>
> I opened the letter from my Dad. Most letters came from my Mum, so it was unusual for Dad to write. It was just full of mundane goings on, with him telling me about trying to fit a kitchen. I started to cry, the letter had snapped me back to home and the people I love, and it was the jerk back to the reality and danger of what we were about to embark upon. I was sat next to 'Jonna' in the turret who simply said, 'Letter from home boss?' It was his way of putting a verbal arm around me as if to say, 'We know, Sir and we get it.'

After the letter, I got back in the focussed mood I needed for the invasion which was starting in just a few hours' time.

The transition from Operation *Southern Watch* to *Iraqi Freedom* took place on Wednesday, 19 March. Flt Lt Andy Johnson, RAF, tactical director on an AWACS E-3D Sentry, kept a diary:

Wednesday, 19 March D-Day at PSAB. Today we were briefed extensively on how we were going to transition at 18:00 tonight from *Southern Watch* to military operations codenamed Operation *Iraqi Freedom*, with the aim of removing the Iraqi governing regime, neutralising Iraqi theatre ballistic missile capability and destroy Iraqi weapons of mass destruction and their capability to produce and disseminate such weapons. The desired end state was a stable Iraq with a new broad-based government that no longer supported terrorism or threatened its neighbours.

This looked like it was going to be a busy and challenging day both conceptually and physically. There were two good bits of news, however. First, we were given a new callsign. Brutus was dead. We were now callsign Bondo. Second, we were issued US-made desert flying suits which were more comfortable than our typical green RAF issue kit.

I briefed the crew on the importance of changing their mindset from peacetime to war ops. I reminded them that just because our war was to start at 18:00 didn't mean that the Iraqi Air Force would have to wait for us to start. Not only would we be searching for threats coming at us, but that all those slow-moving tankers and less protected aircraft would be relying on us. There was also an increased likelihood of incoming Scuds as soon as it was dark at PSAB (16:00).

We were now to be working directly for Bloodhound and our on-station time was 10:00 to 18:00.

In principle, on this first flight of Operation *Iraqi Freedom*, we should be talking to the two American AWACS E-3Cs, callsigns Karma and Luger. Predictably the comms plan was up the chute and we hardly spoke to either. Tracking responsibilities seemed ad hoc and wishy-washy. Consequently, some aircraft were not tracked at all, and others were tracked by two. It really was messy and made me feel very uneasy. Deeper into the orbit time Bloodhound was calling us for updates on messages coming from a tasked F-16 callsign Hammer 53. No one knew about this or who was meant to be talking to Hammer. Utter confusion was evident and to cap it all we had a fire alarm go off. A smell of burning was emanating from the electrical cabinets behind the cockpit. We declared the situation and handed over radar responsibility to Luger while we investigated the alarms. No fault was found but it illustrated that this aircraft, ZH107, was not fit for operations and we returned to PSAB.

Friday, 21 March 0630 Breakfast – 0730 Briefing – 0830 Engine start & Push Back – 0900 Take Off – 1000 On station – 1300 Air to air refuel – 1800 Off station transit to PSAB – 1900 Land & two tin debrief – Eat – Sleep – Repeat.

Not long after arriving on station over the western desert the SATCOM burst to life.

'Cobra 24, troops in contact, request close air support.'

'Bloodhound copied, standby for asset.'

We selected one of the F-16C aircraft, callsign Flesh 13, and passed the details to Bloodhound: 'Bloodhound, Bondo, Flesh 13 he's an F-16.'

Not long after that hand off came another more detailed request. Cobra 22, an American SF ground team, had spotted a convoy of five vehicles and approximately 40 personnel just 500m from their hideout outside a small industrial compound.

'Cobra 22, request immediate close air support.'

'Bloodhound, Bondo, Fuji 62.' Fuji 62 was also a US F-16C.

Out of sight of Bondo, the Air National Guard F-16C from Colorado turned towards the grid reference provided by Cobra 22 and armed his weapon systems for the run-in to the target. The pilot selected from his payload four GBU-12 Paveway 500lb bombs. The Lockheed Martin Paveway bombs were laser-guided 'smart bombs' and could hit a target only one-metre square with 88% hit rate probability. The requirement for such bombs grew out of the Vietnam War when US Air Force pilots were trying to hit supply trucks on the Ho Chi Minh Trail. The task for Fuji 62 was not so dissimilar but 30 years after the war in Vietnam had ended.

The report came in from Fuji 62 and Cobra 22 'Mission Successful, four times GBU-12, two trucks destroyed and 20 personnel.' Bloodhound asked for clarification 'Bloodhound, what type of trucks Fuji 62?'

Fuji 62: 'Type unknown just, err trucks!'

Then came the call we had all been waiting for.

'Two Scuds in position …' The end of the message was garbled and unreadable. We all asked each other if anyone had heard it better. We called Luger and asked what they had heard. They replied negative. We called back on the net asking the callsign to repeat and identify. The man was gone. This was ludicrous! What could be the most important call of the day and the man had not even stayed on the net long enough to make sure he was received and understood. Ten minutes later we found the man via other means and took his message. Two suspected Scud-carrying trucks carrying four missiles each were parked, partially hidden, behind a gas station.

We assigned Bambam 25, but that F-16 called, 'Bingo fuel,' so up popped War Dog 67, a pair of F-15Es. After a few minutes War Dog declared the weather and sandstorm was so bad they were unable to positively identify the target. We could not help with the weather so we all just made notes of the reported sighting and hoped we could do something more later. The decreased visibility also caused a stir for one USAF callsign who reported, 'Fast mover – Zero-Eight-Zero. 20, low, 110kts heading east.' As we all started planning and calling in the probable sighting the callsign radioed up again 'Cancel all – it was just a car doing 120mph on the main road.'

We had to be careful here, it was too easy to make a catastrophic mistake and kill innocents.

Saturday, 22 March [A-day] Standing on the flight line after dark on 22 March was a very memorable moment. The heat of the day was beginning to cool and become a pleasant and warm Kuwait evening. I had wandered down near the runways at Ali Al Salem Air Base to watch the Tornados of IX Squadron take off on their missions to Iraq. One by one the crews, two to each aircraft, climbed aboard and completed pre-flight checks, fired up their engines and roared off into the night sky with their afterburners leaving a bright red-orange glow behind them. Tornado ZG710 was flown by my mate Kevin Main. I had seen him earlier in the crew room before briefing. On most days he would come and sit in our TIIW pods for a bit of peace and quiet away from the engineering noises of the flight line. I didn't realise that I would never see Kevin again.

Just after the last Tornado took off the air attack warning siren went off and we all scuttled off to the underground air raid bunker. Just before 03:00 all clear was sounded so I went back to the flight line and saw the aircraft were already back and parked. I saw the flight controller and remember asking him if all the planes had come back and he said yes. With that I turned in and went to bed.

The next morning, I went into the Group Captain's briefing and there was an obvious air of tension. I knew something was wrong so asked what was going on. I was told that the same number of aircraft had been counted back, as had taken off. However, one of the aircraft that landed was from another squadron and had landed with a problem from another base. We had lost a Tornado. ZG710 with Kevin and his navigator Dave Williams had been shot down as they headed back towards the Kuwait border. What made this loss even worse was that they were killed by an American Patriot missile. A board of enquiry investigated the circumstances of the incident.

The MOD board of enquiry published its findings in May 2004. It confirmed RAF Tornado GR4 ZG710 was destroyed by a US Army Patriot surface-to-air missile, which wrongly identified the aircraft as an Iraqi missile. The crew were killed instantly and did not eject. The enquiry showed that the Identification Friend or Foe (IFF) system was checked by ground crew prior to take off and was in working order. The Tornado was descending at an altitude of 17,900ft when it was hit.

The Patriot battery crew detected the incoming object, and the radar identified it and tracked it as an anti-radar missile. The track was interrogated on the IFF system but there was no response. Having met all the criteria for launching under self-defence protocols, the Patriot battery engaged and destroyed the track.

The board identified several contributory factors: Patriot rules of engagement were not robust enough to prevent friendly fires and the crew though well trained suffered from generic training and not enough threat-specific scenarios which alter each day. The battery was deemed to be operating too autonomously and lacked direct radio contact with higher formations.

The board also concluded that ZG710 had an IFF fault which the RAF crew were unaware of. The investigation uncovered certain power failures in the aircraft led to the IFF shut down but with no failure warning light displayed. There was no evidence that the crew switched off the IFF.

Lastly, it was concluded that airspace routing and control measures should be improved. Other recommendations were also highlighted and later implemented around airborne IFF checks:

Coalition losses of aircraft in 2003 were remarkably low and ZG710 was the only RAF aircraft lost during the war. Kevin Main and Dave Williams conducted a dangerous and demanding combat mission in an exemplary manner yet did not return safely.

Sunday, 23 March What started out as a routine flight for Bondo later turned a nasty corner. After some close air support calls for Caveman teams and our planned refuelling, my colleague Burt reported a burning smell in the aft of the aircraft. The E28 cabinet seemed to be the culprit. This could be serious, so we shut down the systems in it. However, one function it fulfilled was management of the forced air system that affected lots of other cabinets. Burt had to go walkabouts with his mask, O2 bottles and an extinguisher, checking each cabinet. As it needed two people really to go aft, so Adrian Morris – the other tech – went with him. This now meant, while we were still on station, that we had people away from their tasks. In all our previous training episodes our mantra would have been to shout. 'Return to base.' Now, at war over Iraq we had literally hundreds of people relying on us, and so we could not simply shout 'return to base'.

One nasty knock-on of the loss of cabinet E28 was we had to turn off IFF. This denied us our primary means of identification that, in theory, stops us being shot out the sky by our own fighters.

'Bloodhound, this is Bondo,' I called over the radio. 'We are investigating fumes, have lost IFF and may have to go off station at short notice. Will keep you informed.'

The fumes dissipated slightly, and we only handed over duty to the next crew 11 minutes ahead of schedule to help us get back to PSAB and investigate on the ground. Later, I heard that one of our Tornados had been shot down by a friendly fire Patriot missile: it reminded me of how much we needed to stay on the ball. We were all very tired and had flown four long missions in seven days. I was acutely aware of course that the 'Cavemen' on the ground would have hardly slept at all and certainly not been near a bed so we had to keep performing for their sakes.[7]

One such Caveman team on the desert floor, below Bondo, was Zero Six Bravo, a 52-man raiding party from M Squadron, SBS operating in western Iraq hunting for TST like Scud but primarily its task was to find the 80,000-strong Iraqi V Corps and take its surrender in the Tikrit region. Some people on and around the undertaking questioned whether it was some kind of suicide mission. There was a lack of credible intelligence that V Corps was poised to surrender nor was there proof that the region was benign. It proved to be wholly otherwise. The 60 UK SF operators were travelling in rugged, adapted Land Rovers but they were not armoured and the weapons carried were small arms, some 40mm belt-fed grenade launchers and .50cal machine guns – illustrating, perhaps, either the lack of planning or the lack of resources available and 'on call' should they require help. For the SBS it must have felt like a poor man's military.

After being compromised one night by a goat herder (echoes of *Bravo Two Zero*), the patrol attempted to evade pursuit by a growing Iraqi hunter force but was ambushed in a laying up position by well-armed Fedayeen and even several T-72 tanks. Forced to carry out escape and evasion, several Land Rovers became bogged down in wet sand and had to be destroyed by the SBS to prevent them falling into enemy hands. Unfortunately, several were not destroyed and were captured and paraded on International TV in a major propaganda coup. Having been splintered into three groups, each made their own bids for rescue. One pair of troopers evaded into Syria on a quad bike. A second small group were extracted by RAF Chinook on ATV quads and motorbikes. The largest group, with a few overloaded Land Rovers, called for air support when it got surrounded by armoured Fedayeen forces again. In ever desperate voices, the SBS radio team – callsign Vader – asked pleadingly for air support to 'help mallet the Fedayeen, because they are right on top of us.'[8] It was dark and deep in enemy territory many miles from useable cover. Answering the call for help and routed via the AWACS was Honcho 23, a pair of US F-16s from the 160th Fighter Squadron, Alabama Air National Guard, flying out of Jordan. Amid a feeling of utter desolation and disbelief on the ground, the pilots said they could not bomb the Iraqi forces because not only was the weather bad but they were dangerously close to the SBS positions. Additionally, other SBS units were now on the run and could be intermingled near the Iraqis. The risk of friendly fire was too great. However, Honcho 23 did provide help a few minutes later by low-level shows of force. They flew at palm tree height with full afterburners on over the enemy then pulled up sharply creating explosive noises with comets of fire trailing from their afterburners. Two such runs and the deployment of flares from the aircraft further distracted the Iraqi ground troops for long enough to allow the SBS patrol to sneak away once more and be picked up by RAF Chinook. The two USAF pilots were awarded the Distinguished Flying Cross for their bravery and coolness in action that night.

The RAF continued its command-and-control missions at 34,000ft, with the AWACS E-3D controlling missions and co-ordinating effects all across western and southern Iraq. Flt Lt Andy Johnson, RAF was aboard:

> Our disappointment at not having been able to help the SBS guys more than we did the previous flight was to be banished in April when we helped coordinate a CSAR mission. Our mission take off was messy, when first a Nimrod pushed in front of us on the runway then the pilot, Sandy, had to abort take off when an airfield vehicle strayed across our path. Sandy smashed the brakes on and throttled back so fast that we were all pitched right forward in our seats.
>
> Before the CSAR call came up we had been investigating troops at Haditha Dam on behalf of a Caveman callsign, Striker 32. Striker reported coming under accurate mortar fire around 09:15 and requested close air support. We sent in a series of callsigns to help Striker. First a pair of F-16s, Curfew 11 vectored in, followed by British Harrier GR7, Gospel 21. Striker was reporting good hits and wanted more. Hotel 63 was next, the pair of A-10 Warthogs rolled in with their signature multi-barrel 30mm cannon at the ready.
>
> At 09:44 the Scud Sat Comms barked out 'Sprint' over the loudspeaker. This was the codeword for a Caveman unit being overrun. Zulu 99 (US Rangers) was operating near the Haditha Dam and one of their unit had been injured and they were being surrounded by Iraqi forces. The wounded Ranger was callsign Whisky 50.

Haditha Dam is on the Euphrates River 200km north-west of Baghdad and just 100km from the Syrian border. The enormous dam provides hydroelectric power for much of central Iraq and Baghdad and had been deemed a priority target to capture and thus prevent its destruction by Iraqi forces. As early as 23 March US Delta Force SF teams had been monitoring Objective Lynx, the dam, and Iraqi Army activities around it. It was deduced that a larger force would be needed to capture the dam due to the presence of a large number of Iraqi infantry, perhaps more than 150 and upwards of 40 tanks and IFVs as well as nearly 100 AA guns, six Roland SAM launchers and 15 155mm howitzers.

The 3rd Battalion, 75th Ranger Regiment was flown to Iraq from Fort Bragg, NC in C-17s who then picked up 14 M1 Abrams tanks from the 70th Armoured Regiment and shuttled the battlegroup to landing strip Grizzly to the east of Haditha. Grizzly had been established by Delta Force since 20 March.

As the Rangers and tanks engaged the defenders, operators from Delta Force landed from AH-6 Little Bird helicopters and entered the main buildings controlling the dam and the power networks. The battle lasted more than three days in and around the dam buildings and on either side of the Euphrates. On 3 April as fighting died down at the dam, three Rangers manning a checkpoint on the outer cordon were killed by a vehicle-borne IED (improvised explosive device). An Iraqi female driving a car seemed distressed and was asking for water at the checkpoint. As the Rangers approached her, she initiated the bomb and all three were killed. Shortly after, Rangers on the banks of the Euphrates became suspicious of a civilian in a kayak on the river who kept paddling up and down past them and other Ranger positions. They called to him to come to the riverbank, but he ignored them. Some well-sighted sniper shots holed his kayak which started to sink, and this appeared to encourage the man back to the shallows. He was arrested when it was found he was a forward observer, equipped with binoculars, maps and sketches of all the Ranger positions.

Meanwhile Andy Johnson aboard Bondo was due to refuel right about the time the CSAR mission would be underway, so the crew agreed with Bloodhound to go for fuel early and carry on with the CSAR mission when back and on station. Four Blackhawk helicopters, Prince 45, would be escorted by A-10s, callsign Mohawk 15, down to the dam and scoop up the wounded Ranger around 14:30.

However, Mohawk had several problems on his radio and Prince 45 started his run in to the LZ without him. Mohawk then gained contact direct with Zulu 99, the original CSAR callers, at the dam and so understood what was happening and made his presence felt above the helicopters at the LZ. Flt Lt Andy Johnson continues:

> Soon after, I heard that Whisky 50, suffering from gunshot wounds, was now stable aboard Prince 45 and en route to hospital. I was so pleased that this one had come off. There had been some communication breakdowns aboard Bondo and clearly everyone was very tired, but I was pleased with the team performance and impressed how we were all now working together.

CHAPTER 4

Operation *Houghton* – Capturing the Al-Faw Peninsula

When the war started, we had moved up close to the Iraqi port of Umm Qasr with the media. I could see and hear jets passing overhead and distant explosions. I was trying to get some sleep in my tent when I was awoken and told the Brigade Commander, Jim Dutton, wanted to see me. I went rather bleary-eyed into the CP tent and the brigadier said 'Ben, we've lost a CH-46 helicopter, with the Brigade Reconnaissance Force on board.'

I personally knew two of the eight British guys on board and was shocked. Apparently, the US pilot had become disorientated with a combination of dark, sand and smoke from the Iraqis burning the oilfield and just flew it straight into the ground, nose first. It then tipped over onto its back and burst into flames. It was described to me as a burnt-out split metal banana. No one survived.

The next day our column went forward up the road towards Umm Qasr. I was driving a hire vehicle, a white Mitsubishi Pajero. I wanted a Land Rover so as not to stand out but we didn't have enough. A Team from the MOD had gone into Kuwait and hired just about every vehicle they could lay their hands on. The Press rocked up like a scene from *The Cannonball Run* with a host of all styles of hire cars, saloons, 4x4s and even a luxury Lexus. I often wondered how many of these cars got returned in one piece back to their airport rental desks.

On the road not far inside Iraq was a burnt-out Iraqi truck. I remember seeing the driver still sitting in his seat at the wheel, all burnt and crispy. I think he had been hit by an air strike.

Entering Umm Qasr was like the liberation of Paris in 1944. The locals had been persecuted by Hussein for years and they came out to cheer us, so we gave out water and food. Then the troops started setting up defences against counter-attacks and one area was reinforced by piling the big metal ISO containers up, three high, and filling them with sand and stone as a blast wall.

Attached to us was an USMC battalion. That was quite a coup because it is highly unusual to have foreign troops subordinated to another country's command. It showed the level of trust and understanding between the USMC and the Royal Marines. There's no way they would have done that for the French.

LT COL BEN CURRY, RM

The twin-tail Phoenix drone swept across Bubiyan Island and over the Iraqi border, unseen by the Iraqi sentries patrolling the Al-Faw. For several hours the UAV lazily cruised above the Iraqi positions amongst the oil infrastructure, all the while beaming back pictures and data to the ground station manned by crews from 32 Regiment, RA. Phoenix was unarmed and with a wingspan of over 5m would offer an easy target if spotted, but due to the altitude it could operate at, it was rarely seen. Having spotted and recorded the enemy positions, the drone was flown north to double-check the

Map 2: Basra and northern Kuwait

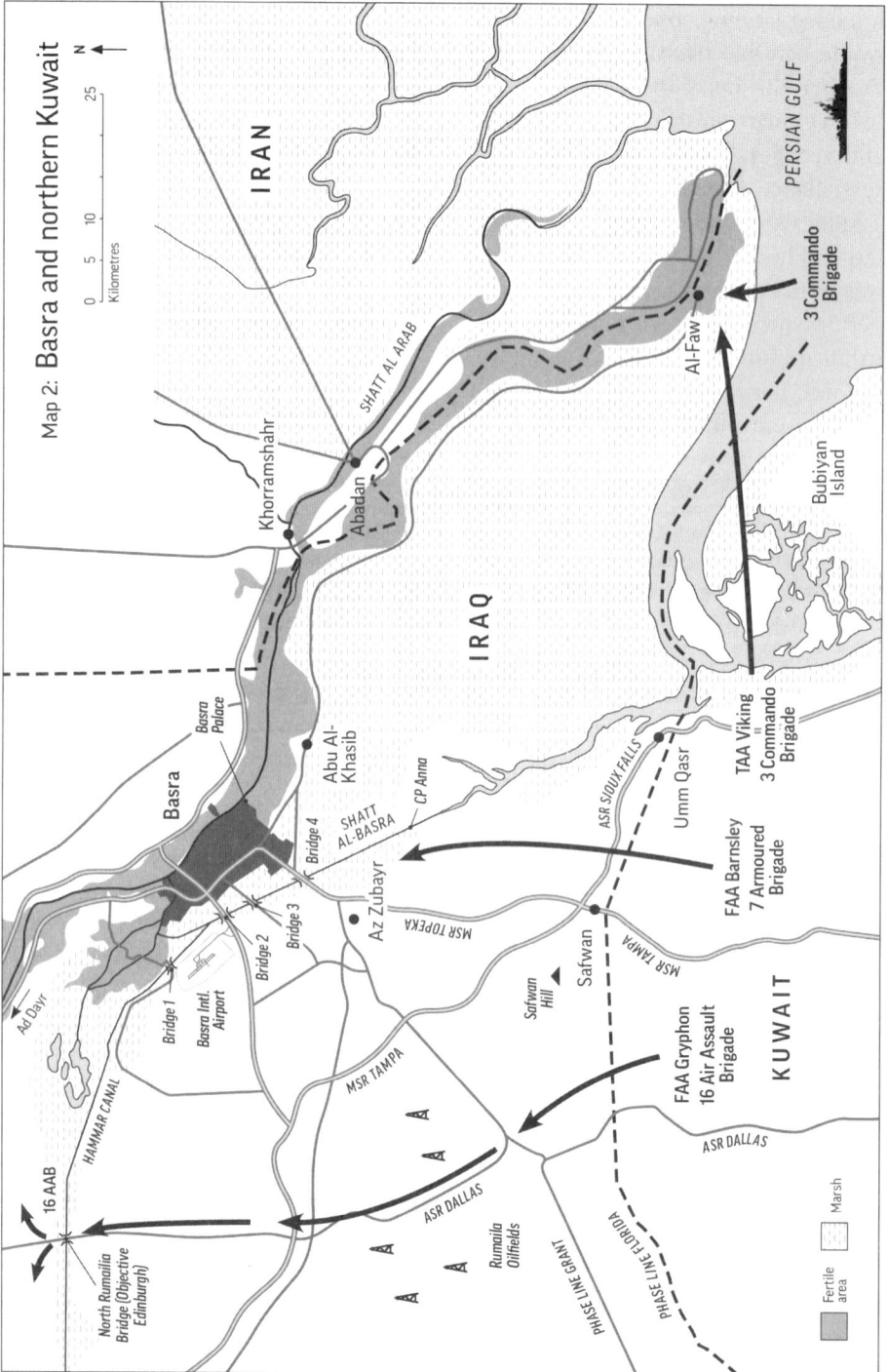

intended landing zones for the US Navy SEALs and 40 Commando, RM at what would be Objective Coronado.

After the invasion began, the Royal Artillery Phoenix teams further assisted 29 Regiment gunners with fall of shot reports as they targeted Iraqi positions and vehicles. The brigade was most innovative with its approach to intelligence, surveillance, targeting and reconnaissance (ISTAR) assets by combining Sea King Mk 7 radar reports, Phoenix imagery and on-ground recce units with their eyes on the target. Phoenix was known as a 'zero length' drone in that it needed no runway and was launched from a catapult on the bed of a truck. The launch teams perfected their performance and drove down time to launch figures from two hours pre-deployment to 50 minutes when *Telic* was underway. Phoenix really proved its worth during the war, particularly on 25 March when a battlegroup of Iraqi T-54/55 tanks was detected moving south towards 3 Commando Brigade. Out of range of the available artillery the only ISTAR asset on scene was Phoenix. The ground control team quickly located and identified the column and called on the only asset it could to help the marines, F-18 Hornet jets of the US Navy. The British Army FAC was dragged from his sleeping bag to co-ordinate the strike, which was successful and defeated the threat. The paradigm of CAS control had shifted.

The other less visual effect of Phoenix was its psychological effect on the enemy. Iraqi troops got used to being watched by UAVs and then soon after being hit by artillery or air strikes. As the campaign moved on at Basra, flights were often undertaken to both watch the enemy but also to encourage him to capitulate. Controllers often watched as the enemy abandoned his equipment or took cover, indicating its mere presence was already generating a suppressive effect.

An unspecified number of Phoenix were lost on *Telic*, but one is thought to have been shot down at low level by small-arms fire and at least one was sacrificed by the controllers who knew it was running low on fuel but deemed it more important to remain spotting the enemy for as long a time as absolutely possible due to the high-value nature of the target. Greater range, endurance and better sensors were all listed as improvements needed at the conclusion of *Telic*. The army got its wish with the arrival in 2006 of the new improved Watchkeeper drone.

Operation *Houghton*

The Al-Faw peninsula is a small piece of flat and muddy land that juts out into the Persian Gulf. It is, however, of vital importance as 90% of Iraq's oil is exported through it, so there is a great deal of oil infrastructure based upon it. On its east side runs the Shatt al-Arab waterway and the border with Iran. On its west side runs the Khawr Abd Allah waterway, sitting upon which is the container port of Umm Qasr. It is roughly 80km by 50km in size and has only Umm Qasr and Al-Faw as its population centres.

Tasked with securing the port and the oil infrastructure was Britain's 3 Commando Brigade. The Royal Marines – nicknamed the Royals – have a very long and proud history going back to their formation in 1664. As part of the Royal Navy, they were originally set up to maintain discipline on and around naval ships and provide maritime infantry for battles at sea. They grew to provide gunners for the guns and turrets on larger ships as well as to make amphibious landings. The term 'commando' was coined in 1942 when Winston Churchill, desperate to maintain the fight against Hitler after the Dunkirk evacuations, appealed for specially trained volunteers who could continue the fight by unconventional means and by raiding the coastlines of Nazi-occupied Europe. Each of Britain's three services had commandos and they gained many well-known battle honours including D-Day and the Rhine Crossing.

3 Commando Brigade Order of Battle:
539 (Commando) Assault Squadron
29 (Commando) Regiment, RA
40 Commando, RM
42 Commando, RM

After the war, with downsizing the commandos became a purely Royal Marine force. Today, they are an elite amphibious force specialising in mountain and arctic warfare and jungle fighting. They provide a key element of Britain's Rapid Reaction Force.

Commanding the RM Brigade on Operation *Telic* was Brig Jim Dutton, RM. After failing selection to become an officer in the army in 1972, Dutton switched to the Royals and went on to have a glittering career, retiring as lieutenant general in 2010 having served in the Falklands and commanding 40 Commando. Just after 9/11 he was posted to the US Pentagon to act as liaison officer and was the first foreign officer allowed into the US National Military Command Center. While there he was tasked with working out what options were available for the UK to provide military assistance in an invasion of Iraq. The Americans were still working on Plan 1003, a 600-page document written in 1998, detailing how next to invade Iraq. Plan 1003 was heavily influenced by the 1991 war, after which the Hussein regime had brutally quelled the Shia population in the south after an uprising. It was, therefore, vital in any future conflict to be able to support the population around Basra with humanitarian aid and that meant seizing the port of Umm Qasr to allow aid vessels to unload easily. The waters approaching and beyond Umm Qasr were mined by the Iraqis and would need to be comprehensively swept, so a good size fleet of minesweepers and RN clearance divers would be needed in any coming plan. Chinese-manufactured Silkworm anti-ship missiles had also been positioned on the Al-Faw dominating the waterways and their northern Gulf approaches.

The combination of the oil infrastructure and the threat that Saddam would sabotage it, the need for a port and the Silkworm missile threat meant that the

Al-Faw was a high priority target. No US troops in Plan 1003 had been allocated to this task, so it fell upon the British to perform it. Working with Rear Adm David Snelson, Dutton began to plan for 3 Commando Brigade to seize the Al-Faw. After fresh intelligence updates on the mechanics of the oil and gas infrastructure, American generals at CENTCOM in Tampa, Florida, became concerned that the task was even larger and more vital than first thought. They added special forces from the US Navy SEALs and Polish GROM teams to the plan. These teams would strike hard and fast in a first wave, seize the vital nodes and then be relieved in place by the Royal Marines to complete the clearance and then defend the positions against the expected Iraqi counter-attacks from the Basra area.

With both 40 and 42 Commando committed, the navy assigned to the Persian Gulf plan HMS *Ocean*, HMS *Ark Royal* and 20 other ships – including two submarines, destroyers, frigates, minesweepers and Royal Fleet Auxiliary supply vessels.

Detailed planning then began with Brig Dutton, Lt Col Gordon Messenger (40 Commando), Lt Col 'Buster' Howes (42 Commando), Lt Cdr John Pentreath (commander of the Naval Air component) and the US SEAL team staff. The main effort was allocated to 40 Commando. It was to capture the buildings and machinery that control the gas oil exports from the southern oilfields. Pipelines flowed through a large MMS which was nearly 2km square, containing offices, storage tanks, pumps and other machinery and maintenance buildings. The MMS became Objective Coronado. From the MMS, two separate 4ft diameter pipes ran underground, emerging a few kilometres south near the coastline at two buildings named M and K, codenamed Penzoil and Quaker respectively. M and K controlled the final flow out to sea to two platforms where ocean-going oil/ gas tankers could be loaded.

US SEAL teams would seize the MMS, sea platforms and pipelines, then 30 minutes later Royal Marines of 40 Commando would move in, set up defensive positions and allow the SEALs to redeploy. Having recently restructured, both 40 and 42 Commando consisted of around 800 men across six companies – four rifle companies, a logistics company and an HQ company. The final unit was the Manoeuvre Support Group (MSG), a highly mobile and well-armed unit with Browning .50 cal HMGs and MILAN missile posts.

Iraqi resistance and reaction were expected, and intelligence suggested the presence at Basra of the 6th Armoured Division, which had more than 60 T-80 and T-55 tanks. To counter this threat, 42 Commando would land north of the MMS and provide a screen for 40 Commando and protect its flank. The eyes and ears of the brigade, the Brigade Reconnaissance Force (BRF) would land further north still to spot and report on any sightings of a counter-attack toward the MMS. The BRF was a small group of experienced marines with reconnaissance expertise and included forward observation officers from 29 Commando Royal Artillery Regiment.

The final element added to the Operation *Houghton* plan was for a squadron of Scimitar light tanks of the Queen's Dragoon Guards (QDG) to land via

USMC hovercraft on Red Beach near Objectives Penzoil and Quaker. These very lightly armoured but fast vehicles, armed with a 30mm cannon, would provide 40 Commando more firepower and manoeuvrability.

40 Commando companies were allocated tasks for the operation and loading tables for the helicopters drawn up accordingly. C Company, MSG and 40 Commando HQ would land in the first wave at the MMS, reinforced 60 minutes later by A Company. B Company would follow the US SEALs at Objectives Penzoil and Quaker. Finally, D Company would fly in directly from the landing ships HMSs *Ark Royal* and *Ocean* to reinforce B Company. They were to be the only unit to fly directly from ships with all the other elements assaulting from bases in Kuwait; TAA Viking or TAA Swallow (42 Commando). It had been agreed that due to the threat of shore-based anti-ship Silkworm missiles, the fleet needed to maintain a distance from the coast which would lead in turn to helicopters launching a long way from shore. This increased the shuttle time for each flight and, therefore, made it impractical to launch the main assault that way.

What became apparent in planning was the need for all the elements of the brigade to arrive near simultaneously – thus dictating the need for the air assault option rather than an amphibious landing. However, as British lift capacity via helicopters was too small, so 42 Commando were to be given help from the vast resources of the USMC. Several weeks of planning and training in the Kuwait desert followed, where the British and American marines practised together to understand methods, terminology and capability. Thirty-seven US helicopters were needed to lift Buster Howes's 42 Commando into Iraq. They were a combination of the twin-rotor CH-46 Sea Knight and the heavy-lift MH-53 Super Stallion. The Royal Marines used a number of Bv206S tracked vehicles and these needed to be underslung the helicopters. Troops trained until the times were acceptable in loading, taking off, fixing the slung loads then landing and unloading. One of the biggest problems encountered, naturally, was dust thrown up by the enormous downdraft, especially from the MH-53s.

It is fair to say that the US SF were still hung over by the disaster of Operation *Eagle Claw* in 1980 – the operation to rescue 50 US embassy staff held captive in Tehran. An RH-53D helicopter and an EC-130 Hercules aircraft collided at a staging point amid a dust storm of swirling helicopter blades. This resulted in the deaths of 13 servicemen and the mission was abandoned. Because of this, procedures for the US pilots in 2003 were extremely risk averse in desert environments, which led to friction between the US and UK operators and planners who could see that the delays built in between each airframe landing, to allow dust to clear, seemed interminable to the forces wanting to get on the ground. The British also discovered that the general standard of pilot experience in US Marine squadrons was lower than that of a British pilot. Few had experience of underslung loads or night flying and the training flights were found to be rather scary.

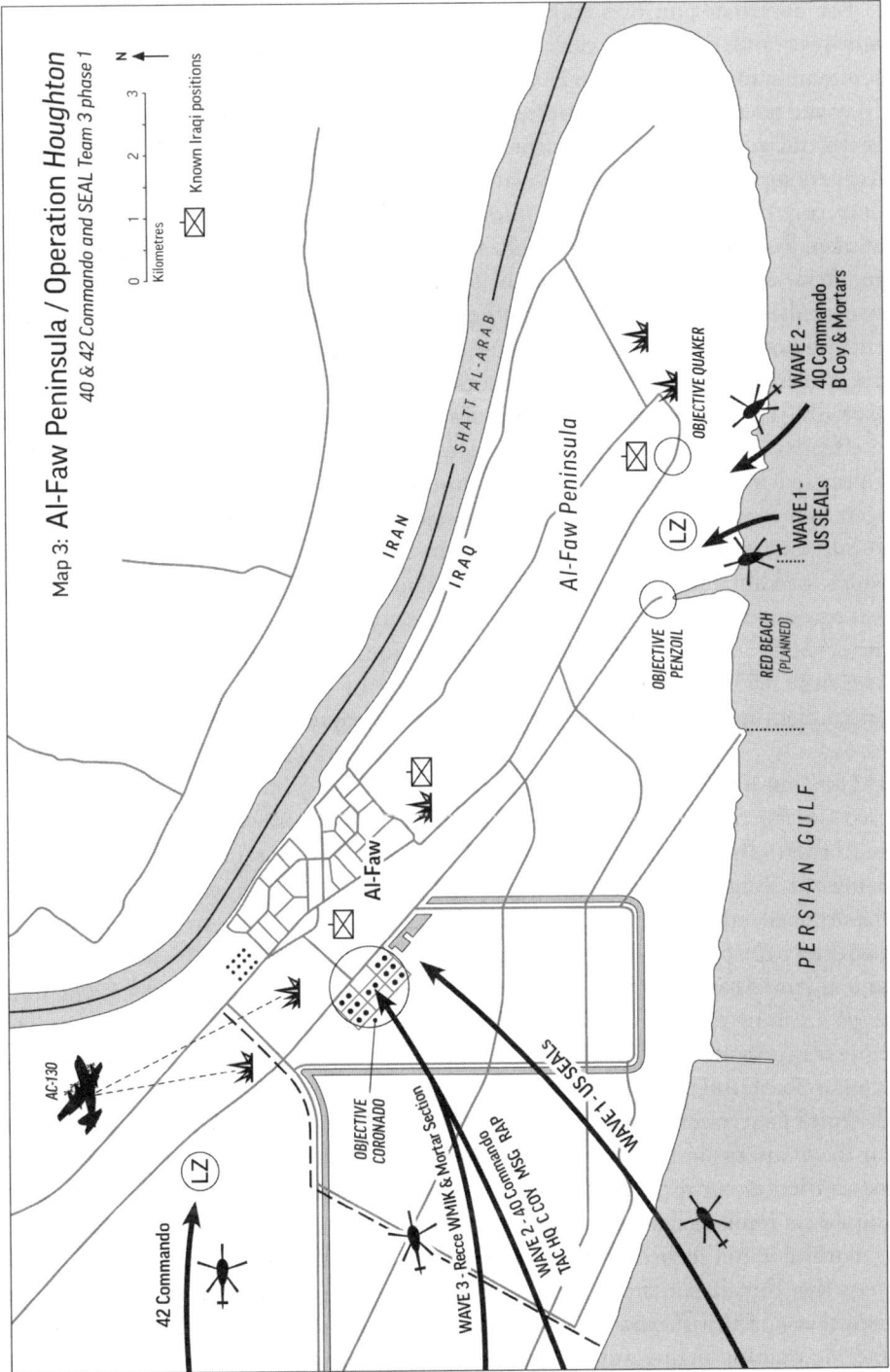

Map 3: Al-Faw Peninsula / Operation *Houghton*
40 & 42 Commando and SEAL Team 3 phase 1

N

Kilometres
0 1 2 3

⊠ Known Iraqi positions

SHATT AL-ARAB

IRAN

IRAQ

Al-Faw Peninsula

OBJECTIVE QUAKER

WAVE 2 -
40 Commando
B Coy & Mortars

LZ

WAVE 1 -
US SEALs

OBJECTIVE PENZOIL

RED BEACH
(PLANNED)

PERSIAN GULF

Al-Faw

AC-130

OBJECTIVE CORONADO

LZ

42 Commando

WAVE 3 - Recce WMIK & Mortar Section

WAVE 2 - 40 Commando RAP
TAC HQ C COY MSG

WAVE 1 - US SEALS

For doctrinal purposes, military units prefer to concentrate their groups for firepower and mutual support. Operation *Houghton* was spreading out the two commando units across a vast area that would preclude that preferred concentration. To make up for the deficit, artillery, naval gunfire support and air support would be on call with specialist associated fire controllers embedded in each unit. Royal Artillery support came from 29 Regiment with its commando-trained gun crews and their 16 105mm Light Guns, divided into two eight-gun batteries. One hurried fire mission for 29 Commando was called on 30 March when a RN Sea King overflew an old desert fort in the centre of Al-Faw and saw a well-hidden and camouflaged Iraqi artillery battery. It had been bypassed by the rapidly advancing 40 Commando but still posed a severe threat should it come into action. Eight guns were called to fire a swift salvo and within five minutes the 105mm HE and airburst rounds were exploding on target, devastating the position.

The 16 guns of 29 Regiment fired over 6,000 rounds (375 per gun) during Operation *Telic* in support of the commando ground forces. They proved once again how vital it is to have responsive, mobile, all-weather integrated fire support.

Supporting the marines in addition to 29 Regiment was C Battery, 3 RHA which would be in position on Bubiyan Island just west of the Al-Faw. The RHA was equipped with AS-90 155mm guns whose incredible range and accuracy would prove vitally important during Operation *Telic*. Each of the four RHA batteries had eight 155mm guns with a total manning of close to 1,000 personnel. The initial opening fire plan for Operation *Houghton* was a 90-minute barrage on the Al-Faw targets which would receive a total of 3,600 rounds of both 105mm and 155mm rounds.

Naval forces in the Gulf included HMSs *Chatham*, *Marlborough* and *Richmond* and HMAS *Anzac*. All were armed with either 4.5-inch or 5-inch guns. American Air Naval Gunfire Liaison Company (ANGLICO) teams in Humvees, with state-of-the-art data and communication technology that could accurately integrate, request and direct all of the fire-support assets, were embedded with each battlegroup down to company level. The ANGLICO teams called in over 600 salvos from the four ships on the gun line co-ordinated through HMS *Marlborough*. They also hailed close air support, usually within 25–30 minutes, in the shape of US Navy F-18s, US Air Force A-10s or USMC AV-8B Harriers. If not on station loitering above the battlefield, rotary wing support coming from AH-1 Cobras could also be called for in about an hour. The offensive support co-ordination of ANGLICO teams was a blessing to the British and one capability that postwar analysis suggested should be replicated as soon as possible.

For the initial stage of invasion, the other deep fires offensive firepower available were the Tomahawk cruise missiles aboard the Royal Navy submarines, one of which was HMS *Turbulent*. Unlike American submarines and surface ships, the Tomahawk missiles fired from a 'Trafalgar' class submarine leave the torpedo tubes by conventional pneumatic launch, then the rocket motor kicks in and they accelerate vertically up out of the sea and into the sky. Marine Engineer Mechanic Anthony Williams, RN was there:

> I was on duty in the control room by the periscopes when the captain got called to the small radio room. After a few moments he came out carrying a piece of paper and said, 'Officer of the watch stand the ship to for strategic launch of Tomahawk missiles.'
>
> We had all been expecting it, but even so when those words came it was still a bit surreal for a moment. We all knew what to do as we had practised hundreds of times. The final arming and loading of the missiles takes a while to get ready and before long my six-hour shift finished, and I went off watch. I went straight to the wardroom where there was a tiny screen that relayed an image in black and white of the periscope view. Lots of us crowded around it to try and get a view of this moment. Many sailors serve for 20 years and never see a missile launched in anger. The periscope was set looking straight forward so it was set to observe the launches.
>
> Just before the first launch the officer of the watch asked sonar to report if there was anything close. They reported that there was only a fishing dhow about 500m to the starboard side of *Turbulent*.
>
> A moment later we heard the familiar 'whoosh' of the first missile as it left the tube, then a few seconds later came the amazingly loud noise of the missile engine firing up. Then there it was on the screen, broaching the surface ahead of us and arcing up into the sky. I often wonder about those dhow fishermen casting their nets in the late afternoon sun and just what they said when suddenly a string of one-ton missiles emerged from their fishing grounds.
>
> There was maybe 15–20 minutes between each missile being fired and I wanted to see the guys in action so went down to the weapons section with two big jugs of orange squash. It was really hot in there and the team of lads all had their T-shirts wrapped around their heads because of their sweat. I saw lots of missiles had messages written on them, like the WW2 RAF bomber guys used to do. One had 'Up yours Saddam'. We fired 21 out of 22 missiles aboard. One missile failed to fire. Largely we were using Tomahawk Bloc 4 and the one that misfired was an American Bloc 5. I can only say that nearly everything that we fired at was to do with the Iraqi Air Defence structure. Radar towers, control buildings and so forth. Every missile hit its target and we were shown pictures later by the captain so we could understand what we had been involved in.

With the job done, all missiles fired, *Turbulent* slipped back deeper below the waves where it was at its best and most comfortable. It returned to the UK having completed the longest British submarine deployment since World War 2 – 11 months. As 'Turbs' surfaced once again for the final approach into the harbour at Devonport, the crew raised a Jolly Roger pennant, which had been designed and stitched by Anthony Williams. It was a black flag with the skull and crossbones and the addition of white Tomahawks sewn onto it, indicating that it had been in action firing deadly missiles. Anthony was not on board to raise the flag when the boat berthed. He had flown home early from Gibraltar to carry out other tasks but years later when he visited the Royal Navy Museum, he was proud to see that the 'Turbs' Jolly Roger had made its way into the museum displays.

Maj Neil Wraith, RM was with 40 Commando and was waiting to be airlifted into the Al-Faw peninsula:

Four-tonner lorries took us out to the helicopter landing site (HLS) and again we waited some more, now in the dark. On one side of me was the BBC's Clive Myrie doing a piece to camera and on the other side sat two marines on their Bergens facing each other, hands out, playing slaps (the playground game where you try and slap your opponent's hand). Another truck arrived with a mail delivery and I got a parcel from my Mum and Dad. It was crammed with sweets – Haribo – and some more cigarettes. At any other time, I would have distributed the food around my kit for later, but my kit had been packed so meticulously and was so full, that I had to either eat it or share it out. We had a sugar rush and then had to bin some of it sadly.

The Royal Marines seem to have a good relationship with the embedded media teams, so much so that they are still invited to reunion dinners. Tom Newton Dunn from the Mirror Group published an article just before the invasion entitled 'How the coalition will invade Iraq'. It gave a frighteningly accurate description of the actual plan. When the media were allocated seats on the helicopters for the invasion lift, they went on the second wave. The CO looked at Newton Dunn and said, 'Best hope the Iraqis didn't read your article!' Maj Wraith continues:

Shortly before 02:00 Thursday, 20 March, our five RAF CH-47s came in and we loaded on. There were 48 marines on my Chinook – more than normal – so it was very cramped. All the seats had been taken out and we sat on the floor with another guy in between your legs or on top of you. Throughout the hour or so flight and orbit time I had one excited NCO keep asking me, 'Are we were nearly there yet?'

Space on board the Chinooks was at such a premium on the first waves that the marines had to go in without their Bergens and rely on their belt kit, fighting order and a small daysack. For Maj Wraith one other vital piece of kit was his home-made 'battle board' which he had been shown why and how to make on his anti-tank officer's course:

It's just a piece of plywood about as big as an A4 sheet, with a clear plastic cover and folding pieces of acetate so you can do overlays on the base map. It's held together with gaffer tape. It's so much better than having a map flapping about in the wind and rain. You can buy Gucci ones on the internet but we prefer to make our own. In any other spare pockets, I crammed about 600 cigarettes.

On the flight in I sensed no fear nor had any, but there was a palpable determination to get the job done. The flight crew gave us the five-minute then two-minute warning signs and we felt the aircraft descending rapidly toward the chosen LZ.

Planners had opted to fly in and land right on the target, Objective Coronado, rather than land outside and fight their way in. The five Chinooks were split between two landing sites within the MMS. Maj Wraith, with TAC HQ, was in the fourth Chinook to land at the MMS and recalls the plan was to land on top of a circular concrete platform that used to be the base for an oil storage tank. As the marines disembarked, Wraith climbed out and felt the concrete base beneath his feet:

We moved to our initial positions quickly and I recall lying in the mud watching a taxi drive up a nearby road as if it was just a normal night in downtown Al-Faw. As a result of the extensive rehearsals and study of photographs, despite it being dark, we all knew exactly where we were. It all seemed strangely familiar, although the lack of opposition at that stage added to the surreality of the situation. It didn't last and the Iraqi infantry regrouped and started engaging us with direct and indirect fire. Our helicopters returned to Kuwait to pick up the second wave and it took them six attempts to land due to the presence of some previously unidentified telegraph poles which were dispatched by the SEALs. Ongoing fighting on the ground continued as C Coy secured the immediate objectives and the MSG established the perimeter against a now regrouping enemy. By the time the second wave actually landed, the initial counter-attack had largely been beaten back and while we continued to get indirect fire throughout the night, the remainder of the objective was secured without delay. One Iraqi mortar bombardment started landing close to us inside the MMS. We looked for cover and I found a gap between two huge metal engineering structures and squeezed myself in. I looked back to the other two guys I was with, and they had rolled underneath a huge pipe which contained something nasty like superheated fuel. I shouted over to Ed and his signaller about the stupidity of their choice of cover. Ed shouted back, 'Is there room in there with you?' I said, 'No, there is only room for one,' and laughed. A few years later he was back on another Telic rotation and he sent me a picture of himself standing in my cubbyhole shelter at the MMS captioned, 'There is room for more than one in here'.

The SEALs were excellent, great to work with and well equipped. They did deploy some sort of dune buggy vehicles but they got bogged in the ankle-deep cloying mud and were pretty useless.

We also had Australian naval gunfire support to our northern boundary from HMS *Anzac*'s 5-inch guns. Friday, 21 March became known as '5-inch Friday' after the amount of naval gunfire support that came in around us. It would be fair to say that naval fire is a very useful area weapon for suppression but never achieved the accuracy of the artillery from 29 Commando or the RHA who supported us.

The support from an American AC-130 gunship was devastatingly impressive.

The water table on the Al-Faw was only a foot or so beneath the surface, making it impossible to dig trenches or bury the dead without first creating a mud bath. Numerous dead Iraqi were found in and around the MMS and other defended areas. Many had been hit by artillery or JDAMs (joint direct-attack munition) and were in a ghastly mess. The dead still needed to be buried, so parties were organised to dig graves in the roadside berms where at least it was above the water table. The next day a party of locals requested to recover their dead and came over and dug up them and removed them. Maj Wraith remembers:

> The first actual Iraqi soldiers I saw were prisoners that had been taken during the first night's assault. Patrolling out through their defensive positions we saw they were expecting an assault from outside rather than a coup de main inside the perimeter. There were a lot of gas masks in their deserted positions which reinforced our fear that there was a possibility of its use against us.

During the morning A Company flew in and headed south-east from the MMS to link-up with B Company, north of Objective Penzoil, and cleared an underground HQ bunker and trench system before swinging around to screen against enemy coming south out of Al-Faw town. TOW missiles fired from supporting 847 Squadron Lynx helicopters assisted A Company in its moves and fights at the bunker. D Company had come in as reserve at Objective Quaker and first linked with A Company and then swept the banks of the Shatt al-Arab and date plantations. Maj Wraith:

> A Company penetrated Al-Faw town and raided the police station and Ba'ath Party HQ with little opposition. A small crowd of civilians and oil workers approached the gates of the MMS, so we stood to, but they were friendly and smiling. I was very wary of one individual though as he wore a Manchester United football shirt. Prisoners were held within natural enclosures in the MMS but just seemed happy to be out of the fight.

A SEAL team and a detachment from B Company went across to the designated beach landing area, Red Beach near Objective Penzoil, to give a final sweep and assessment as to its suitability for an amphibious landing of the incoming Scimitars from the QDGs. Maj Wraith described the beach as 'utter dog shit, thick sticky mud, coils of barbed wire and lots of Iran War era land mines lying around'. Red Beach was closed before it ever opened and the Scimitars returned to Kuwait aboard USMC hovercraft and did the 70-mile journey via road, hooking up with the Royal Marines the following day.

Sgt 'Barney' Barnett was in D Company. A champion boxer with nearly seven years' service behind him, he had served in 40 Commando since joining in 1996 but had spent more and more time boxing for the corps and the Royal Navy. He had just got back from a boxing tour in Australia when the news of mobilisation for Iraq was circulating. He rang his sergeant major and was accepted back into D Company, having to fly out to Cyprus to meet up with the rest of 40 Commando. Despite his boxing bouts and specialist diver and reconnaissance training he was still excited before the battle:

> I was sat on the messdeck of HMS *Ark Royal*, watching Sky News as missile strikes were reported in Baghdad. The reporter also announced that marines had started the invasion. That felt odd, as we were still on ship at action stations. In fact, we were going to be the only UK marines to do a traditional heliborne assault from a ship, as the rest of the brigade flew in from Kuwait. Our company was to fly in the second wave on the Al-Faw peninsula.
>
> We were all excited and raring to go. I get goosebumps even now remembering the smell of aviation fuel wafting down the darkened corridors as we were led up to the flight deck by a young Navy guide with an illuminated wand. We went up the ramp and onto the CH-47. We knew the next time we touched down it would be inside Iraqi enemy territory near the MMS.

Maj Matt Pierson, commander of D Company, had addressed his assembled troops on the hangar deck but he avoided any Henry V style speeches and simply reiterated the plan and told the men to trust each other. They stood with blackened, camouflaged faces, weapons and kit close at hand. This was in stark contrast to the navy personnel who stood in white anti-flash hoods, respirator bags tied at the waist and fireproof gloves on. At action stations, the crew can be at this level of readiness for hours. Watertight doors are secured, movement is restricted, damage control parties and firefighting teams are on standby and the galley is closed. The crew are fed in a process called action messing. Bacon sandwiches and bottled water are passed around or a 'one pot' dinner is served on a plastic plate, to be eaten standing up at station.

After landing, D Company was told to clear the bunkers between Objective Coronado and Objective Penzoil. Maj Pierson could see through his binoculars that there was plenty of activity around the bunker and the associated field defences. Showing immense compassion for his enemy, Pierson called in a naval gunfire barrage, not right on top of the bunkers but just off target to the right, as he did not think he necessarily needed to kill them all and hoped a show of force would persuade them to surrender. Waiting in the Persian Gulf 10km away was the line of four British and Australian destroyers. The barrage soon arrived, crashing down with a mix of high explosive and air-burst shells. The earth exploded sending fountains of sand and mud skyward. Like giant hammer blows the shells reverberated through the night every seven or eight seconds, the blast waves shattering eardrums and sending fear and terror through the bunker garrison. Even Pierson was shaken by the display, as the earth settled and the smell of cordite blew across the peninsula. Emphasising his next move, Pierson ordered a mortar illumination round over the bunker, to prove the next salvo would be right on target. Slowly men emerged from the bunkers stripping off their uniforms, stumbling through rubble and shell craters in their underpants. Three hundred men surrendered.[1]

Capt 'Stu' Taylor, RM of 42 Commando remembers the helicopter insertion problems:

I have done much reflecting on Operation *Telic* and the factor I think about most is around those helicopters in the first lift. In the original plans and air brief, those three CH-46 Sea Knights were allocated to my unit, J Company. The aircraft that crashed was going to carry me, as company 2IC, and others into Iraq. A late tweak to the plans took that aircraft for the Brigade Recon Force lift. I knew many of the lads – like Phil Guy, who I trained with, and Jason Ward, who took my place on the Sea Knight – and they then died. It could have been me. Fate has a strange way of emerging.

Because of the late airframe change, my team was put on a MH-53 Sea Stallion. We had loaded, amidst yet another dust storm, around midnight 20/21 March and were rotors turning ready to go. As commander of the 'stick' (about 20 guys) in the back, I was given a set of headphones which plug into the internal communications and cockpit chit chat. I heard some frantic chatter in the earphones then the USMC crew chief just looked at me and used the universal signal for 'no go' by swiping his open palm back and forward across his neck. I couldn't understand what was going on. He leaned into my ear and shouted over the noise of the by now shutting down twin General Electric turbofan engines, 'mission aborted'.

The big rear loading ramp was lowered and, feeling very deflated and confused, we debussed. We all sort of stood clustered in a huddle, the guys asking what the hell was going on. I didn't know but the Sea Knight had crashed with all aboard killed and the US air commander had paused all flying until the dust storm abated.

As we stood in our huddle there was suddenly a loud bang. It was an ND (negligent discharge). The Commando Gunner Liaison Officer had unintentionally fired his SA80. Fortunately, no one was hurt. We got told to go back to the assembly area and that was when we were told a helicopter had piled in. We didn't know which one. We all knew people across the three helicopters and the mood was very sombre.

People started to gather in growing numbers around the radio nets and listen to the contact reports coming in from 40 Commando who were now fighting on the Al-Faw. Frustration was evident as we knew that we needed to be out there to support 40. A little later we were told who had crashed and it was an immensely sad feeing when we heard of the loss of such a great group of lads.

With the Americans refusing to fly, they blocked the landing sites for anyone else with their huge Stallions, so the CO walked around the HLS and ordered each of the American MH-53 pilots to clear the zone to allow the RAF to come in and take us to the Al-Faw. There is much banter and criticism of the RAF from the marines and the army, but that day, those Chinook and Puma crews really dug in to get the mission done. They had already run out of flying hours, had been working all night delivering 40 Commando and now they re-routed to pick us up, with no real plans or anything, and flew us to our insertion point.

Our mission was, when we finally got delivered by the RAF, 'to raid and secure' which went against our doctrine. We should either 'raid and leave' or secure!

The HLS where I inserted is at grid 29°59'59.0"N 48°24'22.0"E 5km north-west of Al-Faw town. By the time we landed, seven hours after when we should have, it was daylight, about 08:00 on 21 March.

We took up positions along the levees. The ground below the roadways was an absolute quagmire of muddy saltmarsh that we could easily get stuck in. One marine stepped off the Chinook and sank into the mud and broke his leg. Using mainly the raised tracks and roadways, we moved on foot towards our first objective which was some non-residential buildings to our east that lined the Al-Faw road. This basically hugs the Shatt al-Arab waterway which runs down from Basra. We could see activity around the buildings, and it was at this point that my CO had to make a very difficult ethical and moral decision. We had an American AC-130U Spooky gunship with a potent GAU-12 25mm cannon at our disposal, awaiting any fire missions we needed to call down.

The CO, after some soul searching, decided that he could not positively identify the people as soldiers and suggested they may well be civilians. He called off the gunship. We got the company further forward without receiving any incoming fire. Then our snipers from the Manoeuvre Support Team pushed on and identified that most people were in fact civilians, or at least were dressed as such. The CO had made the right call. Some enemy soldiers were identified then and dealt with from afar.

We took some prisoners who were quite eager to surrender. Most had discarded their army uniforms and even arrived in underpants. It was easy to spot the officers, they had clean clothes, manicured hands, groomed hair and upon closer inspection had well looked after teeth. Dentistry was clearly not available to most inhabitants. We processed around 80 prisoners over the next two days, sending them south into Al-Faw where the prisoner-handling team was. We also conducted burials for dead Iraqis, most of whom had been clearly killed in air strikes and by the Spooky gunships. We saw that several trenches with dead bodies in had white surrender flags lying in the bottom. They looked like they were planning on an early surrender but were killed before they could. The RSM and a team of marines searched the bodies for ID then buried them. Some Red Crescent teams appeared next day so we passed details of those we had buried; most were not identifiable, so they could mark the graves or reinter as they needed to.

At 23:30 on 23 March the four 42 Commando company ICs were moved by helo to Umm Qasr. We then moved further north to the old UN compound where we did a recce of the site to allocate areas that the commando would then move into when they came off the Al-Faw. The rest of my lads got taken back to TAA Viking where the commando logistics team did a magnificent job of preparing showers, giving them a good meal and having the quartermasters replenish any consumables or damaged clothes and kit. It was a great morale booster. It's always talked about that when you are in a group of smelly soldiers you don't really notice the smell, but as soon as someone is clean, you notice the smell!

Our second base was called the UN Compound simply because that had been where one of the UN weapons inspection teams had been based. The US Marines had been there for four days when we arrived, and the place was in a real shit state. The water was off and every toilet was blocked with piles of excrement. Partially eaten and spoilt food was lying in piles and discarded ration packaging littered the place crawling with maggots and flies. Hygiene was an immediate issue.

Matt Palmer was company 2IC of K Company. He was a very bright US Marine on attachment to us. He was furious with the mess left by the departing Americans and went and spoke to some of them and berated them. He told them they had embarrassed him and were a disgrace to their corps. They couldn't get out of there quick enough!

Our lads got stuck in with real Royal vigour. Within a few hours some guys had got the water going, the toilets were cleaned and rubbish burned. It was then a reasonable place to occupy.

I chose a little low office block for the company to move into. There was no electricity, of course, but later in the day I and the sergeant major saw three of the lads out the back tinkering with what looked like an electricity box. We had three marines in our company who were RM Reservists called up to fill some vacancies. One of these reserves also worked for the Electricity Board and he said he wanted to have a go at restoring power. The CSM told him that if he could get the power back on, he would get him a crate of beer at the end of the operation. Within two hours the lights were on, the microwave was heating food and batteries being charged. Commando HQ was still on generators, so we were glad for the skill of the reservists.

We made ourselves comfortable and laughed that being in Iraq was better than exercises because we didn't have to book the training area, didn't have to pick up the brass and none of the buildings were off limits to troops.

To get to and from O-groups at Brigade HQ the troop commanders had commandeered a black American-made saloon car they called the 'Sedan'. The driver had been arrested by our troops and sent to Al-Faw on suspicion of being Fedayeen. While on one of its journeys the Sedan sprang a coolant leak, overheated and had to be abandoned near our base. For a memento, a young troop commander took the number plate off. The next day the driver showed up having been released from military custody and demanded his number plate be returned. He explained that without it the local police would arrest him again. It was bizarre that such things would be discussed while only miles away bombs were dropping and combat was in full flow. He got his number plate back; we even screwed it on for him and push-started the Sedan. Without the coolant I am not sure he got very far though.

Lt Col Ben Curry, RM, SO1 Media Ops for 3 Commando Brigade, had reached Umm Qasr on 21 March:

On day 2 [22 March] we started to take some sporadic incoming rounds and an alarm rang. We all grabbed our weapons and went up to the defensive berm. I saw a whole group of US Marines firing but I had no idea at what. I couldn't see any enemy. I spoke to the US captain, and he explained that they had taken incoming rounds from a house with black curtains, pointing in the distance. I looked through my binoculars and judged the distance to the house to be at least 1,000m away. The captain agreed. I asked him what the effective range of their M16 rifle was, and he told me maybe 400m. That didn't seem to dissuade them from wasting their ammo, so I walked away and left them to it. I did then witness them call in an airstrike on the house.

A USMC AV-8B Harrier duly arrived and dropped its ordnance. As it did so, I looked through my binoculars at the house to see the impact and its effects. I had my eyes on when

I heard the impact of the 500lb bomb, but it wasn't anywhere near the house I had been looking at. It was around half a kilometre away. I really had seen enough and went back to my tent.

Our unit moved later to Basra Palace which was a huge sprawling complex. We commandeered a building and the Press moved in with us. Basra was not so welcoming as Umm Qasr and we were far more wary.

Even the Press fought amongst themselves sometimes. I remember Tom Newton-Dunn, a journalist with the *Daily Mirror*, having an argument with a squat little Sky News cameraman inside the palace. They squared up to each other – what it was about I cannot remember – but Tom was about a foot taller than the guy and was taunting him, 'Go on then, go on then, have a go!' So he did, and he punched Tom right on the chin, rocking him back on his heels. Another guy intervened and they just walked away from each other. I smiled inwardly. Tom could be a nuisance but is a nice guy.

On the morning of 30 March, the Press started buzzing about news of a firefight on the waterways north of Umm Qasr involving a Royal Marine unit.

The firefight was to lead to controversy. The unit involved was an element of 539 Assault Squadron, RM on patrol on the Khawr Az Zubayr waterway. This runs north–south from the Persian Gulf at Umm Qasr to Basra and cuts between Basra and Az Zubayr to the west. At Basra it becomes known as the Basra Canal.

The Marine Assault Squadron used a variety of craft for amphibious operations, many of which were covert such as infiltration and insertion of special forces in clandestine night-time operations. In Iraq they were being asked to perform work they were not really suited for. They were tasked to patrol in daylight on inland waterways in craft that were neither armoured nor well-armed. The waterways ran behind enemy lines and thus they could be ambushed easily from either bank of the waterway.

The squadron set up its HQ at an abandoned Iraqi naval base just north of Khor Al-Zubair port so it could patrol in the marshy delta toward Basra and stop any militia infiltrating behind British lines. Nine days of patrolling without firing a shot had started to lead to boredom when the call went up about a contact in the marshes.

The squadron in Iraq had with them two hovercraft, some fast boats and some LCVP Mk 5s (landing craft vehicle/personnel). These would normally be used to land up to 35 marines or even small vehicles onto a beach. They had a range of 320km, with a speed of 20kts with a crew of at least 3. Two LCVPs had been on patrol overnight acting on information which suggested that radio signals were emitting in the marshes, and it was likely that the signals were Iraqi military reporting on British positions or movements. Travelling some distance apart and out of sight of each other, the two craft had turned for home and were heading south on a tributary when the leader came under small-arms fire prompting the second one to try and come to its aid. As the following LCVP entered the main waterway, it too came under fire and was hit by a rocket near the wheelhouse. Marine Hiscock was blown out the wheelhouse and injured by shrapnel in the face. Marine Chris Maddison lay wounded near him in a serious condition. Two other marines were blown overboard into the marsh. Hiscock got back in the shattered wheelhouse and tried to get control of the craft. It was then hit by a second missile. He said:

> There is no way that I was going to leave two of our guys in a contact, but I had injured guys on board. The only thing I could think was that I saw one of them make it to the bank and I thought the other one must be dead.

Meanwhile the craft that had initially been attacked hid in the shadow of a sunken old tug, to take advantage of its steel hull.

At the old navy base downstream C/Sgt Howman called the two hovercraft crews to action and told the marines they were needed to rescue the LCVP crew. Embedded with these marines was a Press team who would accompany the rapid response team. Swiftly, the two hovercraft swept upstream in search of their wounded comrades and the Iraqi ambush teams.

Marine Jones had been injured in the leg in the wheelhouse blast that had catapulted him over the side. Wincing in agony he was hauled over the side and into the first hovercraft to arrive on the scene. A few minutes later the second marine was seen in the reeds near to the bank and he was also rescued. The other hovercraft reported that further upstream soldiers could be seen moving about on the wreck of an old partially submerged tug. They were now engaging the tug with GPMGs and LAW 94 rockets. The second hovercraft moved up to assist, when a British flag was seen fluttering on the tug and the shout went up to 'check fire'. It quickly dawned on the hovercraft crews that they may have been firing at friendly troops. They had, but none of the LCVP crew hiding behind the tug had been hit, fortunately. With rescue helicopters also now over the scene, the hovercraft returned to base with the wounded. Chris Maddison died later that day.

Capt Durrup organised a search party to look for the elusive Iraqi attackers at the mouth of the tributary and main waterways. No one yet had actually seen the attackers from the river and neither had the patrolling helicopters. After the search returned empty-handed Capt Durrup suggested to the commanding officer of 539, Nick Anthony, that the LCVP had been hit by friendly fire. His two key factors: there had been no sighting, nor evidence of, any enemy on the marsh and that 42 Commando had since reported engaging a slow-moving target downriver with three MILAN anti-tank missiles.

The Royal Military Police then intervened as there was a possibility of the engagement being a friendly fire incident. They confirmed the LCVP had been hit by two anti-tank rockets, either from 42 Commando or from Iraqi forces. The RMP report ruled out the 42 Commando theory because the maximum range of a MILAN missile is 2km and the LCVP, according to their calculations was, 2.8km away. In addition, a Russian-made 'Sagger' missile system had been found in an abandoned rubber boat 30km downstream.

The MOD report said that the patrol had been ambushed and that Marine Maddison had died as a result of enemy fire. Growing concern about a cover up grew when some of the embedded media team who had been on the hovercraft that day and the BBC, began their own investigation, with the backing of many of the marines involved. They confirmed it was a tragic friendly fire incident followed by a cover up.

In 2006 at Oxford Coroner's court, Marine Maddison's father said the MOD report was a farce. The court heard that 42 Commando and the MILAN team were protecting a crossing point but had no idea of any friendly waterborne patrols in their area. There was no liaison between the two units and communications between the Brigade HQ and the various units such as 539 and 42 was lacking.

The coroner, Mr Walker recording a narrative verdict, concluded Chris had been killed by a MILAN missile fired by 42 Commando. Mr Walker added that serious failures in the command chain, briefings and communications were contributory factors.

Mr Walker said: 'I've had the privilege during the last few days to hear from men whose courage and bravery when they came under fire is truly remarkable and follows that tradition within our armed forces of heroism and self-sacrifice, of which all of us are rightly proud.' Chris's mother, in a statement said:

> If a senior officer or officers had ensured that all procedures and orders necessary, and usual, had been in place before the initial task force was sent out, the resultant confusion would not have taken place. This omission resulted in catastrophe and the creation of a dangerous situation which ultimately led to the death of our beloved son.

845 Squadron flew to TAA Viking in Kuwait as planned, just 10km from the Iraq border. Rumours, orders and counter-orders came thick and fast at 845 HQ but amidst yet another dust storm it was apparent the attack would not begin that day.

In the early hours of Thursday, March 20, the mood was calm and measured at both TAA Viking and at the FARP. Codewords started to be broadcast on the net indicating events for the SEALs and 3 Commando Brigade were underway. Around 01:00 the US air component commander, callsign Woolly, took off in an AC-130U gunship which he would use as his TAC HQ.

Meanwhile, Lt Cdr John Pentreath, RN was at 40 Commando HQ in a tent at TAA Viking awaiting the next codewords:

> I was expecting to feel nervous, anxious and with some trepidation but had none. It felt just like another rehearsal; everyone was calm, just sitting under the stars. Visibility was still not great after the dust storms, vehicle movements and aircraft downdrafts but not bad enough to stop us. At last, at 01:25 final mission approval came over the net – codeword 'Carrie'.
> The commander seemed happy enough with how it was all going, although ever so slightly slower than planned – it was now around 90 minutes behind schedule. Most of the aircraft were now shuttling in supplies from HMS *Ocean* and *Ark Royal* so activity at Viking quietened down. It sounded like there had been resistance at most objectives but the SEALs and first units of 40

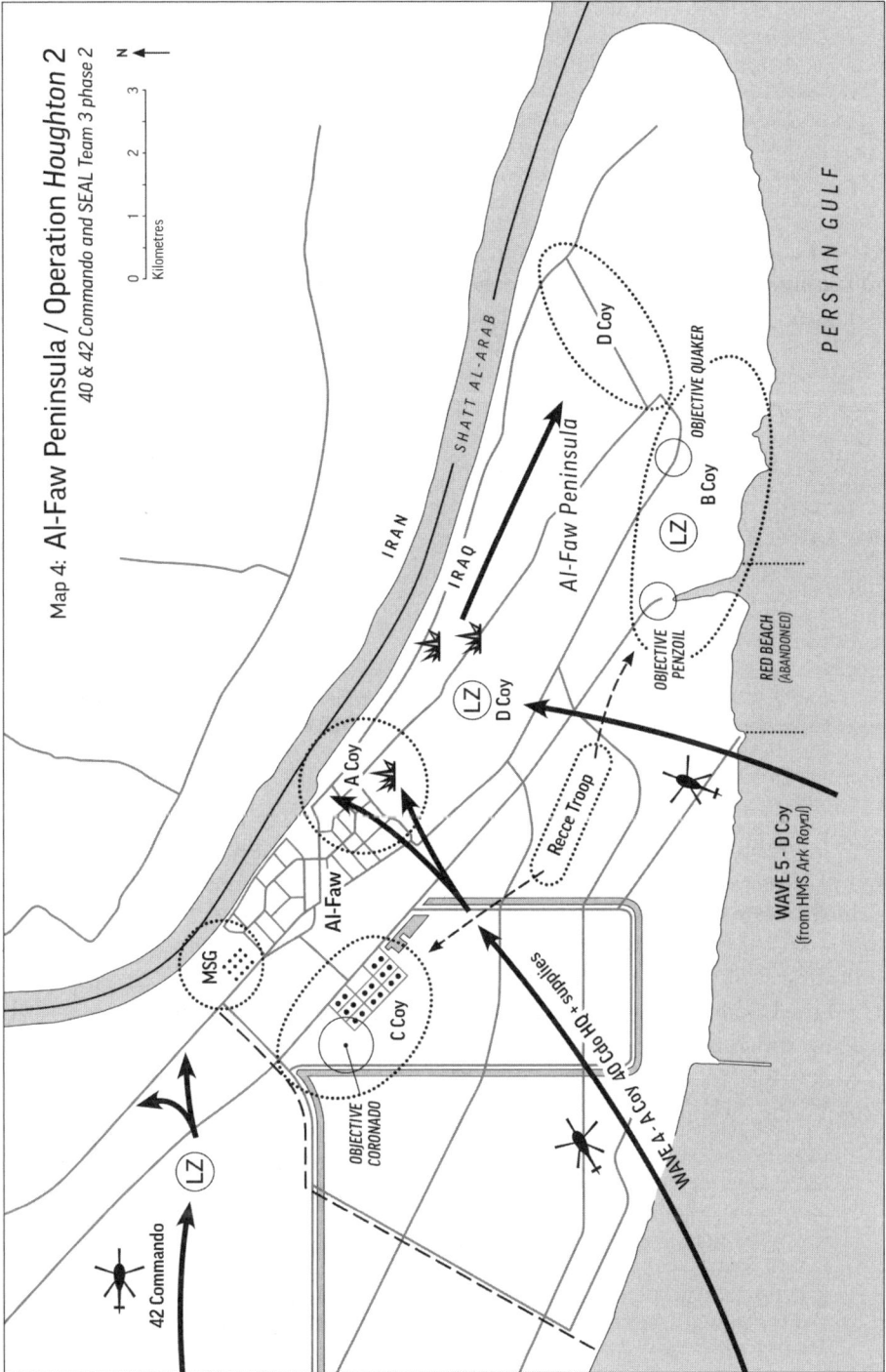

Map 4: **Al-Faw Peninsula / Operation *Houghton* 2**
40 & 42 Commando and SEAL Team 3 phase 2

were OK, thank God! About 10:00 on 20 March I hopped on Richard Harrison's Sea King and came back to *Ocean* via the MMS, where we dropped a load of Bergens. A quite surreal feeling as we coasted in over Iraqi territory and then into the MMS (Objective Coronado) where it all seemed rather quiet. After six weeks of planning and studying imagery, I felt as if I knew the site like the back of my hand. It looked a lot browner, a lot muddier and the radio mast was a lot taller, but all rather as expected.

Back on *Ocean* I was grabbed for interviews before breakfast by Andrew Hastings, Sky News and a BBC lady. Then I debriefed some of the crews and was amazed to hear how bad the first waves had found the visibility. They had performed incredibly well, and I am intensely proud of them, but probably more relieved. Many of 845 saw the explosion as the CH-46 crashed and are upset about it. A sobering reminder of how dangerous this business is.

A crash in the early hours of the next day, 22 March, of two Royal Navy Sea King Mk 7s caused the loss of seven FAA aircrew of 849 Squadron. None of these was from 845 Squadron, but the media kept posting images of a Sea King Mk 4 in winter tiger stripes as used by 845. This lazy journalism resulted in confusion and upset at home as relatives watching TV thought they may have lost loved ones. The team at Yeovilton manned help lines and started cascading phone calls of information that 845 was not involved. Angry exchanges followed between the squadrons and their commanders about planned routes in and out, use of navigation lights and NVGs – all trying to avoid another dreadful collision.

Lt Cdr Pentreath continues:

I have finally had time to reflect on the last few tumultuous days. What a rollercoaster of emotions: concern, anxiety, hope, intense pride and very deep sadness. However, pride is the overarching one. Pride in the way the entire squadron has conducted themselves, with many instances of skill, dedication and commitment. (One aircraft flew for 23 hours continuously with crews hot seating and maintainers working like a Kwik-Fit garage.) There are so many I am struggling to pick out individuals, but I need to think about honours and awards. Last night I flew one of the taskings taking supplies to the MMS and then got diverted to pick up 42 Commando TAC HQ and take them to Umm Qasr port. It seemed there was more resistance there than anticipated. On our fly in we got 'locked on' by gun radar. I had no option to break left due to the tall line of maritime cranes on the docks. It was an uncomfortable few seconds and made for a less than a perfect landing!

Our Sea Kings had been built in the 1980s and so were already quite old. It has a crew of three, it's smelly, oily with lots of leaks and vibrates a great deal. It's noisy too, so it's no wonder many Sea King pilots now have bad backs and are deaf, like me. Having said that we loved it; it was reliable and strong. The crew is two pilots and an aircrewman who is responsible for everything that goes on in the back: briefing passengers and any loading teams, manning the door gun which was the standard 7.62mm GPMG on the starboard side. In the navy the right-hand seat is generally the more junior pilot who does most of the flying. The left-side seat is generally the senior pilot who is aircraft and mission commander who navigates and operates the radios. All functions can, however, be fulfilled in either seat. Our squadron largely flew with the same crew for much of the operation, except for me as commander so I fitted in with several crews to give pilots a rest. We have a very flat cockpit, meaning rank is not so important and everyone can and should feel able to speak up and suggest things, especially over safety. Crews worked 12-hour shifts on days or nights before having the seventh day off and then switching to the opposite pattern.

Generally, we would have a flight briefing around 90 minutes before the flight. This is done in the island – in the tower above the flight deck. That would involve the mission, the intelligence briefing, a threat update and, of course, the weather situation. After the first few days the mission was very generic as it involved taskings to carry forward supplies. Most of the time we kept six aircraft available out of ten, with the others being maintained and repaired in the hangar. We flew in standard Royal Navy DPM combats. We removed all badges of rank and reference to being aircrew in case we were captured. We looked as bland as we could. Of course, we also had our tactical kit, emergency signal beacon, a day sack, personal weapons – SA80 and SIG Sauer P226 pistol – and a life preserver. We would then go out to the aircraft and flash up (start the engine). The right-hander turns on the electrics, goes through the pre-flight checks and then, within about 10 minutes, starts number one engine, which is a gas turbine. If the rotor blades are folded, which they often are on board ships, that engine powers the hydraulics to spread the blades. Once complete, a check is carried out on the hydraulic systems and the generators, next the radio and navigation systems are turned on and finally number two engine is sparked up. Without number two, the gearbox is not connected.

The levers on the roof switch from accessory to main drive and off you go flying. By then I had done about 2,000 hours on the Sea King, so was very comfortable in the cockpit. Flying from the ships to shore we had flight bands we had to adhere to. The whole airspace was divided into the flight bands. Ours, as assault helicopters, was 0–200ft. Most of the time, day and night, we flew at 75–100ft. We realised it was the optimal height to avoid SAM missiles and still allow our defensive aids time to react and deploy (chaff). As we left the ships, we generally flew at 150–200ft until we made landfall. The Tomahawk cruise missiles flew in the band above us at the 300ft mark. One night I was flying back towards HMS *Ocean* when a Tomahawk whizzed straight over me, obliquely only 100ft higher than I was. It flew at 500mph so was gone in a second. We looked at each other rather wide-eyed. It reminded us of the need to stay low.

Dr Sarah Chapman-Trim was on board HMAS *Kanimbla*:

The *Kanimbla*'s own Sea King had to put down in an emergency on the Al-Faw peninsula – a year later the same 30-year-old helicopter crashed on Banda Aceh, Indonesia while flying humanitarian missions following the Boxing Day Tsunami. The co-pilot from 2003 Iraq was the lead pilot in Indonesia when it crashed and was killed with all nine crew aboard. That felt very close to me as I had spent a lot of time with that crew and flying in that helicopter.

The fireworks display seen by many on the upper decks on 20 March turned out to be the two RN helicopters that collided, and several crews were traumatised by seeing that, especially as the day before we had the helicopters and crew aboard *Kanimbla*, and I had spoken to the pilots in the wardroom. They were based in Culdrose.

POWs were held in some temporary holding cells below decks. I went down to the secure area as part of my role to assess them. The prisoners were largely in civilian clothes looking dishevelled and unkempt. The prisoners appeared rather hateful and full of distrust, but they were well looked after.

The follow-on ground elements of 3 Commando Brigade echelon were formed up just near Umm Qasr. Spearheading the Coalition attack on the port was 15th Marine Expeditionary Unit which, for the first time in history, was under command of a British unit, 3 Commando Brigade. Stubborn resistance was encountered from dispersed Iraqi Republican Guard teams hidden in the town, but it was uncoordinated and when faced with several US M1 Abrams tanks heading the advancing armoured column, following a crushing barrage by the Royal Artillery, the fire subsided, for a while.

Marine Steve Penney of the Royal Marine Police Troop:

We moved up a few miles to secure the crossing point into Iraq. To our east we could hear the British guns firing from Bubiyan Island toward the Al-Faw peninsula. One other task we had to do was set up a short diversion and guide traffic off and around a stretch of tarmac (Route 801) which was being used as a helicopter landing site. They didn't want a heavy truck crashing into a parked CH-46 helicopter, so the diversion was important. To guide the convoys, I was on a Harley Davidson 350cc motorcycle driving over soft sand, in the dark without night vision, which was interesting!

I was on the northernmost point of the diversion bringing vehicles back onto the tarmac and had seen numerous helicopters flying over towards Iraq when there was a large flash and a fireball to the north. I thought something big had been hit by our artillery but found out a few hours later that, in fact, it was an American Sea Knight CH-46 helicopter carrying our marines that had crashed, killing everyone aboard.

As well as the convoy diversion we had to secure the breach on Route 801 that leads from Kuwait to Umm Qasr in Iraq. At the berm line our job was to control the breach so that only the right traffic crossed in the correct direction. We stopped and diverted any civilian cars and controlled speed and spacings for troops heading into Iraq. After dawn on 21 March we moved up into Iraq and passed the crash site of the CH-46 next to the road. There was a patch of scorched ground and twisted metal, and it was most difficult to tell that it was in fact a helicopter. I can see why no one would have survived the crash.

The US Marines ahead of us were taking a while to clear Umm Qasr and we could see them banging away with tanks and attack helicopters at some of the buildings in the village, but for a while, having completed our role on the border, we were without a task. That is when we were approached by some guys who I believe were Intelligence Corps or SF but wore no rank or cap badges. One of the Int guys recognised our sergeant from a course they had done in the UK years back. They asked us for help on their assignment. We agreed and spent the next three days escorting them on intelligence-gathering missions around Umm Qasr.

First, we went to the heavily damaged Ba'ath Party buildings and gathered paperwork from offices and filing cabinets; then we went to a private house and put a cordon on the building while the Int guys went in and interviewed a man inside. I suppose as a police troop without heavy weapons, we were able to get about quietly and unobtrusively without attracting too much attention – which is what the Int team wanted. I remember there being very few people showing themselves on the streets and it was all a bit eerie.

We took some incoming rounds on one of the tasks. We were in our vehicles on the move when the driver saw some muzzle flashes ahead and we heard the crack of the rounds passing the Land Rover. We dismounted and assaulted toward the last-known positions, but they had gone.

We had a loudspeaker on the Land Rover so got involved in the Psy Ops as well. The Arabic speaker would use the speaker to call troops to surrender and report to the army. But to be honest no one did, they had either already discarded their uniforms and melted away or had been wasted by the Yanks. However, on the last day at Umm Qasr we moved down toward the port area which was a bit separate from the village. I was on the Harley when I saw some enemy soldiers about 500 metres away. It was obvious the port had not been fully cleared. It was at that time the coolness of riding a Harley about Iraq evaporated rather quickly. I turned around and went back to the base and never rode the bike again!

The clearing of the port area took longer than planned, with Iraqi Fedayeen Militia and Republican Guard soldiers using guerrilla tactics to set up ambushes and snipe at the marines, both US and British. RAF Harriers and USMC Cobra gunships added their firepower to the hunt for the elusive enemy, destroying several warehouses and port buildings as they did so. US Navy SEALs also discovered around 50 Republican Guards setting up positions on old, abandoned ships in Basra port. It was suggested that they were going to mount ambushes from the old ships but were forced to surrender, as did around 400 other Iraqi soldiers in the port. Over the next few days joint US / UK naval mine-hunting teams descended on the Basra Canal entrance and the port to clear it of the mine threat. Navy clearance divers, mine counter-measure helicopters and the Royal Navy minesweepers HMS *Bangor* and *Sandown* served a crucial role in opening the port for supplies and humanitarian aid, the first of which was unloaded only three days later from RFA *Sir Galahad.*

With the port secure and swept clear of enemy threats the Royal Marine Police Troop were allocated other duties. Marine Steve Penney continues:

> We were tasked by our officer to go and pick up some prisoners from a site near Basra. There are salt marshes to the south of Basra and little raised roads like dykes cut through the marshes. He told us the route to use and the four of us went in two Land Rovers. It was dark and we travelled on convoy lights (very dim) along the roads. I was driving the second vehicle moving quite slowly when suddenly the lead Rover stopped abruptly. We switched on our sidelights for a bit more light and all around us we could see land mines sitting on the surface of the road and the marshy grass alongside us. We were in a minefield. My thoughts were, 'Oh Fuck, how did we get here without getting blown up?' My mind raced and we shouted across to each other about what we should do, and I also called him a wanker then we all started laughing. We then extricated by means of the co-driver climbing into the back, looking over the tail gate, and giving directions to the drivers to reverse out of the minefield very carefully. Fortunately, the mines were easily visible sitting on the surface, so we dodged them OK. When we got back, we went into the Ops room and tore into them about the minefield and asked why we were sent along a route with a known mine threat. Some silly bastards had nearly got us all killed.
>
> We had a couple of days of downtime then, knocking around in shorts back at the port. I watched the US guys at the dock with their dolphins they were using for mine hunting and then in the evening we watched the news on a big TV someone hooked up. We found that Al Jazeera gave us the news while the BBC was more like a propaganda channel that we all laughed at.

With the initial invasion phase successfully completed 3 Commando Brigade turned its attention toward Basra. On 24 March, Operation *Leah* began with the brigade moving north towards the city. The bulk of the peninsula is either flooded marshes or thick mud, so movement was restricted to the existing road system. Just a few roads ran away from the town of Al-Faw. The main road ran 80km north, parallel to the Shatt al-Arab waterway and the Iranian Border, up to Basra. The secondary road cut west, 50km to the port of Umm Qasr, close to the Kuwait border. 40 Commando moved north using all available transport, dismounting whenever enemy fire was encountered. Concerted, coordinated defence was non-existent and progress was steady.

Maj Wraith describes the advance:

> We could see and taste a huge oil fire. Clouds of thick black smoke obscured the sky and reminded us of the first Gulf war in 1991. We passed Khorramshahr, passed the oil refineries and stopped just south of Abu al-Khasib, which is a suburb of southern Basra. On 27 March

we heard that an enemy armoured column of 60 tanks was heading south through Basra in our direction. A hasty call went up on the net asking for the ammunition status of the MILAN Troop. 58 came the reply! In the event Challengers of the Scots DG and some air support destroyed much of the Iraqi armour and the remainder melted away.

The story is continued in Chapter 9.

CHAPTER 5

The Tip of the Spear

21 March A bit of a Shit Day! crossed the border [near Safwan] around 04:00 at Triangle Two, following Y Company but had to protect the west flank but not exploit. Surprised by how many road signs are in English and how many shot-up tanks lying about. Took on fuel and moved up toward Basra.

22 March The most amazing day! 2km from the bridge (Objective Golf) it became my day! We had to secure the home bank. There were lots of abandoned but not destroyed enemy field positions and dug-in tanks. The SAS were on the ground and were giving us intelligence. The Yanks had not secured the home bank like we were told they would have but were now watching us as we went in to do it. It looked like a Vietnam film. The sun was setting, and thick smoke was billowing across the city. Huey Cobra gunships were giving it masses and destroyed targets on the bridge. I was quietly shitting myself now.

Lt Chris Rees-Gay, 1 RRF

The combat engineer tractor (CET*), commanded by Cpl Wolf of 39 Armoured Engineer Regiment, RE, rammed the sand and gravel berm with its bulldozer blade for the final time, clearing away the last of the obstruction and opening Triangle Two, the breach into Iraq. This was his first view of Iraq from inside the armoured vehicle and it was a bit of an anti-climax. It was just after 04:00, 21 March 2003, and the Royal Fusiliers Battlegroup (1 RRF BG) was leading the way for 7 Armoured Brigade, which included the Royal Engineers in their CETs and bridgelaying vehicles:

7 Armoured Brigade Order of Battle (led by Brig Graham Binns)
3 Royal Horse Artillery
Royal Scots Dragoon Guards BG
2 Royal Tank Regiment BG (incl elements of 1 Battalion, The Light Infantry)
The Black Watch BG (incl elements of The Royal Scots Dragoon Guards and 2 RTR)

---

* The FV180 Combat Engineer Tractor was a 17-ton armoured engineer vehicle used by the British Army between 1976 and 2013. Its two-crew sat in tandem with dual driving controls facing opposite directions. An 8-ton lifting and moving bucket was mounted on the rear and powerful 8-ton winch on the front. It has since been replaced by the new Terrier armoured vehicle.

1 Battalion Royal Regiment of Fusiliers BG (incl elements of Queen's Royal Lancers)
1 Battalion, Irish Guards
32 (Armoured) Regiment, RE
25 Armoured Engineer Squadron (attached from 38 Engineer Regiment)

The brigade was tasked with advancing to Basra and was doing so a day earlier than anticipated because intelligence identified that Republican Guard reinforcements were moving south to join the Iraqi 51st Division opposite the brigade. Providing close support was the 1 RRF MILAN Platoon and some attached Irish Guards with their MILAN. The berms were so high that vehicles could not scale them, so snipers and night vision-equipped MILAN teams had climbed them at intervals along a 3km stretch of the border to provide both observation and direct fire. They dug their posts into the crest of the berm and scanned their arcs as the Sappers, under command of 2Lt Claire Blewden, finished their job of clearing the breach. Guardsman Mat Matthews, 1 IG remembers:

> I scrambled up the berm, stopping short of the top, scooped out the parapet and pushed the MILAN firing post tripod into place, and slipped backward at the same time. My first thoughts as I rolled down were that the post and I were going to get the full *Saving Private Ryan* treatment – rounds from every direction at me, but everything was quiet.[1]

After the 1991 Gulf War the Kuwaitis built an extensive obstacle belt, 250km in length, along the entire border with Iraq, to deter any future attempts at invasion. Ironically, it was this same zone that was now to cause difficulties when planning for the 2003 invasion. The border zone, all of which was inside the actual border line of Kuwait, consisted of three layers and was around 5km deep.

Approaching the border from Kuwait, you first came across a berm of sand and gravel, 5m high and 10m wide at its base. Just behind that was an anti-tank ditch, 6–8m deep and 8m wide, with vertical sides. 2km further into the zone was a huge stack of concertina rolled barbed wire that was electrified, and on each side of the stack was a chain link fence 2m high partially there to stop animals walking into the electric wire. The zone was completed by another duplicate berm and ditch another kilometre closer to Iraq. This whole zone was demilitarized by the UN and prior to the war being declared you needed diplomatic clearance to enter it. This had made close reconnaissance an issue.

Maj Duncan McSporran, 1 RRF crossed the border east of Safwan. Most of his background had been as a light infantryman and he was fairly new to the armoured role when he took over Z Company in 1 RRF:

> The collective firepower available is impressive. Each company had 15 Warriors, with four at each of the three platoons and three at HQ. I had the 511 command variant Warrior, which doesn't have seating for eight soldiers in the rear; instead, it has two small 'bird' tables

for maps and extra radios. Keith Armstrong was the senior gunnery warrant officer in the company, so he was my gunner. The driver was a fusilier, then I had a corporal signaller and a watchkeeper captain. The primary role of the signaller was to keep the sergeant major and me fed with brews which he made with the BV. Outwardly, the 511 is almost identical to the main fighting version but it does have two extra radio antennas and the rear doors are not the powered-ramp type.

I did like the Warrior, but it was let down in two key areas. Firstly, the gun was not stabilised so you couldn't fire accurately on the move which by the early 2000s was an expected standard.

Secondly, the night-vision systems were rubbish. There was an image intensifier but no thermal system, so that was a let-down. If you looked after her with daily checks and maintenance schedules though, she was a very dependable, rugged and tough vehicle.

We crossed 5–6km from the main highways and I will always remember being totally impressed with the work of the Royal Engineers at getting us across the ditches and berms on the border – the ditch was 5–6m deep and vertically sided. The engineers' fleet was so old it was constantly breaking down and they would have to do on-the-spot repairs. Their work was outstanding. I went through at crossing 1A (tracks) and alongside it was 1B (wheels).

After securing the border crossings, it was planned – and we fully expected to – follow the Black Watch on the advance to contact up towards Basra. Z and Y Companies, 1 RRF, secured the breaches and the Black Watch passed through us but then seemed to stall and we were ordered to leave the breach and make the advance as the lead battlegroup. This was a significant change in the plan and one that we can be proud to say we achieved seamlessly. One area that we certainly benefitted from was that we had in the battalion a lot of senior soldiers who had fought in the 1991 war and whose experience was gold dust.

Some say that the Black Watch had failed to maintain their fleet of vehicles in the desert, and they suffered numerous mechanical breakdowns. Others may suggest less flattering reasons for them stopping. Either way the Fusiliers were seemingly the go-to battlegroup who then took over the advance. 1 RRF only had one Warrior fail all the way up to Bridge 4 and that was a track falling off which was fixed in under two hours.

The movement to the border crossing point near Safwan had been planned and rehearsed in the previous two weeks. It was supposed to be an unopposed crossing 24 hours after the US forces had entered Iraq to the west but when it was executed the crossing was made only three hours after the Americans, with a boundary plan change and became opposed too. The forward assembly area just shy of the border, codenamed FAA Barnsley, had been marked and prepared by elements of the Queen's Dragoon Guards and RRF. It was where 1 RRF BG hastily listened to updated orders which now outlined the upcoming opposed obstacle crossing – possibly the most complicated and least relished of all types of operation.

With news suggesting a brigade of Iraqi Republican Guard tanks were heading south, the Fusiliers and attached units listened to their final briefings tensely but with confidence before they left FAA Barnsley. They began clearing two openings in the berms as the friendly artillery fired a two-and-a-half-hour fire plan. Lt Olly Campbell, 1 RRF, recalls:

> The weight of friendly firepower tore through the air, shaking the ground as it exploded. The engineers worked quickly clearing and bridging each element of the obstacle and we moved with them, dismounted, acting as close protection for the ageing heavy vehicles. Then at the last

berm we scrambled up to the top, heaving for breath in the heat and under the sheer weight of our ammunition. There was our first glimpse of Iraq. But there were no Medina Division tanks or screaming hordes of Fedayeen Militia, there was just a landscape that looked as quiet as the Kuwait side of the berm.[2]

The quiet and anticlimax did not last long. The British artillery was already firing overhead and was soon joined by the RRF's 81mm mortars. Incoming small arms contacts were reported, as was movement at a bunker complex on the limit of the Fusiliers' visibility. Fusilier Terry Ward called in a mortar fire mission on an Iraqi patrol in the distance and L/Cpl Cardwell fired the first MILAN missile at the bunker. It was a rogue missile, veering off into the night sky and probably landed somewhere in Turkey. Swiftly reloading, he fired a second missile, scoring a direct hit. No more movement was seen at the bunker.

The 1 RRF BG rolled forward and through the breaches. With Warrior callsigns 12 and 13 crossing on the left – green crossing – callsigns 10 and 11 under Lt Olly Campbell crossed to their right at red crossing and fanned out scanning the night. With nothing further reported, the attached troop of Challenger 2 tanks from B Squadron, Queen's Royal Lancers (QRL) then thundered past, their combined weight of close to 140 tons of armour obscuring everything in a cloud of dust as they stormed into Iraq.

Lt The Hon Thomas Orde-Powlett, 1 IG, remembers crossing into Iraq:

> G-day came and we crossed the breach fully bombed up. We brought up the rear of the brigade convoy, behind some RAMC vehicles, which did raise a concern! We passed through 7 RCT at night with alarmingly little liaison. We even had to shunt several static USMC vehicles to the side of the road to get forward.
>
> That night we went firm and experienced our first and only shout of 'Gas, Gas Gas'. We spent the night fully kitted up but it was the last time we had to.
>
> The terrain reminded many of us of a Vietnam War film with raised roads and vegetation along the ditches and streams – it was unlike the desert we were expecting. Movement across the low-lying ground, off-road, was not advisable and often ended with bogged-down vehicles.
>
> Towards last light on G+1, the RSDG Recce Troop was pushing ahead in front of our Warriors on the north-east side of Basra, when a contact report broke the radio silence. The column was being engaged by two bunker positions to the east. I was ordered to give them some 'Mick [Irish] Action'. Due to the boggy ground, I ordered a dismounted attack, with support from the vehicle-mounted weapons. We destroyed both bunkers, engaging them with our full array of firepower, from 51mm mortar to LAWs and small arms as well as the Warriors' 30mm main guns and coaxial 7.62mm chain guns. With the position cleared, we leaguered up close by and spent the night engaging the enemy, who foolishly were trying to stalk our position with RPGs, seemingly oblivious to our night vision capabilities.[3]

Cpl Paul Burton, REME was attached to the Black Watch BG:

> Early morning on 19 March we were set at 10 mins notice to move. This meant that we were manned up on the vehicles with engines running. This period lasted for about two to three hours. During the wait, one of the young subalterns from the Black Watch played the bagpipes whilst marching up and down the columns. This event was extremely moving. It made me

proud as an Englishman about to go into battle with a famous Scottish Regiment. Something I will NEVER forget. Whenever I hear the bagpipes now, I am taken right back to 'Barnsley' on 19 March 2003.

Our BG crossed into Iraq about 9km east of Safwan. The berms and a trench had been dealt with by 32 Armoured Engineer Regt. We thought we would be first to cross, only to find a smug bunch of engineers sitting with their feet up waving at us.

Sitting on top of the FV432 as we headed north into Iraq, I soon saw the first examples of the Iraqi Army. A group of Americans were guarding them in a makeshift barbed-wire pen. The Iraqis looked dirty, dishevelled and a bit frightened.

Sometime later we reached the outskirts of Az Zubayr. We were to conduct a relief in place of an American unit. There was a low-walled compound and some low buildings lined it around the outside. I realised later that it was a small military camp. There was a line of American armour outside the gate and we stopped nearby to do the handover. As the Yanks started climbing into their vehicles to leave there was an explosion and a shower of white phosphorus and smoke started filling the street. All the Brits shouted, 'Stand to,' and brought our weapons up looking for the enemy. The Yanks seemed to panic a bit. Then people started shouting, 'It's OK, it's OK stand down!' Apparently one of the Americans, when climbing into his vehicle, triggered an automatic discharger to go off and so it was a negligent discharge. This first encounter with the Americans was not a good one.

Maj John Cotterill was attached to 1 IG:

Having moved up to FAA Barnsley, closer to the border, on 20 March I was manning the net when the 1 RRF entered Iraq. They quickly called up reporting being shot at by American M1 tanks from the west. The 1 RRF 2IC called up explaining that he would take his Warrior and go and speak with the Americans. He headed off and then got shot at as well. Fortunately, the US tanks had missed, and someone got a message through to the Americans and the M1s stopped engaging.

Such 'blue on blue' events – the term used to describe friendly fire incidents where someone fires on members of his own side – are all too common in the heat of battle, despite the efforts of planners to avoid the likelihood. The Americans carry out what they call 'rock drills', which are similar to the British sand table exercises. Rock drills for the invasion were carried out on a piece of ground the size of a tennis court with geographical features all marked out and rocks representing Coalition units were then moved about according to the plans. Hypothetical contingencies were also examined and talked through on the rock drills. Hundreds of people would be at the drills – from artillery and infantry officers, through to aviation, signallers and logisticians. They were all-day affairs. The worst-case scenario was focussed on Saddam using chemical warfare and the medics being overwhelmed with untold casualties. Maj Cotterill continues.

Once we started moving into Iraq following the leading battlegroups, I was in a FV432 command vehicle. Instead of the normal crew of two and eight-man section in the rear, this one had extra radios, map boards and desks areas for two or three men. Before I closed the rear doors, the noise of our outgoing 155mm artillery was impressive. However, once closed down with radio earphones on and engine running, I couldn't hear the artillery again until I got out hours later, 35km north at Shaiba Air Base (north of Az Zubayr).

On arrival in Kuwait the army had equipped each battlegroup with an interpreter. By the end of March 2003, it was realised that what was needed was closer to one interpreter per company or squadron. An army cannot engage with a foreign-speaking population of a city the size of Birmingham with only four interpreters (four British battlegroups were encircling the city). The battlegroups were each around 1,000 strong. The city had a population in 2003 of 1.1 million. Maj John Cotterill had been spending some of his time teaching brigade staff some basic Arabic language and cultural skills. When the need came for more interpreters, he was asked if he would go forward as an interpreter with the Irish Guards. He jumped at the chance. His story continues on page 157 (Chapter 8).

Lt Ian Cross of Falcon Squadron, 2 RTR also assembled at 'Barnsley'. Once the breach was open and 7 Brigade moved north past Safwan, 2 RTR BG moved in bounds, generally as quickly as it could. The smaller packets of balanced firepower would usually include a troop of three tanks leading and a platoon of four Warriors trying to keep up. They would only break out into a tactical formation if they came under fire and needed to engage the threat. He remembers:

> For the invasion we were part of the 2 RTR BG. It was called a square formation in that it had an equal number of tank units as it did armoured infantry units. This meant a good balance of firepower, mobility, armour and dismounts. 2 RTR was grouped with the 1 LI (Light Infantry). They were exceptional and a pleasure to work with. We had done some training with them in Paderborn, Germany so had started to get to know each other. Rather incredibly, my tank troop was paired up with an infantry platoon, whose commander was a subaltern in my Officer Training Platoon at Sandhurst and who had a room opposite mine. Lt Jamie Bourbon was a lovely guy and very good officer, so that made things very much easier. I worked with him all the way through from Kuwait up to our big battle at Az Zubayr where his platoon assaulted the buildings, and we provided covering fire all the way.
>
> We arrived at FAA Barnsley – now I don't think I have ever been to Barnsley in England, but this place stank of fish. Then it was a classic case of hurry up and wait. My main achievement of the day was finishing reading my latest book and adding a few points to my rather ill-prepared small map. My poor troop corporal's engine blew up and he was towed into 'Barnsley', which was a nuisance for him as he thought he would miss the invasion.
>
> Our start time was brought forward, and I was dozing by the tank when 'Strawberry' – my Warrior driver – came and woke me up. As we crossed the border the mood in the turret changed but the jokes and joviality continued interrupted by the occasional retching sick sounds from Wienand. We were pretty jittery when we first moved up as we kept seeing lots of enemy tanks and APCs but on closer inspection they were found to have been destroyed by air power. That's when we made use of the thermal sights. As soon as you scanned a tank, if it was cold, you knew it was abandoned or knocked out. A lot of them were dug in like a pillbox.

Following on the great column of armoured vehicles were dozens of wheeled vehicles carrying all the combat support and combat service support units such as Royal Signal units, REME repair teams, medical platoons and EOD groups. WO2 Andy Abbott, RE was part of this column:

I led our convoy of 30 vehicles through the main crossing point on the road to Safwan. We went through the breach a few hours after the lead column, in the early morning. The convoy consisted of 4-tonners, Land Rovers and plant – JCB desert-painted diggers. We had to paint black Vs on them all. The RMP waved us through and off we went – I didn't know where we were heading at that point. We were attached to 28 Engr Regt as part of 1 UKDIV. Mark Austin, an ITN TV reporter, came in with us to cross the border. He wanted to stay with us but the CO said no.

We headed towards the small Iraqi town of Safwan. It was like a proper desert with no trees, bare-arsed and only a tired-looking ramshackle brick-built border post! It makes me smile now, as after the war my wife asked to see my passport to look at the passport stamp for Iraq!

Just after we crossed the border, we were still leading the slow-moving convoy. I was front passenger when we heard a definite crack of a bullet close by. I was like, 'Oh Fuck what do we do!' I had my SA80 on my lap with only 10 rounds in it and it was my first contact. 'Great,' I thought! I wasn't even sure where the round had come from, but I stuck the muzzle out the window and fired off a couple of shots, and at least let them know we would fire back. Other guys in the wagon behind fired as well. I called in on the radio, 'Contact. Wait, out.' The OC came back on the net and said to keep moving. Ambushes of convoys are more likely to succeed if they can get the vehicles to stop. So, we pushed on and within about five minutes there were two of our helicopters overhead obviously on the lookout on our behalf.

We stopped at last light to set up camp by Az Zubayr but already had been given some local tasks. Our RSM had been our PSI [permanent staff instructor] before the war – Nick Pettit. Nick had got the QGM in Bosnia but was lumbered with the RAF EOD which he didn't like. However, just as the main invasion started, he and his driver (a female TA corporal) went off and tagged onto a leading convoy just to be there, and he got a tasking straight away. Some unit got lost and went into a minefield – he got them out and got the GM (George Medal).

One of our teams (two vehicles and four men) were sent off to do a recce on a task in Az Zubayr in soft skin vehicles, two Land Rovers. I think it was a Police station they were originally sent to visit, but they got hit and ambushed on the way in there.

In the front Land Rover was the bomb disposal operative (BDO), S/Sgt Simon Cullingworth, and his number two, Luke Allsop. Then in the second Rover was the BDO's number three and four. Number four was normally the radio operator. WO2 Abbott continues:

I think they took a wrong turn or something like that and ended up outside the route allocated. You couldn't tell who the enemy was then as virtually all those who had been in green army kit now wore civilian clothes but still carried weapons. Both vehicles got hit by machine-gun fire and RPGs. The lead Land Rover with Si and Luke got disabled and the second Land Rover tried to reverse back but it became clear it was out of action. The two guys at the back bailed out, jumped over a brick wall, and looked for Si and Luke but they couldn't see them. The two lads then commandeered a nearby car and got away. Si and Luke were not seen alive again. What we know now is that the enemy filmed the ambush on a mobile phone, and the footage was passed to the TV station Al Jazeera who posted it online. It showed Si and Luke being dragged out the Land Rover. It is then suspected that they were murdered by the Fedayeen.

Some RMPs asked me to identify some equipment that they had found on a search of the town. The equipment was military, but they weren't sure what it was. I identified it as part of the system we use to disrupt IEDs, and they were then certain it had been taken from the BDO's Land Rover and probably was kit stolen after the ambush. Simon and Luke's bodies were discovered about a month later wrapped in carpet and buried in shallow graves just outside Az Zubayr.

After this incident me and my number two, John, had a chat about what had happened. John was the most miserable git but a very professional soldier. We agreed that we must not get caught up like Si and Luke, and we mustn't get captured and dragged off. So, we agreed to blow ourselves up! We set up some PE4 (plastic explosive) behind the seats in the Land Rover, with detonators connected to a press switch. I know now it sounds silly, but when things were so bad and we had been given so little ammunition, I mean I crossed the border into Iraq with 10 rounds of 5.56mm ammo, we couldn't even fill a mag! What the fuck was going on? It reminded me of Isandlwana in the Zulu wars! It was a shambles, it had all been so rushed. Fortunately, within a day of crossing into Iraq we picked up AK-47s and loads of ammo. We wrapped our SA80s in plastic and stored them behind us and used the AKs as our go-to personal weapons. We fired off plenty of rounds and even some RPGs, so we got used to the weapons and how they worked.

Dogs were a real problem. Packs of wild dogs would loiter around us on a task and then they would get closer and closer until they were right in your face, and we would have to fire off rounds to persuade them to clear off.

We ran out of explosives after the first 24 hours. We were using so much to blow everything up, it was unheard of the amount we were using. So, me and John were tasked to return to Kuwait in our Land Rover and trailer and fill up both with explosives for the unit. We did that and filled up but by the time were on our way back into Iraq it was dark. Everywhere we went we heard distant explosions and constant Scud or gas alarms were being called. We got to a checkpoint and were stopped by a redcap as a Scud alert was going off.

The RMP shouted 'Scud alert, get out and take cover underneath the Rover.' John and I laughed and replied that it would be pretty silly hiding underneath this Land Rover and told the RMP to look in the back. He quickly glanced in and said, 'Fuck me, get away. On yer go quick!' and waved us away. The guy had realised that if we were hit, it would be a bigger explosion than the Scud!

The explosive we used to destroy things was PE4 plastic explosive that comes in sticks about seven inches long that weigh half a pound (250gm) and is an off-white-coloured, hand-mouldable, putty-like substance. We used half or one stick to destroy a mortar bomb. In training or at home we might need occasionally to destroy one mortar or a WW2 bomb but out in Iraq we had thousands of things to get rid of, it was unreal. Saddam had the fifth biggest arsenal in the world. There was so much stuff we physically couldn't blow it all up. We had to prioritise and get rid of the most dangerous, unstable things or stuff that was in a dangerous place. At first, I did worry that this stuff might be booby-trapped but we never came across anything that was. I think they were all in too much of a hurry to bugger off. The IED threat came so much later and was a challenge for the troops later.

One of my first taskings was on the Al-Faw peninsula. There were lots of these GOSPs that were important to keep intact. The marines had captured them and seen that there were some Iraqi artillery positions overlooking the sites. They tasked us to go over and destroy the artillery so it couldn't pose a threat later if any Iraqi gunners came back. There were eight or nine of these guns, I think they were either 122mm or 155mm artillery pieces. What we did was standard for this sort of task. We utilised their own discarded ammunition.

I took the fuse off the nose of one of their 122/155mm shells and inserted a stick of our own PE4. Then connected a detonator with some det cord to the PE4. This was then put inside the end of the gun barrel, or directly in the breach. This was then connected to a 'shrike' that we buried nearby and put sandbags over to protect it. We retired back to a 'safe' place, usually no more than 100m. (Had we been in the UK, it was meant to be 1km!) We then had our hand-held initiator which connected remotely to the shrike, which in turn set off the PE4. That was the nine guns gone.

Around 22:00 on 21 March, the RAF-led Joint Helicopter Command convoy set out towards the airfield at Safwan just inside the Iraqi border. Safwan hill overlooking the airfield had taken a pummelling by Coalition artillery and attack helicopters for some hours but was now in British hands. Engineers had cleared the Iraqi airfield and declared it safe for the helicopter force to move in. Prior to the helicopters landing, the ground convoy would move in and set up the facilities needed to service, refuel and rearm the aircraft.

One of the leading Land Rovers in the convoy was crewed by four men of the RAF Regiment. It is not known exactly why or how but their Land Rover drove off the tarmac route and into the scrubby sand at the side of the road and hit a mine. The resultant explosion blew the vehicle forward some yards, destroyed the front left-side of the vehicle collapsing the Rover onto its chassis and leaving it canted over at 45 degrees. Inside the cab the passenger was wounded and unconscious. The three other RAF men were in shock.

Adding to the unfolding drama was a firefight between some nearby dismounted RAF Regiment gunners and the Iraqi Army who were only a few hundred yards away. The call was put up about the mine strike and the RAF EOD HQ called RSM Pettit to attend. He was by this hour near Safwan being driven by a Scottish Territorial Army corporal named Nina. Nina was the only female in 33 Regiment and had been volunteered to drive for the RSM. Pettit and Nina in their Land Rover led the RAF contingent in their Spartan armoured vehicle towards the scene, without a full understanding of what they might encounter. Even before they got on site, they had to dodge getting involved in a firefight on the edge of Safwan. With Pettit map-reading and shouting directions, Nina threw the Land Rover around corners avoiding passing tracer fire and soon got to the stranded convoy. The stricken vehicle sat 50m from the road, in total darkness. The question that struck the RSM was why on earth the four men were still sitting in the vehicle, in the minefield? The troops had all been taught self-extraction and there were even some RAF engineers in the convoy who should have been helping. It seemed that the whole unit had been stunned into inactivity. CSM Nick Pettit, RE takes up the story:

> We set up an incident control point (ICP), then positioned two of our Land Rovers at ninety degrees with their headlights facing the mine-damaged vehicle. Nina went off to arrange for the medical team to come forward to the ICP and I got on the radio to tell HQ that we would be going in and that the route would be open again in 15 minutes for 7 Armoured Brigade.
>
> I spoke to the RAF EOD Sergeant and said, 'You OK, Mick, ready to go?' He was my junior and should do the extraction. He looked straight at me and said, 'No, not really.'
>
> 'Okay, fine,' I said, 'I'll go.' I knew he wasn't up for it but I couldn't have lived with myself if he had gone in and got blown up, it would be on my mind for the rest of my life.
>
> I was scared. I said to Nina, 'Get that medic team here for the injured lad and for me if I injure myself. Get everyone behind cover in case I hit a mine. I don't want anyone to catch me in the face as I'm coming back out at 100mph.[4]

The stricken vehicle had passed over two lines of Italian-made anti-tank mines without hitting any but drove over one in the third line. The VS-1.6 Mine is a plastic circular anti-tank blast mine. It has very few metal components, making it hard to find. Its explosive contents are small in contrast to many anti-tank mines, and it is for this reason that the RAF Land Rover was still largely intact.

Pettit readied himself to approach the Land Rover and equipped himself with a metal prodder, for probing the sand, a Maglite torch which he had purchased himself just like his Gerber Knife and Leatherman – all good kit that the army did not provide. He also took a roll of white mine tape to mark a safe lane. There was no robotic Wheelbarrow nor armoured bomb suit. Today, it was going to be the RSM on his belt buckle crawling in the sand. With the nearby firefight continuing, he lowered himself down to the sand.

> I could see some of the mines had time pencils and trip wires attached making them very unstable. It was look, feel, prod, repeat. Using the torch, I thought 'I'm going to attract incoming fire here or set off a mine,' But soon I was close to the Rover and could talk to the lads on board. Trying to lighten the situation I shouted, 'I'm 40 years old and an RSM, and you've got me crawling through sand in a minefield to rescue you.' A voice from the back responded 'You think you've got problems! I'm a 44-year-old corporal sitting in a Land Rover that's hit a mine!' The conversation continued and I think took all our minds off the severity of the situation. Your emotions are going 10 to the dozen, your family flash in front of you and you pray. But your training really kicks in so you can concentrate on the job in hand.[5]

Pettit had laid the white tape as he went, thus marking a 'safe' lane for his return journey. Finding that one of the men was unconscious, he hefted him up into a fireman's carry, told the others he would be back for them and then carried out the injured soldier. Once he laid the man down with Nina and the medical team, he returned a further three times into the minefield, each time leading out one of the other RAF men. He instructed each of them to put their hands on his shoulders and to shuffle along in his footsteps in order to not stray off his clear path.

The next day, in daylight, Pettit and his team cleared 26 mines from the location and destroyed them all in place with plastic explosives. It had been an immensely intense experience and was the most memorable day in his war. RSM Pettit was awarded the George Medal for his actions near Safwan and was presented his medal in 2004 by HM The Queen at Buckingham Palace.

The citation, written by an RAF wing commander who witnessed the event reads:

> … the risk to his life was significant and that his bravery and calming influence under real stress was of the highest order. At no stage could RSM Pettit have been sure his actions would not lead to the detonation of the mines and his own death, despite this he continued to work with relentless determination, speed and resolve under the most arduous conditions that are an example to us all. He showed sustained courage and coolness of the highest order.

Also travelling north in a packet of six Land Rovers was the Tactical HQ of HQ 1 UKDIV. It crossed into Iraq at crossing point Dallas embedded with the US 1 MARDIV. Col Jim Tanner was there:

On 20 March I wrote in my diary 'We are at war'. I was embedded with Maj Gen Jim Mattis of the US 1st Marine Division, who I knew from Granby in 1991. A superb guy and a hard soldier. His HQ was also in soft-skin vehicles and that was quite a worry to us. We knew that a small well-armed band of Iraqis could knock us out if they got in close even without any heavy weapons or vehicles.

My role was to command the RIP, the relief in place, of the US Marines by the British when they caught up. As the shout went up to start engines, we turned our little convoy lights on, then swiftly got berated by the US Marines who told us to turn them off. They all had NVGs, but we only had about one set per section. I thought to myself 'well this will be interesting!'

We moved off toward the border breach. Ahead of me in the lead Land Rover was the Signals captain, Cliff Kamara. He pulled away and drove straight into a shallow trench, upending the vehicle. We did laugh. Once clear we headed up onto route Tampa which was the main tarmac Route 80 north. Once on that the marines, strangely, turned their lights on. After two hours of slow movement, we pulled over alongside a long line of AAV Amtracs and could see a whole lot of tracers and explosions to the north ahead of us. That was Safwan getting hit. About 02:00 on 21 March we got our heads down. I was thankful for my warm sleeping bag as it was bloody cold.

We carried out the RIP at 20.00 on the 22nd. Shortly after, some prisoners came into the HQ. Two were young soldiers, one was wounded with a gunshot wound to the stomach. They were bedraggled and beaten. Four officers then came in including a brigadier and a colonel. They were well spoken, educated, and scared for the safety of their families. It was clear that the Iraqi Army had already crumbled as an organisation. The decision was made in Washington to stand down the Iraqi Army completely, so it was out of our hands. We had planned for the transition phase but effectively were stopped by the Americans from doing it. That was a catastrophic decision that shaped the insurgency for the next six years.

BSM Leigh Sharpe also crossed into Iraq in a convoy:

We had several vehicles in our troop, mainly Land Rovers, but I drove the 4-tonner with the RQMS and a guy on top cover with a GPMG, but virtually no ammo. We slowly assembled with 30 other vehicles and moved up towards the border crossing in the dark, with just pinprick convoy lights on. It was slow, stop-start for hours. I could feel my eyelids getting heavy and did what I could to stay awake as it was now about 04:00. After yet another halt I told the top cover guy to come down inside as it was cold, and we were still inside Kuwait.

We crossed into Iraq through the 30ft-high berms and over a newly laid bridge and stopped again. We notched up the heating and then the next thing I knew I woke up with a jolt, blinked my eyes looking in front of me and saw that the convoy in front had gone! The instant dump of adrenaline surged through me and I thought, 'Oh Shit.'

We decided that we should go forward a little to try and re-establish contact. Only a little way further on we saw two British squaddies standing at the roadside and asked them about the convoy. Fortunately, it had only just passed them and was pulling up a few yards ahead.

We stopped near to the Yanks' MSR, codenamed Tampa. We ended up there for about a week. We dug shell scrapes and got the kit ready but never needed it. One night a battery of artillery, AS-90s I think, was quite close to us and started banging away. It was like a free fireworks display, only noisier and scary when you think about who might be on the receiving end.

The major in charge of the medical unit we were attached to was a dentist. One day he took a Land Rover out with a young nurse on a recce. She was his driver and somehow managed to get it stuck somewhere in the sand. They had no comms with them, and he made her stay with the waggon while he walked back to our camp to get help. He left her alone while he walked back. I could not believe it, and if she had not been there waiting when we got to her, we would still all be talking about it today, but in vastly different terms, I am sure.

Engineers came up with a JCB and dug out a latrine trench for us which then had a wooden box placed over it with three holes. So, it looked like the TV show the Goodies on their triple seat bike, hence Goodie box. It was better than having to do a 'shovel recce', except one lad dropped his wallet onto the box, how we laughed. When the Goodies were full, they dug a new one and filled the first one in with the spoil.

The other thing that sprang up were 'desert roses' for peeing in. They were like a grey plastic tube, six inches across, that was sunk a foot or two into the ground, at 45 degrees, for men to pee into. I do remember, oddly, seeing a female nurse try to pee into a desert rose.

One of our guys got a bit sick after a few days in the desert, so he was sent 3km across the flat desert to a field hospital. We went over to see him in the Land Rover, but as we left it was like the strangest thing ever. The corridor to the exit was really windy and sand was whipping about the tents. As we got outside it was incredible, we couldn't even see the ground ahead of us because of the sandstorm. We thought we should try and get back to camp, so started feeling around for the Land Rover. We thought we had found it and got in but soon realised it wasn't ours because the steering wheel was on the wrong side. The grit was swirling and billowing about, and we literally just couldn't see more than a foot. We then aborted the idea and went back in the tented hospital and waited until it passed, which was the next morning. I have seen Hollywood films where big sandstorms suddenly roll up; well, it was like that.

After being near the MSR for the first week, we spent a week at the airport near Basra. Then we were ordered to move to Basra Palace on the river. We had a route briefing about where we were going, the route to follow and 'actions on' along the way. I was driving the second vehicle, following the dentist. The route said go out of the camp, turn east toward the city. He drove off and turned west toward the desert. I am thinking, 'What the fuck is he doing?' The only way I could attract his attention was to blow the horn which risked everyone else thinking, 'Gas alarm'.

I pulled alongside him, and he said, 'Just trust me and follow me.' It turned out that after the briefing he was told by the intelligence team that a local market was blocking the planned route. He just hadn't bothered to tell anyone. It was awful and unprofessional.

In those first three weeks we only took in one casualty, an Iraqi kid. The poor old medics were champing at the bit to deal with stuff. They had surgeons, an anaesthetist, and numerous nurses but nothing to do. One was an Australian girl who insisted on strolling around in a bikini: that was pretty awful to look at.

They never found any WMD because there wasn't any to find. I think it was a scam and a non-event. Thankfully our decontamination skills were never used.

Maj Gareth Davies, RTR of the JNBC Regiment, crossed the border with 1 MARDIV's 7 RCT:

Having crossed the border, I watched USMC Huey Cobra gunships over Safwan Hill to my east, like a scene from a movie. They were pouring fire on the hill like a fire-power demonstration. Next to me stood this real character who was an ex-US Navy SEAL who was now an SNCO marine who was a SEAL team liaison officer. He never wore conventional uniform and carried over his shoulder a Vietnam-era M79 'Blooper' grenade launcher with the strange wooden stock.

Cpl Scott Blaney, REME, crossed the border in his CRARRV in the leading convoy:

We were warned off to go into Iraq with the leading convoy and it was going to be in the middle of the night. We had orders as to the exact time we had to join the procession and move north up the highway towards the border. It was about a 30-minute slow drive to the start line from where we were parked for our last peacetime shut eye. Steve, Kaffir and I had a routine which allowed one of us to sleep in the tank, one to sleep on the engine deck and one on the ground. We tried to sleep those last few hours, but we were soon all awake. Kaffir was normally in charge as the sergeant but for some reason he asked me to take command, while Steve drove and Kaffir stood by as mechanic and on the BV for brews. Sadly, Kaffir has, since the war, committed suicide and I wonder whether his self-doubt started at this moment.

We were all capable of interchanging roles and I was quite happy, so I jumped up into the commander's seat. Kaffir then announced he needed to go for a nervous poo. I told him to hurry up as we were on a tight schedule. He ran off in the direction of a long line of 'thunderbox' portaloos that were stood about 50 yards from us. Impatient to get going, Steve and I ran through some last-minute kit and equipment checks – food, water, GPMG ammo, grenades, cam nets, radio on correct net and everything lashed down. Having done all this Kaffir was still not back so I called up Steve on the headset and said, 'Fire up the APU … OK, start engine.' I was now getting concerned that we were going to be late for the war. I joked with Steve that we shouldn't really care because we might be dead in 30 minutes. I looked over to the line of portaloos and saw the one in the middle of the line had a light on inside, which was probably crapping Kaffir's head torch. I told Steve to drive over to the portaloos, 'First gear, forwards … left stick … forward a bit … stop.' The nose of the CRARRV was only inches from the portaloo and then Steve revved her up. I started laughing at the thought of poor old Kaffir sitting on the crapper with what must sound like hell clawing at the door. We ramped it up a bit then and Steve put it in first gear, then delicately nudged forward a few inches. The portaloo rocked back until it was then leaning at about 45 degrees. Then Kaffir finally emerged from his crapping, from a portaloo three doors along from the one we were pushing on. He bounded over as I shouted at him to get aboard. He leapt up the dozer blade and into his hatch in a few seconds. I ordered Steve to reverse and get us the hell out. To this day I do not know who was in that portaloo, it could have been Commander 7 Armoured Brigade for all I know.

The Media

The 2003 invasion of Iraq involved unprecedented media coverage. One of the most popular networks in the United States was Fox News, which carried a waving flag animation in the corner of the screen and was clearly pro-war. The journalists on the spot walked a thin line in the search for stories and some of them paid the ultimate price. Most of those that died were Iraqis – such as Tareq Ayoub who died when a US warplane bombed Al Jazeera's headquarters in Baghdad on 8 April 2003. Others – like veteran Reuters cameraman Taras Protsyuk and Spanish cameraman José Couso of Telecinco – were killed when Baghdad's Palestine Hotel was targeted by an M1 Abrams of A Company, 4-64 Armor.

British casualties included Terry Lloyd who was the first ITN reporter to die in 48 years. He was in one of two vehicles, clearly marked with 'TV', and travelling towards Basra in the first stage of the American-led thrust across the border. For some still unexplained reason the two-vehicle convoy seems to have driven across the front of a USMC armoured platoon in M1 tanks who were guarding the flanks of the US advance near the Shatt al-Basra waterway.

At the same time a pick-up truck with enemy soldiers armed with RPGs came across a bridge towards the tanks prompting them to open fire. All the vehicles were hit by machine-gun fire and at the inquest it was reported that the TV crews were possibly hit by both American and Iraqi fire. Two of the Press team were killed immediately. Lloyd was wounded in the stomach and a passing Iraqi civilian picked him up and loaded him into his own Mitsubishi intending to take him to get help. Sadly, this vehicle was mistaken for being another enemy vehicle and was also fired upon by the US Marines. Terry was hit in the head and killed.

This event had an immediate effect on British journalists. Lt Col Ben Curry, RM, SO1 Media Ops for 3 Commando Brigade, said:

> None of the Journos like being 'embeds' because it hampers their freedom of movement, and they feel their right to roam is curtailed by people like me. However, after the ITN Journalist Terry Lloyd was killed in southern Iraq most of the journalists decided that they would after all stay close to the British troops.*

Lt Col Jeremy Tuck, RAMC, commander of 5 GSMR, had his own run-in with the Press:

> We crossed the border east of Safwan and travelled through cloverleaf junction where Route 8 crosses Route 1. Around a mile further to the north-west we stopped at the side of the highway in a big lorry park and set up our new field HQ. We remained there until the major war fighting stopped in mid-April, then moved north to Shaiba Air Base.
>
> A few days into the invasion I was being driven in my Land Rover to see one of my detached teams when I saw that an American column had stopped at the roadside and was in all-around defence. A man was down in the road being attended to by a US medic. I got out to see if help was needed and then saw it was an Iraqi civilian who had been shot in the right shin while driving his car and had a shattered tibia. I told the American I was a doctor and he immediately apologised and said that he was being told to leave the casualty and get back to his convoy. This was slightly perturbing as it left us in a vulnerable position with a patient whose history I did not know. The American medic appeared to suggest the man had been shot by persons unknown in the desert, but the wounded man was adamant it was a shot from the American convoy that had hit him. I did some basic scene analysis and saw the line of bullet holes down the side of the car and to my mind it looked even more certain that an American providing 'top cover' in a cupola had fired the burst at the car.
>
> As I was finishing stabilising the wounded man a photojournalist from our convoy came up behind me and started snapping shots of us. I asked him to give us some space and dignity, but he claimed it was newsworthy and carried on at which point I raised my voice and told him in no uncertain terms where to go. It was too isolated to call and wait for help, so we loaded the Iraqi into my Rover and took him back to HQ where he got a proper ambulance.

---

* Terry Lloyd was married with two children, Chelsy and Oliver. His death was declared an unlawful killing by the British coroner but not even at the Coroner's Court could Chelsy uncover who shot him or why. Showing a journalistic spirit that her father would have been proud of, she contacted the US Marines and in 2013 met up with Lt Vince Hogan (ex-US Marines) in a Virginia coffee shop. Hogan had been the platoon commander on the day and had ordered his men to open fire but had no recollection of exactly which of the vehicles were fired at or by whom. Hogan was clearly still dealing with his own demons from the war and far from being a confrontation, the two found the meeting helpful. Accepting his version of events, no matter how much it hurt, has helped Chelsy cope.

The photograph made it into *The Sunday Telegraph* complete with me mouthing off at him.

Maj David Green, RAMC at 202 Field Hospital saw various media teams and a private film maker for extended periods at the hospital:

The MOD would not allow them to film wounded British personnel. I think that's a massive own goal. There is, of course, a balance between privacy and the need for the public interest to be satisfied. However, casualties bring it home to the public that there is nothing sanitary about combat, it's grim. The Public root for our wounded soldiers and want them cared for and to have a speedy recovery. Just look at the success of Help for Heroes and other charities. We can look at the Falklands War as another example. The book *Red and Green Life Machine* was immensely popular and the associated documentary *Falklands Combat Medics* is watched still by thousands with on demand TV. Simon Weston's story with his horrendous burns illustrates the level of interest and popularity by allowing their stories to be told and not hidden away. The Invictus Games is another spotlight on our wounded, so people clearly know soldiers get hurt, why not let the public see the army medics caring for them on the battlefields? Of course, with the caveat that families need to be told first so I'm not suggesting live streaming our wounded is necessary. I think that social media and digital platforms have now transformed this scenario even further, but it was the Vietnam War that was the most televised war, that changed the landscape for ever.

CHAPTER 6

Seizing the Rumaila Oilfields

We set out at daybreak. Towering columns of black smoke clouded the horizon ahead of us, the air growing darker as the pollution settled and spread. It was getting harder to see anything, with some oil wells already burning it was more important than ever to maintain our momentum, get ahead and secure the ground before the Iraqis set every single well ablaze.

I noticed the odd guy on motorbikes ahead of us, coming within a couple of kilometres, taking a good look, racing off again talking into their mobile phones. It didn't occur to me straight away that they were dickers – touts like the street rats spotting for the IRA in Northern Ireland.[1]

L/Cpl of Horse Mick Flynn, CGC, MC, HCR

Paratroopers naturally believe in the concept of air assault and that it is a battle-winning theory. The sheer quantity of air and aviation assets available in theatre gave credence to the expectation that 16 AAB would, therefore, seize the Rumaila oilfields by helicopter assault. It was a long-standing joke in the brigade that 4-tonners (lorries) were frequently used in training to make up for the shortage of UK airlift capability or for when the weather was too bad for flying. Troopers were always told that this is 'only in training, it will never be like that in a real war'.

But despite all the hype surrounding the capabilities of 16 AAB and their helicopters, the lads of 1 and 3 PARA and 1 Royal Irish did find themselves going to war on what they laughingly called 'Bedi-copters' (Bedford 4-ton open-sided trucks):

16 Air Assault Brigade Order of Battle (led by Brig Jon 'Jacko' Page)
D Squadron, Household Cavalry Regiment
216 Parachute Squadron, RSigs
Pathfinder Platoon
1 Battalion, Royal Irish Regiment (1 Royal Irish)
1 Battalion, The Parachute Regiment (1 PARA)
3 Battalion, The Parachute Regiment (3 PARA)
7 Parachute Regiment Royal Horse Artillery (7 PARA RHA)
9 Parachute Squadron, RE
23 (Air Assault) Engineer Regiment

7 Air Assault Battalion, REME
13 Air Assault Support Regiment, RLC
16 Close Support Medical Regiment, RAMC
156 Provost Company, RMP

Sgt D Clarke, 1 Royal Irish, remembers doing so:

> We crossed the border on 4-ton trucks which the lads found hilarious, nevertheless the guys were switched on and ready to go. As we advanced into the unknown all we knew was that the Americans were ahead of us, and we were to relieve them. It was clear the Iraqis were retreating with little resistance. As they retreated, they managed to sabotage some of the pipelines and GOSPs. We approached the oilfields with the air thick and black with smoke as the burning GOSPs lit up the dawn horizon bright red.[2]

Pushing forward to screen the main Para BG was the Pathfinder Platoon. It was 46-men strong, commanded by a senior captain or major. It can act as a Brigade Reconnaissance Force with the men all highly trained and experienced. It can insert via HALO/HAHO (High Altitude Low opening/ High Altitude High Opening) Heli-Abseil/fast rope or Land Rover vehicles equipped with .50cal Machine Guns and MILAN missiles. Generally, the team worked in small six-man teams or multiples thereof.

Typically, the six men would have sets of additional skills such as, Signaller, Demolitions and Bridge engineering specialist, Sniper pair, Combat Medic, Forward Air Controller and Mechanic. For Operation *Telic* they were using their Land Rovers which would assist them covering the many miles ahead.

During Operation *Telic* the pathfinders were tasked with several missions including screening and interdicting the enemy main supply routes up to 200km ahead of the main brigade. They would discreetly observe the enemy convoys and call in air support. Callsigns 34 Bravo and 34 Foxtrot worked together in a 12-man patrol and inserted using four Land Rovers close to Nasiriya, 140km north-west of Basra. They did so knowing that a similar patrol of US Special Forces had been compromised and had lost their vehicles when being hastily extracted under fire from Iraqi forces. The pathfinders skilfully established a series of observation posts along the Euphrates River with views of the enemy supply routes. In amongst a populated area with scrub, arable crops and drainage ditches, using great guile, the patrol commander moved his team each night to avoid detection and so remained undiscovered for eight days, reporting enemy movements. 34 Bravo also went out to confirm if the lost US SF vehicles were still where they had been left, but they had been taken away.

Tasked with reconnaissance of a main supply route between two major towns, 34 Delta had to gather information on road construction, bridge classification (weights it could tolerate) and enemy traffic. The patrol inserted, on the first night, as a three-man team to minimise the signature and had infiltrated across 5km of difficult terrain when the patrol commander knelt in the barren scrubland to examine his next bound more carefully. Suddenly, he heard excited Arabic voices and a weapon being cocked close by, on a low sand berm. Just behind him on the berm he saw an Iraqi soldier peering into the darkness. The paratrooper instantly realised he only had a second or so before he lost the advantage his night vision goggles were giving him. He shot the enemy soldier, ran up the berm pulling out a grenade as he did so and dropped it into the Iraqi trench he saw just on the other side of the berm. As the grenade went off, he climbed back up and he and his FN Minimi-armed gunner fired short bursts into the trench system. The rear man in the patrol then joined them and threw two more grenades into the position. This allowed them then to extract, covering each other's movements. 34 Delta's patrol commander then fired two 40mm grenades from his underslung launcher to further dissuade the Iraqis from pursuing them. The patrol extracted without loss.

As well as 7 PARA RHA and its 105mm L118 Light Guns, the brigade also had C and D Battery, 3 RHA to fire in support of the units north of Basra. They fired 3,000 rounds against the Iraqi 6th Armoured Division that moved down to meet the advancing British forces. Highly effective against tanks and other vehicles, the L20 bomblet round is an Israeli-made artillery shell containing 49 submunitions which are spun out when over the target. The most effective shoot with the L20 rounds from the RHA knocked out 12 of 15 T-55 tanks en route towards Basra. However, they have a significant long-term drawback: an estimated 2% failure rate. This meant that once the British had fired 2,000 L20 rounds in Iraq, around 2,000 deadly submunitions lay on the ground as unexploded devices.

Cpl Freddie Kruyer of 3 PARA remembers:

> Our first stop inside Iraq was to first relieve some Americans. We were a ragtag bunch wearing a mixture of desert and green DPM uniforms, travelling in old Bedford lorries and stripped-down Land Rovers. I don't think we were very impressive. The Americans we were meeting arrived next to us in one of their armoured vehicles. The rear hydraulic ramp powered down smoothly and out stepped a cross between Robocop and a Starship Trooper. The Yank was bristling with equipment, body armour and radios. We must have looked like Fred Karno's Army to them. On the other hand, I thought how difficult it would be to conduct a section attack wearing all that gear.
>
> As we moved north towards Rumaila Bridge we saw a lot of destroyed Iraqi fighting positions, trenches and knocked out armour but no enemy. There were some dead and there was discarded kit and uniforms, but I hardly saw a soldier. The condition of the vehicles and dugouts suggested a complete lack of care or maintenance.

It was not the enemy that posed the greatest problem for the troops on the left flank with 16 AAB, it was the vast wide-open desert. Spanning some 80km north and

30km across, the brigade needed to put a lot of effort into planning its signals set up and keep a logistic chain connected between all ground units. Kruyer continues:

> The biggest issue was the distances to cover to be evacuated. I had to arrange evacuation of a seriously injured soldier after the WIMIK [named after WMIK – weapons mount installation kit] he was driving rolled and crushed him. We could not get comms and had to send a vehicle halfway back to base to act as a re-broadcast. Eventually, a helicopter was sent to recover him. He did have life-threatening injuries and it was almost two hours before he got to hospital but he did survive and recovered.

Helping the ground troops cope with the extreme distances of western Iraq was the job of the Army Air Corps, and time and again on Operation *Telic* 3 Regiment AAC plugged those gaps superbly. During this phase of the operations, 663 Squadron, AAC had moved up to an advanced base just east of Rumaila near the old Baghdad Railroad. The squadron was tasked with providing an aviation reconnaissance patrol (ARP) of one Gazelle, crewed by two staff sergeants, and one Lynx Mk 7 crewed by Capt Richard Cuthill and a corporal. Held at 15 minutes' notice to move (NTM) was a response fire team of two further Lynx. After first light on 30 March the patrol took off into the early morning sun, swinging north over the Hammar Canal (codename Rubicon) towards the outposts and recce screen to the north that were held by 1 PARA and the Household Cavalry (HCR). Brigade HQ had passed a message from 1 PARA that dug-in enemy T-55 tanks had been sighted and the ARP was to investigate further. On approach to the objective area, the radar warning receiver spiked in the cockpit of the Gazelle, picking up hostile radar indications. Apart from this, the patrol saw nothing of note and returned to refuel. Lt Hughes, AAC, acting as watchkeeper at Battlegroup HQ, then took reports of contact further north of 1 PARA, with Scimitars of the HCR in action against Iraqi armour. The ARP was told to return, with the addition of another Gazelle, to assist the HCR. Heading back north at low level, the three helicopters got back to the screen lines held by the HCR and immediately started seeing incoming anti-aircraft fire. 20mm tracer rounds streaked through the air and then heavy artillery also started impacting below the helicopters. This meant hovering in one spot became extremely hazardous for the soft-skinned aircraft. The three aircraft were lined up along a raised road scanning for the enemy who were around 8km south of Al-Qurnah.

The HCR had seen the enemy and was now trying to talk the aircrew onto the target to engage it. L/Cpl of Horse Mick Flynn was the FAC in the little Scimitar CVRT, callsign Whisky 32 (W32). The Gazelles, flying at extremely low level, lined up behind W32 so they had a similar axis of view but elevated over him and soon saw two T-55s, dug in some 2,000m away. Capt Cuthill was then called forward with his Lynx to engage them. More enemy artillery shells were now impacting on and around the embankment near W32 and very close to the hovering helicopters. Cuthill was still not able to identify the target so to aid him further Cpl Flynn

'Kuwaiting' – typical 9'x9' tent and British Land Rover in a Kuwait camp. (Author's own collection)

'Mr and Mrs' – Major N. Wraith RM and Flight Lieutenant J. Wraith RAF in Kuwait prior to invasion – a rare holiday together! (N. Wraith)

Major Wraith and his signaller with TAC HQ 40 Commando on Objective 'Coronado' just after landing on the Al Faw peninsula. (N. Wraith)

Knocked-out Iraqi defence bunker on the Al Faw peninsula. (N. Wraith)

One of B Coy, 40 Commando objectives in Operation *Houghton* – the pumping station, codename Quaker. (N. Wraith)

40 Commando Tac HQ Land Rover WMIK, Operation *Houghton*. (N. Wraith)

Flight Lieutenant Andy Johnson RAF at work on the AWACS during Operation *Telic*. (A. Johnson)

RAF Tactical Imagery Wing at work during a SCUD alert in Kuwait. (A. White)

RAF GR4 Tornado showing the huge RAPTOR pod underslung on the centreline. (A. White)

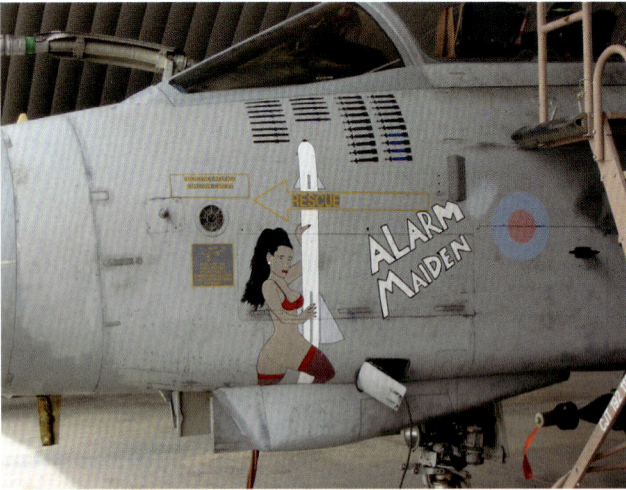

'Alarm Maiden' – an RAF GR4 displaying its 'nose art' and bombing missions tally. (A. White)

HMS *Ocean* at sea on a later deployment in the Gulf. (MOD)

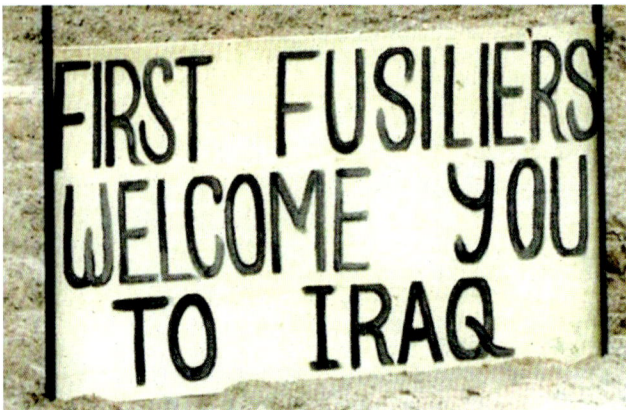

'Welcome to Iraq' sign beside MSR Tampa. (*Journal of the Royal Fusiliers*)

Captain Ed Pugh 1RRF alongside his Scimitar AFV. (E. Pugh)

A Scimitar AFV of 16 AAB alongside a USMC LTVP-7 west of Basra, March 2003. (US Marines)

WO2 Andy Abbott and the remains of an Iraqi artillery piece that he had just destroyed. (A. Abbott)

WO2 Abbott in front of fresh graffiti on a Saddam Hussein mural in Basra. (A. Abbott)

Paratroopers from 3 PARA aboard their 'Bedi-Copter' heading into Iraq, west of Safwan. (Craig Allen)

Soldiers of A Company, 3 PARA advance through the Rumaila oilfields. (Craig Allen)

Major Dan Worthington, 3 PARA talks to men of the Anti-Tank Platoon on their WMIK. Note the MILAN ATGW mounted on top and the LAW missiles on the bonnet. (Craig Allen)

A US AH1-Cobra gunship flies over Basra, a destroyed T-55 in the foreground. (N. Wraith)

A freshly 'up-armoured' British Challenger MBT in Iraq 2003. (I. Cross)

A knocked-out column of Iraqi armoured vehicles near Basra (at front is a T-55 followed by a Soviet built MTLB APC). (I. Cross)

Corporal Burton REME attached to the Black Watch under a cam net, southern Iraq. (P. Burton)

Bridge 4 at Basra, known as Objective Golf for 1RRF. (E. Pugh)

Paratroopers of A Company, 3 PARA cross the Hammar Canal over a blown section of the Rumaila bridge with the aid of assault ladders. (Just after the photograph was taken it was noticed there were large amounts of explosive still in place under the bridge which needed clearing by sappers.) (Craig Allen)

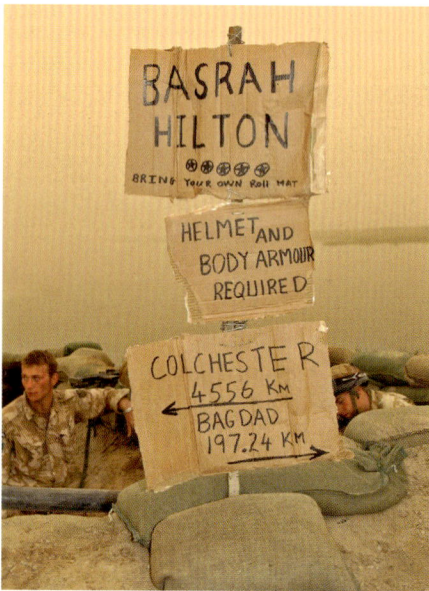

A sign put up on a 3 PARA position north of the Hammar Canal close to Rumaila Bridge. (Craig Allen)

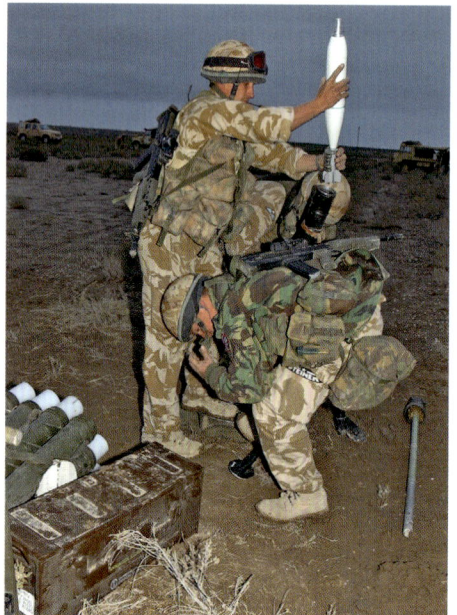

A night-time fire mission for 3 PARA mortars, March 25. (Craig Allen)

Major Neil Wraith briefs men of 40 Commando for Operation *James*. (N. Wraith)

A typical oil fire on Route 6 near 'Odd Job', Abu Al Khasib during Operation *James*, 30/31 March 2003. (N. Wraith)

This large compound in Abu Al Khasib became known as the 'Alamo' for 40 Commando after Operation *James*. (N. Wraith)

'Bombed-Up' – Major Ben Farrell, 1 Irish Guards, prior to the push into Basra, 3 April 2003. (B. Farrell)

Guardsmen of 1 Irish Guards receive a briefing from Major Farrell (seated on left) before they attack across bridge 4 into Basra. (B. Farrell)

An 'M3 Rig' of the Royal Engineers at Crossing Point Anna. (S. Taylor)

A paratrooper of 3 PARA with his SA-80 and the underslung grenade launcher which entered service during the war and proved to be a valuable weapon that remains in use. (Craig Allen)

3 PARA snipers armed with L115 Rifles scan for signs of Fedayeen activity during the move into Basra, 6 April. (Craig Allen)

Saddam mural in Basra suitably altered by the Royal Fusiliers. (E. Pugh)

M42 Type cluster munition with PE4 about to be destroyed by EOD Engineers. This type of munition was widely used by American Forces in Iraq. (R. Fadil)

A typical EOD tasking – hundreds of Chinese Type 58 anti-personnel mines awaiting destruction. These lethal devices are notorious killers if handled after arming. (A. Abbott)

A large and complex EOD task of destroying Iraqi rockets and anti-tank mines; note PE4 explosive and 'det cord' connecting all the ordnance. (A. Abbott)

The smouldering hulk of Saddam's super yacht, *Al Mansur*, lies ruined in the Shat al Arab, Basra. With gold taps and a secret submarine escape pod, the $30M vessel was hit by two bombs dropped by US Navy F-14s. (N. Wraith)

Task Force 22 arrive in Baghdad Green Zone in the hunt for WMD. (A. Abbott)

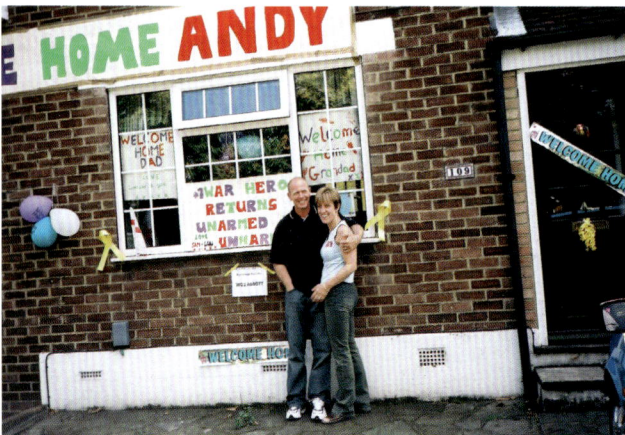

'Welcome Home' banners for WO2 Abbott in Kent. (A. Abbott)

nudged his Scimitar up the embankment a little further in order to get shots off at the enemy. With three rounds of 30mm tracer loaded, he crested the embankment and, at great risk, exposing himself to enemy fire, got the burst of tracer off at the enemy. Using the roof-mounted sight on the Lynx Cuthill observed the Rarden tracer arc out across the scrub and thought he saw the rounds impacting on the armour when a flash filled his sight. However, it turned out that it was not the tracer hitting, it was the muzzle flash as the enemy fired directly at him. Immediately, the round 'cracked' past his aircraft only a few metres away. Capt Cuthill was now lining his sights on a 2S1 122mm howitzer-armed SPG. Russian-made, known as *Gvozdika* (carnation), it had been in use since the 1970s and is based on the familiar MTLB chassis so common in Iraq.

Cuthill locked-on with his TOW (tube-launched optically-sighted wire-guided) missile system, fired and the 2S1 was confirmed as a K-kill. (A gunner can also report an M-kill meaning the vehicle is immobilised but may still be a threat.) Using the shoot and scoot method once more, W32 fired at another T-55 which Cuthill engaged. His first missile was seen to strike but with little visible effect, so a second was fired and that was a second K-kill of the day. Throughout the engagement, other tanks were firing their main armament at the hovering helicopters. One crew reported not only hearing rounds 'crack' past them over the noise of their gas turbine engines, but also felt the overpressure as a round passed no more than 4–5m above their rotor blades. The trio were nearing 'bingo' fuel and returned to their FARP. Another Lynx joined W32 on station and that was successful at destroying a static field gun hidden behind a berm. A first TOW missile was used to blow the top off the berm to gain a better, exposed view of the artillery piece, a D-30 122m howitzer, then the follow-on missile crashed into the gun itself.

As well as the Lynx TOW hits, the Gazelle crews called in several Royal Artillery fire missions which destroyed another 2S1, bringing the squadron's tally that day to two T-55s, two 2S1s SPGs and a D-30 howitzer.

Throughout the day Capt Richard Cuthill had displayed outstanding airmanship, courage and leadership, commanding his own aircraft and the patrol with great skill and determination. He was awarded the Distinguished Flying Cross. L/Cpl of Horse, Michael Flynn, W32, was awarded the Conspicuous Gallantry Cross. He had already served in the Falklands and Bosnia, and later he served in Afghanistan where he was also awarded the Military Cross making him one of the British Army's most decorated soldiers. He left the army in 2012 as a WO1.

***

Thirty-six hours before G-day was due to commence, a call came in over the regimental net at 7 PARA RHA HQ with some urgency. 'Hello CC, this is Zero. Fire Mission, 18 guns, over.'

The gunners who were embedded with 16 AAB had with them 18 105mm L118 Light Guns, just like the guns of 29 Commando Regiment. They had not fired in anger since Aden in 1967 and as the call for a fire mission came in rather prematurely, they weren't quite ready but were not going to disappoint. The fire mission was in response to an Iraqi mortar barrage falling on some US Marines who were still inside Kuwait before the invasion started. The USMC artillery regiment to which 7 RHA was attached, very sportingly had given them the chance to fire the first artillery shots of the war. Cynics may say they were stitching up the Brits in case something went wrong, and it was all in error!

Later the gun group limbered up and crossed the berms into Iraq intermingled with some US M1 tanks and became the first UK ground forces across the border.

16 AAB's Offensive Support Group (OSG) was developing into a potent force responsible for battlespace management, surveillance target acquisition, and offensive fires. It grouped 7 RHA, D Squadron, HCR, the Brigade Pathfinder Platoon, three WLR platforms, a Phoenix UAV and the US ANGLICO team.

Once the US Marines released 7 PARA RHA, it rejoined 16 AAB as it advanced to secure the Rumaila oilfields. One challenge it faced was the terrain, vast open stretches of desert scrub forced the adoption of Soviet-era tactics. Deployment of the guns straight from the line of march up the roads became the norm. Two batteries advanced with the RHQ behind them and the last battery brought up the rear. On receipt of a fire-mission, the regiment could halt, deploy to the roadsides and get into action in less than five minutes. The new artillery pointing system (APS) that replaced the decades-old dial sights brought a quantum leap in swift, accurate firing. The FOO parties with the infantry were also equipped with some new technology. Laser binoculars and hand-held Sophie thermal imagers gave 24-hour capability and tied in the with new APS on the guns. First round hits were common. Bracketing and numerous adjustments became a thing of the past.

APS is based on an inertial navigation system which enables it to be unhooked and into action in 30 seconds. The APS replaces the traditional dial sight and takes into account trunnion tilt, without the requirement to level any spirit level bubbles as before. A touch-screen display tells the gun controller when his gun is laid onto the correct target data provided. This enhancement improves the accuracy of the fall of shot to a greater degree of accuracy than possible with the dial sight.

At the North Rumaila Bridge (Objective Edinburgh) across the 600m wide Hammar Canal, the brigade made a tactical pause as the division HQ did not want any further avenues of retreat out of Basra to be cut, yet. The Iraqis had tried to destroy the important bridge with explosives but only succeeded in dropping one of the spans across the canal. A Company, 3 PARA moved to the edge of the canal to observe the far bank.

Amidst a huge downpour of rain, an Iraqi counter-attack surprised the Para group at the bridge. The first reported contact was from Capt Chris Allen at the 7 RHA observation post on the south bank of the canal. He was under small-arms, artillery and mortar fire from the north bank. The WLR systems kicked in and offered up counter-battery fire solutions to the light guns of 1 Para Battery, 7 RHA, but they were under fire themselves. Iraqi 122mm D-30 guns were firing on them, but to confuse matters the enemy battery was to the east across the brigade boundary in 7 Brigade area.

The torrential rain across the battlefield soon turned the drained Hammar region back to the marshes it had been for hundreds of years, adding to the chaos of the battle. As authority was being sought up the chain of command – from 1 UKDIV CRA – to fire across the inter-unit boundary, the chaos deepened further when the roof of the tent housing the Artillery Command Cell, bulging under the weight of the water trapped on the top, finally gave way in a tidal wave and swamped the radio and data equipment knocking it all out in a fizz of short circuits and error messages. If not so serious, surely some present would have laughed. With all communications to higher echelons now down, the FOO and battery commanders took it upon themselves – after risk-assessing the situation – to let F Battery fire at the enemy D-30s who were by now firing airburst at the British gun line and getting close to killing the crew. The battery commander was seen, without helmet but with red beret and cigar, coolly giving commands and encouragement under fire. The combined fires of 1 and F Batteries silenced the D-30s and ended the counter-attack.

Before the twisted bridge remains were crossed on 23 March, a sharp bombardment of the far bank was made by the Mortar Platoon and guns of 7 RHA. 3 PARA crossed first and, with smoke drifting across the area from a burning oil/gas plant, A Company and some engineers worked their way across, checking for booby traps and installing assault ladders as they went. They managed to jump and climb and got across feet dry. The first platoon across set up two GPMGs on the raised road next to an abandoned sentry-box, and Cpl Davies's men started patrolling forward for signs of the enemy. Several destroyed T-55s, MTLBs and wheeled BRDMs were found knocked out near the northern end of the bridge as well as a very potent four-barrelled 23mm AA gun.

200kg of explosives that failed to detonate were cleared from a pier of the bridge and 9 Parachute Sqn, RE started constructing a medium girder over bridge. This was followed by a 38m untensioned long span (LS) general support bridge (GSB), built across the dropped span by Lt Col Callum Skeat's 28 Engineer Regiment. This was the first operational deployment of the LS GSB, which is built using automated bridge-launching equipment. The engineers also deployed their diving team to check on the condition of the underwater components of the bridge piers and for further explosives. By dawn on 24 March wheeled vehicles were crossing to the northern bridgehead and expanding their influence east towards Al-Qurnah. During this very fluid phase of operations with less than clear lines, infiltration by enemy forces or attack from bypassed ground units posed a real threat and local defence was well to the fore. ARPs flown by the Army Air Corps reinforced the screening process and identified numerous Iraqi positions and units on the move. The OSG was in full swing, bringing every available ISTAR and strike asset to excellent effect.

On 31 March (D+12), Maj David Moreton's 23 Amphibious Engineer Squadron provided an M3 ferry crossing at North Rumaila in support of 16 AAB's expansion north. This allowed AS-90 self-propelled guns and support vehicles of D Battery, 3 RHA to cross the Hammar Canal. The AS-90s were too heavy to cross the GSB.

The first operational deployment of M3 ferry rigs had occurred on the Shatt al-Basra Canal at Crossing Point Anna. The crossing point was provided by a troop of 23 Amphibious Engineer Sqn, 28 Engineer Regt, RE supported by 59 Independent Commando Sqn, RE and 131 Independent Commando Sqn, RE (V).

Some 10km east of the 3 PARA crossing at Rumaila was the small town of Ad Dayr which sits astride Route 6 that runs north from Basra and up to Al-Qurnah. The rivers Tigris, Euphrates and Shatt al-Arab all meet at Al-Qurnah making it a vital location to occupy. As 1 PARA advanced on Ad Dayr the Royal Irish rushed north to Al-Qurnah and the Garden of Eden where they were met by crowds of smiling and waving locals. ISTAR assets over Ad Dayr identified the HQ of Iraqi 6th Armoured Division and calling it a TST soon had a JDAM dropping on its roof. Iraqi 6th Division made use of its South African-made G5 155mm howitzers which outranged the light guns with 16 AAB. To counter this issue, the CRA ordered what were known as artillery raids. Batteries of light guns raced forward to get in range of the enemy guns, emplaced, fired and withdrew before the Iraqi gunners could fire back. It proved an effective tactic that wore down and silenced the enemy until the big AS-90s arrived and destroyed the G5 guns.

By 31 March, 7 PARA RHA's war was over. It had fired over 9,000 rounds including HE, smoke and illumination rounds. The paratrooper gunners had kept all 18 guns in use, meaning each gun had fired over 500 rounds, the most of any of the divisional guns.

Six days into the war, 16 AAB had pushed deeper inside Iraq than any other British brigade. The helicopters of the AAC acted as eyes and ears in a traditional cavalry-screening role. Patrols were being pushed beyond the Hammar Canal and as far north as Al-Qurnah and Ad Dayr, which is 35km north of Basra on Route 6. Operating at these distances in front of their own brigade guns meant they often outstripped the reach of 7 RHA's 105s and even the 155s of 3 RHA. If they were to call for a strike on an enemy, it would probably have to come from American fast air. However, the American thrust for Baghdad was in full swing and most air support was now being abstracted to the northern thrust, away from 1 UKDIV. S/Sgt Bertie Banfield, AAC had an experience as an FAC around Ad Dayr that have left him with very mixed emotions even 20 years on:

Around 26 March we patrolled the flat barren lands south of Ad Dayr looking for signs of enemy moving south towards Basra or the Hammar Canal. Staying under 50ft, and wary of air-defence systems, we hugged the terrain and often flew less than 20ft off the ground to avoid detection, hiding behind the sand berms and just popping up to look briefly. The net was buzzing with activity and it was difficult to get on the air to give sitreps [situation reports]. Although the area looks flat, it is actually criss-crossed with raised roads and irrigation ditches, as well as little clumps of palm trees and date groves near rivers and ponds: all of these can conceal enemy armour. Our normal tactic for this sort of operation would be to do 'relief in place'. This is where one unit flies the patrol and waits in the area for their relief aircraft to arrive and relieve them so that continuity is retained in the patrol area. Well on *Telic*, it never happened, we didn't have enough aircraft. We had seen a fair number of destroyed Iraqi tanks and some Fedayeen pick-ups that were knocked out. Nearing the end of this patrol my pilot Sgt Paul Goddard and I spotted movement about 3km away on top of a berm. Using the x10 magnification GOA sight, I tried to identify the enemy but at that range, with the dust and heat haze, it was not really clear. We suspected they were Fedayeen setting up mortars or some form of weapon system. Having waited what seemed like a long time to get on the air, I started calling for fast air. I was told none was available but depending on the target, the guns of 7 RHA might be in range. I called for a fire mission, fire for effect, with two batteries, giving good grids and bearings to the target. I had the guns 'laid and loaded' meaning they were loaded with HE and the barrels were orientated ready to fire. They reported ready but awaited my further command. The time of flight for the rounds would be 20 seconds to impact.

But I just had a gut feeling that something wasn't right with the target. I felt I needed to get closer and satisfy myself before they were vapourised by HE shells. I worked out in my mind that we could fly really low and at full speed across the ground in between my OP and the three pick-ups on the berm, and then get a good view of them. If it were the enemy, my word of command would bring down a rain of shells within 20 seconds, neutralising the threats. I shared my slightly unorthodox plan with Paul, my crew mate, and he said, 'You want to do what?' We jockeyed into a starting position then started our run to the berm 3km away. Paul powered up the Gazelle hitting 160mph as we skimmed the desert at less than 25ft, the helicopter living up to its name of 'whistling chicken leg'. My eyes were glued on the dismounts next to the pick-ups as we got ever closer, then Paul jinked the Gazelle up just by the berm and put the aircraft almost on its side allowing me to have a perfect view out of the left side of the bubble. A dozen tomato farmers were stacking crates next to the road below me. They were 20 seconds from annihilation as Paul levelled off and steered us away. I stood the guns down and cancelled the fire mission. The tactic was something we had never been taught and was a risk that today I am still incredibly proud I took. It kept those dozen people alive.

Two days later, 28 March was both a tumultuous day at the tip of the spear and a very tragic day. D Squadron, HCR was again probing forward in their little Scimitar CVR'1s north of Basra towards Al-Qurnah keeping the Shatt al-Arab to their right. They had passed the settlement of Ad Dayr just over halfway to Al-Qurnah and were expecting to run into more units from the Iraqi 6th Armoured Division.

Welshman Mick Flynn already had vast experience and was a mature senior NCO – a lance corporal of horse – with experience in the Falklands, Bosnia and Northern Ireland. Commanding his Scimitar, callsign W32, his two recce tanks were following Route Dagger while, roughly 3km to his east, closer to the Shatt al-Arab, was 2 Troop, following Route Sword. He came under fire from a mortar team near a small village who were using an elevated berm next to them as an observation post.

His gunner engaged the observers with his laser-accurate 30mm cannon and killed them in what Flynn describes as both an amazing and terrible spectacle to watch. They then switched aim to the crew and saw they also had a BMP-1 armoured carrier with them. They pumped rounds into both using HE and sabot to pierce the BMP armour. They saw their hits strike home and it backed out of view towards the village. W32 called for a fire mission but was told all guns were out of range. He was also told to go no further north for he might cross into a kill box open for friendly fast air. While keeping observation on the village a Gazelle and Lynx from 3 Regt, AAC arrived overhead.

S/Sgt Bertie Banfield, AAC was on his second patrol of the day:

> We were assisting an HCR unit observing an enemy near Ad Dayr. As soon as we got close, we were welcomed by substantial indirect artillery fire and streams of 20mm tracer coming at us from near the village to our north-east. We saw white flags being waved in the village and a T-55 at the same time. Sgt Ross in the Lynx was acquiring this target when he saw more rapid muzzle flashes and the aircraft was rocked by an explosion just above the disc (blades). Debris fell on the Lynx windscreen. We agreed to withdraw to assess the damage.

Itching to get some effects brought down on the enemy at the village, W32 enlisted the help of the ANGLICO team in their Humvee. He pointed out several tanks and a juicy BM-21 *Grad* multiple-barrel rocket launcher. Minutes later a pair of F-16 jets 'came in hot' dropping their powerful ordnance. All the bombs missed by more than 500m. With ammunition expended the F-16s turned away leaving the Scimitar, W32, to now face the hornets' nest that had been kicked in front of him.

Several more T-55s and BMPs now exited the village, fanned out and generally headed towards W32 which was jockeying for hidden positions behind a series of staggered berms. Moving up on his right flank were the other HCR units of 2 Troop: several Scimitars and Spartan APCs armed with Swingfire anti-tank missiles. More fast air had been called for and A-10 tank busters from the Idaho National Guard were inbound to assist with the growing firefight, 6km south of Al-Qurnah.

L/Cpl of Horse Mick Flynn, HCR saw what happened next:

> There was a deep roar of jets from behind us and I saw the unmistakable silhouette of the of the A-10s banking in. Heavily armed with Maverick missiles and bombs, its signature weapon was the 30mm Avenger rotary cannon which fires a storm of depleted uranium shells that can mince armour at 60 rounds per second. It sounds like a giant ripsaw; everyone knows its distinctive roar. I heard it now in bursts of two seconds. I scanned the enemy positions looking for strikes, hits or explosions. Nothing. That was odd. A thought struck home; the pit of my stomach fell away. I looked right and saw the Scimitars of 2 Troop stopped and on fire. At that moment across the net came the desperate shouts 'Check Fire, we are being engaged by the A-10s, Check fire, Check Fire!'[3]

The message of the friendly fire incident quickly reached S/Sgt Banfield in his Gazelle, who even to this day says he admits to carrying a guilty feeing about the incident with the A-10s. The lack of their own resources meant that the helicopters were not able to be relieved in place and provide the cover and control of the fast air that they would have liked. Of course, the A-10 pilots from Idaho National Guard and the rather loose American rules of engagement have far more to do with it than any British failings. Before the 'check fire' was registered in the cockpits of the A-10s, they swept back and rolled in for another strafing gun run. The utter chaos on the ground kick-started a full-scale rescue operation. Locally, the nearby members of the HCR formed a protective screen around the two stricken Scimitars while the injured crew were helped from the wreckage. The thin aluminium armour was clearly no match for the tank busting 30mm shells.

A casualty evacuation plan was formulated and two RAF Pumas, with combat medics aboard, were scrambled from Shaiba. To provide a screen for the Pumas when they landed, S/Sgt Banfield led two armed Lynx helicopters back to the scene. He co-ordinated their efforts, ensuring the Lynx were well positioned to guard the vulnerable Pumas as they touched down near the burning Scimitars. Just a few kilometres to the east, callsign W32 was still engaging yet more enemy armour that was coming through the maze of berms towards the smoke of the Scimitars, like moths to a flame. The Iraqi armoured crews must have sensed victory amongst the chaos ahead of them and closed in for the kill. Mick Flynn and his crew damaged a T-55 when their Rarden cannon shells hit the turret ring on the lead tank, meaning it could not turn its turret, they also set alight a BMP-1 APC. S/Sgt Banfield ordered one of his Lynx closest to the HCR callsign to assist. The first TOW missile missed but the second was true and smashed into the flank armour of the 40-year-old tank. Bright orange flames were seen within seconds of impact as the intense heat began to cook off fuel and ammunition. The following explosion lifted the turret clean off with a column of yellow orange fire. As the turret came to earth, the chassis blazed furiously and that, perhaps, was the final blow to the morale of the Iraqi armoured troops not yet hit, as they halted and began to retreat.

It had been a most significant day in the history of the Army Air Corps. Eight armed patrols had been flown, CAS and artillery fire had been called and 16 TOW missiles fired resulting in two T-55s and one BMP-1 destroyed. There had been a good degree of courage and skilful airmanship displayed by the Lynx and Gazelle crews, which – especially when combined with formation recce on the ground – had proven the effectiveness of the corps. For his courage, leadership, skill and determination S/Sgt Banfield was awarded the Distinguished Flying Cross which he received from HM Queen in 2004 at Buckingham Palace. Mick Flynn was also recognised for his gallantry with the award of the Conspicuous Gallantry Cross.

The Pumas lifted off from the scene of the destroyed Scimitars with five wounded on board, but L/Cpl of Horse Matty Hull could not be saved and had died inside his vehicle. Eighteen-year-old Trooper Chris Finney had been burned re-entering the blazing Scimitars trying to rescue his colleagues and was awarded the George Cross, the highest award for gallantry when not in contact with the enemy. There were several boards of inquiry into the tragedy, followed in 2007 by a coroner's inquest. Much media attention was attracted, and scrutiny laid upon the incident. Coroner Andrew Walker declared the killing of Hull as unlawful and that the aerial attack on the Scimitars amounted to an assault and was therefore a criminal act. A host of errors were identified in the American attack, including not asking for the grid references of likely friendly forces, attacking without permission from the FAC and disregarding the friendly orange panels clearly displayed on the tank roofs, even though the pilots acknowledged their existence.

The identity of one of the A-10 pilots was revealed by the media, but neither man attended court nor did any representatives from the US government, and they were not held accountable.

Keeping the army squadrons airborne, maintained, fuelled, armed, briefed and with the correct radio channels loaded was the job of the AAC Regimental HQ and its attached REME teams. The high state of readiness, constant demand for aviation support and the fatigue of the desert environment took its toll on both pilots and machines alike, and often the squadrons found themselves with only 50% of their aircraft available to fly. In the HQ, which was set up with tents in the shape of a cross, was the group of AAC officers, NCOs and troopers responsible for both planning and operational matters. The cruciform HQ is found in most British units and goes back at least as far as World War 1. The centre of the shape was the main 18ft by 24ft meeting space known as the 'bird table'. Off this, backed up against the central tent, were smaller 9ft by 9ft tents and Land Rovers containing Intelligence Corps, artillery, engineers, signals, admin clerks and REME. Access was through a controlled point with a defence section protecting the set up. Working at this HQ was Maj Mike Peters, AAC:

> I would usually be one of the first up in the morning, and often last to bed writing something up on a computer and saving it to the 'A drive' floppy disk. I was lucky to have my own tent with light and power, and I made sure I was up for the shipping forecast when I was shaving, at least I did when in Europe. I would then update myself on any overnight incidents and get up to speed on any last-minute changes from the night before. I also checked in on my re-bro teams to make sure they were all OK before the day's operations started. I would then flit between the Future Ops tent and the Current Ops tent for the rest of the day. My very reliable Troop Sergeant Dunk always looked after me with a proper breakfast before it was too hot and there were fewer flies about, and one of his lads would also bring me something for lunch. I quite enjoyed looking after myself in the evening and usually managed to have a few minutes alone and have a small ration meal or something. When we went static at Basra Airport the echelon quartermasters caught up with us and they started cooking meals for us again.

CHAPTER 7

The Cauldron

28 March: Shaiba Airfield – Called to O-group at 7 Brigade HQ. This whole area is fucked but the locals are coping well enough, they all wave and the poor farmers scratch a survival from the soil. I requested that we go forward and take a look at the ground in Az Zubayr with some of the Black Watch. The Black Watch CO, Mike Riddell-Webster, agreed to the proposal to test the local conditions and we went in three Warriors.

When we arrived in Az Zubayr just south of Basra, I saw a British dismounted infantry company in a compound handing out water and food to hungry and thirsty villagers. Just across the next street was another platoon on foot patrol sweeping for hidden enemy and snipers. Then, just a few hundred yards away around the next block a full-on urban warfare battle was going on with AFVs and RPGs flying across the street. It really was just as predicted in Krulak's three-block war. This was a taste of things to come, and it was certainly talked of that Basra could degenerate into a new Stalingrad, which we had to avoid.

On our way back we ran into trouble. Starting to exit the built-up area we noticed ahead on the road the tell-tale warning sign of rocks piled up in a line rather trying to block us off. I was sat in the turret, in the gunner's seat so had control of the aiming and firing mechanisms for the 30mm Rarden cannon and the coaxial 7.62mm chain gun. Suddenly, there was a loud dull boom on our right side. We had been hit by an RPG-7. It failed to penetrate and had no real effect on the vehicle. Warrior is an extremely robust bit of kit. We had one hit by a 120mm HESH round fired by a Challenger on *Granby* in a blue-on-blue scenario. The explosive armour defeated the incoming round but a soldier outside was severely injured by the blast.

I looked through the vision block to the front and suddenly saw a very calm-looking Iraqi with an RPG-7 launcher walk into the middle of the street. I adjusted my eyes onto the gunner's sight and started to line up the crosshairs on the man. He raised the rocket launcher and aimed straight at me. I was on target too but needed to activate the chain gun first before it would fire. I could not remember how to do it, I had to take my eyes away from the sight and look at the controls. In that instant he fired first. At no more than 50m the impact was almost instantaneous. A boom, and a shower of sparks followed, but again no penetration. By the time I got the firing mechanism set the man had walked away as calmly as he had arrived. Looking back, I think that perhaps it was good that the chain gun didn't fire as there were several civilians further down the road and I may have hit them.

When we got back to Shaiba the men ribbed me relentlessly about not firing the gun, which was OK and it was lesson learned – do not sit in the gunner's seat if you are not a gunner.

COL JIM TANNER, HQ 1 UKDIV

In the 1990s, Commandant of the USMC Gen Charles C. Krulak advanced the idea of what he called a 'three-block war' to explain battlefield realities in an era of failed and failing nation-states. Not only was the Marine Corps operating in complex environments and executing a range of missions – including humanitarian aid and peacekeeping, alongside mid-intensity conflict – it was also operating in an atmosphere of pervasive media coverage. With the rise of the internet and cheap video equipment, the actions – or mis-actions – of Marines could spread quickly around the world. Krulak perceived the need to invest heavily in the human dimension of warfare. This was done to ensure that even the lowest-level marine leaders were fully developed and prepared to operate effectively to contribute to the achievement of strategic objectives in this environment of ever-increasing scrutiny.

It was just this sort of environment that British troops would find themselves in Az Zubayr and Basra. EOD expert Sgt Rey Fadil, RE had to deal with instances of civilians and unexploded ordnance:

> There were 11 of us in a group of engineer augmentees ready to go into Iraq on 28 March as reinforcements for the leading parties. I was to go to 33 Regiment, an EOD specialist unit. We had two vehicles, a Land Rover, and a DAF truck. The truck had a fuel pump problem and kept cutting out. I was in the back of the DAF as we got to the border near Safwan, where we rendezvoused with our guide, a Spartan CVRT. The crew shouted out that we were moving off straight away and that it was 'a bit lively down the road'.
>
> The situation was laughable. We were crossing into a war zone in a soft-skinned truck, that kept stopping with mechanical issues, and we had less than 20 rounds of ammunition each.
>
> We took over Basra Airport and had to check it for dangerous discarded munitions. The departing Iraqis had totally trashed the place. Just about every window and door was broken and furniture removed. In the control tower the radio consoles were smashed and there was human excrement and urine everywhere.
>
> I worked in a small team of four men. We had two Land Rovers with trailers. There was a BDO in charge, a number two (me) and then a number three and four who were familiar with all the kit and procedures as the support element. On top of our own personal kit, we carried all the necessary equipment for bomb disposal: explosives, detonators, an initiator device, sandbags, tools, marking tape and a .50-calibre rifle.
>
> Our first task was to assist another callsign with a guy called Andy Abbott who I knew from Rochester. An area on a farm had been chosen to be a forming-up point but intelligence suggested that there was discarded Iraqi artillery ammunition there and that several cluster bomblets had been seen. These posed a serious threat. The CBU-99 and -100 Rockeye II cluster bombs, with their 247 bomblet submunitions with either anti-tank or anti-personnel capabilities, were dropped by the US Air Force as an area-denial weapon. The submunitions could also be fitted with anti-handling devices meaning they were unstable.
>
> We found the low farm buildings which formed a sort of open square with trees and dried out irrigation ditches opposite. In between was a field of tomato plants. As we set up the incident control point, we saw movement in the tomato field. There was an old farmer wearing flip-flops. He was bending down, picking up and then piling the Rockeye bomblets neatly at the side of the field!
>
> We persuaded the farmer that it was probably bad for his health to carry on moving the munitions and he left it to us to clear the field. The BDO (Tony Wyles) and I then took our marker flags and searched the field, marking each bomblet as we went. Once marked you can see the footprint of the area to work in and we planned on the safest destruction method. For this task we blew them up in situ. Each bomblet gets given some moulded PE4 plastic explosive, about the size of a tennis ball next to it. All the PE4 is then connected by detonator cord in what

we called a Christmas tree. The cord is then connected to the electrical firing device. Having done all this we blew them up and sadly, most of his tomatoes as well.

On another day we were diverted from one task to an urgent call from a Royal Artillery unit near Basra. Some local kids had been mucking about on an old Iraqi MRLS rocket launcher and there had been an explosion. The MLRS system contained submunitions like Rockeyes and apparently one of the kids had tried to take it apart. Three or four children were killed instantly, and their bodies were picked up by the locals, until the danger of more of the unexploded munitions was realised. When we arrived the artillery guys put a cordon in to keep the locals back while we set up the Control point. Tony went in and picked up the three other dead children, one by one, and brought them all out. The families loaded the bodies onto a horse-drawn cart. It was very emotional and there was a lot of tears. Tony spoke Arabic and spoke to one man who was extremely distraught. The man explained that one of the dead girls was his and that the previous month his wife had also been killed in an airstrike. Tony was awarded the Queen's Gallantry Medal for his work that day. His assistant, Tomo, got a unit commendation.

2 RTR BG pushed north 30km using Highway 8 until it reached the outskirts of Az Zubay. Lt Ian Cross was in a Challenger 2 MBT:

> I was the lead vehicle when we came onto a roundabout on the edge of the town. I was looking for a little track off to the east but couldn't see it, so we started to go round again when, of course, the rest of the column started coming onto the roundabout too. One officer shouted over, and I just replied, 'just checking!'
>
> After the raids into Az Zubayr and several VCPs on the ring roads, on 27 March we finally attacked one corner of Az Zubayr that we knew was full of militia. My three tanks lined up abreast to provide covering fire for the platoon of 1 Light Infantry who had dismounted, but a couple of their Warriors also gave extra weight of fire from the flank. Alongside me were a couple of Scimitars from Recce Squadron also firing their 30mm cannon. The LI had two hundred yards of scrub and open ground to cross but with so much heavy firepower hitting the enemy buildings they all arrived on the objective safely. Just as per training in Canada and Germany, as our infantry approached from the left of our view, we switched fire slightly to the right so as soon as the infantry started getting close to the building we were aiming at, we moved to the next. We started with coax machine guns and a few rounds of smoke, then we switched to HESH and put bags of HESH on target, absolutely loads of it. The buildings were crumbling down, and many were largely destroyed as the infantry arrived. It must have been incredibly noisy for the infantry with our rounds crashing in so close to them.

The 70-ton Challenger 2 was originally designed for the export market but found its way into the British Army in the 1980s. It fired two main types of anti-tank ammunition: APFSDS and HESH. APFSDS – armour-piercing fin-stabilised discarding sabot – nicknamed 'Fin' combines a collar, the sabot, that surrounds a Tungsten long-rod penetrator. The sabot falls away after the round leaves the barrel and the Tungsten dart is propelled at an incredible 2,000m/sec with such kinetic energy that it simply pierces steel like a hot needle through butter, smashing into the interior of the target taking with it white molten hot blobs of metal that split, smash and ignite anything combustible. Flesh and bone stand no chance. Tanks or armoured fighting vehicles that are loaded with fuel and high explosive shells can easily be set alight by this devastating impact and it will often lead to explosions as the ammo 'cooks off' with the resultant explosions sometimes lifting the turret, weighing several tons, clean away from the chassis.

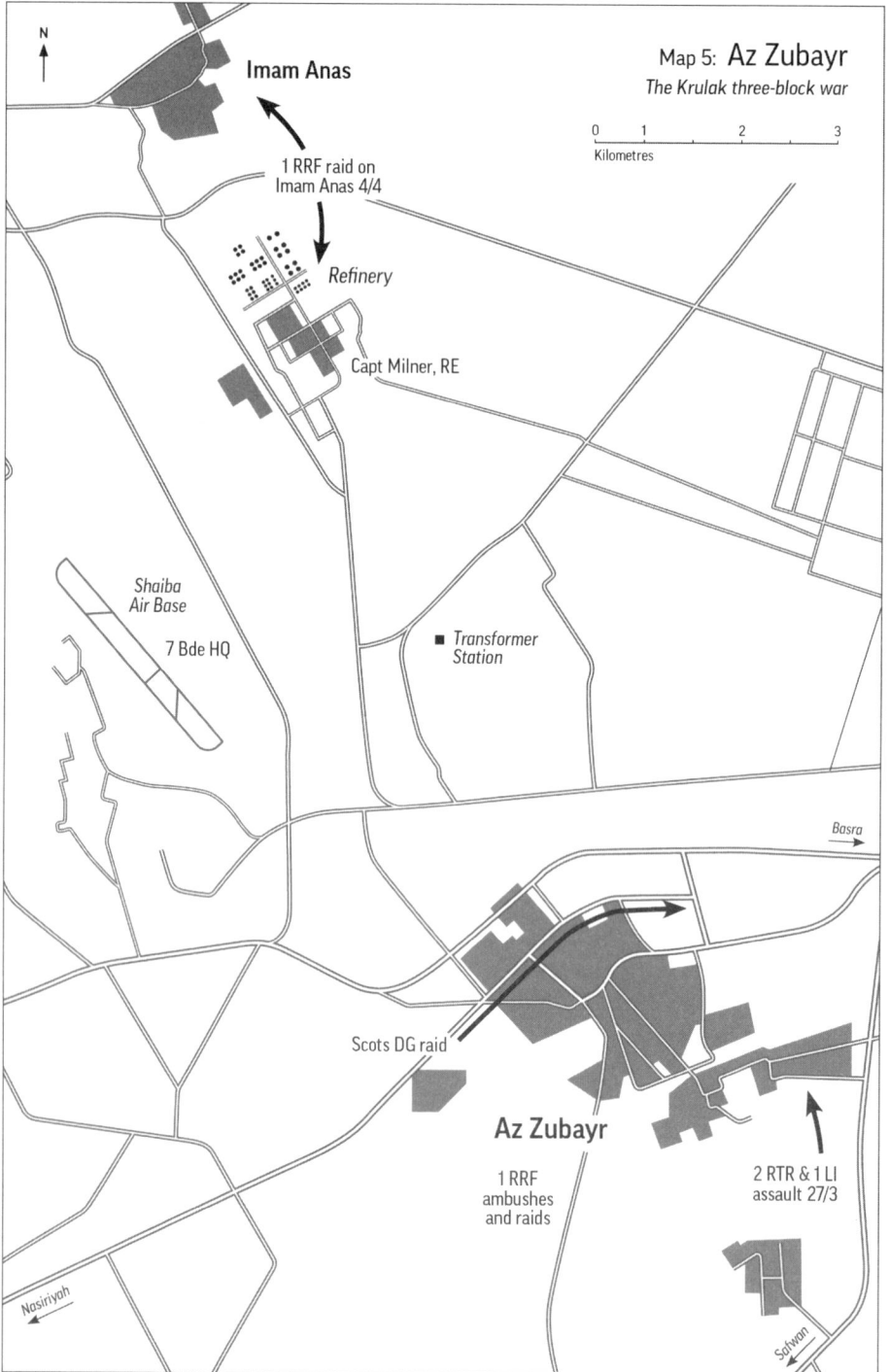

N

Imam Anas

Map 5: Az Zubayr
The Krulak three-block war

0   1   2   3
Kilometres

1 RRF raid on
Imam Anas 4/4

Refinery

Capt Milner, RE

*Shaiba
Air Base*

7 Bde HQ

■ *Transformer
Station*

Basra

Scots DG raid

Az Zubayr

1 RRF
ambushes
and raids

2 RTR & 1 LI
assault 27/3

Nasiriyah

Safwan

HESH – high explosive squash head – has a load of HE behind a thin metal cap. On impact the HE flattens out like a cow pat and explodes in an instant. This may not lead to penetration but the enormous explosive shockwave travels through the armour and causes 'spall' – fragments and splinters peel off the interior and fly off inside. Whilst Fin is the first choice of a gunner to take on an enemy tank, HESH may be best used against slightly softer targets such as IFVs like the Soviet-made BMP or BTR 80. HESH is also a great bunker buster or for use on buildings.

The Challenger 2 is operated by a crew of four who have to work together smoothly and efficiently to get the best out of the machine. It is also vital that the four men can tolerate each other in the stifling confines of the interior. Men fought, ate and slept inside the tank for many days at a time, leaving no room for privacy or niceties. Without really thinking, the men inside the Challengers were working as close-knit teams that utterly rely on each other in life-or-death situations. Without their months of training, the crew of Three Zero would not have been able to endure the tempo of operations in Iraq. The combination of modern equipment and the highly trained slick machine of the RTR really came to the fore on these operations. Lt Ian Cross again:

> The set-up of the commander's and gunner's sights in CR2 meant we could operate as a hunter-killer team, which sounds dramatic but simply means that the commander can hunt for his next target through his own vision devices and when he settles on a target – for instance an enemy tank – he operates a switch which lases the target and starts locking the gun onto it by swinging the turret around. I would also shout the designation for the appropriate ammunition for the task, so for a tank I would shout 'FIN, TANK!' Below me, 'Verge' was loading the big fin round. As soon as he was ready, he pulled this manual guard across the side of the breach to illustrate he was ready to fire safely, and shout 'LOADED'. At this point 'Vinnie' would lase it again to double-check the range, shout 'ON' then 'FIRING' and I would just check that it was on the right target and say, 'GO ON'. Vinnie by then would have used his index finger on the safety flap that covers the trigger guard on his handset controllers, then pressed and fired, I was already scanning for another target. It was taking just a few seconds per round. The proficiency we achieved was better than a Soviet autoloader in a T-72.
>
> In Az Zubayr we were firing mainly at the buildings which often needed more than one hit so we would be shouting. 'HESH, BUILDING', 'LOADED', 'ON', 'FIRING' ... 'GO ON'. The team would load another until I said stop and then we moved the barrel to the right for the next building and repeated it.
>
> When we went for replen [resupply] after the Az Zubayr battle, we were on the edge of town getting bombed up again when someone shouted that militia had been stealing a pick-up truck from a hospital compound literally across the street.
>
> We drove straight out into the middle of the street, and the little truck quickly lurched out in front of us with the militia inside. I lased the truck, shouted, 'COAX, TRANSPORT, GO ON' and Vinnie brassed it up with the machine gun. We could not use the main gun for fear that we would have blown half the hospital frontage off.

As the Black Watch took over the bridge sector, 1 RRF was used to start sweeping up trouble-makers in the rear areas between Az Zubayr and Basra where growing resistance had proven troublesome to convoys and isolated units. It was clear that the enemy was now virtually unseen and so various imaginative patrols, raids and ambushes were sprung by the Fusiliers in order to unsettle and destabilise the Fedayeen leaders. Armoured raids targeted Ba'ath Party buildings and used a Warrior to knock down a concrete mural of Saddam. Snipers from the RRF Support Group inserted covertly into areas to watch for signs of the militia. One such mission identified a series of houses in the village of Imam Anas, 8km north of Az Zubayr, that possibly housed militia and party officials. Operation *Selous* was planned for first light of 4 April with Lt Olly Campbell's 7 Platoon striking targets in the village, while 9 Platoon under Lt Tom Kibble raided the large refinery that employed half the village just nearby. Using cover of night and a stealthy approach march on foot, with commanders using NVGs, the Fusiliers lay in the dew-covered sand of pre-dawn and awaited the signal to strike. Lt Tom Kibble remembers:

> With 10 minutes to go before H-Hour I launched my sections forward the final 300m. We had held off at the final lay up because there were so many dogs in and around the houses, they would have put up an alarm. Bang on H-Hour we went in. Each team had a sledgehammer, so all the doors went in easy and with the shock and surprise all the occupants were subdued. One guy put up some resistance, but he was quickly dealt with. 43 arrests were made, two RPGs, two AK-47s and two Lee-Enfield .303s plus stacks of ammo were seized.

Soldiers' views and recollections of events in wartime have been and always will be different to that of officers. L/Sgt Bob Giles provides a somewhat different view of the night-time raid on Imam Anas by 1 IG:

> In the race between me and Saddam to draw first blood, I lost. Around the start of April whilst directing traffic in the pitch black, we were attacked by what was apparently a lone individual armed with an RPG.
>
> I say directing traffic, although the traffic was in fact the Fusilier battlegroup. Our task was to sit on a junction and provide security and also to act as a traffic control point. Harry manned the turret and radios in the wagon with Eddie, with three of the lads from the section in the back. They were acting as a sort of quick reaction force should the remaining three, which consisted of me, Chris and Lee, get into any bother. Us three were patrolling about, up to about 50m from the wagon, directing vehicles from the battlegroup in the right direction as they formed up for a dawn attack on a village full of people wanting to be attacked.
>
> At first, all was very quiet, and Lee asked me, 'Where's this battlegroup then?' We could hear it, jockeying around in the dark, which should be no surprise as a battlegroup consists of about 2,000 men in 250 or so vehicles. Just as I was about to suggest we were in the wrong place the engineer assets in the form of about half a dozen JCB diggers rocked up. JCB diggers in themselves were nothing unusual, as a battlegroup is totally self-sufficient and consists of all wondrously varied vehicles and characters. What was odd is that they should be at the front with no Warrior or tank protection, but these things happen in the confusion of a night move as I had learnt from my days in the Recce where, as lead element and route markers for such moves, you were happy if anyone turned up at all!
>
> Eventually the odd Warrior turned up and a plethora of wheeled vehicle and lorries soon meant we had a full-scale traffic jam on our hands. The three of us makeshift traffic wardens were doing our best to contain the chaos when one Bedford truck decided to do its own thing, pull out into the road and jam everything up. As I approached one of JCBs to ask it to pull

backwards to allow the twat in the Bedford to make good his vehicles escape, there was a flash and an almost instantaneous ear-piercing explosion. Chris and Lee, out of sight to me due to the darkness, went to ground immediately, whereas I swivelled 180 degrees and legged it.

Not that I got very far though, as I hadn't taken into account a huge hole in the ground which was also masked by the darkness. It later turned out to be an old Iraqi trench system, or maybe a cunning 'trip' system, in which case it had done its job. Falling totally prostrate on the other side was painful enough, but what actually took me out of the picture was that during 'air time' my respirator haversack had swung round and placed itself between my stomach and the ground, thus on impact with the aforementioned surface, I had the wind completely knocked out of me so badly that I was unable to even make a groaning noise to alert people of my discomfort.

In the dark, all alone, I heard Harry come on the radio, and ask what the fuck was going on. At which point I heard Chris scream 'Bob's down! Bob's down! I remember thinking I'd better get my breath back soon in order to get on the radio and prevent a full-scale panic. However, my lungs had a different take on it all and refused to operate for at least what seemed another lifetime. Chris and Lee scrambled back to the sanctuary of the wagon and got inside, at which point someone, and for some reason I think it was Marshy, was asking 'Where are you Bob? Bob? Bob, where are you?' Eventually I managed a strained 'I'merrllrighterr.'

On my return to the wagon, the ridicule and laughter – and the fact my hands, fingers and knees were pissing blood – were compensated by the fact Marshy handed me one of his medal-winning brews.

On finishing Marshy's brew, the three of us ventured out again and quizzed the JCB driver over the event. Sure enough, he'd been sitting in the cab of the digger when a non-uniformed Arab stuck his head out of the bushes and fired an RPG round from about six feet away, hitting the bucket. If it hadn't been for the bucket, the would-be sniper would have unintentionally hit me, Chris or Lee before making good his escape. What a good start to the campaign that would have been! In short, Saddam deserves to be congratulated for scoring first in our personal duel.

Lt Zoe Ferry followed the leading columns over into Iraq about 9 or 10 hours after the invasion started:

The first stop we made was near Az Zubayr. We slept by our vehicles in a disused industrial complex, and I remember waking up with a rat on my chest. The other conundrum was going for a poo in privacy. The engineers had dug 'long drops' with a wooden plank to sit on and little privacy boards in between. I waited for ages until it was quiet then as soon as I sat down some guy appeared next to me. Even with the privacy screen we could see each other's heads. There was another time I just needed a wee so went behind the Land Rover. There I was mid-business, and a cheer went up. A bunch of guys had climbed on the roof of a truck to see me peeing, I was so embarrassed I stood up and wee went all over my trousers which I could not get changed for two days. To top all that off I started receiving unwarranted creepy love letters in the squadron. I would come back from a shower and find handwritten letters pushed in my bedspace. I found it unnerving and distracting. The blokes thought it was funny, but I certainly didn't. Later things improved when the Mobile Shower and Laundry unit turned up: that was bliss. All my kit got a wash and we had some female-only time in the showers without blokes gawping.

As the invasion started, I controlled the Ambulance matrix, rather like a 999 Ambulance service control room does, despatching ambulances where they were needed most. Fortunately, British casualties were very few and most of our evacuees were wounded Iraqis, either soldiers or civilians. We took most back to 202 Field Hospital. If I wasn't too busy, I would go in and see the staff at work or visit my sister on the ward. While I was there early in the campaign,

> I did see one dead British soldier who was very waxy coloured and had a large hole in his chest. I remember hearing he had kids and thought how terrible it would be for them.

The same day as Zoe crossed the border with the invasion forces the *Reading Chronicle* ran a story on the twins both being at the front. A few days later *The Mail on Sunday* ran a two-page spread with the headline, 'I saw Cherie weep for her son going to university. I've given my lovely twins to a war I can't believe in.' The article was in reference to an interview Zoe and Gayle's mum Christine had given reporter Fiona Wingett from the *Mail*. Like many other anxious mothers at the time, she was waiting for news from her children posted to the front, yet she was the only mother with twin identical girls there. Christine did not believe in the cause of the war and told her girls that before they went but still understood they were doing their jobs and supporting each other. What made it all the more bitter was the story Christine had seen previously of Cheri Blair crying when her son went a few miles away to university, while other people's children were now fighting a war. The article concluded quoting Christine Ferry 'Saddam Hussein is no doubt very evil, but I believe there were still alternatives to war. To put all our young people's lives at risk, you hope Tony Blair knows something we don't – and if that's not the case, God help us all.'[1] Maj Ben Farrell of 1 IG was in the thick of it all:

> It was not only my birthday, but it was also my first wedding anniversary on 23 March and I remember thinking what an impact this has on people who are left at home. My poor wife was at home and my little girl Tilly who is now 20, had just been born three months before, and there I was trundling around in a Warrior outside Basra.

1 IG had moved as an armoured battalion following 1 RRF between Az Zubayr and western Basra, then spring-boarded further across a series of bridges onto a piece of ground that sits alongside Route 6 national highway to the north of Basra. The route was a single track through swamps and thick mud. By positioning themselves on the barely perceptibly 'higher ground' they cut Route 6 and effectively screened the city from any Iraqi troops trying to move south into Basra. They were most certainly putting themselves in harm's way, as intelligence suggested the Republican Guard was heading towards them. Along the route the recce elements came under small arms and even mortar fire, but it soon melted away after return fire or when heavy weapons were brought forward. The final objective sat around 8km north of the Qarmat Ali waterway where it splits from the Shatt al-Arab. Maj Farrell continues:

> Once we got into that area, we had a bit of a scrap. The open scrubland was about a kilometre wide so we, 2 Company, opened into formation facing north as 1 Company guarded the rear. To the east, fire was coming in from a troublesome bunker position, so I pushed 4 Platoon out to engage the bunkers. 2Lt Orde-Powlett dismounted his platoon with Sgt Perry. Two bunkers and trenches were now identified and engaged with as much firepower as they could lay down. Guardsman Ward and L/Cpl Williams fired 94mm LAW rockets at each bunker whilst the Warriors pumped 30mm cannon shells in. Two sections then assaulted forwards, led by 2Lt

[Tom] Orde-Powlett, while the remaining section and the Warriors continued covering fire. Both positions were cleared, and the platoon began to reorganise and re-mount their vehicles when four unseen Iraqis launched a brave but futile counter-attack with RPGs and AKs. They were cut down by our machine guns. I received a cool sitrep over the radio from one of the guys, Paul Fagan, who said, 'The position has been engaged, they (enemy) will be taking no further part in tonight's activities.' His tone was very calm and professional, and it set the pitch for the rest of our campaign. That action was our first together and it set the bar for how we would proceed going forward. I was so impressed with Tom's performance that day I wrote him up for a Military Cross.

Lt Thomas Orde-Powlett, heir to the Bolton estate near Leyburn in the Yorkshire Dales, was awarded the Military Cross for his actions, courage and leadership that day. He now runs Bolton Castle in Wensleydale with his father Harry, the eighth Baron Bolton.

After their first 'scrap' the Irish Guards had a brief and rare view of Basra from some high ground and Maj Farrell describes being able to 'look down into Basra.' Within 24 hours the Micks were back on the flats at Basra International Airport and the 'high ground' was left unoccupied. It's difficult to tell whether this was because the planners failed to realise it could actually be key terrain or simply because there was insufficient infantry and too much ground to hold.

If there was too little infantry, the same could also be said of the number of tanks. Challenger 2s were very much part of the combined-arms operation now well underway around Basra and Az Zubayr.

Zero Bravo, the callsign of the tank belonging to A Squadron commander, Maj Tim Brown, RSDG, crept forward in the pre-dawn light. They were moving into Az Zubayr to attack the Police station – intelligence said it was a hideout for some of the Fedayeen leaders. Creeping along next to Zero Bravo was Zero Charlie with the squadron 2IC Charlie MacDermot-Roe in command. The idea that two such tanks can 'creep up' on an inner-city target is absurd but that is how it felt to Tim Brown:

It was just before first light, and we were completely closed down [all hatches closed] so there is virtually no noise coming in from outside, just the reassuring hum of the engine. It gives the false impression that you are moving much more quietly than of course you are! The streets were completely empty, and we were now only about 75m from the objective. We lased the building and reported our position to get the green light to fire when this old man walked out into the road junction just in front of me. This old chap looked like he hadn't a care in the world, he looked straight at us in our main battle tank as if we were a milk float or newspaper van on our delivery rounds. I told the gunner to hold fire and we waited until he was out of our view. I then said to my gunner, Vince, 'Fire'.

Cpl Vince Mcleod takes up the story:

This was the first time we had fired at a building with the main armament, so we loaded HESH and fired. The shell struck in the blink of an eye. The impact was impressive, but it was the shockwave that was even more so. Every piece of litter, bins, grit and dust was scooped up and swirled around in a tornado and we couldn't see a thing. I shouted, 'Christ what happened/ Have we hit an ammo dump?' the HESH round had clearly passed through the front room of the building and the interior wall before exiting the rear. Another Challenger fired as the dust began to settle and the double impact was cataclysmic. The huge swirling dust storm of debris eventually subsided and where once had been a concrete-fronted building there was only grey sky. The clearer picture revealed smouldering debris and several khaki-clad soldiers dazed and dusty.[2]

The typical load of ammunition in a Challenger 2 tank for *Telic* was 29 Fin rounds, 18 HESH, 3 smoke rounds, 20 smoke grenades, 6 regular hand grenades, 22 boxes of 7.62mm ammunition totalling 4,400 rounds for the coaxial chain gun and the roof-mounted GPMG. The crew, in addition, were also issued two shortened SA80 assault rifles with 100 rounds of 5.56mm ammo for the loader and driver who were the only ones with room to store them. Most commanders and gunners also had a Browning 9mm pistol but the history of dismounted armoured crew relying on such hand-held weapons would suggest that if things had got that bad, it was probably over anyway!

Sgt Will Montgomery, RSDG was manning a vehicle check point (VCP):

> I was rubbing my face to try and stay awake, this being the third night without any proper sleep. We had been manning an overwatch position on a VCP outside Az Zubayr for 10 hours on 24 March. Suddenly, the radio in my headset crackled into life. Just the urgency of the voice and the background gunfire was enough to tell me someone was in a ferocious firefight. I listened with a mixture of horror and exhilaration. This town is turning into a fucking nightmare.
>
> My squadron commander, Maj Brown then called me, callsign 31, and informed me of a mission we were needed for. A soldier was missing. L/Cpl Barry Stephen from 1st Battalion, Black Watch Mortar Platoon had gone missing from his FV432 armoured vehicle during an engagement on the edge of town. I was the closest callsign and we were required to make up and lead a four-vehicle search and rescue party for 'Baz' Stephen.
>
> The three other vehicles were Warriors of the Black Watch led by Lt Col Riddell-Webster.
>
> I was told my callsign would lead the other vehicles toward a grid reference in Az Zubayr a mile away, where it was possible L/Cpl Stephen could be. My heart sank, and I was virtually shitting myself, but as soon as I thought of the Black Watch soldier, lying injured or crawling in the street, or captured or dead a sense of purpose took over.
>
> Two facts really struck me: one was I had never been into the town, so I was having to navigate at night through a maze of narrow streets using my hand-held GPS; second, I was the only tank.
>
> We had not seen a single human and were deep inside the town when the electrical system failed inside 31 and I shouted, 'Shit, shit, shit!' My gunner, 18-year-old 'Daz' joined in with expletives on the intercom. I shut down the GUE. [The GUE is a secondary auxiliary engine that powers the turret and other electricals.] It had been playing up for days. Without switching back to main power and resetting, we could not traverse the turret or use our night vision equipment. It only took 30 seconds but it felt like hours! With it all back on we continued to the grid which was like an open market square or car park in the town. Shops and houses stood on the edges and in one corner a mosque. I felt it was like a bad trip, hallucinating at the green and white screen on my optics. Daz called 'spooky or what?' As he said that, I switched my magnification to 'high' after I thought I had seen movement in the corner 250m away. Then I saw them clearly. A group of about 15 enemy armed with AK-47s and RPGs stealthily setting

up in doorways and alleyways facing us. I think they thought we hadn't seen them. I called for permission to engage and lased the target for range. My training kicked in and all the years of training and drills on Sennelager paid off. I handed off for Daz to take over and fire. 'It's not firing,' he called. I shouted, 'Of course it bloody will, let me take over.' I squeezed the trigger for the coax 7.62mm machine gun and a stream of rounds poured at the group with dozens of tracers marking their flight. One guy crumpled in a heap and the others jumped for cover. By now the infantry from the Warriors behind had deployed and begun searching for Barry Stephen. The occasional shot and fleeting figure crossed our sights but in order to avoid a blue on blue we were ultra-careful. After some time, a voice came over the radio, 'This is Zero Alpha, we have found the body of L/Cpl Stephen, we are extracting.' Then as if a light switched on, the square lit up with tracer as the enemy opened up on us with everything they had. Tracer and RPGs clanged against the metal of our vehicles and showered sparks on the tarmac. All our gunners returned fire with deadly accuracy. The Warriors' 30mm Rarden cannon thumping three-round bursts into balconies and doorways, and 7.62mm chain guns sprayed enemy in alleyways and open spaces. We covered the Warriors who got away first and we reversed back to cover the withdrawal. Never turn around while in contact is a golden rule of armoured warfare so I had to guide the driver backwards giving instructions, 'Left stick, right a bit' and so on. Two dull thuds rang on the tank armour in quick succession, 'You're getting hit by RPGs,' came over the net. I prayed that the rocket-propelled grenades would not damage the delicate night vision systems or comms kit. With more distance now between us and the enemy grenadiers we swung round and faced the right way. 'Get us the hell out of here,' I said.[3]

L/Cpl Stephen had been acting as top cover on his FV432 covering his mates when he was hit by an RPG round in the chest that threw him off the back of the vehicle. He was dead, but he was back with his mates. Prior to *Telic*, Barry was with the regimental recruiting team in Perth, Scotland and had volunteered to rejoin his beloved battalion rather than miss the action.

As 7 Armoured Brigade began its advance early on 21 March with 1 RRF leading, 2 RTR was in reserve and moved up to FAA Barnsley ready to follow on. Brig Graham Binns had insisted that each of his brigade elements would provide 'agility and responsiveness'. Hence Lt Col Hankinson stood ready to take his 64-vehicle armoured convoy forward at a moment's notice:

> At a critical point in the set-piece border clearance a significant Iraqi armoured threat began developing on the flank. Joy of joy, the brigadier ordered 2 RTR BG to move immediately up the main highway (Route Topeka), avoiding the congested UK crossing. I had the extraordinary experience as a tank commanding officer of leaping into my MBT and declaring on the BG radio net, 'Move now, follow me, orders on the move,' in the utter confidence that my 1,000 soldiers, 32 Challengers and 32 Warriors would respond as requested.

Of course, the 64 vehicles of 2 RTR and 1 LI responded accordingly and advanced up the main highway towards Basra arriving south-west of Az Zubayr by nightfall.

Az Zubayr was known to contain Iraqi Regular Army and militia troops and, it was predicted, a hostile population – a prediction that was a partial truth. To avoid high civilian casualties and much collateral damage, a full-frontal immediate attack was avoided. Instead, a series of roadblocks was established to deny enemy movement.

Shortly after dawn on 23 March, VCPs established outside Az Zubayr manned by 8 Troop, Cyclops Squadron reported hostile crowds approaching. 33-year-old Sgt Steve Roberts, known to everyone as 'TC' was dismounted at the checkpoint. A proud Cornishman, Roberts had been in the army for 16 years and was a well-respected tank commander. Roberts tried to placate the hostile crowd, but it began to throw stones and when one individual threatened the sergeant directly, he drew his pistol but had a stoppage. Fearing for the life of his commander, Tpr Gary Thornton aboard the Challenger on overwatch swung the coaxial chain gun into action. Thornton fired a burst of 7.62mm rounds at the Iraqi, but at such close range it also fatally hit 'TC'. Unfortunately, Roberts had been one of the crews to surrender his body armour and was not offered any protection. The whole regiment felt the loss as did of course his mourning widow, Samantha.

At his inquest, Coroner Mr Andrew Walker was scathing of the army and Ministry of Defence. 'Sgt Roberts was killed by friendly fire because of the army's unforgiveable and inexcusable failure to equip him with body armour. He went into battle lacking the most basic equipment.' The coroner concluded 'This is unforgivable and inexcusable and represents a breach of trust that the soldiers have in the Government.'

The Shatt al-Basra Canal runs roughly north–south, between Basra and Az Zubayr, from the Euphrates to Khor al-Zubair. Four bridges span this key obstacle. The Coalition numbered them 1–4, north–south. Early on the 23 March, Egypt Squadron, 2 RTR found itself at the bridges together with a platoon of the Black Watch, a MILAN section, a sniper team and some USMC reservists who operated as FACs. Positioned on the eastern outskirts of Az Zubayr with views over the roads that connected the bridges, 'Egypt' soon spotted Iraqi teams armed with rifles and RPGs. Lt Col David Catmur, 2 RTR takes up the story:

> The crews were quick to realise the devastation, both real and to morale, caused by a single burst of the coax chain gun, particularly when the turret was initially pointing away from the enemy, but the commander, unknown by the enemy, had already used his independent sight to laser him so that the computer could then, in one movement, bring the turret round and fire the guns. By similar methods, but using the main gun, Lt Pinkstone and his gunner, L/Cpl Williamson, in callsign 10 dealt with several enemy trying to establish a defensive position in a building. The reality of the range capable of being achieved also hit home, when Tpr King, gunner in callsign 11, hit a lone gunman at over 2km with his first burst.

Az Zubayr

Dropping JDAMs and using Challenger tanks may not be thought at first to be a surgical option in warfare, but with the accuracy possible from these platforms, it was a very surgical strike indeed that was enabled on Az Zubayr at dawn on 26 March. Special Forces had identified a complex being used as a command centre for the Fedayeen militia, codenamed Objective Brain, that was to be destroyed with prisoners captured if possible. The plan was to use three troops (nine tanks) of Challengers from Cyclops Squadron, 1 LI's A Company and half of Recce Squadron with a FOO. Opening the raid was fast air from the USMC (Harriers) dropping JDAMs. A Sky TV crew was also on the ground. Lt Sam Clarke was with Cyclops Squadron:

> While the day before the city was clearly visible from the forming up point, the rain that fell during the night was now creating a dense fog that hid the buildings. Crew waited in anticipation, scanning the hazy skies for the expected aircraft. Most never saw them but a couple of minutes after the expected time a series of shattering crashes reverberated across the fields and the armoured column moved off into the city, with the infantry securing the routes alongside. It soon became clear that perhaps not all the bombs had detonated as there were several buildings in the complex still standing intact. The CO instructed the Cyclops tanks to destroy the remaining buildings, which was completed in five minutes of rapid firing. Cyclops then fanned out to encircle the complex and city block as a show of force, allowing the infantry to capture a number of stunned Iraqi personnel. The column withdrew leaving a no doubt shocked Ba'ath Party leadership.

The surgical strike had killed at least a dozen enemy with no loss to the raiders of 2 RTR BG. 1 UKDIV wrote the operation up and the action was later cited in an army doctrine paper as an example of offensive action. It was a classic example of shock and awe, caused by the JDAM and tank fire. However, the militia in Az Zubayr was still active and evidently was trying to re-locate some of its troops prompting a hasty operation later in the afternoon of 26 March.

Once again Sam Clarke and his men from 7 Troop, Cyclops Squadron were to go into action to interdict the enemy who apparently were using pick-ups and minibuses to move their troops. 7 Troop led off on the dual carriageway that took them into the eastern suburbs of Az Zubayr. This time the enemy was ready, with RPG teams in waiting, hidden in the alleys and side streets.

> We were ambushed from both sides by RPGs and HMG fire. All three leading tanks were struck by RPGs but no serious damage was inflicted. All three tanks returned fire. Sgt Topping – callsign 31 – concentrated on the right side of the road (north); Three Zero Lt Clarke concentrated on targets ahead while 32 Cpl Dale concentrated on the left-hand side. We used both main guns and coax in this intense and violent action, which saw numerous two-man teams neutralised and further militia sent scrabbling back into the city. On the way back 31 spotted a Soviet-made MTLB with militia around it. Three rounds of HESH were enough to remove that threat. Sgt Andy Topping got a commander's commendation for that day.

What these fierce encounters had demonstrated was that the tanks of 7 Troop had scarred armour and some damaged personal kit, that was stowed on the tank exterior, but that Challenger 2 was virtually impervious to RPG attack and could operate in an urban environment. With the armoured raids and precision air strikes the head of the serpent in Az Zubayr was effectively cut off. The local population then needed convincing that the troops were there to stay and that they could help restore order and get the city working again. The timely delivery of bottled and tanked drinking water for the locals was a very well-received act by the battlegroup.

With the town somewhat pacified, attention could now turn east across the Shatt al-Basra Canal, to the 1.5 million people in the city of Basra.

As 2 RTR punched into the cauldron of Az Zubayr, a JDAM strike was being organised by 17/16 Battery, 3 RHA controllers at 7 Brigade HQ. Eleven precision guided munitions (PGMs) were on their way to hit eight different buildings that made up the Ba'ath Party complex in the heart of Az Zubayr. This deadly combination of an armoured ground force in concert with the 2,000lb JDAMs would have a decisive crushing effect on the enemy and its will to fight. This was also the first time conventional UK forces had synchronised a PGM strike linked with a ground manoeuvre. It was an unconventional plan by a battery commander but one that achieved its aim.

CHAPTER 8

Hackles Raised

We were at the FUP (form-up point) just by the dual carriageway when some bearded geezer with a cockney accent appeared by the Warrior and asked for Lt Rees-Gay. The bearded guy reassured me saying, 'You'll be alright lads, it's only a few rag heads who can't shoot for shit!' It was the SAS aka the Hereford Gun Club.

We were now hurtling down the motorway, yet again in broad daylight. I looked out the back and I could see the white pick-up right up our arse with three of the Hereford Gun Club in it, mad bastards. In the turret Cpl 'Biceps' Burke and Fusilier 'Elmer' Fudd were in full-on shouting mode. Biceps was shouting to Elmer to traverse left and right so much that I thought the turret was going to unscrew. All this was to the tune of 'The Ketchup Song' I had put on at full blast in the back for morale reasons. Biceps spotted an already knocked-out T-55 that had a load of enemy standing on it. Three rounds of 30mm HE were despatched in a burst and needless to say only smoking boots remained. Biceps then shouted, with urgency, 'Traverse right, traverse right!' Elmer, of course, swung left, and Biceps shouted, 'Traverse right you knob! MTLB, MTLB.' Elmer then declared the MTLB was already destroyed, and Biceps shouted, 'Well if it's knocked out why is its fucking turret turning towards us?'

Elmer muttered, 'Oh fuck,' then despatched three HE and six sabot [armour piercing] into it and giggled. The last sabot round ricocheted off the armour and hit a civilian lorry at the roadside. The driver was last seen doing an impression of Linford Christie down the road to Basra.

CPL PEARCE, 1 RRF, IN THE INFORMAL DIARY OF 12 PLATOON

Bridge 4, known to the Fusiliers initially as Objective Golf then later as Stirling, carried a four-lane highway across the Basra Canal from Az Zubayr in a north-easterly direction into south-western Basra. It is today known as Zubair Bridge. The canal is 90m wide but the overall bridge with the approach ramps is around 500m. The approach to the ramp towards Basra was dominated on its left by an industrial complex that overlooked the road. This was a gated compound with a courtyard and low-rise offices on three sides, measuring 400m square. Some refer to it as the bus depot. It was already damaged by artillery before the arrival of the Fusiliers. Much of the surrounding land was open scrub and in places muddy and marsh-like if not built upon. To the north of Objective Golf, three other bridges were going to be assaulted by the other battlegroups. Codenames were Bridge One – Ludlow, Bridge Two – Oldham, Bridge Three – Leicester.

1 RRF's Y Company commander, Duncan McSporran, tasked 10 and 12 Platoons to take and clear Bridge 4. The bridge approaches (home bank) would be captured by 12 Platoon then 10 Platoon would pass through and secure the far bank. An SAS patrol using a white pick-up truck would accompany 12 Platoon and assist on the bridge.

Lt Chris Rees-Gay, OC 12 Platoon, had callsigns 32 and 33 (Warriors) on the right-hand carriageway to secure the right embankment; 31 and 30 (himself) took the left side. They advanced in a line across the highway. Not far behind were a troop of Challengers from the QRL. Lt Chris Rees-Gay takes up the story:

> As soon as we made the final approach to the bridge we spotted a T-55 tank on the far bank and engaged it with our 30mm. The Challengers then saw the T-55 and it was destroyed. As this action took place, I ordered the sections to debus, and they split off left and right for their objectives. Numbers 1 and 3 Sections swept over their respective embankments and quickly cleared the underneath of the ramps and met up under the bridge. They then came under sustained machine-gun fire from just north of the far bank. We returned fire and 33 also added some cannon fire and the position was destroyed. (One Iraqi was shot hiding in the superstructure of the underside of the bridge and plummeted into the water.) A second, well-hidden machine gun then opened fire on Platoon HQ from 500m north of our position but on the home bank. Sgt 'Chesty' Wellard made effective use of the platoon 51mm mortar before the enemy was neutralised by a HESH round from the QRL tanks.

Having silenced the enemy on the far bank for now, Lt Rees-Gay had to clear the bus depot that still posed a threat to anyone using the bridge approaches. The lieutenant gave brief orders that each side of the complex would be cleared in sequence with one section clearing, one section in fire support and the third section in reserve. The three sections covered each other and moved up to a firm base at the gateway to the compound, nearest the northern building line. As soon as Number 1 Section began their assault, with bayonets fixed, automatic Iraqi fire erupted from the central part of the complex facing them. The covering fire returned was both accurate and devastating, with the tracers lighting up the darkening scene, the gunner on board 31 added his 30mm Rarden cannon fire to that hitting the Iraqi post. The section cleared the first length of building then turned 90 degrees left to clear the rearmost building of the compound where the Iraqi resistance had shown itself. The blast of grenades and short bursts of automatic fire echoed through the buildings and Cpl '94' Richardson fired two LAW rockets at one of the positions, his accuracy being questioned later! The final section was launched on the return leg of the building and the depot was soon declared clear. Cpl Pearce continues:

> We always loved a bit of OBUA [Operations in Built Up Areas] and got stuck straight in. Of course, the platoon commander turned up, and as officers do, stated the bleeding obvious. One enemy popped up at a window and I fired at him, but I was running so think I missed but probably scared him. No enemy in the complex … my arse!

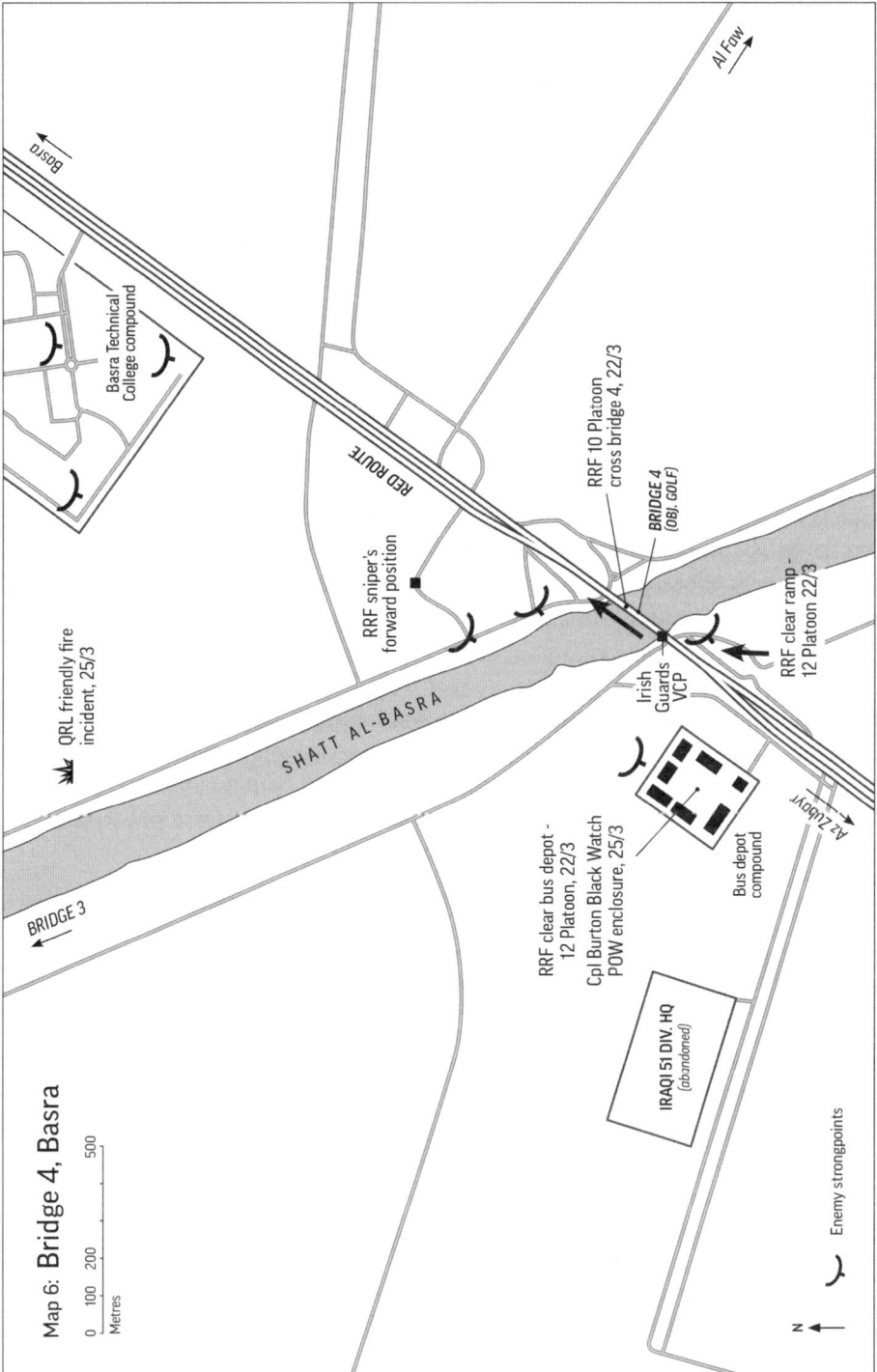

Map 6: Bridge 4, Basra

0 100 200   500
Metres

Basra

Basra Technical
College compound

RED ROUTE

Al Fow

RRF 10 Platoon
cross bridge 4, 22/3

BRIDGE 4
(OBJ. GOLF)

RRF sniper's
forward position

RRF clear ramp -
12 Platoon 22/3

Irish
Guards
VCP

QRL friendly fire
incident, 25/3

SHATT AL-BASRA

Az Zubayr

BRIDGE 3

RRF clear bus depot -
12 Platoon, 22/3

Cpl Burton Black Watch
POW enclosure, 25/3

Bus depot
compound

IRAQI 51 DIV. HQ
(abandoned)

Enemy strongpoints

N

The whole fight had taken 90 minutes and was completed with copious illumination rounds being fired from the 51mm and battalion 81mm mortars. Over a dozen Iraqi prisoners were taken and half that amount again were killed. Lt Chris Rees-Gay:

> I had changed my mind halfway through Sandhurst. I thought I wanted to fly helicopters aged 21, but I realised that in the end that did not involve leading men into battle which I grew to like, so I swapped from the Army Air Corps to infantry, which meant only one regiment, the Royal Fusiliers. That decision took me to Iraq as a boy and I returned a man. Everything I had trained for at Sandhurst, BATUS and on my platoon commanders' course had prepared me for that day of battle at Bridge 4 and I was immensely proud of what the platoon had done, every man gave his all.

OC 10 Platoon, Lt Chris Head took up the momentum of the attack as his platoon moved toward securing a hold on the far bank:

> It was nearly dark as we started up the bridge, like a rollercoaster as it drags you toward the top, you can't see the other side of the bridge until over the crest.[1]

Cpl Wheeler was ecstatic to be lead vehicle, his driver edging him forward passed wrecks of abandoned and wrecked cars with the eerie glow of illuminating flares floating down above them. A strict limit of exploitation (LOE) had been imposed on 10 Platoon, meaning there was a line in the sand they must not go beyond for risk of being hit by fast air or artillery support. Just shy of the LOE the four Warriors pulled up to start dismounting at the end of the far ramp of the bridge. A small group of enemy showed themselves willing to surrender and Cpl Kitson and Number 1 Section began to lead them back up the ramp when a firefight started from buildings to the left of the ramp. Lt Head released Number 3 Section to assault the building with bayonets fixed and that show of aggressive force put paid to any more firing that night. Lt Head continues:

> All-round defence was set up including MILAN posts with their thermal image sights looking up and down the canal banks and along the road into Basra. By dawn 23 March civilians began to show themselves near the bridge and more bedraggled Iraqi soldiers came in to surrender. The Fusiliers were under orders not to allow any vehicle or foot traffic out of the city for now as the risk of infiltration was too great.

A simple roadblock and Warriors dominated the carriageway to vehicles but the pedestrians kept coming and eventually a crowd gathered and action needed to be taken to prevent a rush at the Fusiliers. A Warrior gunner was authorised and fired a burst of cannon fire at an abandoned Iraqi vehicle – the resulting noise and showers of sparks sent everyone, including the Fusiliers, diving for cover. Soon the bridgehead and the bus depot came under sporadic and inaccurate mortar fire. It did keep the Fusiliers inside their Warriors and the pedestrians back inside the city. The Fusiliers' position at the bridges was maintained over the next 36 hours with the QRL tanks confirming eight K-kills of T-55s and BTRs roving about on the far bank.

Objective Leicester – Bridge 3 – was the road bridge 4km north of Bridge 4 and was the objective of Maj Dickie Trant's C Squadron, QRL group comprising two troops of Challengers and a platoon of Zulu Company, 1 RRF. American scout tanks had reached a point 3–4km south of the bridge but had not moved on to test the defences. One Challenger lost a track when it hit a mine hidden in a culvert, which strangely had already been driven over by a dozen other vehicles. It was repaired by the next day.

The call for fire support or fast air to begin the attack on Bridge 3 fell on deaf ears and so Maj Trant committed his troops at 18:15, 22 March. Bridge 3 was an altogether smaller affair than Bridge 4 and tanks had to jockey for position to take it in turns to engage targets with HESH rounds. Dismounts in trenches were found to the left of the bridge on the far bank and soon destroyed with HESH and chain gun fire. A dug-in T-55 was seen 2,000m north along the canal bank and successfully taken out with a Fin round, while two BMP armoured cars were also destroyed at 1,200m range. This continual degradation of the Iraqi position then flushed out two T-55s from the rear of their positions. Breaking cover from some low buildings, the two tanks sped south along a dirt track and were targeted at 1,500m range by 20 and 22 (C Squadron QRL Challengers). Both old Soviet-style tanks were hit and destroyed, the second suffering a huge internal explosion creating a vast fireball in the sky. Small-arms fire and skirmishes continued until 23:00 when it became clear the position was secure.

Maj Paul Nanson and his Y Company, 1 RRF were the last to leave the border breach and so it was dark by the time they reached Bridge 2, another major highway-carrying bridge that led towards Basra across the canal. US Marines had already secured Basra International Airport, but Bridge 2 was still in enemy hands.

Defensive positions were established and clearance patrols were sent out to probe the enemy lines instead of trying to launch a difficult full-frontal assault. Challenger tanks also maintained an obvious presence to dissuade the Iraqis from forming any stiffened resistance or counter-attacks. Sgt Gardner (QRL) destroyed a T-55 and BMP as they carelessly exposed themselves to him on the bridge ramp.

At 05:00, 23 March, the group rushed forward in their Warriors and Challengers from their start line codenamed Cloverleaf, moving the 2km onto the bridge where sappers confirmed it was not wired for demolition. As the Warriors dismounted their Fusilier sections on the bridge, the Iraqi defenders opened fire. They had been waiting. Like Panzergrenadiers in World War 2 or even the British infantry at Cambrai in 1917, the Fusiliers withdrew into file behind the cover of their Warrior and let the armoured vehicle absorb the hard-hitting machine-gun rounds. Direct and indirect fire rained down on the Fusiliers huddled behind the Warriors but still they edged forward until they got closer to the enemy. Then, all outgoing fire was increased and gradually the Fusiliers won the firefight and kept the enemies' heads down. Sensing the need to swing the balance yet further the way of the Fusiliers,

Sgt Gardner was sent in with his Challenger. Several HESH rounds later, two BMPs were burning and a defensive post lay smouldering at the roadside. The intense firefight had lasted nearly an hour.

The northernmost of the bridges to be seized was codenamed Ludlow and sat just north-east of Basra International Airport, which was codenamed Kittyhawk. US Marines operated ahead of the QRL and were relieved in place upon arrival of the QRL/RRF groups. Both Kittyhawk and Ludlow fell relatively quickly and with less opposition. Lt Chris Rees-Gay noted in 12 Platoon, 1 RRF diary:

> Now holding the eastern bank lodgement at Bridge 4. Went over the bridge at 13:00 and at 17:00 message received that 20 x T-72 heading south toward my position. Two engineers also reported captured in an ambush.
>
> It was a very long night. We only told the section commanders about the tank threat, no need to worry all the lads. We did have them prepped with the LAWs. In front of us sat a screen of the three Challengers. They sat there all night with their big diesel engines purring, very reassuringly. The T-72s never came. The next day, 24 March, we handed over the bridge to the Black Watch.

Maj Duncan McSporran, OC Y Company:

> We absorbed five counter-attacks at the bridge in the 24 hours after its capture, including two with armoured vehicles, and we inflicted very high casualties on the soldiers and militia trying to retake the bridge. Our sniper section (four men) deployed in what was no man's land in front of the Technical College to spot and neutralise gathering threats and enemy artillery spotters, which they were highly effective at. Civilians were never far away, and my guys were incredibly disciplined in maintaining the difference between the two groups and not opening fire on them. The concept of ridding the population of the tyranny of Saddam was easy to get across to the boys, they got it.
>
> As we sat on the far ramp of the bridge after the assaults died down, I was hit with a wave of relief and an enormous sense of gratitude. No matter what happened after that, no one can point at us and say, 'Well you screwed it up.' We had achieved what we set out to do. Bridge 4 was the Brigadier's key terrain that he told me was the most important and we got it. There was immense pride in 'Zulu' across all ranks.

Firing in support of 1 RRF were the 16 155mm guns of J and 17/16 Batteries, 3 RHA. Over 1,000 rounds were fired at the Technical College opposite the RRF positions. These barrages were usually followed up by some precision Hellfire/TOW missile strikes from US AH-1 Cobra or UK Lynx gunships. It was found that the US Cobra was the precision CAS weapon of choice in Basra and Az Zubayr due to its agility, firepower and willingness to fly lower than the less well-armed and unarmoured Lynx. (The Army Air Corps was very soon after issued with the formidable Apache.) Four JDAMs also hit the college further reducing the occupants' capacity to fight.

Cpl Paul Burton, REME was attached Black Watch BG:

> Our next stop was a compound on the southern side of the Basra Canal and west side of the MSR. It was the old bus depot recently cleared by 1 RRF.

We were attempting to cross the bridge for a good week or so. Every time we patrolled over the bridge, we encountered enemy fire from a compound that we later found to be the Basra Technical Collage. I can remember us facing mortar attacks as well as constant small arms. We did return fire with mortars and called in air strikes on the compound. At one point we waited for 24 hrs for air support but when it came the US Cobra helicopter did a good job with its TOW missiles. To this day I still don't know what the enemy strength was. They did not seem to let up and the constant attacks seemed relentless. Our strength was just company level with the Mortar Platoon attached.

We also had a small SF team with us, and they were used to interrogate any enemy forces that we were able to capture. Once we had captured several enemies, we found out that they were Saddam's 'Fedayeen forces', known to us to be willing to sacrifice themselves for their cause. This did make me feel quite scared, and the reality of what was going on soon started to hit me. I was tasked to guard these Iraqi soldiers and to start with I felt sorry for them. They were all crammed into a concrete building within the compound. At one point when we were under a mortar attack, they tried to get me to take shelter in the building with them. I realised that I had very little chance, with around 40 prisoners and a magazine of only 30 rounds!

It became policy to have your bayonet fitted when guarding prisoners as this seemed to be the best way to protect yourself and they seemed to be scared of it. After a very short time, I realised that they could not be trusted and the chance of them trying to escape was high. I used my bayonet in an aggressive manner on more than one occasion to keep them under control. I did not use the bayonet to its 'fullest' potential, but I did come remarkably close.

Most of the POWs did appear to be relieved that they were in our hands. The exception to this was the Fedayeen prisoners. I can remember during the early days, when we were under threat of a Scud attack and in full CBRN kit. The prisoners seemed to be very frightened and requested that we give them respirators. This added to our own belief at this stage that the threat of chemical weapons was a very real one. In most cases the prisoners had got rid of their uniforms and were barefoot. I guess initially they were trying to avoid capture by pretending to be civilians but also to show us that they were no threat to us.

On another day I took over guard of four Fedayeen prisoners in a small room. The room was in the old bus depot near Bridge 4. The room opened straight out into the compound so if the prisoners got out, they were free to get away. They were tied up and had hoods on their heads. The soldier I took over from said, 'These guys are trouble and will give you grief. Don't you dare let them escape.' Within a few minutes one of them tried to take his hood off and stand up so I pushed him down and shouted sit down. I was a bit frightened and realised that I needed to stay in control, or they would try and get the better of me. It makes me angry now that I was forced to use violence on them, but I had to do so without shooting them.

On 25 March the fog of war led to a tragedy between Bridge 3 and 4 on the eastern bank of the canal outside Basra and the resulting mess needed the services of the REME CRARRV team to clear it up. Cpl Scott Blaney, REME:

On 25 March we were stationed close by the set of bridges across the Basra Canal, west of the city. I took a radio message that we were needed to recover a badly damaged Challenger belonging to C Squadron QRL. We soon understood that it was a 'blue on blue' and that the QRL Challenger had been hit by two HESH rounds fired from a tank belonging to Egypt Squadron, 2 RTR.

I had been involved in clearing the 1991 Highway of Death out of Kuwait City where hundreds of tanks, APCs and trucks had been hit by air power as they tried to escape north back to Iraq. We were tasked back then to use the dozer blade on the CRARRV to clear the road and bury everything, including burned corpses and scattered pieces of torso. It was an unholy mess, the images of which are still with me. I knew therefore that the blue on blue was probably going to be nasty. I was still surprised at the mess the C2 was in. It was still smouldering when we got there and had clearly suffered a catastrophic fire. I think the rounds hit the engine deck but I'm not sure. The scene was reminiscent of my first tour in Iraq in '91, it was not a nice day.

The OC wanted it taken away before the Press descended and we were told to cover up the tank with a tarpaulin, but it was too hot. We dismounted, hooked up the Challenger for recovery and took it back on a low loader to Umm Qasr port.

An inquiry and coroner's court hearing were held after the war and great scrutiny was laid upon the actions which led to this tragic incident. War is chaos and in the smoke, fog and heat of battle, friendly fire has always been a sad but common theme. In the 1991 Gulf War 25% of US casualties were suffered in friendly fire incidents and nine British men were hit by a US warplane, ironically involving one of the same regiments involved in 2003 (Royal Fusiliers).

Early on 24 March the Black Watch BG (consisting of infantry from the Black Watch and a troop of three Challenger tanks from Egypt Squadron, 2 RTR) took over duty at Bridge 4 on the Basra Canal. They were using as HQ the compound that Chris Rees-Gay's 12 Platoon, 1 RRF had cleared before. The 1 BW group positioned Warriors and tanks on both sides of the canal. A further troop of detached tanks from C Squadron, QRL was working about 1,000m to the north near a dam at Bridge 3 under the 1 RRF BG.

Crew from 2 RTR reported seeing movements and hotspots with their thermal image sights to their north, which they believed must be enemy according to their latest intelligence. The RTR asked for permission to engage, and this was granted. Their first HESH round fell short, but the blast blew one of the crew off the turret. A second HESH round hit the commander's hatch and killed two of the crew. Cpl Stephen Allbutt from Stoke and Tpr David Clarke from Stafford. The other two crew were also badly injured.

The official MOD inquiry identified several causal factors, including planning, incorrect target identification, communication failures, lack of command and control, fog of war and fatigue. It listed the main shortcomings as:

1. The passage of information regarding interunit boundaries, locations of friendly forces especially at key features.
2. Command and control of the battle space, especially around unity of effort.
3. Combat identification, target recognition and arcs of fire.

The combination of these factors led to 2 RTR misunderstandings about arcs of fire and enemy threats which then led to an erroneous appreciation of the situation.

The board concluded that the incident could have been avoided if the following had occurred:

A. Complete and accurate briefings with up to date unit boundaries clearly marked.

B. Black Watch and RTR Orders had included existence and significance of the operations at Bridge 3.

C. Troops at Bridge 4 should have been tactically briefed before going east of the canal, with the inclusion of QRL tanks working to the north.

D. RTR tank commanders had been more inquisitive regarding lack of task details and demanded more information at briefing.

E. RTR Challenger tank commander had not been disorientated and placed his radio reports on the wrong side of the canal.*

Every reader of a book about desert warfare knows that desert nights are the friend of airmen, providing cover of darkness from which to deliver stealthy and unexpected attacks. But every desert-qualified helicopter pilot knows, light levels of less than 1 millilux, featureless terrain and a myriad of uncharted obstructions make for a very demanding environment that stretches aircrew abilities to the limit. It is this scenario that faced pilots of 662 Squadron, AAC when they were pulled from 16 AAB on 25 March and diverted to help 7 Armd Brigade on the bridges at Basra. The group of five Lynx departed the 16 AAB area having not yet fired a shot in anger, but earlier that day had been engaged at low level by an RPG duo from the back of a pick-up truck near MSR Tampa. The transit of 50km south-east to 7 Armd Brigade HQ was not only in the darkness described, but also in worsening weather conditions. High winds and a heavy downpour darkened the night sky yet further until dramatic bolts of lightning lit up the horizon but shut down the pilots' NVGs temporarily. Unexpectedly tall radio masts and highway lanterns loomed in front causing several rapid and jerky avoidance manoeuvres amongst the Lynx. Regular alarms rang out in the cockpits too, the radar warning receivers letting them know they were still in an enemy land. Once landed at Shaiba Air Base, the 7 Armd Brigade briefing team met the pilots from 662 and commenced a very thorough briefing. Int corps, artillery deep fires officers and even some scruffy-looking bearded individuals, who did not introduce themselves, provided up to date information, imagery and new maps.

Two Lynx of 662 were to attack the Basra Technical College just across the other side of Bridge 4, which had been captured by1 RRF and was currently held by the Black Watch. The target, 2,000m from British lines, was being used by the enemy for a host of functions. It was a supply depot, observation post, mortar baseline and meeting place for the Fedayeen and secret police. The target had already been hit by bombs and artillery fire, but the Lynx crews were asked to cause as much destruction as possible, which was probably music to their ears. The team to carry out the attack was led by Capt Neil Passmore, AAC. After the briefing the raid team conducted

---

*   Salmon (2005).

its own map recce and agreed its own actions and Capt Passmore issued his orders. Each Lynx was loaded with eight ITOW (Improved TOW) missiles and filled up with JP8 fuel. The crew donned their combat and survival gear and walked out to their aircraft sitting on the apron at Shaiba. It was still dark and lightly raining as the two helicopters flared up and took off. Fires burned across the Basra skyline throwing a sinister light across the marshland they had chosen for their ingress. The lead helicopter's navigational system started playing up and giving spurious suggestions but fortunately the crew was well trained and quickly reverted to compass and stopwatch to bring them in on target just as planned. The pair approached their limit of exploitation at the canal just after 03:00 on 26 March and soon saw the lurking hulks of British Challenger tanks sitting on the bridge away off to their right front. Capt Passmore brought his aircraft to the hover looking through his NVGs and thermal-image weapon sight. He soon acquired the target buildings. In front of him ran a huge line of electricity pylons and wires carrying part of the Iraqi national grid. The wires were slung pylon to pylon and sagged at about 40m above the ground. Capt Passmore remembers that the questions in his mind were:

i) What are the limits for firing ITOW under high voltage wires?
ii) What would be the effect of ITOW on buildings?
iii) How quickly might we expect return fire?

He gave the order to fire, and each Lynx fired in turn, both firing seven missiles each at the target buildings. Some of the impacts resulted in dramatic secondary explosions in buildings that clearly contained ammunition dumps. Not wishing to wait around any longer, even to admire their handiwork, the Lynx pair peeled away and returned to Shaiba. As Capt Passmore commenced his final approach to Shaiba, reports reached him from an observer on the ground saying all three target buildings were demolished, an ammunition dump was continuing to explode and a water tower had fallen over.

Passmore got his answers as follows:

i) TOW can be fired from the 3m hover, underneath high voltage lines, at targets 2km away with no problem.
ii) If TOW hits a mortar ammunition dump the secondary explosions are most impressive.
iii) Even if you fire all seven missiles and linger 30 seconds more watching your work, you can probably still get away.

Capt Passmore had used exceptional flying skills, leadership and courage on the raid and was subsequently mentioned in despatches.

Forty-eight hours later, on 28 March, troops of the Black Watch were conducting their dawn VCP duties on Bridge 4 when they came under fire. Hundreds of early riser Iraqis were already going about their business, amid the war, and many were already gathering on the eastern approach ramps of Bridge 4, waiting to get out through the VCP and make their way to Az Zubayr market or wherever else they felt they needed to go. Fedayeen technicals (pick-up trucks with HMGs or mortars mounted on them) were darting in and out of the side streets to the bridge ramp and firing both at the British on the bridge and at the waiting civilians. Showing enormous self-control, the Black Watch held their fire for fear of hitting the civilians.

Two Lynx crews from 662 Squadron were on 30-minutes NTM at Shaiba and sprang into action when the FAC at the bridge, callsign Wild Eagle 3, requested aviation support. As the two Lynx scrambled, permission was first given to engage, then rescinded. Maj Orr piloted one Lynx with his gunner S/Sgt Shepherd beside him; the other crew was Sgt Farmer and Sgt Allen. Orbiting in a holding pattern a few miles west of the bridge, the aircrews waited for permission to engage which they duly got at 08:30. S/Sgt Shepherd:

> The Fedayeen must have seen us approaching as they quickly scattered into the nearby housing estate as we took up firing positions. Looking through my magnified sighting scope, I could see the grisly view of dead, wounded and panicking civilians. Suddenly Wild Eagle called up 'reference large mast, base of mast, right 200m, two times technicals!' I fired at the vehicle as it moved left to right past a group of trees and then it stopped behind a low building. It didn't come out the other side, so I had to abort the missile and I put it onto some waste ground to avoid any civilians.[2]

Meanwhile, in the second Lynx Sgt Farmer had his eyes glued to his sighting system as he fired off his first TOW at the other technical. The Fedayeen machine gunner on the back of the pick-up was standing, feet braced against the chassis, firing the gun on its pedestal mount at the now scattered and cowering crowds. The driver then pulled the truck forward and behind a building. Sgt Farmer now had the same dilemma as that which faced S/Sgt Shepherd only a moment before, what to do with the missile. The problem was solved as the vehicle reversed back into view. Sgt Farmer smoothly guided the 20kg missile for the last few seconds, before it hammered into the pick-up at 800kph, the 5kg of HE obliterating the pick-up and blasting the gunner 15m in the air as he was engulfed in a fireball, just like his other two crew mates. Maj Orr had by now jockeyed his Lynx into an enfilade position, affording S/Sgt Shepherd a better view of the first technical. He launched the third missile of the engagement and, perhaps seeing the launch, the driver accelerated harshly and then started turning sharply towards a narrow side street attempting to evade the fiery end that had befallen his friends a few moments before. It was not to be, the TOW slammed into the rear of the pick-up instantly turning it into a mangled fireball of twisted metal and smoke. The remaining technicals retreated into the side streets, realising they were no match for the two Lynx which had lived up to the 662 Squadron motto of 'Death Dealing Eye'.

The incident captured the attention of the media, with Sky News releasing the story before the rotors had even stopped spinning. Images showed the civilians under fire and running for cover at the bridge while the Lynx delivered death from a distance. Of course, that was only half the story. Omitted was the nature of the risks taken by the two crews who had operated well within range of the enemy small arms as well as air defences and that they had to prosecute the attack with great skill and determination to bring the atrocity to an end – not to mention the quite superb unconventional gunnery skills needed to hit such fast and erratic targets.

Carrying out VCPs on the bridges to Basra was serving a purpose but the mood of the division was that a more offensive stance was needed to start knocking off balance and dislodging the Fedayeen – not only in the no man's land just across the canal, but also in the shanty towns and estates on the western edge of Basra. The tactic became known as 'raid and aid': penetrate the city to destroy an enemy strongpoint, weapon, symbol or person, then provide humanitarian aid (water) if appropriate to do so, then withdraw back to the bridges. The Americans called them 'Thunder Runs' but lacked the clinical targeting the British looked to deliver.

A Squadron, RSDG was selected to deliver the first penetrative raid deep into the city on 29 March. The push for the raid came from Number 10 in response to the news footage that showed the Fedayeen gunners machine gunning civilians near Bridge 4. Politically it was felt that the atrocity could not go unanswered. The tanks would need to go in and strike back. The eleven Challenger tanks were commanded by Gulf War veteran Maj Tim Brown. Tim had been a troop leader firing the tank main gun in 1991 and so had plenty of experience at desert warfare in the armoured role. His squadron had already been in action in and around Az Zubayr and the Police station, but this operation would encompass more of the squadron fighting together than before. There were three objectives for the squadron: firstly, destroy a 100m TV and radio mast that was central to the propaganda being pumped out by the Ba'ath Party 24 hours a day. Second, pull down or destroy a large statue of Saddam that dominated a road junction and triangular park 6km into the city from Bridge 4. Lastly, destroy a known Fedayeen HQ building that sat halfway between the bridge and the statue.

Maj Brown, callsign Zero Alpha, was missing his wife Sonja and little boy Tom but had made the conscious decision not to have any contact with them after the invasion started, and to keep focussed and not get distracted by home events. With his head clear but extremely tired, he had been putting the plan together for the raid that was set for the next morning. He had chosen to use only three of his four troops leaving Number 1 Troop at the FUP, which was the by now well-used old bus depot just west of bridge 4. His axis of advance was straight up Red route, across Bridge

4 and into the city. All three objectives were along that road so little navigation was called for. Red route was a four-lane road, with two lanes in each direction. He planned to have 2 Troop on the left side of the road, led by his most experienced troop leader, Capt Walters, and 3 Troop on the right. 4 Troop would sit 50m behind 2 Troop and Squadron HQ would sit behind 3 Troop. The Squadron HQ group consisted of his own tank and that of the 2IC plus two armoured Samaritan CVRT ambulances and the huge REME CRARRV with its bulldozer blade and recovery winch. Following would be four Warriors carrying a platoon of B Company, 1 Black Watch. It was to be an audacious raid into the heart of a city of a million people that would destroy some of its vital symbols and infrastructure. It was sure to be no walk over. Enemy tanks were known to still be lurking in the side streets and the high-rise nature of the buildings alongside the axis would provide elevated fire positions for RPG teams and snipers to pick off exposed commanders and disable the tanks. If the population turned against the armoured column, it could easily be blocked in and swamped by the angry populace, an ugly scene not lost on the planners but not shared with the men at briefing.

Having given his orders, the squadron broke down into troops to further brief themselves and once content all ranks knew the plan, the men ate a little, prepared the vehicles in their leaguer for the next day and retired to the comfort of their chosen bed space. Remarkably, it was only a week into the war and many of the men had already got into a routine and were ready for what the next day may hold.

Most of the men not on stag (sentry duty) pulled out their doss bags (sleeping bags) and threw them out on the large expanse of engine deck at the rear of their Challenger. The doss bag was too hot for the desert night but did provide a small layer of mattress comfort to take the edge off lying on the tank or hard ground directly. With the comforting thought that they had a whole five hours of sleep ahead of them before they needed to be rolling, the men dozed off.

An explosion shook the leaguer. Various voices from their doss bags shouted curses at the Royal Artillery, the men thinking that a nearby AS-90 battery had opened fire on a distant Iraqi target. A second, louder and brighter explosion shook the gathered troops of the RSDG and sent white hot splinters and shards of steel flying around the site, slicing through the DAF truck of HQ echelon. More rounds soon followed, and it was deduced they had been bracketed by a multiple-barrel rocket launcher, probably a Soviet-made BM-21. The tank crews could either try and get inside their tank or if they had been on the floor asleep, crawl under the tank. A third rocket hit which set one of the fuel bowsers alight. Two men were hit by shrapnel and the shout for medic went up. Maj Tim Brown, RSDG took immediate action:

> Sgt Watson (my operator) and I dived under my tank. We were torn as to our next action. Do we stay put in a pretty safe place or do we risk it, get out and climb up into the tank where there is even better cover and the radio which I needed to take control of the situation. We agreed to go for it and in record time bounded up the tank onto the turret and dived through

the hatches. Vince, my gunner, was dropping into his seat just ahead of me as I pulled the hatch closed. I then put out a 'Charlie Charlie One' call. That's like a roll call telling everyone to respond in callsign order to let me know if anyone is hurt. Having seen the impacts of the rockets and the burning vehicles I was pretty sure we would be callsigns down. Gradually, incredibly, everyone called up.

The injuries received were all HQ echelon staff. One REME soldier, Craftsman Burrell, who was on stag, had been incredibly lucky. A large splinter a foot long had hit him in the chest, it embedded itself in his body armour knocking him over but did not penetrate. Maj Brown looked out at the squadron, now lit by the dying flames of the bowser and exhaled loudly and felt a sense of both relief and triumph. The raid would still go ahead so his next radio broadcast on the squadron net followed, 'This is Zero Alpha, raiding party prepare to move.' He couldn't hear it, but the troops were cheering.

Areas of the city adjoining the Red route axis had been zoned and designated alphanumerically (see Map 8) The first zone on the right was Bravo, a squalid area of mainly single-storey humble dwellings – shanty-type homes, strewn with rubbish, wastelands and fetid swampy pools. A subobjective during the raid was for a team of SAS to be covertly inserted into Bravo to hunt, identify and neutralise an elusive and troublesome Iraqi mortar team that had been continuing to use the cover of the shanty town to fire on troops at Bridge 4 and the bus depot.

Maj Tim Brown, RSDG continues:

> I met these two SAS guys while at the bus depot. They had been operating behind the lines on and off all week gathering intelligence and spotting targets. What struck me was they had traditional Arab garb on, wearing *dishdasha* and *shemagh* and were tanned and bearded, but they had British Army uniform trousers and military type boots on. It struck me as most odd, and I wondered how they had not got spotted. They hoped that the raid would stir the enemy mortar team into action thus allowing the SAS to spot them and end their activities.

Adjoining Bravo on Red route was Zone Charlie which housed the enormous TV tower. Set in a walled compound with guard towers and some maintenance buildings, it dominated the west of the city. Opposite Charlie was Zone Delta which contained, amongst many other three and four-storey buildings, the Fedayeen HQ target complex. The most distant objective, the statue of Saddam, sat in Zone Foxtrot at the first major junction and within the memorial gardens, rather like London's Marble Arch. Overlooking the junction and Red route was the Basra College of Literature.

Zero hour was 05:00, 29 March, just a few minutes before the first rays of sun crept up over the far side of the city. The 18-vehicle raiding party sat in formation with engines idling just east of the bus depot. Flicking his squadron net radio to transmit, Maj Brown watched the final seconds tick away and transmitted, 'This is Zero Alpha, move now.'

Engines gunned and tracks squealed on tarmac as they moved across the start line and towards the ramp that took Red route across Bridge 4 and into the city. As the column headed up the ramp the gleam of the Basra Canal shimmered silver below them. All eyes in the tanks were glued to vision slits, periscopes and gunsights. In the rear of the Warriors the Jocks of B Company sat squashed amongst all the extra kit looking at each other with no external view to be had apart from the man closest to the rear door, who had a vision block.

The leading tanks now crested the hump at the centre of the bridge at 25kph and could once again see the sprawling mass of the city spread before them. On command, all the drivers then sped up, hitting 65kph on the down slope of the bridge. A thousand tons of British armour thundered forward in a truly amazing spectacle with echoes of a bygone era, when British cavalry galloped towards their enemy, using speed, shock and power as at Waterloo, Omdurman and Audregnies.

2 Troop, with furthest to travel, began to edge ahead as they entered the city. Then a ferocious barrage of RPGs and HMG tracers lit up the morning and smashed into the Challengers. The machine gun rounds bounced off harmlessly other than destroying kit stowed on the exterior. Most RPGs missed due to the aggressive speed the Challengers were using. Callsigns calmly called up with contact reports and targets to look out for. Fedayeen were everywhere, from trenches and bunkers at the roadside, to rooftops three storeys up. Their bravery and courage were not in doubt, and many were seen in the open taking aimed shots at the British before being cut down by coaxial machine-gun fire.

Inside the turrets, loaders worked feverishly pushing round after round of 120mm HESH shells into the breach so their gunners could pump the shells into bunkers, buildings and trench systems. A section of enemy in Zone Charlie was positioned in one of the guard towers blasting passing tanks until a HESH round destroyed the tower, sending the dying men cartwheeling into the air as the tower collapsed in on itself.

Squadron HQ and 3 Troop reached their objective at Zone Charlie and began to focus on the TV Tower. Close by to Maj Brown, 4 Troop had also stopped and was engaging the Fedayeen complex objective in Delta Zone. Capt Walters led 2 Troop further into the city and was soon out of view and also out of the main Fedayeen killing area, but not out of danger. Maj Tim Brown, RSDG:

> We all started pumping HESH rounds into the vast concrete base at the foot of the TV Tower. We had discussed this before the operation and agreed that it was the most likely method to succeed quickly. The TV mast was made of steel girders that symmetrically split into four huge steel lattice legs, on each corner. Additionally, four thick steel hawsers were stretched out to massive concrete anchors a hundred or so metres from the tower.
>
> We put six or seven rounds into the base, as had everyone else. Not a twitch or shudder was even registered. Meanwhile a quick look behind us and I saw that 4 Troop were pulverising the suspected Fedayeen HQ.

Even the REME were in amongst the fighting. The CRARRV is normally equipped with a single GPMG on the roof for local protection, but the crew had purloined another GPMG from somewhere and so had one firing in each direction providing a valuable asset guarding the rear of the column. Astonishingly, writes Niall Edworthy in his book *Main Battle Tank*, the third REME crewman was seen hanging out his hatch, exposed to the waist, with a pump-action shotgun, furiously blasting any Fedayeen daring to get close to the CRARRV:

> My gunner and I agreed the HESH rounds were just not cutting it, so Vince said he would use Fin rounds directly on the supporting stanchions on each corner to see if that would do it. Although we were at close range, the size of target was tiny and took great skill and concentration amid battle to hit. Vince made some minor adjustments as the Fin round slid into the breach, then squeezed the trigger. The tank rocked as the breach burst open releasing yet more hot gasses. The Fin round sliced through the steel leg, and it buckled and wobbled. I looked down at the back of Vince, his face glued to his sights. He was in a form of trance as he traversed onto the next stanchion and repeated the same procedure. Leg two was now sliced through but the tower stood firm, incredibly. The other tanks with me continued to fire HESH at the anchors, then the third stanchion was despatched skilfully by the third depleted uranium Fin round. I was so intent on looking at the third leg, I missed the top of the tower wobble at first, then realising that it was about to crumble I shouted 'Fucking hell! Driver reverse!' This thing was coming down straight towards us.

All the tanks reversed back as the tower crashed down. Maj Brown then called all units to extract and reminded them to reverse out, keeping their thick frontal armour facing towards the threats. 2 Troop had already destroyed the 20ft high iron statue of Saddam Hussein with his arm outstretched. They fired a single HESH round into it, leaving only his boots stuck in the ground, the rest of Saddam was in small pieces littering the park. All units now had to run the gauntlet once more of the shanty town in Bravo. Not as fierce as before but angry nonetheless, Fedayeen once more sprayed the Scots Dragoon Guards with small arms and more RPGs. One keen-eyed Challenger commander called up on the net warning Zero Bravo (Maj Brown) of a Fedayeen RPG gunner seen running along a nearby balcony. Maj Tim Brown recalls:

> I swung my sight around and, sure enough, I saw a guy crouched down on a balcony no more than 50m away. Machine-gun fire from Zero Charlie was smashing into the walls just below him. I lased the gun onto him, with HESH loaded and was about to fire when the man ran a few more steps and dived into a doorway, and as he dived amid the flying debris and chunks of concrete, I saw he had desert combat trousers on.
> I realised what I was looking at and shouted on the net 'STOP! STOP! STOP! Check Fire, friendlies in that building.'

In that fraction of a second as Brown sought to get a positive ID on the man lunging through the doorway, he realised it was one of the bearded SAS men in the *dishdasha* with army combats on, who he had met at the bus depot. By holding his fire an extra second, Maj Brown had saved the life of a decorated SF soldier who would go on to command Special Forces in the future. Later, the SF man went to find Maj Brown and thanked him for holding his fire. He said, 'Thank you. When I saw your barrel coming on to me, in all my time serving in the SAS, I have never been so close to death.' Brown answered, 'You don't know how close you were.'

Once back at the bus depot, Maj Tim Brown cleaned himself up and was put in front of the BBC cameras and reporter Ben Brown to do a piece about the raid. At the conclusion of the interview the reporter asked the major if he wanted him to call anyone on his Sat phone. He gave him the numbers for his wife and for his parents but none of them were at home. Later that evening the BBC ran the story and Tim's parents were with friends watching the news as their son came on the screen.

With the dust settling from the fallen TV Tower near Bridge 4, plans were coming together for a similar excursion across Bridge 3 by the RRF. Sporadic mortar fire, suspected rocket launchers and BMP armour had been seen on the forward edge of the city across from bridge 3 and the CO, Lt Col Paterson, wanted to take offensive action. A dismounted recce patrol led by Capt Pugh was tasked with crossing the bridge into no man's land on the night of 29 March, where they hoped to identify and plot the enemy positions for targeting in a subsequent armoured raid. As a memento Ed Pugh kept the patrol report he wrote that night:

> Iraq smells. Not only did Basra smell of shit, but it also smelt of burning oil. There was so much oily smoke in the air you could taste it where the Iraqis had set some of the wells alight. It genuinely was like something apocalyptic; the view was like a scene out of a disaster movie or war film.
>
> One of the burning structures was in the no man's land east of Bridge 3. I think the Iraqis set it alight to shroud their positions in smoke and to hinder our thermal image night sights. My mission was to patrol no man's land and gain information on location and strength of the enemy. Our time out on the patrol was 23:15, 29 March and we returned at 01:50, 30 March.
>
> I chose a rather rank heavy team for the patrol, with myself leading, C/Sgt Cockrill, Sgt Duthie (sniper), Sgt Thompson and three corporals. Cpl Carroll was bloody hard and unflappable, if you got in a fight, you wanted him next to you. In hindsight this group of NCOs was rather foolish, and we could have lost too many of my highly experienced soldiers.

The eight-man patrol moved out quietly, their faces blackened with camouflage cream, using the cover of the burning oil well to their advantage. Hugging the left side of the raised road, they reached the blazing oil fire without incident but found the heat intense and had to skirt it quickly. They then veered north to investigate an area of wasteland and rubbish piles where some digging had been seen in the daytime. Nothing of note was found so they moved back towards the raised road to observe the area on the other side (south). Their personal role radios (PRR) allowed virtually silent conversation to be had between the patrol commander and the patrol elements. These were relatively new pieces of kit and afterwards Capt Pugh describes them as a real winner. Pugh noted enemy trenches in the area and possibly some berms concealing dug-in vehicles. Around 01:00 vehicle noise was heard by the buildings on the edge of the city:

We got ourselves even lower into the dirt and I used Sophie (hand-held thermal imager) to scan the building line. I saw the BM-21 (multiple barrel rocket launcher) edge out from a building on the main road and then fire straight at us. I was zoomed in on it as it fired so it was super white hot when I saw the seven or eight missiles fire out. They were so low in trajectory I thought they were coming at us, but they shot overhead thankfully and impacted up near the bridge in front of the friendly quick reaction force QRL Challenger team. The shockwave as they impacted was memorable to say the least. It was like standing in body armour, and someone very strong whacking you across the chest with a big shovel.

Over my PRR one of the team alerted me to movement on the other side of the road 200m away. Using Sophie again, I spotted three enemy crawling along the ground. They were on a collision course for our extraction route, so I called a snap ambush. We all got into position lying on the side of the berm. I initiated the ambush by firing a Shermuly parachute flare that helped light up the crawling Iraqis. We all poured lots of rounds at them and they all were hit and stopped moving. Of course, that woke everyone up to our presence.

I called for extraction (by two Warriors) and the two QRL Challengers came forward giving covering fire, as we gradually withdrew, overlapping each other along the berm towards the arriving Warriors. Each half of the patrol then split, mounted into the Warriors, and withdrew to company HQ for debrief.

The CO, Lt Col David Paterson, was brought up to speed with the patrol report and together with the company commander, Maj Paul Nanson, decided that they should move straight away at first light to attack what was clearly a well dug-in and aggressive company-sized position.

The assault would be carried out by three Challenger tanks of 2 Troop, B Squadron, QRL and 9 Platoon, 1 RRF mounted in four Warriors. Behind 9 Platoon would be a TAC HQ, FOO, MFC (mortar fire controller) and an ANGLICO Team. Another team lending support was a US SF team with a drone which did an overfly of the Iraqi position while the briefing was on at the O-group. Everyone gathered around the monitor watching the live feed of what was new battlefield technology. The drone showed six dug-in BMPs and confirmed the patrol sighting of trenches connecting a series of bunkers. The final 'add on' for the assault were two Royal Engineer CETs which were tasked with trying to extinguish the flaming oil fire in no man's land.

Just after first light a preparatory artillery bombardment hit the Iraqi lines. As the first salvo of 155mm shells fired by 3 RHA impacted, the attack commenced. It was hoped that the Warrior dismounts would not even need to get out of their armoured carriers and their main armament and chain guns would be enough to destroy the infantry. HESH rounds soon found their mark busting the bunkers, and Fin shells hit several of the dug-in BMPs. RPG teams soon started engaging the column but once again the British heavy armour defeated the RPGs. One of the tanks drove down off the raised road onto the trench lines and carried out 'neutral turns' spinning the tracks while sitting on the trenches, causing them to collapse and bury those inside. After 40 minutes in contact, word was passed that the Sappers in the CETs were starting to poach inside their vehicles, with the intense heat of the blazing oil well proving too much for them despite dumping tons of sand across the source of the blaze. Maj Nanson called for extraction and as he did so the crew of a QRL Challenger spotted the elusive BM-21 rocket launcher, reversing away between two blocks of houses. One well-aimed HESH round obliterated the truck-mounted weapon system and acted as an encore of the performance by the Fusilier BG. The vehicles carefully reversed back under covering fire from the Mortar Platoon, towards and across Bridge 3, firing smoke grenades as they went.

With the confirmed destruction of the BM-21, at least two BMPs and perhaps 60 infantry the assault was a success. The Iraqi command post in the buildings was still operating the next day and so an American AC-130 Spectre gunship, callsign Slayer, was called in by the ANGLICO team and pulverised it into brick dust with its 105mm and 40mm cannons.

Following the RSDG and RRF raids, and the good work of 662 Squadron near the Technical College, it appears the Fedayeen were less keen on venturing onto the main road or even being in sight of the bridge. The locals soon began to venture back out and try to cross to Az Zubayr or Umm Qasr. Endless streams of locals trying to flee the city meant a growing pressure on the VCP teams to communicate with them. For the next phase of operations at Bridge 4, the Irish Guards moved up and relieved the Black Watch and immediately a call was made for more Arabic speakers to be made available, preferably one per company. Maj John Cotterill was one of them:

> I jumped at the chance of getting forward with the Micks as an interpreter, and quickly traded my 9mm Browning for an SA80. I climbed on the back of a CVRT which took me to Bridge 4 on the edge of south-western Basra. On 30 March I reported to Number 1 Company, The Irish Guards who were part of the Scots DG BG. Each battlegroup was 'square', that is to say, it had a balanced mix of two armoured (tank) squadrons and two armoured infantry companies in Warriors. We spent four days there and it was very busy. Nothing was allowed into the city and there was a constant stream of civilian traffic exiting it. We had to stop and talk to the occupants of every vehicle approaching our VCP. First, they were searched to ensure no weapons were leaving the area and then checked against lists of known targets. Most were tomato farmers and families in cars escaping what looked a potential battle in their city.
>
> I was the only Arabic speaker at the bridge so was constantly needed to converse. 'Who are you? Where are you going? Show me your papers. Where are the Fedayeen Militia? Are they building defences? After a while some of the people started offering us bits of information about what was going on in the centre and where the Ba'ath Party people were living. Countless people upon questioning about Ba'ath Party membership would haul up their *dishdasha* or shirt and show me horrible torture wounds that had been inflicted by the party officials. Most of the victims were Shi'ites and had been much repressed by Saddam. The overwhelming attitude of 99% of people in Basra at that time was positive to our presence and the toppling of Saddam Hussein. The later insurgency was, I am certain, backed by anti-western extremist Iranian-funded groups.
>
> There was growing media attention we had to manage carefully at the bridges. Sky, BBC, CNN and so forth all turned up. We gave a French crew a tough time because they were not contributing to the war effort. On another bridge (2 or 3), a TV crew interviewed a soldier as

he was speaking to two Iraqi brothers, who for some reason then went back into the city. The Fedayeen got to hear about this interview that must have gone out on Al Jazeera or Satellite news and the two brothers had a visit from the militia, who killed them.

Our checkpoint straddled the four-lane highway that ran across the bridge. Armoured Warriors were parked in such a way as to create a chicane that vehicles had to negotiate. Gunners inside the vehicles covered the approaching traffic and dismounted Irish Guardsmen were in defensive overwatch and manning the checkpoint with me. Two Challengers from the Scots DG were also very close by with their main 120mm armament aimed at Basra. Occasionally RPGs were fired in our direction from the buildings near the Basra end of the bridge. Immediately the Challengers would respond, firing HESH or their chain guns at the offending buildings. We also came under mortar fire at the VCP. Fortunately, the engineers had been along with their digger and dug us some deep trenches, so as soon as incoming mortars burst nearby, we could jump into the trench. Moments later the guys would all be out again talking to people at the windows of their cars just like in Northern Ireland. This went on seven or eight times a day. The troops' ability to 'flick the switch' between war fighting, sheltering in a trench from shrapnel fire, then immediately engaging with non-English speaking civilians, joking with kids, searching car boots in a professional and courteous manner and, of course, not interfering with their women folk was hugely impressive. I thought at the time that there probably wasn't any other army in the world that could have done that switching between passive liaison and aggressive action. Years and years of experience in counter-insurgency work in Ireland and Bosnia really showed through and I was proud to be part of it.

Manning the VCP was a job rotated through each platoon. In between duties on the bridge the other platoons pulled back to Az Zubayr for rest, feeding and local patrols. L/Sgt Bob Giles, 1 IG:

I was on the VCP at the bridge again when a guy, an extremely tall and skinny man standing at around 6ft 8in, approached me with a girl of about three or four years of age on his shoulders. Like hundreds before him, and hundreds after him, he quietly pleaded with me to show him special dispensation and let him return to Basra. Exhausted, and won over by the little girl's friendly and trusting brown eyes, I ushered him through. Sick to the back teeth with British army chocolate, I staggered after him after only a few feet and pushed a bar of the retched stuff into his daughter's hand. One less hater of devils in a couple of years I thought. He thanked me and encouraged his daughter to do likewise which she did whilst trying to balance on the towering shoulders and open the wrapper. I swear I saw them both again only days later under very different circumstances.

The crowds on that road, no matter how desperate, were not the enemy. Some tried to push through en masse, but never with any conviction and certainly never acted in a threatening way. These were the people of Iraq, not the regime, and it still amazes me today how they generally just accepted their fate and facelessly went about the business of surviving. Later in Basra, these same people would dismantle their own city whilst fighting raged around them, but still in that neutral, almost automotive way, like they were following an instruction they had learnt all their lives that in this given situation, this is how you should act. They were instructed well.

Just before this period of the war ended and we assaulted Basra, the people leaving the now-smoking city were victim to an Iraqi mortar attack on the bridge leading out of the city. A great deal was made of this by the army, inviting the media to come and take a look what the Ba'ath Party was prepared to do to their own people making a dash for the newly freed Iraq. In fact, that was bollocks. I never once saw organised government violence towards other Iraqis. There was plenty of evidence of individuals taking retribution on other individuals as the regime unravelled, but never targeting of civilians by the military.

What in fact was the case, was one of our checkpoints had set up too close to the city and therefore was in range of their mortars. The reason why Iraqi civilians were hit that day was because they got in the way of an attack on British troops.

Not all traffic at the VCP was civilian but one unexpected convoy came as a surprise to the Micks and Maj Cotterill:

> I was busy speaking with a car of Iraqis at the VCP when I became aware of a commotion behind. I looked up and saw a huge American military convoy of Humvees and soft-skin vehicles approaching. It was so long a convoy I couldn't see the back of it. It had approached on the wrong side of the road and was heading towards Basra. It was simply incredible. There were our two Challengers, both with smoking guns, not having fired very many minutes before, Guardsmen in fire positions with GPMGs set up, and yet here was a bunch of Americans seemingly oblivious and about to blunder into what was still classed as uncleared enemy territory. I stepped across and waved down the Humvee, which was a risk in itself. I spoke to a young captain in the front and asked him where he was going to which he simply responded, 'Baghdad.' I followed up by asking about his specific planned route and he said, 'Straight through Basra.' I laughed and told him it wasn't in our hands yet. He said, 'Oh, right. Well we had better find another route.' He then had to turn around his whole convoy of maybe 50–60 vehicles and head back whence he came. The target was clearly too good to miss, and we were soon mortared. Miraculously, all the vehicles got away, but it begs the question, how on earth was the guy briefed on taking a route like this through a war zone with a soft-skin supply column?

Without making an all-out entry into the city, the brigade commander now took a gamble by mounting a series of raids intending to demonstrate to everyone that the British were in control, dictating the terms and send a message to the Fedayeen. The first raid was in the area codenamed Breadbasket. This was an industrial complex on the edge of western Basra close to Bridge 2. B Squadron, QRL and Z Company, 1 RRF were to cross Bridge 2 and push on eastwards along Highway 31 until it met Route 6 running north–south. The junction of the two roads is a major interchange with on and off ramps to go north, south, east or west. It was codenamed Loop.

A plan was laid for three tanks to advance onto the Loop, each then turning outwards and facing in different arcs on the various carriageways. The four Warriors of 12 Platoon would plant themselves inside the ring of Challenger steel and conduct a VCP. As the Warriors manoeuvred into position, a T-55 was spotted and engaged by a Warrior and a Fin round from Maj Trant's tank which comprehensively brewed it up.

Lt Chris Rees-Gay, 1 RRF:

> **3 April** 'Op *Certain Death*' The platoon is attached to B Squadron, QRL for a VCP. So much for some down time, I have not washed or showered for seven days. I am minging. Went toe to toe with a T-55, had a stoppage and shit the bed but Zero Bravo, Maj Trant (QRL) waxed it. We had a team of US SF with us and an interpreter which was cool. There are more tomato sellers than grains of sand in Basra!

The VCP descended into more of a battle with RPG-firing Fedayeen popping out of the run-down huts and drainage ditches around the Loop. Scything chain gun fire would drive the Iraqis back into the buildings that were then hammered with HESH rounds. It was a brutal but effective tactic that kept 12 Platoon and the QRL alive. For 10 hours the VCP sporadically stopped traffic and then immediately got on with fighting its local battle. Callsigns were running low on ammunition so with some valuable intelligence gleaned and several prisoners captured, the VCP was withdrawn. Later that day, for the first time, staff officers at 1 UKDIV suggested that Basra need not be taken after the fall of Baghdad. Across the city, C Squadron, QRL mounted a similar raid complete with a REME CRARRV and an ITN film crew who recorded the CRARRV toppling a Saddam statue. Locals stood by and watched and in some cases cheered. The members of the RRF/QRL BG did not know it but the powers that be were planning the final entry into Basra, content that conditions with the population were now right. The waiting was almost over.

CHAPTER 9

The Battle for Pussy Galore

L Company from 42 Commando was helicoptered in as a support unit, landing at Blofeld and moved in to assist both MSG and D Company. Capt Lynch got an MC that day fighting with the MSG.

I could hear marines on the net giggling as they gave contact reports and situation reports. They reported that they were 'entering Pussy', 'withdrawing from Pussy', then 29 Commando Artillery reported that they were 'pounding Pussy' before finally the MSG alerted us that they were now 're-entering pussy'. This was all the time accompanied over the radio by the sounds of fierce contact and the sounds of small-arms fire and RPG impacts.

Having largely cleared the eastern suburbs around the General Hospital, we set up 40 Commando HQ in what we soon termed the Alamo. It was a low commercial building surrounded, nearly all the way, by a high wall. The first task we did was a practice at 'stand to'. Everyone was allocated an area to protect including sections of the wall, windows and the flat roof which had a parapet around. No sooner had we done this, it got dark and we came under attack, and all ran back to our positions. Enemy came at us from all sides through the surrounding buildings and palm trees. We utterly smashed the hell out of them, totally blitzed them, it was great.

Maj Neil Wraith, RM

On the morning of 30 March, Operation *James* started, a full combined-arms assault on the outskirts of Basra against a town called Abu al-Khasib. Maj Neil Wraith, 40 Commando, remembers:

This was a 19-hour contact battle that saw Challenger tanks supporting a full-frontal four-company-wide marine assault on the suburb. (Two things I was always taught that we would never do were: an opposed amphibious assault and a full-frontal Commando assault – we ticked off both of those in Iraq.) I watched the Challengers moving across the start line just as the sun was coming up and remember thinking that someone was going to have a really bad day!

The adjutant and I had done most of the planning for Op *James (Bond)*. As was normal, we broke the area to be assaulted into sections with codenames. This makes it very easy then when under fire to identify where you or your friendly troops/enemy are. We decided this time to use James Bond as the codeword theme. So, Moonraker, Solitaire, Blofeld, Dalton, Oddjob and Moneypenny all appeared on the maps as either phase lines, conspicuous buildings or road junctions. Towards the far end of our area of operation we named two close neighbouring road junctions as *Pussy* and *Galore*.

The plan was initiated by the movement north of the RSDG Challenger tanks along the main road which borders the southern side of Abu al-Khasib. They would push past Moneypenny and Blofeld and go firm at Taku, a major junction 3km west of Blofeld. The Brigade Recce Force would then push to the eastern side of the town and probe the enemy defences. A, B, and D companies would then follow the RSDG along the main road led by the MSG, before at their allocated spot turning right and attacking into the suburbs next to each other. Maj Wraith continues:

> The most significant fighting took place on the western edge of the suburb although at one stage we had each of the companies in contact concurrently across the AO. I was with the CO's TAC HQ and spent much of the day, near Moneypenny, coordinating the battle while sat in a rubbish dump surrounded by used hypodermic needles and being belt-fed cigarettes by our Mortar Troop Commander.
>
> The enemy we encountered were across the full range of conscripts who did not have much will to fight, through Republican Guard who were considerably more determined to un-uniformed militia who were at times fanatical. Some clearly surrendered at the first opportunity, some fought to the death, some used the confusion to desert.

D Company and the MSG encountered stiffening resistance first at Galore then at Pussy. Sgt Barnett, D Company, 40 Commando remembers:

> On Op *James* we pushed forward into southern Basra clearing out pockets of Fedayeen loyal to Saddam. We came into contact the moment we crossed the start line at Blofeld (one of the Bond villains in *Thunderball*). Whilst trying to secure a six-storey college building, this was the first time I took someone's life.

Around a dozen Iraqi had set up a strong defensive position in the large office-like building that straddled the axis of advance for D Company towards Dalton. Using suppressive fire from .50 cal HMGs and a GPMG, the lead troop used fire and manoeuvre to assault the building. Four Iraqis were killed, and the remainder surrendered as soon as the marines stormed the building. One was shaking in fear but pretended to be dead lying next to the bloody corpse of his comrade. Maj Pierson then sent some of his company beyond Dalton to clear the huts and palm groves up to Moonraker (the Shatt al-Arab waterway). The other part of the company was called upon to reinforce the MSG, under Capt Lynch, who were pinned down in a firefight at Pussy Galore. The reinforcement column led with its Pinzgauers and WMIK Land Rovers and set off towards the noise of the MSG firefight. Sgt Barnett continues:

> I can't remember the exact distance but a very short while after moving off we were ambushed. I was initiated by a barrage of RPGs – they blew up our front Pinzgauer and then we came under effective indirect fire from mortars. Unbeknown to us at the time, the Fedayeen were using the Shatt al-Arab waterway behind the houses to shuttle mortars about. We couldn't see them setting up or moving their mortar positions and they hit us again and again. We were in contact for around 4.5 hours.

Miraculously, a second RPG had embedded itself in the radiator grille of the second Pinzgauer but failed to detonate and a third RPG struck a pile of ammo and Bergens stacked in front of Cpl Blackman's seat, before ricocheting off over his head. As marines jumped out adopting all-around defence, they saw a saloon car trying to get away from the ambush scene with four Fedayeen in. It did not get far before being riddled with fire and came crashing to a halt, all the occupants now slumped lifeless within or toppling out. The 20 or so marines in the column were now all out of their vehicles and fighting for their own lives in a new separate battle and were far from reaching the pinned-down MSG. Maj Pierson realised it had been a trap and would now have to extricate his own men. He could not use the main advantage he had, artillery, as the enemy were too close in contact and the positions of his own men was unclear. He needed to know where and how strong the enemy was, which meant he had to get the remainder of his men in the fight and pin the enemy. Using his final troop and the TAC HQ team, he organised a move forward, fighting their way to the dismounted column. Iraqis mounted darting attacks in small unpredictable movements from rooftops and side alleys. The marines in the ambushed column began to reform and fight a retreat, pulling back and gathering each other as they went. At the head of the now static column stood the two damaged Pinzgauers. As well as having a MILAN post on, the vehicles had radios and maps which the Royals were not going to allow to fall into enemy hands. LAW missiles were fired into them destroying them and setting them well ablaze.

Marine Gareth Thomas was in a D Company fire team of four men when, crossing an alleyway, they came under a long burst of machine-gun fire. He dived for cover behind a wall and became separated from his team who he could soon see were pinned down across the street, cut off from their company. He was unable to get at the enemy, so he worked his way down to the Shatt al-Arab (Moonraker) in an effort to outflank the enemy gunners. He saw a small boat moored just beyond where the enemy were. He swam to the boat and towed it back to the bank. Climbing up over the bank and seeing the enemy on the other side of the wall, he dropped a grenade on them, killing all three Iraqis. He called to his stranded team, and they ran to the boat and rowed it back to D Company's lines. Gareth was awarded the Military Cross for his bravery.

After 90 minutes of intense, confusing fighting Maj Pierson accounted for all his men back together, with no loss of lives. Over 30 Iraqi were dead, and the pendulum of battle began to swing the way of the marines. Now that Pierson knew where his own men were, he could call down 81mm mortar fire on the enemy, who then started to retreat.

Brig Dutton was not enjoying the day at all. His MSG was tied down short of its objective, the D Company rescue column had been ambushed and nearly needed rescuing itself, and then a logistics column moving on Dalton also came under fire. With echoes of the movie *Blackhawk Down* about multiple aircraft and vehicle columns getting ambushed in Mogadishu, Operation *James* appeared to be in the

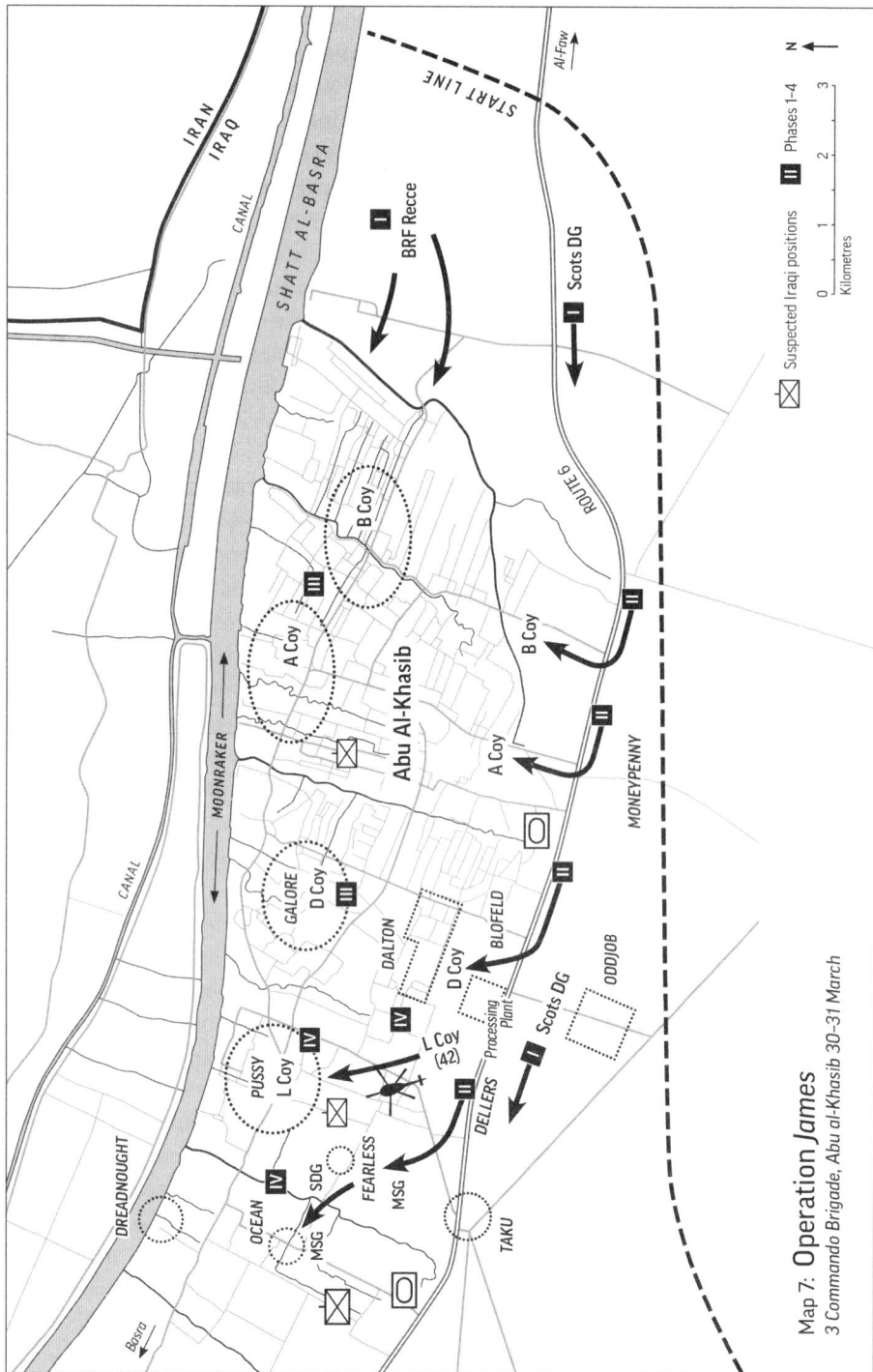

Map 7: Operation James
3 Commando Brigade, Abu al-Khasib 30–31 March

balance with the Bond villains taking the upper hand. It was time for *James* to bring in some support. L Company, 42 Commando was brought forward in a heliborne landing near Blofeld, close enough to get in and help but far enough from the downtown firefights not to get shot down. In the meantime, the logistics column had extracted safely, and D Company was also out of contact. As the Chinooks flared and landed, L Company was told to meet up with D Company and go firm for the night.

On the extreme left flank of Operation *James* the MSG group was heading for Pussy and Galore. This marked two important road junctions on the west of Abu al-Khasib. The most westerly was Pussy, a crossroads that reinforcements from Basra would have to come through to reach Abu al-Khasib. Capt Lynch and his 50 men of the MSG were a well-armed mobile unit and on *James* were supported by a troop of three RSDG Challenger tanks. The MSG had five Pinzgauers, originally six but one had rolled over and was written off. Three vehicles were armed with MILAN posts and the other two each had a pair of mounted GPMGs. Two Land Rovers carrying signallers and the FOOs and a Humvee with the American ANGLICO team completed the MSG column.

The slow start to the mission had worried Capt Lynch as it meant the cover of night was receding to reveal them to all the waiting eyes. However, as the dawn broke, his leading troops spotted hundreds of anti-personnel mines scattered along their route of advance. These lethal devices could easily pierce the soft-skin vehicles and cause lots of casualties. One of the tank commanders called forward the CRARRV with its bulldozer blade which it used to push the mines out of the way and down the side of the road embankment. The tank was impervious to the small mines and no damage was caused. The engineers' activity did not even attract any enemy fire. A basic rule of soldiering is always to cover an obstacle by fire to prevent the enemy easily overcoming the obstacle.

With a Challenger leading, followed by the Pinzgauers, the MSG finally got underway through the date and palm groves and the mud and brick houses along the roadsides. It was not long before the Challenger crew reported movement ahead. Two marines went forward on foot to ascertain if the people seen were civilian or enemy forces. A rapid burst of a Soviet-made machine gun quickly illustrated that the people were black-clad Fedayeen, and they had been waiting for the British. Capt Lynch's mixed column came to a stop across 300m of the raised road. Unable to manoeuvre to either side due to the marsh and mud, his options were limited. RPGs were hitting their mark on the column and concentrated small-arms fire was becoming intense and more accurate. It was a killing ground. A Pinzgauer soon suffered a fatal RPG hit and the damaged vehicle had to be stripped and abandoned. The MSG FOO called down artillery fire and very quickly the 105mm rounds from 29 Regiment were impacting and air bursting in the palm trees only 100–150m ahead of the British, in what some would say was *danger close*. The artillery fire allowed time for the MSG to pull back out of the killing ground. The three Challengers went forward to see what more they could do and rounded a bend to be confronted with a whole crowd of Fedayeen clambering all over the stranded Pinzgauer. A 120mm HESH round was instantly sent on its way, blasting the Pinzgauer and obliterating many of the men on it. Using their thermal image cameras, the tank troop reported that the dense undergrowth and palms were concealing more than 75–100 enemy. This was too much for the MSG to deal with alone and they were glad to hear Brig Dutton had released the brigade reserve, 42's L Company, who were flying in to come and assist in the battle.

Sgt Barnett continues:

> When I came under direct fire again near codename Galore, a US SOF Delta Force fire team was with us and we were close to the American JTAC/ANGLICO who was attached to us, so no doubt the insurgents were aiming for their Humvee. My fire team and I fired and manoeuvred towards the house where the fire was coming from. I ordered one of my marines to fire a LAW94 into the building, which he did with great effect and the firing ceased. I then remember I set up a VCP with a Pinzgauer that had a MILAN on it one side and then another with a .50 cal. We were taking accurate fire and I managed to positively identify that the fire was coming from a water tower around 500m away, I got the gunner to engage the water tower with the MILAN missile, neutralising the enemy position.
>
> I'm not sure how much time passed, it seemed like an age, and we then started to take indirect fire again. On scanning and searching for the enemy, further down the road I noticed a white Toyota 4x4 with a mortar barrel in the back. I engaged the two people in the back and then what I believed as the driver in the right seat. The Toyota then continued down a dirt road and turned off out of sight. For days I couldn't work out how the vehicle continued and got away! Discussing the contact, a friend kindly pointed out it's left-hand drive in Iraq! Doh!

As L Company HQ arrived, Capt Lynch was asked if the area was secure. As if in answer to the question an RPG whistled through the gathering and exploded just beyond them. Fedayeen had infiltrated past the Challenger tanks on the road and were now surrounding the MSG and leading sections of L Company. Firefights broke out at close quarters in the trees and control was starting to be lost. If the Iraqis reopened the road junction Taku, they could roll up the rear areas of the entire Commando in Abu al-Khasib. An increasing amount of small-arms fire came from three directions forcing the marines to take cover. L/Cpl Justin Thomas of the Machine Gun Troop saw that more heavy fire was needed to regain the upper hand. He leapt up onto his Pinzgauer in full view of the enemy and swung his GPMG into action. Pouring belt after belt of the heavy rounds into the wood line, the bullets shredded the palm fronds and gouged huge splinters out of the trunks and smashed into the Fedayeen soldiers with lethal effect. Thomas stayed on the red-hot gun for more than 15 minutes pounding and pinning the enemy to such an extent that his own troop then managed to take back the momentum and increase their fire. Cpl Thomas was later awarded the Conspicuous Gallantry Cross (CGC) for his actions in the battle at Pussy Galore. The CGC is second only to the Victoria Cross in the awards for gallantry. It was first awarded in 1995 and was introduced to remove the distinction of rank in gallantry. Justin was only the ninth recipient of the award, and the first in Iraq. His citation described his actions:

Lance Corporal J. Thomas, 40 Commando, Royal Marines

Lance Corporal Thomas deployed on Op *Telic* as a GPMG section commander in Manoeuvre Support Group of 40 Commando, Royal Marines. Despite his lack of formal command training, his leadership in combat has been of the highest order. Yet it is an individual act of immense bravery that stands him out from his contemporaries as worthy of lasting recognition. On 30 March 2003, a Commando attack was mounted against an enemy in battalion strength in the Abu-al-Khasib area near Basrah. Lance Corporal Thomas' troop was tasked with securing a key junction on the vulnerable western flank. After initially good progress, it was just after first light when they were ambushed in the open by continual volleys of RPG and small-arms fire from a well disguised enemy position in the cover of date palms some 250 metres away. This initial contact lasted three hours during which the troop managed to extract safely to a reorganisation location ready to meet and brief reinforcements from 42 Commando. At this critical juncture in the battle, the assembled troops came under sustained and effective RPG and small-arms fire from a new undetected location of 15–20 enemy troops some 350m away. Realising that many of his comrades were now exposed, Lance Corporal Thomas ran from his position of comparative safety and climbed onto his open top vehicle to man a pintle-mounted GPMG. With his No. 2 feeding ammunition and with no protection afforded by the vehicle, Lance Corporal Thomas single-handedly returned a heavy weight of sustained fire for a continuous period of nearly 15 minutes to enable 20 other members of his troop to safely move into cover and to regroup. As small arms and RPGs landed all around him, his determination to suppress the enemy did not waiver, nor did his courage in the face of considerable threat to his own life. This singular act of selfless bravery ensured that his troop were able to extract safely from effective enemy fire without loss in order to launch a successful counter-attack. Had casualties been taken, the progress on the Commando's western flank would have been slowed and potentially placed the remainder of the unit in a vulnerable position. Lance Corporal Thomas' section had a further three contacts that day as they set about achieving their mission, yet his leadership and personal example were never found wanting. Lance Corporal Thomas' extreme bravery in the face of a well-armed and determined enemy undoubtedly saved numerous lives that day and was fundamental to mission success. Throughout a demanding sequence of operations, his section's performance has been invariably impressive, due largely to his natural command presence. Categorically, his exceptional courage and inspirational leadership under effective enemy fire deserve lasting public recognition.*

L Company now linked up with MSG and the three Challengers to continue the fight for Pussy Galore. MSG headed back up the road and despite the reinforced heavier British presence, the Iraqis showed no sign of retreating. Tanks and dismounted

---

*   In 2009 Justin Thomas put his medals up for auction. He had by then left the army and said he needed the money to help buy a house. Dix Noonan Webb sold the rare group for £88,000. It was the first ever Conspicuous Gallantry Cross to go for auction. Thomas said, 'I'll be sad to part with it, but I have to do what's right for my family, and I know it will be better than it sitting in a drawer.'

marines advanced at a cautious walking pace now, working in close co-operation to avoid further losses.

Late on 30 March, the longest day just got worse. Still advancing north towards the vital junction of Pussy and the tree-lined water's edge of the Shatt al-Arab, the mixed column once more came under attack. A group of determined and well-trained Iraqis, perhaps Special Forces, had crept into hidden ambush positions at the side of the single-track road and awaited the RSDG tanks.

Sgt Charlie Baird was commanding the lead tank, callsign Two One. His driver was Tpr 'Mac' Macawai from Fiji. Known for their commanding size, Mac was a little smaller than most of the regiment's other Fijians but it was still a tight squeeze for him in the driver's seat of the Challenger. Mac was the newest driver in the squadron but worked hard and showed promise as he edged the 70-ton steel monster along the dirt roads. Following about 100m behind was Troop Commander Capt Le Sueur in his Challenger Two Zero and it was he who probably had the clearest view of the attack on Two One. Like a ripple effect, a salvo of RPGs shot out of the trees and streaked the 100m towards the tank. Then the scene erupted as machine gun tracers flew toward the tank as well. The first RPG hit the front of the turret and exploded in a shower of multicoloured sparks. Machine gun rounds smacked into Mac's vision block turning his clear view into that resembling a shattered window. As Mac instinctively braked, causing the tank to lurch to a stop, the crew were thrown forward. Another RPG in the salvo exploded on the commander's hatch which also smashed two of his periscopes. The force of the explosion, close to his head, stunned and concussed Baird into a stupor. Tpr Ferguson began to return fire with the chain gun, but it too seemed damaged and soon had a stoppage. Disorientated, stunned and no doubt scared, the crew began shouting orders and requests at each other but with Sgt Baird concussed, confusion reigned. It became clear that this was a well-prepared and camouflaged position. Trenches ran parallel to the road hidden by the undergrowth and trees, allowing the RPG teams to pop up and fire then do so again from a new alternate position. Capt Le Sueur noted that not a single shot was aimed at anyone or anything other than Two One. He called Sgt Baird and urged him to remain calm and get control of his crew. He also reassured him that he and Cpl Dougal in Two Two were on their way to assist and would not leave him stranded. Baird switched to the internal net and told Mac to reverse and take instructions on directions. Looking to the rear out of his only non-shattered periscope Baird began to guide his driver backwards towards safety.

Two Zero and Two Two were by now firing furiously at the attacking troops. HESH and chain gun fire hosed down the RPG teams that dared show themselves and the tree line began to disintegrate under the immense firepower of the two Challengers. Baird continued shouting instructions trying to make himself heard over the roar of engines and the machine-gun fire crashing against the armour plating of the tank. 'OK, keep her straight, left stick, OK good, slow down, left stick, left stick! NO! Right stick!' came another shout. In the confusion Mac yanked the left stick and it was the wrong one. The tank, so close to the edge of the road and the drainage ditch caused the road to crumble and the tank slid backwards into the ditch. Two One was seen to wobble almost facing vertically at the sky then toppled towards her right track and came to rest at 45 degrees with her belly exposed. Mac gripped his controls, jammed it into first gear and floored the accelerator. The great engine roared like a beast in its death throes. Both sets of tracks objected to this harsh treatment and broke away like flailing arms with the drive sprockets spinning like crazed Catherine wheels. The main gun hung limply like a wounded warrior's sword hand, pointing down at the road. Then as if like a hunter firing the killer blow a final RPG shot out from a small farm shack only 40m from Two One and hit her on the gunner's sights. Captain Le Sueur tried raising Two One repeatedly but there was no reply.

The call had already gone out over the squadron and battlegroup net that a tank was immobilised and needed help. A REME recovery team had scrambled in their CRARRV, meanwhile the other tanks continued to provide covering fire and kept the circling Indians away from the wounded wagon train. Inside the tank the crew were at near panic levels shouting at each other and pleading with Baird to get them out. Of course, they knew that help was on its way and that sitting inside a Challenger tank behind some of the best armour in the world meant that it was safer inside than out. But the constant bullet and RPG strikes continued to wear them down and increase their worry that they would soon be overrun and somehow die horribly inside the tank.

Cpl Dougal in Two Two was working his tank like a honed killing machine as more and more Fedayeen rushed in for the kill, seemingly careless about the threat he posed or the risks they faced.

> Over to Dougal's left another RPG operator knelt and raised his launcher getting poised to fire at Two One. With his scope magnified the Iraqis face filled his sights as if he was only feet away. He was shaved and well-groomed in his black pyjama-like outfit. 'When are you going to learn?' Dougal muttered to himself, 'Why don't you fuck off home?' The paramilitary put his eye to the RPG sight and lined up on Two One. Dougal was quicker and squeezed off a 20-round burst from the 7.62mm chain gun. Bullets hammered into his chest and shredded the man where he knelt. He fell backwards in a black lifeless heap of blood-streaked clothing. [1]

The next strike on Two One was from some other form of anti-tank weapon, possibly an American-made LAW. It struck the turret, did not penetrate but did cause a huge bang and some hot spall fragments flew around the turret. Despair turned to panic and the crew, fearing an internal explosion flung open their hatches to escape.

In what must have looked like the 7th Cavalry racing to rescue the besieged waggoners, the squadron commander, Maj Biggart, in Zero Bravo and Cpl Morgan in the CRARRV, callsign Juliet Three Three, came screaming up to the scene alongside Capt Le Sueur. The deafening noise of the battle was a shock to Biggart when he opened his commander's hatch to survey the scene only 30m in front of him. An RPG shot across the top of his turret, missing him by less than a metre. Having surveyed the scene with his own eyes though, he now knew what needed to be done. He shouted across the squadron net at the crew of Two One, ordering them to stay inside and not abandon their tank until told to do so. Maj Biggart then got all callsigns to fire everything they had at the two-storey building in the trees from where most of the enemy fire was coming. The three Challengers all lined up their 120mm main guns as if in a synchronised movement. Inside the turrets the loaders selected the HESH rounds needed and pushed them into the breach. Fired almost in synch, the big tank shells ploughed through the upper storey, exploding in a fiery blast ball sending chunks of masonry, bricks and shattered timber high into the sky. The process was repeated with more than 10 rounds utterly destroying the building in less than a minute. The heavier fire and RPGs slackened although Fedayeen with AK-47s still shot from every angle. Now Maj Biggart saw a chance for the crew to extract and for the CRARRV to recover the Challenger. Sgt Baird and his crew drew breath and, on the signal, all left the safety of Two One and climbed out into the maelstrom of fire.

Incredibly, the entire crew got out without being hit and reached the cover of the ditch under the tank. By now the CRARRV was only metres away and two of the crew from Two One jumped inside it for cover while Baird and Mac crouched behind Maj Biggart's tank. The REME fitters, then set about recovering the Challenger from the ditch. They had to fix winch chains to Two One and back onto the CRARRV. They carried this out coolly while under fire. Juliet Three Three took the strain and started to try to pull the Challenger up out of the ditch. Two One, like a stubborn stranded bull elephant didn't budge an inch. The combination of the angle of the tank in the ditch, the broken tracks binding up in the suspension and the limited angles available to work with due to enemy fire meant the winch just wouldn't cut it. The strain was immense and then the high tensile steel rope snapped like a tendon, whipping around like a deadly cobra.

With the winch line broken, Three Three was now useless. Morale took a dive lower down the slide when it was realised that the £5,000,000 tank may just have to be destroyed by friendly fire if there were no other options. Unusually, however, a second CRARRV had been sent to 3 Commando Brigade and this was now called forward from the road junction at Taku together with another tank, Four One, as escort.

In the intervening period, awaiting the arrival of the new REME vehicle, news seemed to have travelled locally attracting yet more Iraqi militia about the impending doom of the tank in the ditch. The sun was now setting on Pussy Galore as the second CRARRV arrived. Commanded by Cpl Garrett, the crew jumped into action to repeat the efforts at towing. Maj Biggart briefed the team in cover, making it clear that they would not be leaving the tank behind. He also called in a smoke barrage from the Royal Artillery to help mask the recovery fitters as they once more fixed the steel winches in place. Bullets were still pinging against the tanks like hailstones and now, the Fedayeen were bringing harassing, if not accurate, mortar fire down. Biggart also requested a troop of marines from 40 Commando to come forward alongside the armoured unit to provide more close protection as night fell. Until that point Maj Biggart had kept the marines in reserve due to the high risk of friendly fire in the close quarters of the battle. There were now four tanks firing main gun and chain guns at the enemy positions. To add yet more firepower, the spare crewman on the CRARRV, Cpl Simons, and the Challengers' gunners raised up out of their turrets to man the pintle-mounted GPMGs. This extra firepower was certainly slowly taking a toll on the Fedayeen whose accuracy and rate of fire was slacking.

The winch hawsers failed for a second time, dropping morale to a new low. So low that no one even spoke for a minute or so as they stared in disbelief at the still stricken tank. REME Cpl Jason Garrett spoke first suggesting that he had another idea. He would have liked to use a small lump of PE4 explosive to blow the tracks away which is what tank recovery teams had been doing since WW2 – but something the MOD Health and Safety team had prohibited due to too many accidents in training. That decision now looked likely to cost £5,000,000 in one go. Instead, Garrett would use the CRARRV cutting equipment to cut the tangled mess of tracks away, freeing up the wheels which would make the whole operation easier. The new plan was agreed and again the REME fitters went to work. As if the image of them working on the tank, only 100m away from dozens of frenzied enemies, was not enough, the fitters now crouched next to the tank using arc-welding kit with a bright glow and showers of sparks as if to say, 'Here we are, shoot at us.'

For two hours the team worked amid the incoming fire but eventually had to give up. The combination of the flooded ditch concealing some of the tracks, the incoming fire and the toughness of the tracks meant they had made little progress. Fortunately, the thermal imaging tank sights and the proximity of the highly proficient marines meant that fire from the enemy was notably reducing. One final idea was put forward by the REME. They had a metal recovery frame known by its shape simply as an A-frame. They were rigid recovery options for use on tarmac roads, not for complex assignments in a ditch under fire. Nevertheless, with superhuman effort the REME and the emboldened crew of Two One heaved the two A-frames into position and fixed them onto the hulk in just 15 minutes. The combined 150 tons of the two CRARRVs now pulled ever so slowly, and the hulk of Two One began to rise from the ditch like a phoenix. She then teetered on the edge before slumping down onto the track in a cloud of grit and sand.

With muffled cheers and much back-slapping, smiles spread across the intrepid recovery team and Maj Biggart ordered the slow withdrawal back to Taku. The column reversed, keeping their thick frontal armour towards the enemy as the marines also fired and manoeuvred alongside them. The Fedayeen had lost and were in no mood to try and intervene further. It was dawn by the time the unit got back to the relative safety of Taku.

Two One was recovered to Shaiba Air Base where it was examined and repaired. Fourteen direct RPG impacts and more than 20 other RPG strikes were counted. None had penetrated. Thousands of bullet strikes gouged paint and damaged external storage bins. Most of the vision blocks and periscopes were smashed; all the gunsights were broken. The smoke grenade dischargers were mangled, headlights and horn blown off and the chain gun barrel was damaged. The unknown anti-tank missile had caused the most damage on the front, penetrating a fist-sized hole, three inches deep into the armour and causing the spall inside, but it still had not penetrated. Three days later Two One rolled out, repaired, and fit for service. The two REME corporals were both mentioned in despatches for their leadership, calmness and disregard of their own safety.

The battle for Pussy Galore had been won. The operation had been resumed with tanks and marines returning to the scene of the epic recovery just a few hours after they had left. This time 200 more marines were also converging from the east as the men of D and L company caught the defenders in the flank. Two hours later, Operation *James* concluded, and all objectives were reported taken. The door to Basra was open.

The unit recorded having expended 287,000 rounds of 5.56mm ammo in the battle as well as 165,000 7.62mm GPMG, 894 grenades, 356 LAWs, 120 MILAN missiles and 2,780 81mm mortar rounds. 29 Commando Royal Artillery also fired 5,236 105mm rounds in support of the commandos on Operation *James*. Maj Neil Wraith continues:

Next morning Brig Jim Dutton visited us at HQ and listened to a debrief of the operation and said how pleased he was with how we had performed. He did then say rather quietly to Lt Col Gordon Messenger, 'For the sake of historical record is there any chance we can change the names of these codewords?' We never did.

A few days later, after we had established ourselves in what became our final position (a fertiliser factory), a football match was organised with some locals. I went along as part of the security and got chatting to a group of Iraqi lads, all but one of whom were keen to talk. One of them pointed at the clearly nervous one and said that he had once been in the Iraqi Army, I asked how long it was since he left and with a broad smile this lad said, 'Two days ago.' (They beat us in the football by the way – we were wearing combat boots though!) Some of the official locations we took reinforced in our minds why we were there – clear evidence of torture, indications from locals of mass graves. The overwhelming sense we got from the civilians was welcoming, friendly and relieved that the Saddam Hussein regime was gone. An injured Iraqi soldier being stretchered onto a helicopter gave the lads a thumbs up and shouted, 'I love Tony Blair,' and a young boy came up to me in the street one day with an Iraqi bank note with Saddam's picture on it and tore it up, threw it on the ground and stamped on it with a big grin on his face.

We suffered around 25 casualties during *James* but astonishingly, no fatalities. Eight men were wounded from B Company which was a result of our own 155mm artillery falling short at the start line, or perhaps the guys being too eager to get forward and getting too close to the falling rounds. One guy was hit by two bullets on his helmet, but they did not penetrate the Kevlar. One guy was hit in the torso, but his chest plate body armour defeated the round. Four guys were badly hurt when their 4-ton lorry rolled over, and they fell out the back. We also lost three Pinzgauer vehicles, a BV-106 ambulance and two MILAN posts were destroyed. We captured over 400 prisoners.

Operation *James* was the last major kinetic battle 40 Commando were involved in. The Royal Marines rapidly switched to a more stabilisation and policing role. After three weeks in Abu al-Khasib the Commando moved to Khor al-Zubair port then back on to HMS *Ocean*. They flew home from Kuwait on 7 May.

CHAPTER 10

Basra Falls

There was never any talk originally of taking Basra, so while we were in and around Umm Khayyal (20km due south of Basra) for about six days we ran a sort of policing operation with some locally cultured informants. We were encouraged to clear out Ba'ath Party officials and we were quite successful at weeding them out. We even found two mail sacks of cash on one of our searches. We used some of the money to pay locals to get the infrastructure up and running. We also arranged a football match to help with the hearts and minds style of operation. The game got well photographed and the story made it back to the UK news. We lost 9–0.

Orders then arrived that we would be leaving to go into Basra. This worried us. During those six days we had struck a rapport with many locals, others had been working with us and there was a strong feeling that if we pulled out there may be reprisals against those who had sided with us. The CO asked who was coming to relieve us but the answer was no one.

Some of our company was helicoptered up to Basra and about half went in the few Land Rovers and commandeered vehicles we had on fleet. As the vehicles left the town the marines could hear the shooting start in their wake. It was a moral moment that didn't sit well with us.

CAPT STU TAYLOR, 42 COMMANDO

During the period 31 March to 4 April 2003 the British Army's mood changed noticeably as commanders and troops alike began to sense a noticeable trailing off in resistance to their raids across the bridges, such as when Maj Tim Brown had brought the TV tower crashing down. In the north M1 Abrams tanks of the US 3rd Division nosed out onto the runway of Baghdad International Airport and other tanks carried out what the Americans termed 'Thunder Runs' through the suburbs of the capital city – a term first used in Vietnam when the armoured units fought at Huc in the Tet offensives of 1968. Intelligence reports passed to Gen Robin Brims, commander of the 1 (UK) Armoured Division, on 2 April suggested that the mood of the local Basra population was still not entirely convinced that the coalition had won and would stay in situ. It was neither ready to rise in revolt but was hedging its bets. To gain the final advantage and gather the population's open support, Gen Brims and his team planned Operation *Sinbad*, the launching of simultaneous concentric attacks on the city from both the west and the north. The RSDG would strike first in the south-west quadrant towards a key road junction, Objective Granite. The Fusiliers would head to Objective Quartz in the north of the city which was the large Al Najibiya power station, the University and the Naval Academy. Finally, the Black Watch would push towards the central business district, Objective Slate. Gen Brims said:

> I had complete freedom to do this at the right moment. I was never under pressure from commanders above me, only from my subordinates who were understandably keen to get it done. I resisted until circumstances were right to do it in a less bloody way.[1]

Troops from 16 AAB swept around to the north and completely cut the road to Baghdad, and the Commando Brigade reorganised in readiness to assist with Operation *Sinbad*. 42 Commando was the more rested of the two commando units and was told to move forwards. Capt Stu Taylor of 42 Commando:

> I led our small convoy of nine vehicles toward Basra. I was simply told to get to the RVP at the Technical College on the eastern side of Bridge 4. However, we were not allowed to use Bridge 4 as it was presumably under fire. The instruction was to reach a point known as CP (crossing point) Anna on the Shatt al-Basra where someone would meet me to guide us. The CP was manned by 28 Engineer Regiment, RE using M3 amphibious bridging vehicles.
>
> As far as we knew, beyond the waterway was enemy territory that was very challenging to traverse due to the mud other than by following the raised roadways. The Sappers were using the M3s in raft form and they agreed to ferry us across but knew nothing about our planned rendezvous.
>
> I checked my map from which I had trimmed off all the superfluous stuff and areas unlikely to be needed and had folded in front of me. We were in the right place. I called up on the radio and was told to head north several kilometres to RV with a Scimitar CVRT from the QDG. We met with the QDG and I jumped out to chat with the vehicle commander who then informed me that we were not permitted to go along the easy route, parallel with the waterway, as it had not been cleared. He pointed at his own map saying *you must go via this point and then this junction*. My heart sank. The waypoints being highlighted were on the area of the map that I had so enthusiastically trimmed off! Realising my issue, the QDG guy offered me the series of coordinates which I could punch in my hand-held GPS and a list of notes to accompany them telling me to turn left or right.
>
> With this done, we were on our own. It was pitch dark, heading into enemy territory. I felt rather like David Stirling in World War 2 operating behind enemy lines. As we crawled forward at no more than 10mph I had my cocked weapon across my knees, I really was cacking myself. In the distance I saw a fire which upon getting closer was a burning Iraqi tank. Other than the flicker of the flaming tank there was no light. It was so dark the drivers were worried that they would steer off the raised road, slide down into the ditches or mud and get stuck. We made the decision to move on sidelights to at least give them a fighting chance of keeping the convoy on the road. Minutes later I saw more lights coming towards us. Shifting in my seat uncomfortably I readied my SA80 into my shoulder in anticipation. When it got closer, we could tell it was a car, but we kept our guard up and it too slowed down as it inched passed us. I don't know who was in it, but they were probably as scared as we were and drove on into the night. Flashes lit up the night away to our right: that was the Royal Artillery doing their thing.
>
> Using the GPS, I gave countdowns to the driver so he could look out for sideroads and junctions. Then the radio sparked up with 3 Commando Brigade asking for my location. It was a 15km journey by direct route, but we were now four hours in and a long way from arrival. There was no secure comms, so I had to work out my grid, translate that into code via the old BATCO system, then transmit it. This all took time and was slowing us down considerably.

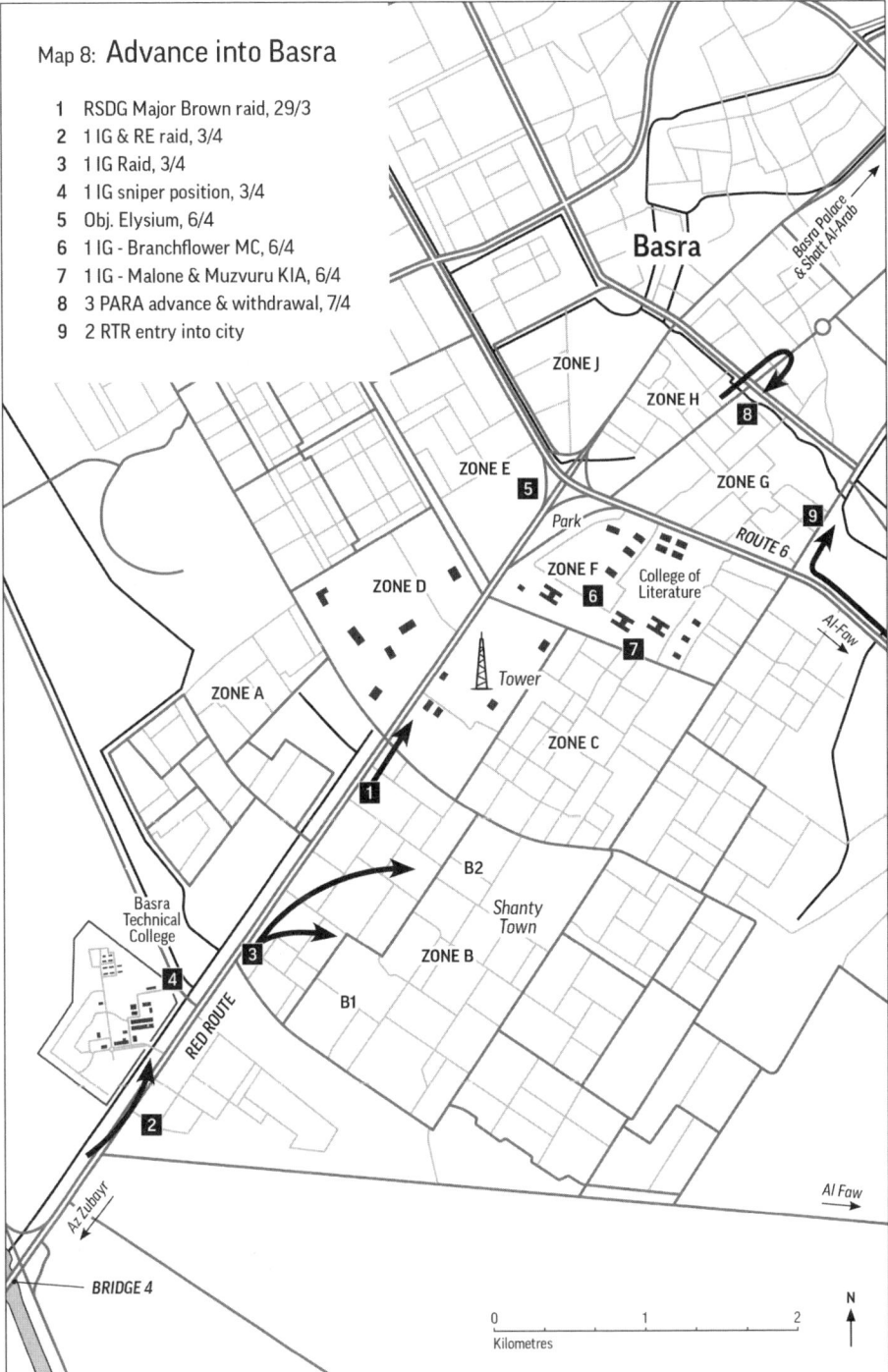

Map 8: **Advance into Basra**

1   RSDG Major Brown raid, 29/3
2   1 IG & RE raid, 3/4
3   1 IG Raid, 3/4
4   1 IG sniper position, 3/4
5   Obj. Elysium, 6/4
6   1 IG - Branchflower MC, 6/4
7   1 IG - Malone & Muzvuru KIA, 6/4
8   3 PARA advance & withdrawal, 7/4
9   2 RTR entry into city

Basra

Basra Palace & Shatt Al-Arab

ZONE J

ZONE H

8

ZONE E

5

ZONE G

Park

ROUTE 6

9

ZONE D

ZONE F

College of Literature

6

Al-Faw

7

Tower

ZONE A

ZONE C

1

B2

Basra Technical College

Shanty Town

4

3

ZONE B

RED ROUTE

B1

2

Az Zubayr

Al Faw

BRIDGE 4

N

0   1   2
Kilometres

I transmitted my location, and the reply came back querying our location, they couldn't understand why I was so far away. By then I was totally knackered, I'd been on edge for four hours and so just pushed on.

Without further incident we made it to the RV. We pulled up to a metal gate manned by a young marine who walked up to my Land Rover window to ask me for the password. At that time, we were using the American system where the challenge was given by the sentry, using two words in a sentence, to which you had to reply with the other two code words in a sentence. For instance, the words may be RED JACKET followed by the response BLUE CAR. The marine leaned on my window and said, 'Have you seen a guy wearing a red jacket?' Knackered and lacking any sense of humour I replied, 'Fuck off.' He opened the gate. It had been a hell of a journey, a real drama and one which I will not forget.

Once inside the compound I was brought up to speed with what other units and brigades had been doing. I realised that outside of my own company and 42 Commando, I had very little knowledge of what anyone else had done. I knew roughly where 40 Commando had been but had absolutely no idea what 7 Brigade had done and for all I knew the Paras must have gone home.

In the first days of April the next stage of taking Basra was launched from the springboard of the bridges over the Shatt al-Basra Canal. It was a series of what was termed 'raid and aid'. Company-sized groups of 14 Warriors and a troop of two or three Challengers would trundle into the city, acting on intelligence about a Fedayeen strongpoint – a Ba'ath Party HQ or a mortar position – and would find and destroy the position and any Fedayeen that happened to show themselves at any point. Vast quantities of bottled water were also taken and when the combat indicators allowed, these aid supplies would be given out to the local population. Running water had failed some time previously and bottled water was in high demand. The impression of giving out aid and then the interpreters talking to the local populace allowed further intelligence gathering on other targets and provided HQ with a feel for the mood of the city. 'Raid and aid' was not a recognised tactic and had never been practised at Warminster or anywhere else, the troops adapted on the move, yet again showing flexibility and innovation.

Flexibility and innovation also had to be shown by the Royal Artillery when it came to achieving effects at long range in urban areas with little or no collateral damage. Lt Col Nicholas Ashmore 3 RHA:

How to put a PGM through the roof of the Ba'ath Party HQ in Basra was not one of the scenarios we had trained for during the training year in Larkhill. However, that was the exact challenge we faced. Fortunately, there were some new assets at 7 Brigade HQ that had not so far trained with us, but which would make that exact scenario possible on 25 March 2003.

Real-time intelligence was being fed into Brigade HQ through a number of feeds. Human intelligence was being fed to HQ on Thuraya mobile satellite phones, via covert SF assets on the ground in Basra describing what they were seeing and hearing. Trusted Iraqi sources were providing intelligence, and the Phoenix UAVs were adding live images of the city. This amalgam of information was fed into the

US ANGLICO command system which processed the data and crosschecked it into a 10-figure grid reference of the suspect target building. A tactical air request for a PGM was generated and sent via a secret US email system for action. The Ba'ath Party HQ in Basra was a high value target and was to be the first to benefit from a PGM through the roof. Two 2,000lb JDAMs with GPS guidance systems sailed down to earth and detonated inside the HQ building. It was largely reduced to rubble, but the failure in intelligence was that most of the Ba'ath Party had left a month before.

A few days later, on 4 April, SAS reports fed in of Ali Hassan al-Majid, better known as 'Chemical Ali', the King of Spades in the US Defence Intelligence Agency's personality identification playing cards and Iraq's fifth most wanted man, being in Basra holding a meeting with key party and militia officials at a large residence near the Shatt al-Arab. After some initial delay, a strike was authorised and directed on target by the SAS using a hand-held laser. Two RAF Tornados and a pair US F-16s from the 524th Fighter Squadron raced to the target. The Americans arrived first. The first two laser-guided 500lb bombs dropped by the F-16s missed: one failed to explode and the other went rogue hitting two streets away. Circling back a second and then a third time the F-16s dropped four more bombs, three glided right onto the target pummelling and collapsing it. Unfortunately, civilian casualties were reported at the rogue bomb sites and the death of Chemical Ali was announced but it was sadly premature. Ali was captured in August and later tried for war crimes and genocide. Found guilty of numerous crimes he was sentenced to eight death sentences and was hung in 2010. He lies buried next to Saddam's sons in the Hussein family graveyard.

The bombing raid aimed at Chemical Ali is an example of what were known as TST – time sensitive targets – that could be based on fast time intelligence of a gathering of high-ranking officers or officials in a building or bunker, or something that in itself is valuable to destroy such as a Scud launcher. In one case news arrived from a source in Az Zubayr of a meeting starting of the Special Security Organisation (secret police). Within 45 minutes the meeting was rudely interrupted by a 1,000lb JDAM coming through the roof. There is no record of what the minutes of the meeting say about the aerial interruption.

Not all Royal Artillery work involved precision munitions and 9,513 rounds of 155mm ammunition were expended by the gunners of 3 RHA during *Telic*, nearly 300 rounds per gun. Many gunners, on debrief, commented that it was 'just like being on exercise', which is testament to the training they had been given. The AS-90 proved to be incredibly accurate and capable of destroying buildings and bunkers with an opening round. It was the only guaranteed offensive support asset available to the division for the entire 17 days of war fighting. It played a pivotal role in liberating Basra and provided a huge confidence boost to the supported arms.

Part of the RSDG BG including the Irish Guards moved east across the canal and set up a forward operating base at the Basra Technical College which had been so heavily engaged by the Fusiliers and Royal Artillery earlier. In fact, the college had been hit by 1,000 rounds of 155mm (6-inch) shells and numerous Hellfire and TOW missiles fired by US Cobra gunships and British Lynx helicopters. To finish off the bombardment two 2,000lb JDAM bombs dropped by F-18 Hornets had also obliterated parts of the main building. It was found that the USMC Cobra helicopter was the best suited for close air support in the city. Its combination of manoeuvrability, speed, psychological impact and accurate firepower was simply superb for the troops on the ground. The British Lynx just could not be so assured defensively and lacked the firepower of the Cobra. It was not long before the Army Air Corps would also have the battle-winning AH-64 Apache in its inventory but not for *Telic*. WO1 Tymon, AAC described in the squadron reports how he commanded a Lynx flight over the city in early April 2003:

> We were woken at 05:00, 3 April and told that there was to be a brief over at 7 Brigade HQ for a likely insertion over the city at 06:30 in support of Scots DG. The brigade was being told to provide support to the local population after the Fedayeen and Ba'ath Party had imposed a night-time curfew. Patrols had been coming under mortar fire and it was hoped that aviation would be able to pinpoint the mortars. The air defence assets in use by the Iraqi forces were still considerable and consisted in Basra of up to eight tracked ZSU-23-4 *Shillka* [four-barrelled 23mm self-propelled anti-aircraft guns], numerous technicals with DShK 12.7mm machine guns and the other great threat was a number of shoulder-launched SAMs that were man-portable but the Iraqis favoured riding them around on motorbikes in shoot and scoot missions from the alleys and rooftops of the Old City. So, with more than a little trepidation and blissfully ignorant of how the day would unfold we walked out to the aircraft. [2]

Each of the Lynx and Gazelles had encrypted radios that have to be regularly given an encryption key by means of what is known as a fill gun. The gun is a hand-held device that can upload crypto variable data to the radio system by means of a hard-wired connection. Technical faults and battery power interruption can lead to radios dropping the key and this means a manual refill by means of plugging in to the fill gun. The Lynx had a common problem of dropping its fill. For operational security reasons the 'fill gun' would not go in the aircraft but stayed at the base. WO1 J Tymon, AAC continues:

> All three of our aircraft had dropped their fill, so before we took off, we needed to arrange for the fill gun to be brought out. There followed an impressive performance of frantic despatch rider, Cpl Wyman, alias the 'White Helmet', racing across the dispersal area ever more burdened by the self-induced pressure of his failing crypto equipment. 'White Helmet' did a sterling job amid his stunt rider performance despite receiving a barrage of abuse (encouragement!).

Twenty-five minutes late, just after 07:30, the aviation patrol arrived, just 15m above ground level, on the start line. With the two Lynx forward and the Gazelle in the rear of formation they crossed the canal near Bridge 4. Beneath them the RSDG had already begun their move up the main road toward the College of Literature. WO1 J Tymon, AAC:

> Sgt Booley flew with me, Sgt Fenton commanded the second Lynx and S/Sgt Lyndsey was in command of the Gazelle, also known as the 'Araldite Pursuer' because they are held together with glue! We carefully edged forward into the city, passing the Technical College and began to pass the 'shanty' town on the right of the road. We saw a smoky flare rising up from the city centre, lazily gaining altitude. We felt no threat in the first moments of seeing the smoke trail, until its trajectory suddenly arced and spiralled towards us. It was a SAM missile. 'Missile Scatter,' was shouted by someone over the intercom and instantly the two Lynx pilots yanked on their controls to turn outwards from formation as the missile tore through the gap straight at the Gazelle which had not moved. The missile narrowly missed but was close enough for the crew to smell the burnt missile fuel.[3]

In a typical British understatement, the shout went up on the radio net, 'Cheeky buggers.' The ARP continued with renewed vigour not only looking for the initial mortar targets but also focussed on finding the SAM team.

Prior to their final push into Basra, 2 RTR ended up swinging around to the Abu Al-Khasib area near the Shatt al-Arab where the RSDG and 40 Commando had just fought Operation *James*. They would use that area as a firm base to springboard into the southern area of the city, approaching from the south-east. Staff officers at HQ 7 Brigade were using the codename *Sinbad* for this operation and had allocated codenames for staging points on the various axis of advance, themed around brands of beer.

The main axis of advance north for the 2 RTR BG was up the main road that 3 Commando Brigade and the RSDG had been using. A large crossroads at the head of the route was codenamed Mackesons. A smaller road that ran east from Mackesons – Route Pumpkin – would become the main axis then in towards the Basra Palace on the river. Staged along Route Pumpkin at intersections were Guinness, Murphys, Hook Norton, London Pride and finally, at the water's edge, was Skull Splitter. The palace itself sitting on the river, 1,200m south of Pumpkin, took the name Spitfire, naturally. Clearly the staff officers preferred ale to lager.

South of, and parallel to, Pumpkin, there was a short alternate route that led east into an old suburb. This was Route Carrot. The smaller track that led to the suburb crossed a minor canal – Nahr al Kadaq – over which ran a bridge codenamed Hobgoblin. Route Carrot took the user to the outside of the old suburb, but once at the suburb it took a 90-degree left turn at Abbot Ale and headed north to meet up with Route Pumpkin.

These unlikely routes, Pumpkin and Carrot, were chosen as the two axes for a squadron of 70-ton Challengers to manoeuvre through. Hardly 'great tank country' as the cavalry would say, yearning for wide-open plains upon which they could unleash their speed and power. The forthcoming fight in the dusty suburbs of Basra threatened to be claustrophobic, chaotic and a defender's dream. Tanks would lose all their advantages when confined in streets so narrow they could not traverse their guns, let alone pass each other for mutual support. Would Hobgoblin hold the weight of a Chally? Would teams of RPG-wielding fanatics pop from every alleyway and window to rain fire on them? Would militia throw the age-old Molotov Cocktails from high up on rooftops down onto the tanks turning the crew into flaming candles? Were snipers concealed in wait, ready to pick off unwary tank crew who dared exposed themselves? The crews of Falcon began asking all those questions and more as the plan was revealed to them while they sat in a date grove at the side of the road. Lt Ian Cross of Falcon Squadron:

> We had pulled up along the roadside under the trees and were aboard the engine deck of our tank when we were called forward onto the start line. At this point we had not had a briefing. The line of march positioned the two junior troops ahead, Squadron HQ in the middle and me and the other troop at the back. Not long after that we rolled forwards and the two junior troops crept ahead towards Mackesons about 4km further on. Lt Matt Stevens was then engaged with, I think, RPG and small-arms fire just before Route Carrot. My troop was waiting to go forward next to Zero Charlie, the squadron 2IC, when Major Woodward the squadron leader, who was keeping an eye on things ahead of us, called us forward to his position. He waved me over, so I went and climbed up his tank to speak with him. Lt Nick Ridgeway from 17 Troop also came and joined us. That was when I marked the collection of beer names on to my map, for Operation *Sinbad*. I was told that my objective was to reach Spitfire going over Hobgoblin on Carrot, through Abbot Ale then join Pumpkin and head east through London Pride. Nick was to go to Mackeson, then simply turn east on Pumpkin and push on through to Spitfire and expect to see my troop emerging from his right at some stage near Murphys. So, the O-group for taking Basra was about 90 seconds long.

The RTR was not fighting alone. 42 Commando, dismounted, waited in the shade of the date groves and sat in the lee of shabby-looking buildings waiting for the cavalry to help them fight a most unorthodox battle, and one which they all said they had never trained for nor ever expected to fight. Lt Ian Cross again:

> As Maj Woodward slipped back into his commander's seat, he must have knocked the firing mechanism for his smoke dischargers, because unexpectedly all six of them fired off for no reason. I remember thinking, 'Oops, he won't be using them again.' The marines joined up with us as we approached the right turn into Carrot. They started to fan out, left and right, clearing bushes and shacks along the way. A few hundred metres ahead was *Hobgoblin*, the small bridge over the drainage canal. It had been purposefully obstructed by the Iraqis and needed clearing. The REME CRARRV was called up and soon came alongside to see what they needed to do. Marines waited in fire positions looking and watching. There were bullets coming down the road at the CRARRV and at the obstacle, not lots, but they were certainly ricocheting off the street and metal. The REME sergeant got out, without body armour on, still attached by his helmet mike umbilical cord and proceeded to walk just in front of his tank giving directions to his driver as they went.
>
> We were locked down in the tank with the hatches shut but we were shitting ourselves just watching, it felt like a proper war scene. The REME sergeant supervised the removal of the obstacle which was holding everyone up, then calmly jumped back in his CRARRV and reversed it out the way for us to go through. It was the greatest act of bravery I ever saw.

With Route Carrot open once more, 16 Troop could resume its advance. To the north 17 Troop under Lt Nick Ridgeway had turned onto Pumpkin with little trouble and was heading towards Guinness. Lt Ian Cross continues:

> One small part of my orders had been to take note of a radio frequency change. Normally we would transmit as required on the squadron net to keep them in the picture but for *Sinbad*, as we were going to be the first tanks into Basra, we had been told to switch to the Brigade Command Net as they wanted to listen. As we cleared the roadblock at Hobgoblin, I gave a glowing commentary of events and explained the picture as we moved up Route Carrot. I was receiving very little back other than a simple, 'Roger'. This was a bit surprising, as I expected to get some staff officer asking me questions. Then the radio buzzed with a voice saying, 'Hallo Three Zero. We are not quite sure what you are or even where you are, but it sounds very exciting. We are HMS *Liverpool* in the Persian Gulf, over.'

In order to keep up the momentum Lt Cross took the lead, anxious his troop would not fall behind the parallel progress of 17 Troop on Pumpkin. Approaching point Abbot, he noticed how the road was getting narrower and the buildings were getting taller, with most facing the road being three or four-storey concrete and brick structures. Old cars, donkey carts, piles of rubbish and wooden market stalls crowded the street. Balconies overhung the street while dozens of air-conditioning units clung limpet-like to all the buildings adding further to the cramped nature of the old street. Road signs and streetlamps leant at crazy angles, and it seemed like each one had extra black power cables strung from it, illegally powering something somewhere. The cobweb of cables hung low over the road, yet another hazard. Lt Cross felt a slight fear of foreboding as the old streets closed in on him. Like most Iraqi streets, markets were never far away, stalls laid out with every manner of fresh food, meats, fish and vegetables. Domestic goods, plastic utensils, cotton, hardware and timber: it was all on sale and not a hint of food standards or health and safety anywhere. The swarms of flies over the exposed meat and fish on the displays, and the pungent odours, still provide memories veterans recall today. Lt Ian Cross:

> Royal Marines kept trotting along around us as we moved on at a sort of fast walking pace. I could see them left and right through my vision port, sweating profusely. It occurred to me that this was all wrong. It was too hot. We trained to fight in Germany; the marines even train in Norway so were even hotter. It was the wrong time of day – daylight, we had given up the tactical advantage of our excellent TI equipment and NVGs. We couldn't use speed as it was too narrow and we would outstrip our support. It was so tight and confined we couldn't traverse the gun fully. If you have a barrel strike on a building it can upset your sighting. Everything about this attack shouted out at us that it was wrong on every level, and it was the opposite of what we trained for. It was turning into a bit of a nightmare and reminds me of the scene in Ridley Scott's movie *Black Hawk Down* when the convoy of American Ranger vehicles continually gets ambushed in the streets. We felt like ruddy great targets, terrified, and hardly able to move or fight back.

To make matters even worse, the column slowed down to a brief stop just prior to the 90-degree turn at Abbot Ale, to allow the marines time to reorganise. Within a few seconds Three Zero began to sink into the road surface. A combination of the massive heat of the day, poor road building, drainage and water pipes under the surface cracking and of course nearly 70 tons sitting on top caused the road to crumble and subside. Tpr 'Strawberry' Field felt the slippage and quickly edged Three Zero forward out of the gaping dip in the road, with Three One and Three Two gingerly traversing the sink hole as well. The operation, of course, in a small way, bears similarities to another armoured thrust up a narrow road, when in 1944 XXX Corps – led by the Irish Guards – swept into Holland up a single narrow road en route to relieve 1st Airborne Division at Arnhem. Perhaps the growing sense of dread setting in with 16 Troop was because they, too, remembered that Michael Caine never made it all the way the up the narrow corridor in *A Bridge Too Far*.

Lt Ian Cross:

> We could hear more and more frantic shouting outside. We heard helicopters going low overhead and the radio traffic was incessant to keep momentum and drive on. It was very chaotic, and we were right on centre stage. I have never felt so alive, and I loved it. I was 25 years old, had come to Basra expecting to die and yet still got on with it. I had crossed that Rubicon. I had said goodbye to my parents on the doorstep of home and kissed my girlfriend Jo goodbye in Germany and was accepting of what came my way. I had made a transition to a military mindset which helped me cope. Even the lovely daily letters from home never dragged me out of the mindset.
>
> As we got to the right-angled corner, there were little barricades making it even harder for the marines to keep up with us, we had to really inch around the bend slowly to navigate it safely. We were concentrating so much I can't even recall if we were being fired at or not. The tank deafens the noise outside so much that time sort of stands still.
>
> We left the very real danger of the old buildings behind us at Abbot and headed toward Murphys where I could see Four Zero of 17 Troop moving along on Route Pumpkin. We slotted in behind and after a few minutes stopped at Objective Hook Norton where we formed a defensive leaguer and stayed overnight parked on a roundabout, with the marines looking after us. 14 and 15 Troop had by then pushed past and they stopped at London Pride for the night. It was at this roundabout that I tried dismally to shoot out with my pistol the bright streetlights, that miraculously were still on. We didn't sleep overnight as it was too dangerous, so we all stayed on watch. We felt staggeringly tired but also overjoyed that we had made it through to that point and started feeling like we were already a veteran crew.

No local militia were daft enough to try and attack these bristling hedgehogs of firepower overnight. They knew that their own local knowledge was useful but that to try and use the cover of night would put them at a distinct disadvantage. Reeling from the armoured incursion into their city, they were trying to reorganise for the next morning with what little they had left in both weaponry and organised manpower. Capt Stu Taylor, 42 Commando:

> The morning brief was that we would now clear the final approaches to the palace. We had Falcon Squadron, 2 RTR attached to us for the final phase, and so following the brief we moved up to the start line. The evening before, a recce patrol had been shot at but little enemy activity was detected, and it was decided to wait until dawn on 6 April to push into the palace. It was benign enough that most of the journey was done in soft skin vehicles without any resistance. We then formed up just in a side road off the main road that runs north–south next to the river that leads to Saddam's palace, which sits almost like a fort in a moated island.

Falcon Squadron fired a few HESH rounds which put paid to any final resistance, and we rolled into the palace grounds. It was obvious that the place had already been looted and damaged. The main wooden doors were locked so some guys used a Land Rover to force them open.

Lt Cross, Falcon squadron, 2 RTR:

> The next morning, we resumed towards the palace, again working with 42 Commando. We moved up to the approach road running parallel to the Shatt al-Arab, where we sat facing south towards the palace gates. Falcon was the first armoured unit to get in the palace. There was no fighting, but sporadic small-arms fire was common. We took the squadron inside the palace grounds which were enormous, parked up and got our red wine boxes out. We spent two nights at the palace, and we enjoyed our drinks party on its roof that first night. Don't ask me how several boxes of red wine made it to Basra from Germany, but they did.

In the north of the city the Fusiliers faced a complex operation in a heavily built-up area with key buildings to capture that would doubtless be defended. Z Company with C Squadron QRL would aim for Objective University and the bridge across the Qarmat Ali. Y Company with B QRL would aim for Objectives Academy, Power and the Cigar bridge across the Shatt al-Arab. The recce platoons would screen to the right (southern) flank and prevent infiltration from the old town.

O-groups were held on Saturday, 5 April, with Maj Charlie Eastwood and WO2 Satchell again creating a large walk-round model showing northern Basra in detail, for the briefing of the Fusiliers and troopers of QRL. It was anticipated that the attack would go in on 8 April and that 6 April could be a quiet day for personal preparation.

Company commanders were asked for a daily briefing at 10:00 on 6 April so Maj McSporran's Z Company duly arrived at Brigade HQ at the airport five minutes early as is the military norm. He was asked to wait outside the CP by a staff officer who then ushered a team of Special Forces operators inside. It was apparent to the gathering company and squadron commanders that, as with every phase of this campaign, the situation was changing rapidly. They all then went into the CP and Brig Binns announced that Operation *Sinbad* had been brought forward 48 hours and would commence in just over two hours' time! Early reports had arrived at his CP that morning from Black Watch and RSDG patrols indicating that the city was very quiet and showed little resistance. Brig Binns had decided to seize the moment and kick-start *Sinbad* asap. Within a few minutes more of confirmatory detail, the OCs left in a cloud of dust and the brigade staff began to strip down the CP and prepare to move into Basra.

At 13:00 Z Company and C Squadron QRL rolled into Basra, with the tanks leading up the same route to Loop where they had mounted the VCP days before and headed to the University. To their south B QRL and Y Company advanced on what was considered the main effort towards Academy and Power. A shortage of armoured mine clearance equipment meant that C QRL had no mine-clearing capability, so were slowed momentarily when the lead troopers spotted anti-tank mines across their path. Improvising, they used their chain gun to blast and explode the mines, destroying six in this manner, and opening a lane to get through. A T-55 and a BMP were soon despatched near the Qarmat Ali waterway before 4 Troop QRL broke down the gates to the university and entered the campus as uninvited guests. Several underground bunkers and dug-in D-30 artillery guns were quickly despatched by 120mm HESH rounds but opposition was light. C Squadron reached its limit of exploitation and sent a group to assist B Squadron with taking Academy and its complex urban terrain. More underground bunkers were tackled, two of which were crushed by the tanks driving over them. The Fusiliers of Z Company were close by and on a tight rein owing to the likelihood of running into friendly troops at close quarters.

In what many described as a perfect combined-arms operation, 8 Platoon of Y Company worked closely with a troop of Challengers in clearing Objective Academy. The platoon commander indicated his targets and the two Challengers fired two HESH rounds through the end wall of the building, creating perfect mouseholes for his platoon to grenade, enter and then clear. A small river in the Academy – codenamed Ouse – was found to be defended by a string of bunkers. L/Cpl 'Benny' Hill was told to clear the bunkers and a watchtower overlooking them. With both his Charlie and Delta fire teams deployed, Hill cleared the tower but as he went to leave, he was rocked by an explosion just outside and a cry over the PRR of 'contact'. L/Cpl Hill remembers:

> I tried to get Delta to indicate where the enemy was but they were all firing at different points and were taking incoming rounds themselves from across Ouse. I knew they were pinned and Charlie would be needed to help get them back. The radio net was drowning me out and I could not get through to Platoon HQ. When I looked back at Delta Fireteam, I realised one of their team was lying in front of them, face down in the open near a bunker. I knew I had a man down and tried to call for medics. The ground around Delta and the wounded man, who I know now to be Fusilier Kelan Turrington, was a blaze of tracer rounds. I instructed Charlie Fireteam to give covering fire while the Delta lads pulled Turrington behind cover. As they did this the medic arrived. Then the firing stopped, and the Warriors arrived. We were told to mount up and move on to Power. We had to leave Kelan behind. It was the hardest thing I have ever had to do.[4]

Despite the best efforts of the medics, 18-year-old Fusilier Turrington from Cambridgeshire succumbed to his wounds that afternoon. To compound the misery of the loss, the initial thoughts that he was killed by an Iraqi shot were discounted at a UK Coroner's Court who ruled in a verdict that he had been hit by machine-gun fire from a British vehicle.

With the marines and 2 RTR probing forward from the south, the Fusiliers in the north, the Irish Guards pressed inwards from the west of the city in the planned concentric attacks. Maj John Cotterill, 1 IG takes up the story:

> We set up on the tarmac playing area of the Technical College. As was normal I slept in my doss bag under a cam net, now against the side of a Warrior rather than the FV432. I had not long been asleep when we were mortared. Huge rounds, probably 120mm, came and hit the

college and the playground. We all jumped up and headed for cover inside the Warriors, but everyone was still in their sleeping bags and so it looked like a surreal sack race as everyone bounced toward cover while maintaining the warmth of their bags. More and more people piled into my Warrior and eventually the last ones tried to jump in, but it was so full they rolled out still in their bags. Everyone was laughing hysterically. They literally fell about with laughter amidst the shelling.

After the mortaring we could see football-sized holes in the tarmac where the big rounds had impacted. Shards of metal and jagged splinters were everywhere, and fresh scars showed up on the side of the Warriors. Clearly, we had been lucky not to have had people killed. We may have been saved by the knowledge the Iraqis now had of our ability to locate their mortars and destroy them by counter-battery fire.[*]

They barely had time to bracket us and fire a few rounds before they had to move fast to a new location, mounting most of their mortars on the back of pick-up trucks. This meant the mortaring was rarely longer than a few minutes before they had to stop or face certain death from incoming AS-90 rounds.

Maj Ben Farrell, 1 IG, was at Bridge 4:

Before we pushed across the bridge we spent the night in the old bus depot compound nearby. I was given my orders which I then passed down to my platoons. It was weird, I thought to myself, how long I had been preparing and training in the army for this moment. My commissioning course at Sandhurst, my platoon commanders' course, gunnery courses, courses on observation, deception and subterfuge – yet when it finally came down to it, we were going straight up a four-lane highway from which we could not manoeuvre and just had to have alternate turrets facing left and right arcs!

We were in very good shape for the attack. We did rock drills with green packets of army biscuits representing our Warriors, then escalated to a full-dress rehearsal in the desert where we moved in convoy and talked through 'actions on' and likely eventualities. We were as ready as we could be, despite it not being an actual tactic we had previously prepared for in Canada, where it was all about open plains. At dawn on 3 April, we were ready and launched the attack over the bridge.

The Technical College was a sprawling estate spread out over a square kilometre on the left (north) side of Red route into Old Basra. Consisting of accommodation, sports and teaching blocks with open 'green' – or rather brown – areas, it had been receiving fire from British units across the bridge since 22 March due to the dug-in Iraqi forces who were using it to observe, direct and fire from. The move forward to

---

[*]   Britain was using a MAMBA (mobile artillery monitoring battlefield asset) weapon-locating radar. Manufactured by Hägglunds SAAB in Sweden since the late 1990s, the system is also known as ARTHUR (artillery hunting radar). It is a passive electronic scanned array C-band radar for acquiring enemy field artillery, rockets or incoming mortars. The system detects and tracks hostile projectiles in flight. It tracks the up-going trajectory of shells, calculates their point of origin and likely impact point. It displays this to the operator or – if they are digitally enabled – transmits it direct to units concerned with either destroying the enemy artillery or who may soon be on the receiving end. It can locate guns at 20km and 120mm mortars at up to 35km with an error average of 0.4% of the range. For example, at 20km it would be accurate to the exact spot or up to no more than 80m out. This accuracy allows counter-battery fire to quickly be brought down upon an enemy position.

take the college and set it up as a new forward base was not so much hampered by enemy fire but it was delayed most of the day by a stream of civilians coming towards them out of the city. The idea of an empty battlefield was dispelled. Many veterans describe being surprised at how many civilians would suddenly appear with little care and start driving or walking around the supposed battlefield. Lines of pick-ups, yellow school buses and taxis poured onto Bridge 4 into the path of the 1 IG BG. This posed an unexpected problem and shows the flexibility and resilience of the British trooper to be able to switch from pure war fighting to a semi-peace-keeping role and back again, that few others would be able to do.

Once clear of the bridge and the civilians the Micks moved on and the Royal Engineers came forward with their AVRE, carrying a fascine and, more importantly, a bulldozer plough on the front. They smashed through the wall of the Technical College exactly where they had planned to, followed in by a pair of Warriors and the dismounted Micks. The college was secured. Wishing to reinforce success the Irish Guards moved further along Red route, once more in convoy formation. Rarden cannons were soon banging 30mm shells at the buildings on the right that had previously been identified as housing Fedayeen and soon were seen disgorging RPG-wielding militia. As the empty 30mm cases ejected out of the turret, they rolled down the armour and clattered against thin metal storage bins on the chassis making an almost constant clanking sound like that heard at marinas when ropes and sheets flap against the masts.

The rapid-firing 7.62mm coaxial machine guns were also barking out thousands of rounds at the dismounted enemy who were running to get into positions at the side of the route. Prior to the attack the Guards had allocated and marked on maps each quadrant of the city alongside the main Red route. Blocks A1–A4 were first on the left after the college, while Blocks B1–B3 and C1–C3 were on the right. The plans went up to Block F which was the College of Literature also on the right at the first major junction. Maj Ben Farrell again:

> Just before we moved on, my gunner, CSM Simon Dammant who was a Grenadier Guardsman attached to my company, came up with the idea of strapping his small video camera to the barrel of our Rarden. We secured it in place with black nasty (gaffer tape) and now today, years later, we can sit and watch the real footage of our battle moving up into Basra.
>
> I had two radio channels going in my ears – one on battalion, the other on the company net – and was really trying to concentrate, and of course I was also supposed to help load the Rarden cannon, but Simon was so very good and competent (he was a gunnery sergeant instructor) that he did it all on his own with his eyes shut. I looked down at him as he was traversing the turret left to engage a new target, and I said, 'Are you OK, sergeant major, what's going on?' He just smiled at me and said, 'Sir it's fine, I'm having the best day of my life.'

The Guards cleared the small buildings in quadrant B1–B3 and it was during one such clearance that a young lance corporal in 1 IG had a very nasty close encounter with an enemy combatant. Maj John Cotterill:

Part of the team had gone across the street to clear a house rumoured to house more Fedayeen. I was watching the team enter the house from the rear. They left the last man as linkman standing in the doorway looking back out guarding the rear of his team. In the rear yard, just a few metres away was an outside privy or shed. The door swung open and the biggest Fedayeen guy I ever saw came charging out of the loo with his AK-47 on his back and a huge carving knife raised above his head. I thought the knifeman was too close for the Mick to be able to react in time, but fortunately he was very alert, and swung his barrel upwards into the belly of the charging Fedayeen and literally blew him off the end of his rifle with a five-round burst.

The young soldier subsequently suffered with some nightmares after that close encounter, leading to screams and groans in his sleep which woke up his sleeping pals. I take my hat off to the Company Commander, Major Farrell, who did not just CASEVAC him away. Instead, he brought forward a psychiatric nurse to the company lines who sat and talked to him about the incident. He was told to write it all down. Now bear in mind the whole incident took no more than a few seconds, it took him 10 sheets of A4 notes to write down all his thoughts and memories. The process was obviously helpful as he had no more nightmares. This was another strong illustration of the lesson slowly being learned that the army should where at all possible, keep soldiers with their own unit and mates if suffering from such mental health issues, and not unload them to random strangers down the line.

Maj Ben Farrell, 1 IG:

L/Cpl Smith [name changed] had eye contact with the guy the whole time and after he shot him, he leant over him and they continued to stare at each other as he was dying. It really shook him and stayed with him. He is no longer in the army but I know he is healthy and doing well, I am glad to say.

With quadrants B1–B3 cleared of enemy, the Guards went firm with their gains at the college and awaited further instructions. A number of 81mm and 120mm mortars had been seized in the push past the college, these were laid on the ground and driven over by Warriors or Challengers to ensure they were not put back into use the next day. The final push to secure and take Basra, Operation *Sinbad*, was being formulated at 1 UKDIV HQ so the men of 7 Brigade would not have to wait too long for it. During the wait for *Sinbad* the six-man Sniper Section, 2 Company 1 IG was deployed on the rooftops of the Technical College to spot and engage enemy activity in the city. They were not easy to see, as most by now were not wearing army uniform. Maj Ben Farrell:

Sgt Waring and his team are worthy of note as snipers here. Amongst the civilians they observed enemy dragging anti-tank mines across the main road, Red route, and asked for permission to engage. It was probably out beyond 600m range. The moment after doing so successfully, one of his team got up, quickly moved to the other side of the roof and threw up. The reality and 'up close' views a sniper has are not for everyone and clearly take a toll. Moments later I went down to the base of the building, and we were mortared. A mortar shell landed only about 20m from me but fortunately it buried itself deep into the wet sand before exploding and so most of the explosion was contained in the sand. If it had been tarmac or a stone floor it could be very different.

H-Hour for Operation *Sinbad* was shortly after first light on 6 April when the RSDG BG (including 1 IG) began moving back up Red route. A battery of AS-90s fired in support and several USMC Huey Cobra gunships flew low overhead. Elysium was the codename for the objective for the battlegroup. It was at the large cloverleaf junction of Red route, the road from Bridge 4 and Route 6 that comes in from the north and continues down towards Abu al-Khasib and south on to the Al-Faw. Elysium was around a square kilometre of Basra's city centre including the College of Literature and Freedom Square – but still perhaps did not quite measure up to Homer's *Odyssey*.

Freshly arrived Fedayeen troops manned their defences and stubbornly resisted the mammoth armoured column as it inched forward to its first objective. Maj Ben Farrell again:

> I saw a Fedayeen soldier jump from his trench and run towards the Challenger of the RSDG squadron CO. The Fedayeen held a hand grenade which, as he got close enough, he threw at the 70-ton tank. The explosion would have hardly registered inside and as it detonated, at least four other turrets turned and aimed at the Fedayeen.
>
> One most amazing thing happened to me here at this junction. Amongst all the noise, tracers and smoke, I watched a saloon car taxi pull up no more than 30m from my Warrior. The rear-seat passenger got out with an RPG, which he fired at me. He then got back in his taxi and drove away; we were so astonished we didn't even have time to get a shot at them before they disappeared up a side street.

The column moved forward at an agonising slow pace, covering the 5km to the objective in three hours. The leading Challenger rammed the gates to the college allowing infantry to enter. The two companies of Irish Guardsmen fanned out in order to clear the obvious defence positions and some of the three-storey college buildings that overlooked the roads. Lt The Hon Thomas Orde-Powlett, 1 IG remembers:

> Sporadic RPGs were fired from windows at the passing column, but the Chobham armour proved its worth. Sections then dismounted and cleared the buildings of enemy, who seemed determined to martyr themselves and may have been high on drugs. It became clear that the SA80 was a truly excellent weapon but the stopping power of a 5.56mm round could be brought into question, and some enemy took several bursts, at close range, before going down.

L/Sgt Robert Giles, 1 IG:

> Our snipers out in front of us in no man's land continued to take a good account of the Iraqi military but the big 2,000lb JDAMs would have done even more damage. It had been decided that we now needed to go and finish the enemy in the centre of the city. We loaded up the Warriors on 6 April for another 'raid and aid' mission; extra ammo, water and food were all loaded in. Our dismounted sections all crammed into the back of the Warriors and sat tight as the column of vehicles and tanks trundled into Basra proper. No sooner had we entered the outskirts of the city than we started taking hits. RPG rounds and small-arms fire rained down but proved completely ineffective against the Chobham armour. The whole thing was caught by a video camera taped onto the barrel of the company commander's wagon (Major Farrell) The footage makes unique viewing, and *The Grenadier* magazine wasn't slow at recognising the potential value of the film.
>
> We battled our way from location to location, destroying any resistance as we met it, with the dismounts still safely hidden behind thick armour. The company commander was insistent that no dismounts should deploy if it were not completely necessary, and it proved to be a

sound policy as any enemy was swept aside with cannon and chain gun alone, and deployment of troops from the back of Warriors would have achieved nothing whilst subjecting them to an unnecessary danger which would have taken lives.

Brigade was being informed by the column as each location was either neutralised or confirmed as having no enemy present. After a few hours there was nowhere else to go apart from the centre of town, and the stronghold of Iraqi resistance in around the city's university campus. The collapse of Basra was nearly complete almost as soon as it had started. L/Sgt Robert Giles, 1 IG, again:

> We drove like mad towards the College of Literature. Our vehicle, accompanied by Challengers, smashed through the outer railings of the university and into a huge open compound. Handrailing the outer perimeter were pre-dug trenches spaced about 50m apart. They were manned to the last by non-uniformed combatants armed with RPGs and AK-47s.
>
> As we drove into the compound, they let us have everything they had. From inside the vehicle, it felt as though the armour was slowly being eaten away, as rocket after rocket came crashing down on us. In reality, they hardly even scratched the paintwork, but from inside the wagon, I felt like a goat in a cage which was being torn open by wild things outside, as the rockets shuddered against the outside armour and shook us all around inside.
>
> I could hear Harry screaming instructions to Eddie in the turret about which enemy to engage. Through the rear window, I could see hundreds upon hundreds of orange and green tracer rounds flying in all directions and hitting the back and sides of our wagon. Tanks and Warriors were firing at targets unseen to me when the biggest shudder of all hit the vehicle.
>
> An RPG gunner had run out directly in front of our vehicle, aimed and fired at us, destroying Harry's delicate sighting system. I thought Harry and Eddie were dead until I heard Harry shout, 'The cheeky bastard!' The RPG gunner then ran past the vehicle and into my narrow tunnel of vision. At first, I didn't know that this man, who seemed to be dressed in brown pyjamas, was the man who had just tried to destroy us, and thought he was a civilian trying to escape the mayhem. However, the Challenger tank about 30m behind us had seen it all and levelled its huge 120mm gun on to him. The Iraqi militia man halted in his tracks and raised his arms in the air. It was too late, a fraction of a second later he disappeared into an amazing bulge of smoke and debris as the tank engaged him from what could have been no more than 15m. I screamed out with a joyful amazement, 'Fucking hell!'
>
> I pleaded with Harry to let us out of the back, as I was convinced that if we didn't get out soon, something was going to penetrate the wagon, and this would be my metal resting place. He calmed me down, however, and reassured me that the tank had dispatched the last of them.
>
> 'That was it then,' I thought. We were in Basra, and now we had to defend it. We stayed static inside the Warrior for a while and gawped out at the dead in the compound through the object window. One apparently dead Iraqi was seen slowly moving for his rocket launcher, after trying to play dead. He had 14 rounds put into him by one of the turret crews, and I felt every one smash into his arms, legs, torso and face as I watched him shot from my little window in the back door of the wagon. Watching another human being shot like that is nothing like Hollywood would have you believe. There is no drama about it. You simply watched the life ebb away from them with no more resistance than a person in a deep sleep trying to throw away an uncomfortable dream.

Number 1 and 2 Companies, 1IG, then spent the evening and much of the night clearing the university buildings, room by room – an exhausting business with so few troops. Each building was entered and cleared from the basement up to the roof with the Guardsmen often having to force entry through locked internal doors, barricaded corridors and operate in some very dark confined spaces. Scattered bursts of gunfire, one or two small fires and the occasional crump of a grenade being thrown into a room broke the otherwise dark and still night. The Micks were joined by several men of the SBS who had inserted into the city to help identify targets but were now back in friendly lines and loaned their skill and firepower to the clearance patrols.

Sgt Fletcher and his platoon in 2 Company 1 IG had pushed right into Objective Elysium to clear an enemy stronghold when two supposedly dead Iraqis came back to life and shouldered their RPGs. As the two rockets fired across the open ground and crashed into the nearest Warrior, the section assumed the prone position, quickly fired back and returned the Iraqis 'to the dead'. More Iraqi small-arms fire then was heard going close over the heads of the prone section. Sgt Fletcher called for target indication on where the fire was emanating but no one could see the source. Sgt Fletcher called for the youngest and newest soldier to stand up and draw fire. Guardsman Anton Branchflower from Salford, the LSW (light support weapon) gunner was only 19 and fresh into the platoon so he dutifully stood up and looked for the enemy, knowing he would get shot at. He immediately saw two enemy shooting at him but rather than return into cover, he remained standing, shouldered his LSW and pumped round after round at them thus allowing the whole of his section to see the now revealed enemy and all his mates also returned the fire, killing the Iraqis. Shortly after a machine gun fired at the section from a small dugout, once more forcing the section to go to ground. One enemy was seen in the dugout preparing to throw a hand grenade at the section, Guardsman Branchflower stood his ground and engaged the enemy grenadier who fell, mortally wounded, while still fumbling with his grenade. He dropped it in the bottom of the dugout where it detonated and killed the other machine gunner. Guardsman Branchflower said:

> I'd never seen such a scary face in all my life. He had wide, staring eyes and a terrible grimace. I felt physically sick. It was either him or us: me and my mates. So, I shot him.'

Clearing the College of Literature took several more hours of fierce close-quarter battle. L/Sgt Hanger of 5 Platoon was still working his Warrior turret supporting his dismounts when he saw an enemy running amongst the assembled group of British vehicles. Knowing his coax machine gun would not depress low enough nor traverse quickly enough at such close quarters, he grabbed his SA80A2 and quietly lifted the hatch on his cupola, raised his torso up until he could see the man and shot him, before dropping back inside his Warrior.

As light faded on 6 April the troops were instructed to go firm and 're-org' on the objective while preparing to stay put overnight. They were told that they had secured

---

*   Anton was called to Buckingham Palace in February 2004 and awarded the Military Cross by H.M. The Queen. He sold his medals at auction for £9,000 a few years later.

a start line from which 3 PARA would deploy the next morning. The close confines of the Old City streets that stood ahead of the Guardsmen were assessed as being more suited to an attack by light infantry such as 3 PARA. Firing began to subside and became isolated shots. Vehicles shunted into defensive postures as ammunition statuses were called and replenishments requested. Number 1 Company, 1 IG under Maj Peter MacMullen, continued to prepare for its overnight stay and L/Sgt Holland (Coldstream Guards attached 1 IG), L/Cpl Martin, Piper Chris Muzvuru and L/Cpl Ian 'Molly' Malone sat back in their Warrior to reload magazines and take on fluids. Then an enemy soldier who had been in hiding rushed from the shadows armed with an AK-47 and fired into the back of the Warrior. All four soldiers were hit. Sadly, Malone and Muzvuru died of their wounds.

Chris was 21 and the first black piper in the Irish Guards. He was born in Gweru, Zimbabwe and was known as 'Muz' to his mates, one of whom was fellow Guards bandsman Johnny Stranix. He was from Shooters Hill in Plumstead and was a regular with Muz at the Red Lion pub. The regulars from the Red Lion raised £3,000 to buy a silver-tipped set of bagpipes which were then presented to the regiment in honour of Muz who they considered one of their own. Sadly, the Zimbabwean Government under Robert Mugabe viewed Muz as a traitor and called him a 'Buffalo soldier' prohibiting his body from being returned to Zimbabwe. Piper Muzvuru was flown to Brize Norton and given a military funeral. Eventually he was transported to Zimbabwe and buried in an unmarked grave to avoid desecration by supporters of Mugabe.

Ian Malone was 28 and from Dublin. He had been in the Irish Guards for six years and was also a trained piper. His family said he was extremely proud to be in the army and they took some comfort from knowing that he died doing a job he loved. He was an excellent chess player and is well remembered for beating all the officers in a tournament. His Dublin funeral attracted more than 3,000 people and is the first time since 1922 that British soldiers were allowed to march through the streets of the Irish capital.

Writing for the *Micks' Journal* after the war, Maj Farrell wrote:

> By lunchtime the next day, 7 April, British troops occupied all of Basra. Number 2 Company was moved to the Sheraton Hotel but found it well ablaze on arrival, with a 1,000lb unexploded bomb sitting on the side of the swimming pool. We moved on to Saddam's cousin's house alongside the Shatt al-Arab, which made a suitable alternative. Our two weeks here have given us time to reflect on our involvement in the war. Personally, I cannot praise the Guardsmen and NCOs enough – to a man they have been brilliant. Brave, tough, resourceful, compassionate and determined: a winning formula that has continued into the peacetime support operations. It has been an extraordinary privilege to command Number 2 Company. All our thoughts and prayers have been with the families of L/Cpl Malone and Piper Muzvuru. These two wonderful Micks have made the ultimate sacrifice and we will always remember them. Less than a week remains in Basra now and we are all desperate to get home safely having been blessed with a good deal of Mick luck in so many ways.

Maj John Cotterill, attached 1 IG:

On 6 April our 'raid and aid' mission was still in progress near the College of Literature at Basra University when the Brigade Commander ordered the RSDG BG to go firm and remain in the city. We then moved into the faculty buildings and set up a perimeter. Just beyond our position were the narrow winding streets and close alleyways of Old Basra. These were not suitable for Warriors so 3 PARA was brought up on foot to pass through us and clear the old town and bazaar. I remember watching the column of Paras go plodding past us, then the next day they came plodding back the other way looking really depressed, because there was no one for them to fight.

On 8 April we moved into a big private house a couple of streets back from the Shatt al-Arab waterway not far north of Basra Palace. Our whole company was inside the house and gardens, and for the first time since Camp Rhino I slept inside a building, well actually on the roof, but still not in a bed.

By this time, the Iraqi Regular Army had melted away, the Fedayeen had been destroyed or run away and the civil police had dissolved. Law and order started to break down and mass looting started. The role of British troops then started to change to include that of civil control. Looting, mainly at night, would be discouraged by householders who seemingly all possessed an AK-47 just like a British person would have a mobile phone. As looters approached one house, the owner would fire a burst of automatic fire into the sky as a warning, then the same would happen all down a street until finally someone did not fire. Then the looters would strike. Businesses would be looted for anything and everything and troops were told to try and stop it by aggressive patrolling and tackling the armed looters. Maj John Cotterill:

Our orders were to arrest or stop armed looters. We didn't bother about lone thieves running down the road with something nicked, that was a police role, we were trying to locate the organised gangs who were all armed with AK-47s. We had to confront them and either arrest or shoot them if they did not surrender. So, as the only Arabic speaker, I went out on the first night patrol on 10 April with the Guards.

A local man ran up to us and explained that there was gang of armed looters in a car up the road. He called them Ali Babas. Together with a lance sergeant and with me holding onto my informant, we hurried up the street where he was pointing. It was pitch black as most of the electricity was cut off. We reached a small crossroads and there, coming along the road, right to left, was this black American 1970s-style sedan rolling along very slowly and bouncing on its suspension rather like those rapper cars of the 1990s. There were four blokes inside the car, the passengers all cradled Kalashnikovs. Sitting in the open boot of the car was another guy, a really fat bloke with his legs over the rear bumper holding a belt-fed RPK machine gun. It struck me that this looked just like one of those firearms training simulators where a film is played before you on a screen and you have sub-calibre weapons to act upon what you see and either shoot or don't shoot depending on the scenario playing out. You then can examine where your rounds hit on the screen to test your accuracy. The looters saw us and in what looked like slow motion started to turn their weapons towards us. Without a word the lance sergeant and I selected automatic on the fire selector lever, aimed and fired several short bursts at the Sedan. Being only maybe 10m from the car, we were not going to miss. We killed four of the gang and one was wounded. The car stalled and rolled to a stop. We went forward to check the car and I slung their RPK over my shoulder and kept it for the remainder of my time in

Iraq. Before we had a chance to search things more thoroughly, a call came over the radio that one of the Guardsmen on another patrol had been wounded and we were to return to base. To add to our haste, we saw someone drop a grenade from the roof of a building which exploded across the street as we pulled back from the crossroads.

A young Guardsman across the street had also seen the rooftop enemy drop the grenade over the parapet. He was armed with the newly arrived FN Minimi squad support weapon, which had yet to be fully integrated into the army. He swung the Minimi straight up vertically in the air, and it was a fairly tall building, he fired off a short burst which hit its target. There was no way he could have done that with the GPMG so when I returned to the School of Infantry, I used that example to sing the praises of the new weapon.

At the next corner I glanced back to the sedan and saw that the wounded man lying in the road had already been surrounded by a group of men who were kicking him to death. With 25 years in the Regular Army behind me, I never thought that my first confirmed strikes on an enemy would be in a dark dusty street in Iraq. Later that night I felt particularly fulfilled about the encounter with the looters. I felt there was something atavistic about killing a man in combat and taking his weapon. They were the first men I had killed but they would not be the last.

In the north of the city 1 RRF patrolled and swept the streets for snipers and Ba'ath party members. They also acted on reports from locals as to the whereabouts of wanted people or arms caches. Capt Ed Pugh:

The great thing about being in Recce is that you often have much more autonomy and freedom to roam. We capitalised on this freedom after the main war fighting ceased in mid-April and had a good cruise about the city. We literally did cruise up and down the river on patrol craft. We went to the house that allegedly belonged to Chemical Ali, in north Basra. It was being systematically looted. I remember in the bathroom, two locals carefully chipping off the ceramic wall tiles one at a time and taking them away. We also went to one of the colleges. Parked outside was a large red tractor and trailer. Inside the trailer was a large pile of computers, monitors and furniture. Coming out of the stairwell was the apparent farmer getting in his unusual harvest. I got the interpreter to ask the gentleman what he was doing. He replied, 'He says he is stealing all the computers.' We asked the farmer if he would stop and put the computers back. The reply came back, 'What will you do if I don't?' I knew we would have to threaten him, but I was also not about to start acting as judge and executioner. I looked at his nice-looking tractor and said, 'Tell him that if doesn't stop we will shoot up his big tractor tyres.' It seems that did the trick as he unloaded the trailer. I know full well that within hours he or someone else returned and nicked them anyway.

We had won the war, but no one had a single plan, not even on a post-it note, on how to implement a single step forward. All around us was a broken city and a million people, who were, by and large, happy to see us having deposed Saddam but needing help in getting their city working again and that is something our government had singly failed to even consider. Scandalous.

All the units now in Basra got tasked with patrolling their quadrant of the city. On 10 April a unit from the Irish Guards was called to reports of multiple shots fired between two rival factions in a shopping area. The platoon of Micks also took fire from some Iraqis on the roof of a shop as they arrived and carried out a building-clearance operation to neutralise the threats. The battle continued inside the building, which necessitated the use of grenades. Several Iraqis were killed, others were detained and numerous weapons seized. L/Sgt Bob Giles, 1 IG:

Our Warriors were loaded with the prisoners from the shop and taken back to the company location. As a result, we all had to walk back the 500m to what I believed would be a well-deserved round of mutual back-slapping after an excellent job well done. I felt like a champion. All my time as an infantry soldier had just come to fruition with that attack on the shop. They were dead, we were all alive, without even a scratch.

Six Platoon headed off and I put my section behind them at the back. After a while they had started to slow up, so I stopped to allow a gap to appear between me and them and became aware I was standing on one of those makeshift roundabouts you find in the middle of a four-way junction. It was no more than a blob of white paint and I thought for a millisecond what an excellent target I must be making. Then, to my left, there was an almighty explosion. I glanced over and about 100m away I could see two large doors which must have measured about 3m in height, hurtling across the street. I only became aware after that we were in the banking sector of the city and the doors were from one of the bank's frontages. We had a Warrior guarding it up until about half an hour previously and had only pulled it away to give support for the incident at the shop. The Fedayeen hadn't been slow to notice this, and as part of a bigger plan, they were attacking all the targets that may have financial worth before making good their retreat from the city. We had just walked into the middle of a Fedayeen bank robbery.

I headed for the side of a building and was walking quickly towards where the explosion had gone off. 'Northern Ireland all over again.' As I lifted my radio mike to my mouth to report the incident, one of the most horrific sights I have ever witnessed unfolded in front of me.

The street had been full of civilians and passing cars, and as the bank doors were sent flying across the street, the local population had not been hesitant in rushing towards what they thought would be all their birthdays come at once. As they ran towards the now wide-open bank, the militia inside, eager to protect any possible bounty for themselves, opened fire with a number of weapons on the crowd from inside the bank. Men, women and children leapt from the back of passing vehicles. Some were shot before they hit the ground. Others who were still sitting where they had been when the explosion went off were slumped, dead as bullets hit their face and chest. I could see women dressed in black burkas, head to toe, being hit by bullets which made their clothes dance up and spit out dust like a rug hung on a washing line being beaten with a stick. At least fifteen people were hit and surely more. My contact report went something like:

'Shit. Hello zero, this is Whiskey 2-3 Bravo. Contact, one hundred meters rear of Sheridan hotel. People being shot and....'

I never got to finish my contact report.

The whole world stopped as if a pause button had been pressed so it could get its breath back. All I knew was something had smashed into my chest. I became aware that I was just about to put my left heel to the floor as I walked forward but was rocked back on it. The world had gone mute. There were no sounds, just a sense of something in between a mild electric shock running through my body accompanied by a buzzing after shock that lasted the smallest of fractions of a second. What followed probably lasted for no more than 60 seconds but takes half an hour to tell due to the billion sensations that went through my mind and body. Still standing, I looked at my left breast, which seemed to be the epicentre of whatever the fuck had just hit me. There was no blood, and the first thought that went through my head was that I had just been hit by a riot-type baton round. Noises from the outside world began to fill my ears again and I thought to myself, 'Well I'm not standing here to be hit by something else.' I somewhat nonchalantly about turned and walked 10m to my rear and sat down behind the cover of a building in an alcove which formed the corner of the junction I had been standing in the middle of. I had no idea that I had just had most of the contents of my left lung blown out of the back of me at approximately 1,000kph by a 7.62mm AK-47 round, leaving a hole the size of the rim on a pint glass, just below my shoulder blade. The round had missed my front body armour plate and had lodged in the rear one. Apparently, my heart had been missed by half an inch, but right then I just figured something had hit me in the chest and at worst had broken a rib.

Why would they be firing baton rounds at us. You've been shot you silly bastard. What else could it have been? What if I haven't been shot and I tell everyone on the net I have? I'll look a right twat! And there's no blood! I don't feel like I've been shot! In fact, I feel quite good, a little tired maybe. I got on the radio and said,

'Hello Zero, this is Whiskey 2-3 Bravo, I think I've been shot. Over.' No Reply. 'Hello Zero, it's Bob, I've been shot.'

I found I hadn't got the breath to say it again, and I was getting interrupted on the net by some tit reporting on lorry loads of fruit again. Zero hadn't heard me but L/Cpl Simon Campbell had and he constructively butted in whilst someone was reporting a particularly dangerous wagon load of tomatoes.

'Shut the fuck up and get off the net, Bob's been shot. Bob's been shot.'

I was all alone. The whole of my section was across the street about 20m away. I remember thinking to myself, 'That'll teach you to take point when you're supposed to be in command.' I could see Gary looking at me as if to say, 'What the fuck are you doing sitting down? There's a gun battle going on up there!'

I took my helmet off, subconsciously submitting and letting everyone know that was me, game over, I'm done. Apart from the difficulty in breathing, and a pain no worse than a slightly pulled muscle in my chest, I actually felt great. A warm glow covered me, and I felt what I can only describe as just having woken up in the sunlight after a really deep relaxing sleep. I know now that what I was in fact doing was dying. My body was closing down and my lungs were filling up. Dying then would have been an extremely comfortable way to go, but I was snapped out of it as my lungs wanted to breathe again but couldn't.

Parky from 6 Platoon came running round the corner with Percy. 'What are you doing Bob?' 'I've been shot,' as I kicked my legs around trying to get more air. 'No, you haven't you silly cunt.'

It was then that this tall man, who seemed like a giant, came round the corner. I had already become paranoid that whoever had done this to me would walk around the corner and stare at me with his brown eyes before finishing me off. As a consequence, I had positioned my rifle so that I could fire at anyone I didn't like the look of, but with the bayonet still mounted on the muzzle I didn't have the strength to lift it into the aim. 'I'll just have to blow their toes off,' I thought. Me and Parky just stared at the unusually tall man. Dressed in western clothes, but obviously a local, he appeared to be out strolling, with a small girl in tow. He gave me a cursory glance then looked at Parky without breaking step. I'm still convinced it was the father and daughter I gave the chocolate to on the VCP roadblock.

Maj Ben Farrell, 1 IG:

In leadership everyone around you has a view on everything and wants to tell you it until it's really critical, and then there's silence and everyone is looking at you and also looking at Bob. I then clicked on to what needed doing and told people to start first aid, get the medic up, get into all-around defence and so forth. I was looking at Bob and I said to him, trying to reassure him, 'Look Bob, it's going to be OK you will be fine.' Of course, he looked pale and totally awful, and I wasn't sure he would make it. Sometime later he was in hospital, and I went to see him, and he said, 'I thought I was going to die,' to which I said, 'What do you mean?' Bob said, 'You had never called me Bob in my whole service, so I knew I was in trouble.' I laughed and said 'You're right. I should have told you never to move without covering fire, it was your own fault!'

Bob Giles and Ben Farrell remain friends to this day and even go on desert motocross safaris together. L/Sgt Bob Giles again:

Parky and Percy were gone as soon as they appeared. I have long since ribbed Parky that he ran away and left me, but in fact he used his initiative and went and summoned a Warrior to pick me up. If he hadn't, none of us would have made it out of there alive as the fireworks were really about to start.

I hadn't noticed any firing coming in our direction until I heard Si Campbell say over the radio that he was coming to get me. I looked over and in between me and him was a light show of green tracer. It was bouncing of the road surface directly in between me and him. We were right in the shit and were pinned down.

The company started to get into CASEVAC mode, with many things going on around Bob that he wasn't aware of. A nearby Warrior had been summoned to act as battle ambulance, and Maj Kevin Burgess, RAMC was also running to the scene. Bob's own section and 6 Platoon started to put in a defensive circle around him and the alcove to defeat the rest of the Fedayeen and provide as sterile an environment as possible. L/Sgt Bob Giles:

Parky had got hold of Cliff who was in command of a Warrior and quickly painted him a picture which told him there was one man down and a shit load of ordinance being fired at a section which was cut off on the wrong side of the street.

I saw Cliff pull up just short of the junction, take his rifle and put around 20 bullets into a man who was directly above my head. Wood splinters showered around me, which was somewhat unnerving as I no longer had my helmet on. It's been said that the gunman Cliff dispatched was the man who fired at me, but I have other theories. Suffice to say, the individual in question was part of the bank robbery gang.

There was still heavy fire cutting the street in two, which had my full attention in case it should start to creep the 10m or so towards me. Then, what I can only describe as bloody stupid, or a total lack of self-concern to save a fallen comrade, I saw Si and Lee come bounding through it, dancing, swerving and kicking up their legs in order to miss the heavy weight of fire. I didn't notice at the time, but the rest of the section thought Lee was dead when he stumbled amongst the green tracer, only to pick himself up and cross the street. The pair of them raced over to me.

The rescue Warrior now pulled up alongside Bob, facing the smouldering bank down the street. As the rescue party started to pick Bob up, a Fedayeen getaway vehicle came out the bank car park. It was a pick-up truck with a belt-fed machine gun on it, which was pouring rounds straight at the front of the Warrior. The bullets did not penetrate but were ricocheting off in a shower of sparks in every direction. The Warrior gunner deftly swung his 30mm cannon to bear and squeezed off a dozen rounds which completely pulverised the pick-up, blowing great chucks of it off and doing the same to the three Fedayeen who had been living souls until then. L/Sgt Bob Giles:

We were aware that any casualties that required extraction from Iraq would be flown to Cyprus, and as Lee and Simon prepared to lift me up from the street, Simon kindly reminded me, 'You lucky bastard, you'll be on the piss in Aiya Nappa in twelve hours.'

I remember thinking, as I sat there alone, before I was rescued, that I was about to start panicking. If I panicked, I'd go into shock, and if I went into shock, then I was dead. So, I had spent the time alone thinking, 'What will be will be, and no amount of fretting was going to change anything.' I had even mentally hummed that Doris Day tune with, 'whatever will be, will be!' in it, to myself. So, there was no way I was going to stare at my own blood as it soaked up the Basra dust and bugger up all the good work I had done in calming myself.

It was all I could do to stop the two of them spinning me round to take a good look at the puddle of red that had once been inside me before they literally 'threw' me into the back of the wagon. 'I can't breathe!' I told them as I lay unceremoniously on my front, face sticking to the PVC seating in the back of the Warrior. I felt a hand grab me by the scruff of the neck and hoist me upright. That was better. Strangely I could breathe perfectly again. Lee was hugging me tightly around the waist.

'What are you doing?' I asked him.

'I'm holding your guts in.'

'Well, that would be great, if I'd been shot in the stomach, but I haven't, have I?'

'I'm going to hold your guts in anyway'.

I was told later that I only had five minutes to live at that point, had it not been for the intervention of Doc Burgess. I wanted to administer my own morphine, but the guys stopped me fortunately as to give morphine with a lung injury can be fatal. We had only gone a hundred yards in the Warrior when it stopped abruptly, and I was dragged out. Maj Burgess had arrived and wanted to get a chest drain in me, but it was too cramped in the Warrior. I was starting to lose focus and become unconscious, but I remember Maj Burgess saying, 'What I am about to do is going to save your life.' He stuck a plastic pipe, 10 inches long, into my chest cavity. The blunt end scraping around inside sucking the blood and snot out. They sucked two and a half bags of blood out the cavity before it started to dry up. Apparently if more than three bags are drawn out you generally die soon after.

The rescue Warrior drove the short distance back to the Company HQ at the Sheraton Hotel where a CASEVAC helicopter would be coming to pick Bob up. While awaiting the helicopter, the gathered medics put intravenous drips into Bob's arm, stripped his kit off to fully expose his torso and dressed the two wounds: a tidy small entry wound and a ragged fist-sized exit wound near his shoulder blade. The CASEVAC helicopter suggested a safer grid square to affect a pick-up as the area around the Sheraton was now also under small-arms fire. This meant being loaded into a vehicle again, this time a Samaritan CVRT ambulance. A few minutes later, Bob was cross-decked from the Samaritan onto the helicopter. L/Sgt Bob Giles:

> We arrived at the prearranged helicopter pick up and I was dragged out of the back of the vehicle into silence. No more engine noise or shouting or firing of weapons or chattering voices. I look back now and realise it was at this point that I left the physical act of fighting the war in Iraq behind, and the mental battle that I am still fighting today started. There must have been the din of the helicopter engine and rotor blades, but I don't remember them. I just remember this overwhelming sense of peace and silence as we lifted off the ground and up into the darkening sky.

CHAPTER 11

Going Home

There are two things that take me back instantly to Basra. I was working for a drain-clearing company in Somerset and we went to a pub with a drain blocked by a fatberg. We opened the manhole cover, and I was instantly back in Basra. The repulsive smell that pervades the back streets is like shit and old cooking oil. It's a really disgusting rancid smell and it reminds me of Iraq. The second thing that jogs me back to Iraq and easily upsets me is seeing discarded clothes in the street. We knew that the Iraqi Army were taking off their uniforms and throwing them down and putting civilian clothes on. So, when we saw these piles of khaki clothes, we knew that enemy were not far away, but just hiding from us. It would put us right on edge. Even now if I see clothes or a dropped jacket at a roadside, I get a thump in the chest of adrenaline and anxiety. It doesn't last long, and I can even smile about it soon after, but it's still happening to me.

Some of those memories keep me awake at night. For many years after *Telic* I had nightmares. I would be half awake sweating and looking for my weapon in my bedside. My current wife has been very understanding and these incidents are getting rarer thanks to her.

CPL PAUL BURTON, REME

Globally recognised visual signals symbolising war coming to an end quickly come to the mind's eye – Russian soldiers climbing with the Russian flag atop the Reichstag building in 1945, King George VI waving at VE-Day revellers outside Buckingham Palace in The Mall, helicopters balancing precariously on top of the US Embassy in Saigon, Vietnam. However, the reality can sometimes be less clear-cut. On 9 April 2003 the world watched live as a USMC tank pulled down a large statue of Saddam Hussein in Firdos Square, Baghdad. A huge chain was fixed, symbolically, around the neck of the statue as it was yanked down to the ground in a crash. The footage became iconic. Basra was already liberated; flights were landing from international locations and the overt military resistance had practically ceased. Two days later, the enormous Iraqi V Corps in north-west Iraq finally surrendered to the US 173 Airborne Brigade. Around 15,000 surrendered but it is believed that many again had simply melted away, mostly carrying their weapons with them, which added still further to the vast amount of hardware already sloshing around in Iraq.

On the same day, the US Defence Intelligence Agency released the 'Most Wanted' personality identification playing cards. Similar ideas for these decks of cards showing the most wanted goes as far back as the American Civil War. In World War 2 they carried silhouettes of Japanese, Italian and German aircraft to aid recognition. In Iraq the 52 cards each carried a picture or silhouette of a wanted person from the Ba'ath Party, the Revolutionary Command Council, army and security chiefs and high-ranking Hussein family members. The card also carried the job title and last-known address or locality.

Saddam was the Ace of Spades and just like a house of cards, when he was captured, the rest came tumbling down. Chemical Ali was King of Spades, and he was captured and hanged. As of 2021 all but four of the 52 have either been captured or killed. Many of those captured have since died of natural causes or been killed by ISIS or other factions. A US$1 million reward is still available for the Jack of Diamonds, Tahir Jalil Habbush al-Tikriti, former Head of Iraqi Security and Intelligence who slipped away in the chaos of the ground war and is suspected of now operating in Syria. There is a great deal of smoke and mirrors around al-Tikriti, with some journalists even suggesting he was paid off by the Americans for providing intelligence; others say he wrote a letter in 2003 linking al-Qaeda with Iraq.

As the overt war fighting ceased, Saddam Hussein's regime collapsed, and it too melted away. Hussein was captured hiding in a drain near his hometown of Tikrit, northern Iraq, in December 2003. He was hanged in 2006 for war crimes. For the men and women deployed on Operation *Telic,* April and May saw rising summer temperatures soar as moves were made in Whitehall to get them home and replace them with those lucky enough to be deploying on *Telic 2.*

Cpl Paul Burton, REME:

> As the months wore on, it did start to get hotter and hotter. Any metallic object, especially the weapons, became so hot that any contact with bare skin would cause a burn. We ended up having to wear our sleeves down and sometimes even gloves.
>
> In the desert the night times were extremely cold, icy even, and it wasn't uncommon to find a frost by the morning. Once we were in Iraq and in the built-up areas the heat didn't do much at night and it was often high 30s centigrade (80s Fahrenheit). The hottest temperature I saw recorded was 55°C (131°F) I had not been issued with desert boots until quite late on into the campaign. I wore the normal Black Pro boots that I used in the UK. They are designed to be used in normal temperate climates. Eventually, the soles of my boots melted and fell off. I was walking about with no soles on my boots for a day or two. This hastened the issue of my new desert boots which was well overdue and very welcome.
>
> On one of our first patrols in Basra we had not long started when we came across a woman who had been hanged. There was a rope around her neck, and she was hanging from a pole at the side of the road. I was told that she had been accused of sleeping with someone out of marriage. We got her cut down and carried her to a house. It should have been more shocking to me, but I realised now that I had undergone some rapid changes. I know now that I changed in just a few days.
>
> During early July I was told that I would by flying out of theatre very soon, ahead of the rest of the Black Watch as I was TA. I was given a few hours to make sure that my kit was packed and ready to go. The RMP carried out a check on all of it to ensure that I was not in possession of any war trophies or ammunition. I said goodbye to the Black Watch lads and revealed I was TA. They gave me so much stick, but it was OK: they had accepted me. They even said that if ever I wanted to wear a kilt, make sure it was Black Watch Tartan.

I was then taken in a 4-ton lorry to Basra Airport where it was a case of hurry up and wait for the flight. Later that day I boarded the RAF TriStar heading for Hamburg. When we landed there, most of the flight disembarked. Initially, I had been told that I would be going to the Black Watch barracks in Fallingbostel but as soon as we had landed, I was told I was heading to Brize.

For the whole time that I was transiting out of theatre, I was not told what the process would be once I had arrived in either Germany or UK. On arrival at Brize Norton the few of us that were on the flight were told that there was transport back to Chilwell. During the bus ride back to Chilwell I was able to communicate with home to tell everybody that I was in Britain. That came as a shock to everybody.

On arrival at Chilwell during the afternoon, I spent a couple of hours handing back kit, weapons and completing paperwork. The last stage was to sign off as a mobilised reservist and be handed a rail warrant for home. I eventually got back to my house that evening. I even caught the end of Coronation Street. Incredible to think that only 24 hours before I had been involved in a firefight while on patrol in Basra, and here I was on the sofa in front of Corrie.

I had received zero decompression. I believe that this is in part what has led to nearly 20 years of depression and contributed to the end of my marriage within five years of returning from Iraq.

Outside of home I found myself looking for trouble. Not necessarily to start it but I relished getting involved and breaking it up. This was true at work as well. My temper got worse, and I had such a short fuse. Wincanton took me off the driver roster because they were worried about me having road rage. I even smashed the office computer up and broke the phone once when I had an argument with a guy. That was when they referred me to occupational health. The nurse was ex-RAF and she recognised what I needed, and I started having therapy sessions with a guy who was also ex-forces. That really helped me and started me on a long road. In fact, this interview will help me, a lot, too.

WO2 Andy Abbott and his team of sapper EOD experts were still clearing tons of unexploded or dangerous ordnance in the Basra area.

As the operation went on, it got hotter each day and we started to strip off increasingly due to the excessive heat. By the end we were even doing 'naked dems' [demolitions] – so literally stark bollock naked setting off PE4. Only one of us was naked, the other lads stayed dressed, obviously, there was a war on! On one dem we cleared the cordon area and even had to fire a flare up as a helicopter kept hanging about only 200–300m up, and if we blew it, it would be seriously hit. This was a giant job with rockets, mortars, landmines and artillery rounds. When it blew, the shockwave was immense and I realised we had underestimated our position of safety. I dived for cover but lumps of mud and steel kept raining down on us and I thought someone was going to get proper hit. We were all OK and laughed, nervously, afterwards.

Two weeks into the war and there was such looting it was crazy. We were based in one building and went out for the day on a task and when we got back the whole building was stripped bare of every bit of furniture, fittings, and fixtures. Like locusts had been through. We saw this petrol tanker trailer, being dragged down the road by a farmer on a tractor, and the trailer had no back wheels, so it was dragging along sending huge showers of sparks out behind it. It was going down the main high street. We were just thinking, 'This is so crazy.'

We went out on a joint task at Al-Qurnah, there was eight of us in four vehicles. We got surrounded by a load of villagers and got very heated. One of the elders brought out a dead child and was protesting that we needed to do something. (I think the kid may have been killed by a mine or an airstrike.) One of our team spoke a little Arabic which helped diffuse the situation a little. We extricated rapidly because if it had kicked off, we knew our chances were slim with only a little ammunition.

A few days later WO2 Abbott was asleep between his two Land Rovers and was awoken with a start from his midnight slumber. Abbott blearily came to in his doss bag at the side of his Rover. Having been knocked out for 24 hours with a serious bout of D&V (diarrhoea and vomiting), he had been in a deep sleep. They were parked near Al-Amarah, close to the Iranian border in a secure four-walled compound that had been property of the Ba'ath Party. As Abbott looked up, he saw a Parachute Regiment soldier leaning over him, shaking his shoulder. 'Sir we need you for a tasking.' Abbott slightly perplexed at this rude awakening replied, 'We are EOD, but we don't blow shit up in the dark, it's too dangerous.' The irony of his own comment was not lost on him, but the young Para protested, 'Sir we need you to come and see a vehicle we stopped.' Relenting at his urgency Abbott got up, woke his team from their slumbers near and under the Land Rovers and a few minutes later arrived at the scene of the vehicle stop.

At the side of the road to Iran, lit up by the headlights of two Para vehicles, sat a dark coloured small SUV with its boot and a couple of doors open. A few yards from the road lay the motionless, dead body of a young Iraqi male. Bullet holes punctured through the side of the car and a tyre was flat. The SUV sat low on its springs, something Abbott and the EOD teams had learned to look for from years of dealing with car bombs in Belfast and Londonderry. But this was no fertilizer bomb. There were no occupants, but it was piled high with weapons and ordnance. The Para checkpoint commander briefed Abbott and his team. The car had been seen to approach the checkpoint but then quickly did a U-turn and drove away. The Paras had a chase vehicle on standby and soon caught it up and forced it to stop by shooting at it. One occupant had died but 3 others were apprehended as they untangled themselves from the piles of Kalashnikovs, PKM machine guns, RPGs and mortars. Intelligence suggested they were gun runners, illegally moving and selling weapons along the border area. One of the males also had a large amount of cash that he could not account for.

Abbott's team was asked to unload the SUV and clear it of booby traps. Without the luxury of the Wheelbarrow robot vehicle so often seen in Northern Ireland the EOD team reverted to the old-fashioned way of tying wires to one weapon at a time and pulling it out from a safe distance. AS each one clattered to the ground it often pulled another one or two with it. Also found under the weapons was several passports and some more cash.

Satisfied the vehicle posed no more threat, the EOD unit stood down and returned to the compound in time for breakfast. Over the MREs and fresh tea, Abbott waded through opening several sacks of mail, all addressed to him but giving out most of the contents to his team. As he worked with a large team at the Post Office when not being called up, many of his colleagues sent him mail through the BFPO system, so much so that on one delivery there were 10 sacks of parcels all addressed to him! None of the contents went to waste but he did cherish those direct from his family even more.

Flt Lt Andy Johnson in his AWACS E-3D was also missing his family and he and his team had allowed their thoughts briefly to turn to that of home when on a mission over Iraq and it could have had tragic consequences.

> My last flight over Iraq was on 14 April. In the whole eight hours on station, we had one single request for support from Task Force 20 and called in Lurch 52 to go and drop some GBUs from his F-16. Despite the lower workloads, I noticed we were making mistakes and some routines had become slack. It was a dangerous spiral to descend into with so much at stake, it was, therefore, a good result that during the flight debrief at PSAB it was announced that we had flown our last flight on Op *Iraqi Freedom*. We were knackered and we were tired of killing. It was time to go home.
>
> I went home via Akrotiri on an RAF VC-10, then a Hercules into RAF Lyneham. Another flight flew us to Waddington where my wife Jo and my two kids met me. I have tears in my eyes now when I think of how pleased I was to see them then.
>
> I had been taking Temazepam the night before flying in Iraq in order to try and get some deep sleep. However, sometimes I found this didn't help at night, but the next day halfway through being on station I was hit with waves of tiredness. Many of us resorted to energy drinks. I got in the habit of having three each flight! Drugs at night to sleep and caffeine-heavy energy drinks in the day is not a recipe for a healthy lifestyle. I had prolonged sleeping problem after Op *Telic*. I know it is a small price compared to what others are dealing with, though.
>
> One other helpful process I was lucky to be involved in was attending a conference in Las Vegas where I was put up at the MGM Grand Hotel on the Las Vegas strip. Over 350 delegates including me talked about our experiences in the air war. Lessons were captured and shared by working groups that looked at all the different facets of the air operations.
>
> Unprecedented air power had been available to the commanders in Iraq and air-ground weapons had achieved extraordinary accuracy. We had more ISTAR – Intelligence, Surveillance, Targeting and Reconnaissance – assets than any prior conflict. This sometimes caused overload of information and options for some scenarios. Another area that was highlighted 'more work needed' was IFF in combat situations, especially with helicopters now buzzing the low-level airspace.
>
> Of triumphant note for me was the expression that CSAR and CAS to SF (Caveman) units had been excellent. At conference I sat next to a pilot from the Air National Guard who had been callsign Mohawk on the CSAR at Haditha Dam. He stressed to me several times the isolation and difficulties he had that day and said, 'Thank you, you must remember it felt like we were on Mars without you.'

Dealing with the vast number of Coalition aircraft operating over Iraq was a task of its own. Americans were flying B-1s, B-52 Stratofortresses, F-117 Nighthawks, F-14 Tomcats, F-15E Eagles, F-16 Falcons, A-10 Warthogs, S-3B Vikings, KC-135 tankers, C-130 Hercules Spooky/Spectre gunships as well as HH-60 Blackhawk, AH-64 Apache, MH-53 Stallion, CH-47 Chinook and CH-46 Sea Knight helicopters. In addition, the British flew Tornado GR4s, Harrier GR7s, Jaguars and Canberra PR9s as well as Puma, Chinook, Lynx and Gazelle helicopters. Finally, the Australian forces flew a small number of F-18 Hornets. An astonishing

41,400 sorties were flown by 1,800 aircraft in the first 28 days of Operation *Iraqi Freedom*. The roles undertaken were, of course, varied, and involved dropping munitions, 68% of which were guided 'smart' bombs or missiles. 32% were unguided.

Just shy of 20,000 guided munitions were expended (19,948), one third of which was a single type: the GBU-12 LGB (500lb Laser-Guided Paveway Bomb) of which 7,100 were dropped. The next most popular was the GBU-31 JDAM with 5,000 dropped. This, like the Paveway, was a converted 'dumb' 2,000lb bomb with a tail fin and GPS system fitted that improves accuracy. Missiles in the form of AGM-65 Maverick (900 fired) and AGM-114 Hellfire (560 fired) were the most prolifically used.

A further 9,200 'dumb' bombs were dropped, mostly being the standard Mk 82 500lb bomb. Over 500 cruise missiles were launched from ships and submarines. Psychological operations were flown, dropping a total of 32 million leaflets. (The equivalent in paper of 120,000 toilet rolls!) Logistics flights moved over 12,000 tons of supplies in C-130 Hercules and CASEVAC missions included 136 sorties, evacuating over 1,500 patients. CSAR teams flew 55 missions saving 73 personnel. Only seven aircraft were lost to enemy fire: four Apache helicopters, two USMC Huey Cobra gunships and one A-10 Warthog. A further 13 aircraft were lost due to friendly fire, engine failures, malfunctions and pilot errors. Estimates place the Iraqi response at around 2,000 surface-to-air missiles being fired. 417,137,230lb of jet fuel was offloaded by air-air tankers – that is enough fuel to keep a Boeing 747 airborne for 11 years.

Some of the Coalition's vast air fleet was, by mid-April, based at Shaiba Air Base, but much of the airfield had been turned into a logistics base and giant car park for armoured vehicles no longer needed on the streets of Basra. Lt Ian Cross's Falcon Squadron, 2 RTR, was there:

> We moved out to Shaiba airfield then and it went to rat shit. There was no cover, the food got worse and then D&V set in with loads of guys going down with the shits. The brigade was trying to get onto a more peaceful footing and that meant no tanks on the streets. We were old news already and seemed to have been forgotten. The speed of degradation of the regiment at Shaiba was shameful. Chaps were having to burn their clothes they were so soiled from diarrhoea and very quickly a large proportion of 2 RTR was not in a fit state to fight again should we have been needed.
>
> Our route home was pretty much a return of the outbound trip. We stopped briefly in Cyprus where I stood outside RAF Akrotiri having a last cigarette before boarding Crab Air back to Brize Norton. I decided then that if the Iraqis hadn't killed me, cigarettes certainly were not going to either, I stubbed it out and I never smoked again.
>
> When we reached the squadron bar back home, after all this ended, I met Maj Woodward for a drink. He was welling up in tears and said, 'Ian, when I sent you into Basra, I never thought I would see you again.' I asked him why, to which he said, 'Brigade had told us to expect up to 70% casualties and the reason I sent you in was because I knew you would tell me what was going on and send a report before you were taken out.' He was an emotional thinker and it had clearly played on his mind. It is not something I will ever forget.

We took a few days off as troop leaders, together in Denmark as a sort of R&R, then were released on leave back to the UK. That was peculiar, it was like life had carried on as normal, but we knew we had been doing some very unusual things. Some other people's comments were unusual. At a bar in Manchester a bunch of us were queuing to go in when the doorman somehow found out we were army and he waved us all inside and said, 'Welcome back guys.' We got great seats and people kept buying us drinks. The polar opposite occurred at a pub Jo and I were drinking in down Borough High Street in London. There was a group of students talking about the war and they were saying how the British were murdering people in Iraq. I was so riled I had to say something and told her it was not like that. She called me a baby killer. It angered me so much Jo steered me away and we left the pub, but I couldn't believe that this was being said to me. I felt hated. There was no welcome home and being called a murderer was a real hammer blow that made me question everything.

Units such as the RAF Tactical Imagery Wing, the Army Joint NBC Unit and 3 Regiment, Army Air Corps were also stood down and began to get ready to return to England. Maj Mike Peters, AAC:

When we cleared down to go home, we were told the brigadier (Brig Jon 'Jacko' Page CBE, OBE) was coming to see us and we were, therefore, expecting at least a thumbs up from him. He kept us waiting for over an hour. He had been in the Paras in the Falklands and then an armoured squadron commander on Op *Granby* in 1991. When he did arrive, he said to us all, 'Well, I had to wait for you in the Falklands, and I had to wait for you again on *Granby* and it was only because I insisted you got into battle that you did so this time.' It was such an infantile thing to say as a brigade commander, the troops were fuming, in fact we all were.

Maj Gareth Davies, RTR JNBC was still in Iraq:

As the invasion phase became the ground occupation phase I went with another officer to Shaiba Air Base in the Land Rover. As we arrived, I realised that this was an ex-RAF base. There was a squadron HQ building just like every RAF base in the UK, and on the roundabout was a gate guardian aircraft. I think it was a Sea Fury. I found out later that a neighbour of my father had flown Spitfires there in the 1940s.

As we unloaded our kit, I saw walking towards us another RTR officer mate of mine, who I had not seen since we left the UK. He had a towel and a washbag under his arm. I put my hand out in greeting and he said, 'Don't want to be rude mate, but I haven't had a wank in weeks, I'm going to the showers to knock one out, so I'll speak to you later.'

One of my last jobs before we left Iraq was with a Latin American US Marine in a Humvee. We were tasked with finding the father of an injured Iraqi child. The child had been hurt in some form of explosion and he and his mother were evacuated by air to Birmingham, Alabama. The father had been unaware of what had taken place and they wanted me to take a Sat phone to his house so he could speak to his wife who was now in a hospital in Birmingham. I had been given a sketch map of where to find the house but no real proper address. Miraculously, we found the house and managed to get the wife on the phone to the relieved father. It was all very bizarre, standing with this man who was clearly living a basic and spartan existence while he chatted on the phone to his wife thousands of miles away. He was so thankful and relieved to hear from his wife. We felt pleased that we had helped in a small way. Sadly, I think the child died a few days later.

As we drove away, back towards Shaiba, a little kid about nine or ten years old ran alongside the Humvee and shouted in a high reedy voice, 'Hey mister, fuck you!' That brought us back down to earth!

Sqn Ldr Andy White, RAF:

I remember the weekend prior to going out to Kuwait I was in King's Lynn town centre looking to buy some essential personal supplies for the upcoming *Telic* deployment, and I came across a 'Stop the War' gathering. It really yanked my chain, so I went over to them and asked them if they realised Saddam Hussein was not far off being Adolf Hitler, he had supressed and gassed minorities with weapons of mass destruction. I said he had invaded other countries like Kuwait. I was absolutely convinced the protesters were wrong and we were justified in what we were going out to do. In my mind it was the right thing to do.

As time went on afterwards, we learned that there were no weapons of mass destruction and our own aerial reconnaissance had also turned up nothing, my views changed. Lots of British servicemen and countless Iraqi civilians died for what was essentially 'regime change' which we had been told the operation was not about. We were lied to by the UK government, who provided a twisted narrative. I was so annoyed by Tony Blair and the lies; it leaves a very bad taste.

But, Operation *Telic* 2003 was the highlight of my career. I am very proud to have been in command of the largest deployment of photo interpreters and analysts since World War 2. Our use of new untried equipment in a war setting proved the systems were full of promise and helped us deliver exactly what was asked of us. I suppose as servicemen we all want a war at some stage in our career, and I got it.

The maritime component of the task force also weighed anchor and set sail for home ports. For the Fleet Air Arm, it meant one more difficult decision. Lt Cdr Pentreath, 845 Naval Air Squadron, discussed speculation about the future of *Ark* and *Ocean* remaining in theatre in his diary.

28 March Rumours suggest 845 may disembark and work from Viking. I feel it is much too early to withdraw the ships while there is still a war ashore. I can understand ship frustrations as they now have little to do but maintain us and the marines but maybe they need reminding their role is a landing platform and their prime role is to support us. I hope we can hang onto them as if we lose that link, we lose an enviable escape ticket home.

Pentreath got his wish and *Ocean* remained in theatre until 1 May. They were engaged 24 hours a day in ferrying equipment and supplies forward to 40 and 42 Commando throughout the rest of March and April. Wounded or sick marines were lifted back to *Ocean*. On 29 March Pentreath flew for 13 hours in and out of a FARP at Az Zubayr ferrying supplies in from *Ocean* and moving 42 Commando:

We spent the afternoon moving teams from 42 who were searching various industrial sites for Seersucker missile launchers after one or two had fired from the area. Many people wave and smile as we fly over the town which makes me feel better, although I think they are probably still scared of Saddam's evil.

On 1 April one member of his squadron, Wren Riley, fell overboard from *Ocean* just after dark. Marines launched rescue boats while 845 Sea Kings lifted off to search for her. After an hour in the water, she was rescued and taken to the sick bay, a lucky escape.

Half of 845 Squadron had to stay in theatre and await relief from new outbound units. The lucky half would be heading home on HMS *Ocean*. This troubled

Lt Cdr Pentreath, who was of the opinion that their sister squadron, 846, had not pulled its weight and they should be the ones remaining in Basra:

> We had a few weeks aboard *Ocean* as she sailed back towards England, which allowed me and the CO of 847 to get some plans drawn up. Royal Navy ships do homecomings very well, with sailors lining the decks as families wave on the quayside. However, the FAA has usually fallen flat with aircraft landing back ashore at varied times and ground crew arriving in coaches separately. We were determined to try and do it better. The unlucky half of the squadron in Basra had finally been relieved while we sailed west in the Med. They flew in RAF planes back to the UK where they picked up replacement aircraft for the Sea Kings they had left at Basra. We then hoped to get everyone in the air just as *Ocean* entered harbour at Devonport for a flypast and then fly on together, loaded with all the ground crew up to Yeovilton. We were going to have 10 Sea Kings, 6 Lynx and 6 Gazelles in formation. As usual, no plan survives first contact, and it all went downhill when we hit a fog bank off Cornwall. Some Gazelles had to put down temporarily as the fog was so thick at Culdrose. We eventually gathered most of the aircraft over HMS *Ocean* at Plymouth just as the sun broke through and thousands waved at us from the famous Hoe. A short while later, the stragglers from Culdrose joined up and the whole wing clattered over Yeovilton with about 500 families cheering below us. It was a fabulous special day.

For the rest of April, 3 Commando Brigade took over the security of the Rumaila oilfields from 16 Brigade, releasing them to go north to Maysan Province. It was in Maysan, at Majar Al Kabir on Tuesday, June 24, that an event took place that caused shockwaves both in the British military and at home. Six RMPs from 156 Provost Company, RMP were killed by an angry mob at the Police station in the town. They were Sgt Simon Hamilton-Jewell, Cpl Russell Aston, Cpl Paul Long, Cpl Simon Miller, L/Cpl Benjamin Hyde and L/Cpl Thomas Keys. The incident showed the lack of clear direction and liaison between the units in Maysan and the MOD was accused of another cover up. It also was another, large, thorn in the side of Tony Blair and of course meant six more grieving families.

With new troops arriving in Iraq, 42 Commando and their brothers in 40 got to go home in May. Capt Stu Taylor, 42 Commando:

> Before we finally left the palace on our final evening, the CO reminded me that a few months before, he and I had stopped in his car in Plymouth to get a McDonalds. He had remarked to me, 'Where do you think we will be in three months' time?' To which I replied, 'Sitting on the roof of Saddam's palace, watching a sunset with a gin and tonic!' Well, it wasn't quite like it, but it sure was close.
>
> At Az Zubayr port we waited for our withdrawal notice and to pass the time a BBQ was arranged and, as was customary, marines love dressing up, so we had a fancy-dress party. There was an air of jubilation and victory amongst us. It even felt good to go and take a crap in a presidential bog.
>
> Of course, the longer you are away from home the more you get paid, and you can get a bonus of about £1,500 for being away six months. If you go beyond that to the next increment, you get yet more money. So, when the talk of our likely routes home came to gossip in the mess tent, we heard that Richard Branson was fronting up a Virgin Atlantic 747 to get us home quickly. Alternatively, the grey fleet would take us home on HMS *Sir Galahad* (a new one after the other one was sunk in the Falklands). I was hoping to be on the ship so it took

longer and I could get the big bonus. I also thought that the sea journey would allow the guys time and space in private to relax and decompress before arriving back to normality. In the event, we went home Crab Air on a TriStar stopping at Cyprus first. As we refuelled, the aircraft broke down and we had to deplane. Humour was running short when it went from two hours to six hours waiting at the little terminal inside the base. Then we were told it would be the next day before we could move so we stood down in the barracks and went to the RAF bar and spent the night drinking beer and whisky till the small hours. The RAF Police got called when some emotions boiled over, and, I think, scores were settled, and it turned rough for a few minutes. Bearing in mind what we had been doing, it was expected and nothing more came of it. A diverted C-17 Globemaster came in and it swept down the runway to load us up. We did a head count and realised that we were one short. The CO said to me that if the late marine did not turn up soon, the plane would go without him, but that I would have to stay and find him. It wasn't what I wanted to hear, and I knew that my wife was expecting me back and would be very upset.

Minutes ticked by with us all sitting in the hold looking out the rear ramp. Suddenly a taxi was seen on the perimeter road by the taxiway. Marine Dick jumps out of the taxi and runs towards the plane. He wore nothing but a white bedsheet wrapped around him. Jumping onto the ramp, panting and looking utterly ridiculous Dick said, 'You won't believe me!' With a press of a button the loadmaster shut the ramp and the engines fired up for take-off. It transpired, so Dick said, that he had sneaked out of camp to the local bar where he chatted up a Swedish air hostess who took him to her hotel room. When he woke up, she was gone, his clothes were gone and he was tied to the headboard. Hours later we touched down at Exeter Airport and disembarked in front of the cameras and our families. By now the Julius Caesar lookalike in white sheet had borrowed some plain clothes and he slipped off the plane last to avoid the inquiring looks.

On reflection of *Telic* my view is that the army and marines were very much still stuck in an outdated mindset, framed by 20 years of peacekeeping and policing actions in Northern Ireland and the Balkans. We had been patrolling with berets and just 20 rounds of ammo, in single vehicles but with very restrictive rules of engagement. To then switch to weapons-free full-on war in Iraq was a big jump and not everyone made that jump easily. As the war transitioned back to the policing and insurgency phase, some units and individuals struggled to acknowledge how dangerous it still was and treated it as a benign environment: it was anything but. I think that's what led to the six RMPs being murdered. My unit's only casualty was the lad breaking his leg getting off the Chinook, so we got away surprisingly lightly. Some lads have even said that they didn't feel they had been in a proper war. They expected trench-clearing with bayonets, but some never fired a shot. At an informal debrief the CO said to them, 'Be careful what you wish for,' and true enough they were all soon to be involved in further roulements on *Telic* and in serious combat in Afghanistan. Some lost their lives to IEDs and so forth over the next few years.

Britain had committed 12% of its military forces on Operation *Telic*. The US committed just under 5% of its military to Iraq and for the Australians the figure was just 2%. Despite the low percentage, Australia was still in the top four of nations contributing to the invasion aims. The profile of forces deployed by the Howard Government in Australia largely followed that in Afghanistan – Special Forces backed by an air and naval component. The Royal Australian Air Force flew Orion maritime patrol aircraft, and 75 Squadron, RAAF flew its 14 F/A-18 Hornets on 350 sorties dropping 122 laser-guided bombs. At sea the destroyer HMAS *Anzac* had fired its five-inch gun in support of Operation *Houghton* and provided on-call fire support through ANGLICO teams to 3 Commando Brigade as it moved north up the Al-Faw. The transport ship HMAS *Kanimbla* had performed a variety of tasks with its 350 embarked troops, navy clearance divers and two helicopters, including capturing an Iraqi ship with 86 sea mines hidden aboard. The Australian Navy vessels set for home in late May 2003. Dr Sarah Chapman-Trim was aboard HMAS *Kanimbla*:

> A ship is a hungry mistress. Just because she may be moored alongside, doesn't mean no one has to be on her. Around a third of the crew are normally needed to carry on functions, even while in port. To enable this fairly after Op *Falconer* (Iraq), we sent home one third of the crew early, by air, so they could get some leave then be back on board to fulfil that dockside function. Before they flew, I did what is known as Return to Australia (RTA) assessments on them all. People were encouraged to open up about their experiences and any troublesome issues. Two guys had also served in the Falklands War and clearly carried with them some trauma from that war too. Most people were fine, others clearly were stressed and expressed sincere thanks for the system putting me in place to at least make people feel cared for.
>
> I returned on *Kanimbla* after our allotted time in the Gulf and later that year was lecturing at the international naval conference, I thought about the senior officer who had once laughed at me and my ambitions and wondered if she would be laughing now. Op *Falconer* (*Telic*) was one of the highlights of my naval career and I am proud of what I helped deliver in my supporting role.[*]

For other members of the *Telic* force going home was not yet an option and they were deployed onto other tasks. One operation was mounted by the British Army to try and recruit and motivate local Iraqi workers to return to work in vital infrastructure settings, such as electricity and water supply. To finance this operation, it was decided to use money held in the local bank vaults. Maj John Cotterill, attached 1 IG:

> We took a patrol into central Basra, to the central business district where there were numerous banks. Looters had made tremendous efforts to break into the Basra banks including their vaults. They were using bullets, explosives and RPGs to try and smash their way in. It was clearly a dangerous pastime as there were pools of blood and bits of bodies where the looters, in such confined spaces found out the hard way about back blast and ricochets on steel doors. As we arrived at another very solid, stone-built building, the Bank of Basra, I was standing right outside the main doors when suddenly an Iraqi came running out of the door to the bank. He was wide-eyed and holding a bayonet. It was a typical cheap AK-47 bayonet with a brown Bakelite handle which he had then wrapped strips of white cloth around to make it more comfortable to hold as a knife. He was about 10m away from me, coming straight at me. I shot him, he kept coming and I stepped back, knelt and shot again. He kept coming so I shot a third time and he pitched over, dead. It had taken four rounds from my 5.56mm SA80 to stop him. I was stunned. When I finally had stopped him, he was virtually touching me. The linkman Guardsman behind me called to me saying we had to move on, but I told him to wait as I needed to check my grouping on the dead Iraqi. It sounds bizarre, but I needed to see if and where I had hit the target – all good hits in the centre mass.

---

[*] HMAS *Kanimbla* was awarded the meritorious unit citation for its role in the Persian Gulf in 2003.

For the next two weeks, we returned to the same Bank of Basra and continued trying to get into the basement vault. We knew we would need specialist equipment, so I went off into the back streets and came across a workshop with a guy using oxyacetylene cutting gear. Using my Arabic, I asked if he would come and help us break into a bank, for a payment of course. He was very happy to oblige. He also brought with him a concrete pneumatic breaker and a team of guys to work together breaking and cutting their way in over a 24-hour shift. We had a team of 12 Micks constantly on sentry at the bank for the whole two weeks it took us to finally get in.

At night the local 'Ali Babas' would try and use the cover of darkness to get close to the bank in order to grab some loot. They were not aware we had night vision sights on our weapons and could easily see them slithering along on their bellies in the gutter or alleyways. We didn't shoot them as they were unarmed but we would let them know we saw them and encouraged their departure.

Mounds of cash were eventually loaded onto Bedfords and removed to the palace for onwards distribution. An absolute mountain of bank notes; Iraqi Dinars were counted, and it totalled 56 billion Dinars, which equated to US$18 million. Certainly, enough to pay the oil and electric workers for some time to come.

10 Field Squadron, RE had been camped in Kuwait until May 2003 and went north to Basra as the war fighting ended. They were tasked with a series of jobs making the area safer and helping get the local infrastructure working again. In command of Support Troop within the squadron was Capt Jon Milner:

Our base was at Basra Airport alongside 53 Squadron. I was in command of Support Troop which has all the heavy plant like diggers, fuel bowsers, dump trucks and DROPS lorries.

Our first big job was at Shaiba Air Base. Weapons, bombs and rockets were turning up by the ton and had to be stored securely. To start with, it was just stacked at Shaiba but numerous locals kept stealing it, so we had to construct a sealed, sheltered ammo compound for all the weaponry coming in. Sentries and snipers were put out on picket to keep away unwanted visitors while we worked. There were several HAS (hardened aircraft shelters) around the base, all of which had been partially destroyed by Coalition air strikes. One or two, though, were still of sound construction and we used them as a base for building the ammo shelters around, bulldozing berms, erecting fences and gates etc. The result was a secure and shaded depository for tons of weapons.

The largest single task we had was working with a group called Prime Power. These are a mixed civilian and military outfit from the US Corps of Engineers, and they are a globetrotting unit of problem solvers that get national grids up and running after wars or earthquakes. They flew into us on Blackhawk helicopters to help us get the Shaiba Refinery powered up again. Captain Geoff Van Epps and his team were superb and together we got the job done.

Shaiba oil and gas refinery used surplus gas to power gas turbines that generated electricity which in turn pumped fuel direct to petrol stations across southern Iraq. With the refinery knocked offline, traditional fuel bowsers were having to deliver petrol along increasingly treacherous road journeys, which was leading to shortages and bad press. Prime Power brought in 30 generators, each the size of an ISO container, that could generate one megawatt each. All 30 were lined up at Shaiba and when they were turned on, the 30MW power kickstarted the gas turbines and powered the fuel pipelines back into action. The flare flame that burns above the tower shot up 60m with the increase in efficiency. Even British

Prime Minister Tony Blair passed his thanks on to Prime Power and the Royal Engineers at Shaiba. Van Epps was so pleased he ordered in 20 pizzas for the Sappers, which made a welcome change from their rations and canteen food. Capt Jon Milner:

> After Prime Power came the CIA. They had a unit set up with portacabins and tents at Basra and came asking for help one day. They had a satellite dish that needed to be erected a lot higher up than they could reach for it to function properly. We had a crane and so offered to get it hooked up on a mast in return for a pallet of Gator Aid that we could see out the back of their portacabin. Quid pro Quo.

S/Sgt Mark Goldsmith, 28 Engineer Regiment, 165 Field Support Squadron, RE moved to Shaiba Air Base after Kuwait:

> We had a place there near HQ 7 Armoured Brigade. Our diggers and plant machines were busy making defensive berms, flattening out areas for tents, including our own, making trenches for shelter and defence and of course helping make the base more comfortable for everyone there. This included the need for field hygiene facilities, also known as bogs. We took great pride in the gradual development of these facilities from the entry level 'Mk I Shitter' – the desert rose plastic pipe for wee, and shallow trenches for a poo which was set alight with diesel. Then as the campaign went on and we had more time we progressed through the 'Mk II' which featured hessian wrapping around six-foot iron pickets to give some privacy for the squatting individual, then subsequent marks featured timber-frame toilets with an actual plastic toilet seat over the long drop, then a bit of wrinkly tin as a roof on the 'Mk IV'. Finally, we launched the 'Mk VI Super Shitter' complete with timber sheet sides, lockable doors and even loo roll holders. Plastic contractor Portaloos arrived later but they were a retrograde step because of the 45°C heat just cooked people in seconds.
>
> One evening at Shaiba a scream and shout went up causing everyone to grab their gear, helmets and weapons and start heading to their stand to positions. I then saw that one of my team, Cpl Steve Warren, was running towards me and it was he who was shouting and looking down at his groin. He had been in his tent, in his doss bag and was only wearing boxer shorts. He was very red-faced and looked in a panic. He said, 'I've just been bitten on the balls by a fucking Camel Spider.' The subsequent bruising and swelling were intensely painful for Steve but the rest of us, of course, found it hilarious. We sent him off to the field hospital and I ended the evening with my troop sergeant who made lovely coffee with a splash of Baileys in it that he had got smuggled out hidden in his post in miniature bottles.

Probably the only WMD found in Iraq were the Working Military Dogs which were built a new kennel by 10 Field Squadron, RE at the air base complete with shaded runs and air-conditioning. Overheating was not only a problem for dogs in the increasingly hot Iraqi summer but also for aircraft and any crew sat in them. The RAF had a problem with the Canberra and its crews overheating when on the apron for more than a few minutes. Canberra was a Cold War aircraft built to operate in the cold air above northern Europe, not the 50°C heat of the Middle East. It was found that the extreme heat could overload the electrical circuits and even start to boil the crew under the glass of the cockpit canopy which would distort, then jam if not opened quickly. The Sappers of 10 Field Squadron were asked to come up with a solution. Capt Jon Milner:

We brought over a bunch of empty ISO containers and put them on top of each other making a U-shape out of three stacks of three containers. The nose and cockpit of the aircraft could get inside the U-shape just leaving the tail fin protruding. We then dragged thick ropes and hessian screen over the top of the ISO containers, which we also covered in scrim and camouflage nets, and secured them tightly to the ground thus creating a shaded spot for the aircraft to taxi into the moment after landing.

Just after we built the aircraft shades my hand went all weird and I had to have an operation. I am not sure if I was bitten on the bottom of my finger by an insect or if I had a needlestick type of injury that got infected very quickly but it resulted in my hand swelling up like gangrene. Initially, I was given some anti-inflammatory pills but the next day it was yellow and looking awful. The doctors said I would be operated on that day and would then be flown home within a few hours. On hearing this I asked my Troop Corporal to grab my Bergen with my gear so I could take that home. I was operated on at the field hospital at Shaiba under general anaesthetic. They opened my hand and cleaned out all the pus and gunk. I woke up in a lovely clean bed in the air-conditioned recovery ward at Shaiba. Then I was flown out from Basra by the RAF to the UK, I can't recall if it was RAF Lyneham, but I was put on a bus that took me to Selly Oak Hospital in Birmingham. Selly Oak was just a general A&E hospital. I was still in full desert combats with my Bergen, and it was only 24 hours since leaving Basra. I found myself sitting amongst the population of Birmingham and felt very out of place. Me in my soldier's desert war uniform with what looked like a wounded hand wrapped in bandages. It didn't feel right. I decided to pass the time with a look at my personal gear in my Bergen which my corporal had grabbed for me. How delighted I was to find the sum total of the kit he had packed amounted to a breeze block, three Porno mags and some dirty undies. Thanks guys, you were amazing.

The work of 10 Squadron, RE shows just one small cog in the working parts of the efforts to get Iraq back on its feet after the invasion, but it provides a window into the tempo and style of the operations that were to follow *Telic 1* with a focus on peacekeeping and self-help regeneration amidst the growing turmoil and chaos of the Iranian-backed uprisings.

As the tempo and style of operations changed in May 2003 it was clear that no WMD had as yet been found and with much pressure from governmental levels the military formed search parties for one final effort of finding the 'smoking gun' which at best thus far looked like a dribbling water pistol. WO2 Andy Abbott, RE:

One high point for me was selection to be part of the JFEODG (Joint Forces EOD Group) in late May. Some of that work remains secret even today. I was called to Basra Palace and spoken to by a brigadier general about the role that the OC had selected me for. I would be working alongside an RE staff sergeant and a captain from the RLC High Threat EOD team. We were to help look for WMD.

The prewar searches for WMD had found nothing but the Coalition was seeking to justify its war. Our team was to go up to Baghdad with a mixed unit of US Delta Force, Rangers and UK SF troops, interpreters and some scientists. We were given the codename Task Force 22.

Our briefing was from a man in civilian clothes who simply introduced himself as 'Martin' and said that he worked for Mr Blair and Number 10. I imagine he was from MI6 and that he definitely wasn't called Martin! We were given a list of 22 sites we had to search. These consisted of industrial units, hospitals, factories, and some large private houses. One was owned by Saddam's own biochemist, a lady who was thought to have buried ampules of anthrax in the garden. There were no signs of poverty with her, it was like a palace, and I remember there was even a gold revolver on the wall. She started to kick off when the SF guys arrested her, and the kids started wailing but it all seemed very false.

On another, quite different, search near Tikrit, there was a giant Iraqi Air Force bombing range. After we went through the main gate, we drove for about 25–30 minutes along this dirt track and passed hundreds of unexploded air-dropped bombs all over the place, some stacked up, others sticking out the sand. It was such a mess. That search was following information from a scientist who said that chemical weapons had been buried in a big container on the range. They searched the spot which showed sign of having been dug before, but again nothing was found. I'm certain the Iraqis had this stuff before, but it was long gone now. One of the US team told me the Iraqis had a system of removing people from the chain of command to reduce the risk of anyone finding anything or being able to pass on that information under interview.

While in the Green Zone in Baghdad we went to a hunting lodge owned by one of Saddam's sons. It had been bombed but there was intel it may hide WMD in underground tunnels. The search came up with nothing again, but I did see a large Saddam painted mural just outside. As an avid West Ham United fan, I am a true Hammer (our club crest involves two crossed hammers) and I felt it was my duty to let the locals know of my level of support. Grabbing some spray paint (army issue) from the trailer I then sprayed a pair of hammers on the mural so that I could get a photo and send it in to the supporter's club. John offered to take the photo, so we got ready to take the picture. What I had not realised was that in between time with another tin of paint, John who is not a Hammer had sprayed a pair of cock and balls as well, so it wasn't suitable for the supporters' club, but it made us laugh. We finished that day by gatecrashing an American BBQ at their camp in the airport. The Yanks really take care of the servicemen and women and lay on much better food for them. We spoke to the chefs and asked for a tray of sirloin steaks, and they said, 'Sure but what can you give us?' We offered two AK-47s. They were happy and we got our great steaks with a cold beer.

Our searches in Baghdad and up to Tikrit in the north found nothing of importance. The film *Green Zone* with Matt Damon was based on this group and the searches we did. It was an interesting time in my army service. We didn't find anything but that didn't alter the outcome of the war although it framed some people's opinions further about the reasons for it in the first place. Looking back on it I realise I was part of history because of what we did and what we didn't reveal.

We came home via Cyprus to Chilwell. I had been there four months on tour. Before I got a chance to change my tour uniform, I got shouted at by the RSM for being a scruffy bastard crossing his parade square, that really brought me back down to earth that we were home!

I had five minutes on paperwork and a doctor asked me if I was OK – that was the extent of the PTSD screening.

Within three days I was at home with my wife Sue via my Mum's in Lincolnshire. There was some nice welcome home stuff in my street – posters and flags to welcome me back. It was a nice touch by the neighbours and their kids. I had four weeks of paid leave owed me from the army then, so we went to Rome for a holiday, and I enjoyed eating the local grub. I had lost so much weight on *Telic* more than a stone, I think.

The rapid drawdown of the forces in Iraq was part of the plan. By the end of May half the 46,000 troops deployed initially were home and by July they all were. The strategy from Whitehall was that the Iraqis would take over and run the country seizing their own destiny. However, the continual drop in numbers undermined the effectiveness of those still 'in country' and the list of forces available changed each week causing confusion at command level. Both Brig Graham Binns and Gen Robin Brims had been due to take on new jobs just before *Telic*, so they, too, were replaced at what was a delicate time in the recovery of Iraq from the war. Some of the last to go home of the original units to arrive in Iraq were the doctors, nurses and support staff of the army hospitals and other medical units. Lt Zoe Ferry RLC, attached RAMC:

> When I got home, I was on my own and had travelled independently of my unit for some reason, but my twin sister (nurse) was still in Iraq, my Mum was away, and my other sister was at work, so I had to get a taxi from the airport. My first journey took me to Tesco so I could get a big fruit smoothie. I was still in my desert DPM uniform, and no one even looked at me, no one gave a shit. It had all been lies by Blair, there were no WMD, and the Government knew it. I look back and feel a bit ashamed, I was very naïve.

The work Lt Zoe Ferry and others did at 202 Field Hospital should be remembered for more than its assistance to British forces. Far more Iraqis than British soldiers were cared for there. On one typical day there were 125 casualties: 26 British, 74 prisoners of war and 25 Iraqi civilians. The hospital began to see an unexpected influx of civilians, many of them children. The CO faced a growing dilemma around dealing with Iraqis. The Kuwaiti authorities had forbidden the British from allowing treatment of any Iraqis on Kuwaiti soil, but they kept arriving. RAF Chinooks, US Blackhawk MERT (medical emergency response team) flights and traditional army ambulances kept arriving at the entrance to the hospital. They would not turn them away, yet the balance was in danger of tipping. The hospital had only a limited number of beds, nurses and medical supplies and its mission first and foremost was to save the lives of British soldiers.

Lt Col Sarah Philips, a surgeon, was from south-east London and said she was used to dealing with gunshot wounds, but what she was asked to deal with on *Telic* was different as they were not equipped to deal with children in a military hospital.

One child, called Hassan, about ten, was playing in an alleyway at the side of his house in Basra when an explosion blew him and his brother across the road. Two inches of bone above his ankle was splintered and left a gaping eight-inch gash on his leg. His family had to leave it until morning and got a taxi to try and take Hassan to Basra Hospital. En route they were stopped by a British patrol who took Hassan and his father to the field hospital as it was more dangerous to let them drive across the city through areas still being fought over. The British Army surgeons tried to stabilise his leg with external pins, but no paediatric size pins were stocked because it was equipped to deal with adult soldiers. The surgeons adapted some hard plastic tubing and made a makeshift splint and covered the wound with a string vest type skin graft.

Ali Karrar, another young Basra boy, was wounded when he picked up an unexploded submunition which detonated, wounding him in several places. He arrived at hospital alone and nothing was known about his family – a truly awful and terrifying experience for a little boy. Nurses started to strip him of his bloody clothing, looking for more small but potentially lethal wounds, when they found a rolled-up US dollar bill taped to his hand. Ali would not give up his dollar until one nurse offered him a US $5 bill as a swap.

Ali had been wounded by lots of tiny metal fragments. One took off his little toe, another entered his shin bone, while the most worrying for the Doctor (Major Phil Henman) was a penetrating wound into his abdomen. He was quickly taken to surgery and whilst nurses swatted flies off the blood-soaked sheets Ali was sewn up and stabilised. X-rays showed that a metal splinter had punctured the bowel in four places, contamination was evident and could have become fatal and so he was then operated on for a second time. This intervention certainly saved his life.

British military admissions remained at a trickle, but the hospital was declared full, mainly with locals. News of the hospital attracted civilians from Iraq who were not only wounded but were suffering from pre-existing illnesses and comorbidities for which they couldn't get treatment in Basra and went to the British seeking aid. This was a serious headache for the management of the hospital as their limited resources were not equipped to deal with numerous family members, non-English speaking patients, dietary differences, cultural issues and the sheer volume and complexity of pharmacy requests. It was eventually decided that the British would run a convoy of nine patients and a dozen close family, into Basra Hospital. It was not possible prior to departure of the convoy to get a response from the hospital in Basra so they would be arriving unexpectedly. The route was not totally safe, there was the risk of the vehicles being attacked by Fedayeen, so curtains were kept closed and armed guards travelled in each vehicle. A combination of hired coaches, army ambulances and a couple of Land Rovers completed the column. It was a tense ride for all the adults, both British and Iraqi, but the kids thought it was a grand day out.

Col Jackson then completed a clinical handover of each patient before the column withdrew back to Kuwait. Young Ali Karrar, still with a $5 bill clutched in his hand, had been told that his father was waiting for him but upon arrival in Basra he could not be found.

In two months in the sand, 202 Field Hospital treated hundreds of Iraqis with combat injuries and just 22 wounded British soldiers. Dozens more civilians were also treated. After two months in the Kuwaiti desert, it was moved north to Shaiba Air Base but by then most of its TA soldiers had gone back to their day jobs. Lt Col Tuck, RAMC recalled:

> I had a very, very long journey home complete with the obligatory argument with some jobsworth on Crab Air. We were welcomed back by the Army Surgeon General which was very nice. I had zero decompression time and was straight back to Preston to sort out other soldiers' post-operation tour leave.
>
> Just after I got home, I went to a dinner party with a bunch of friends and was assailed by one individual on how I managed my conscience at taking part in an unjust war. I responded that we had deployed to do the will of the democratically elected UK government so if there was any soul searching to be done, perhaps they as Labour voters should go and look in a mirror.

Years later I reflect that the war, however, was indeed an unjust war and I regret that the PM at the time, Tony Blair has not been brought to account nor will he be.

The wounded L/Sgt Bob Giles of the Micks flew to Britain from Basra after spending some time at 202 Field Hospital. He was taken to Heartlands Hospital in Birmingham only a few miles from his family home where he had continued treatment to heal his left lung and two ribs that were missing a few centimetres of bone.

> The pain was now just too much. I'm not proud of it, but if someone had lent over me and said, 'Listen son, we can end this now. Just give us the word and we'll put a bullet in your head,' I would have welcomed it. I was stuck in a body that was torturing me but wouldn't let me pass out. It wouldn't let me breathe, and even attempting to do so was too much pain. 'I could die here, on an operating table, after being wounded in battle. I'm ready and everyone at home will be OK with it, come on, let me die and stop this unbearable pain of not being able to breathe.' I couldn't even cry. I was just laid out on my back, gasping like a fish out of water, wide eyed. I thought that now it was I who had that wide-eyed terror look that I had seen in so many Iraqis, but the odd thing was I wasn't scared. Not of death, I would have welcomed it. I wanted it. I just wanted the pain to stop and for everybody to stop faffing around and let me die. I passed out again.
>
> I woke only seconds later knowing I had wet myself. A nurse was looking straight into my eyes. All of a sudden, I could breathe a whole lot better, and the pain was slightly more manageable. 'I'm sorry but I've just peed all over your table.' 'I know love, never mind though, aye? Is there anything we can get you?' 'Yes, a cup of coffee, two sugars and a fag.'

Bob's recovery journey was already underway and part of it was the need he felt to thank those around him who had been so key in saving his life. Guardsman Lee Wheeler and L/Cpl Simon Campbell were top of his list, and he wrote up recommendations that they both should be rewarded for their gallantry. Officers would normally be needed to witness these incidents, but such was the power of his written word and the corroboration given that indeed they were both awarded the Queen's Gallantry Medal. The report said their 'swift actions, bravery and professionalism' helped save their section commander's life. Bob was also keen to thank Maj Burgess for his role with the chest drain and giving lifesaving drugs.

> From the moment I left Iraq, my regiment never once asked me how I was, how they could help or even offer me rehabilitation and physio to get me back in to work; they did nothing. I was off on the sick for four months and in that time the battalion had several piss ups and a medal ceremony, but I never got even a phone call or a bunch of flowers.
>
> All the senior NCOs and key officers had moved on after Iraq and so when I finally got back to battalion, they were like 'who are you?' No one gave a shit. I know there are several dozen other soldiers like me in the Guards who were treated equally as bad. To me, it destroyed the saying that suggests the regiment is family. When the two lads went to Buck House to get their gongs (medals) in 2004, the Queen asked them if I had survived. When they said yes, she asked for me to come right away. We were only based around the corner at Wellington Barracks, so they called me, and I got my best kit on and went to the palace. When the three of us walked back, the new RSM saw us and asked where we had been. I told him, 'To get their Queen's Gallantry Medals.' The RSM just grunted and walked away. He had not been to Iraq, so he didn't give a shit either. I went through a very long period of getting very angry and annoyed with the army.

Incredibly, Bob Giles made a full physical recovery and went on to serve for 23 years and was commissioned, reaching the rank of major. He today has the 7.62mm bullet, and the rear armour plate it ploughed into after leaving his chest, mounted in a smart frame on his office wall as another reminder of 10 April 2003, and how close he walked to death.

A total of 179 British Armed Forces' personnel have died on operations in Iraq since March 2003. Of those, 136 were killed as a result of hostile action. The 43 others died because of accidents or illnesses or have yet to be officially assigned a cause of death pending investigations.[1]

Thirty-three of those who died in Iraq did so in the period focussed on in this book, that main period of war-fighting operations between 20 March and 30 April. Two major Iraqi divisions had been defeated and Basra had been occupied without an urban warfare bloodbath. On the whole veterans and other written sources agree that the vast majority of the population engaged with in southern Iraq originally gave a warm welcome to the British forces. Their pitiful living conditions opposite the vulgar opulence of Saddam Hussein and his henchmen also reinforced the feeling amongst the service personnel that good may come of the ridding of the regime.

Sadly, the lack of planning and poor execution of Phase IV (after the war) sowed the seeds for the subsequent rotating troops to face a growing insurrection. Washington and Whitehall's lack of engagement with the Iraqi people was also a growing concern for the British military patrolling the streets of Basra and Az Zubayr, who felt they were no longer in control and were losing the consent of the population. The incoming command team for Operation *Telic 2* was tasked with 'creating an environment where it will be safe to draw down on UK Forces and in which the Iraqis will become responsible for their own security'.[2] The success of *Telic 2* or any of the other *Telic*s (13 in all) up until 2009 can be judged by the reader. What is clear is that the legitimacy of the US-led occupation was eroded and many other countries' governments backed away from association with it. The political and military credibility of the UK was damaged, and the authority of the US in the Middle East has greatly diminished. In 2007 British Lt Gen Graeme Lamb, deputy commander in Iraq, said 'this is as complex as anything I have ever done … this is three-dimensional chess in a dark room.'[3]

Hundreds of thousands of people have been killed in the two Iraq wars. 4,500 US military have lost their lives plus another 1,500 contractors. The credible estimate for civilian deaths between March 2003 and 2020 sits close to 200,000. Alongside the cost in lives, it also cost the British taxpayer £9.2 billion.

In line with the aim of this work, giving voice to the veterans of *Telic*, it is right that the last line should go to one of them, Col Jim Tanner, HQ 1 UK DIV:

> In 2009 I was flying home from a trip to Saudi Arabia – sat on a flight next to Labour MP, Coventry born, Bob Ainsworth. He was a Labour MP for about 25 years and in 2003 was the

Under Secretary of state for Home Affairs. In fact, later in 2008 he became the Secretary of State for Defence under Gordon Brown which is why he had been to Saudi.

I asked if I could talk to him about the Iraq war in 2003 and he said yes, he would love to as he didn't sleep well on aeroplanes, and it would pass the time.

What had troubled me for many years, was that as a soldier, you can't not want to be involved in a conflict like Iraq, it's the soldiering that you join up for and that you want to do. However, you must remove yourself from any of the shenanigans and politics that surround it. I said to him.

'I feel lied to, deliberately, by our Prime Minister, because I am sure he knew there was no weapons of mass destruction and he just wanted to be a war leader in a bomber jacket just like Bush'

Ainsworth nodded and said 'You think you were lied to! I was lied to, and I was his mate!'

Glossary

1 IG	1st Battalion, Irish Guards
1 LI	1st Battalion, Light Infantry
1 MEF	1 Marine Expeditionary Force
1 RRF	1st Battalion, Royal Regiment of Fusiliers
16 AAB	16 Air Assault Brigade
1 MARDIV	1st Marine Division, USMC
1 UKDIV	1st (UK) Armoured Division
2IC	second in command
A-day	Operation *Telic*'s start of air operations
AAC	Army Air Corps
AEW	air expeditionary wing
ANGLICO	Air Naval Gunfire Liaison Company
APFSDS	armour-piercing fin-stabilised discarding sabot
APS	artillery pointing system
ARP	aviation reconnaissance patrol
ATGW	anti-tank guided weapon
BFA	battlefield ambulances
BG	battlegroup
BSM	band sergeant major
BV	boiling vessel
CAOC	Combined Air Operations Centre
CASEVAC	casualty evacuation
CBRN	chemical, biological, radiological and nuclear
CENTCOM	Central Command
CET	combat engineer tractor
COMATG	Commander Amphibious Task Group
CRA	Commander Royal Artillery
CRARRV	Challenger armoured repair and recovery vehicle
CSAR	combat search and rescue
CVRT	combat vehicle reconnaissance (tracked)
DROPS	demountable rack offload and pick up system
EOD	explosive ordnance disposal

FAA	forward assembly area
FAC	forward air controller
FARP	forward arming and refuelling point
Fin see APFSDS	
FOO	forward observation officer
FUP	form-up point
G-day	Operation *Telic*'s start of ground operations
GOSP	gas oil separation plant
GPMG	general-purpose machine gun
GSB	general support bridge
GSMR	general support medical regiment
HCR	Household Cavalry
HESH	high explosive squash head
HLS	helicopter landing site
IADS	integrated air defence system
IFF	identification friend or foe
IFV	infantry fighting vehicle
IG	Irish Guards
INC	Iraqi National Congress
ISTAR	intelligence, surveillance, targeting and reconnaissance
(I)TOW	(improved) tube-launched optically-sighted wire-guided)
JDAM	joint direct attack munition
JSOTF-W	Joint Special Operations Task Force-West
KI/CAS	kill-box interdiction/close air support
LCVP	landing craft vehicle/personnel.
LI	The Light Infantry
LS	long span
LSW	light support weapon
Map SP	a map supply post
MBT	main battle tank
MFC	mortar fire controller
MLRS	multi-launch rocket system
MMS	monitoring and metering station
MSR	main supply route
NBC	nuclear, biological and chemical
NTM	notice to move
NVGs	night vision goggles
OSG	offensive support group
PGM	precision guided munition
PR	photo-reconnaissance
PRR	personal role radios

PSAB	Prince Sultan Air Base
PSAO	permanent staff administrative officer
QDG	Queen's Dragoon Guards
QMI	senior quartermaster instructor
QRL	Queen's Royal Lancers
RAMC	Royal Army Medical Corps
RAPTOR	reconnaissance airborne pod Tornado
RCT	regimental combat team
RHA	Reserve Hardship Award
RHA	Royal Horse Artillery
RHQ	regimental headquarters
RLC	Royal Logistic Corps
ROE	rules of engagement
RPG	rocket-propelled grenade
RRF	Royal Regiment of Fusiliers
RSA	Reserve Standards Award
RSDG	Royal Scots Dragoon Guards
RSO	regimental signals officer
RTR	Royal Tank Regiment
SF	special forces (UK/US SF)
SOP	standard operating procedure
SSE	sensitive site exploitation
TA	Territorial Army
TAA	tactical assembly area
TD	tactical director
TF	task force
TIIW	tactical imagery and intelligence wing
TNTLS	tactical navigation and targeting system
TST	time-sensitive target
UAV	unmanned aerial vehicle
USMC	US Marine Corps
VCP	vehicle check point
WMD	weapons of mass destruction

Endnotes

Chapter 1

1 Christopher Meyer, *DC Confidential* (2005).
2 Ibid.
3 Sir John Chilcot, *The Report of the Iraq Inquiry* (2016).
4 Peter Beaumont, Antony Barnett and Gaby Hinsliff, 'Iraqi mobile labs nothing to do with germ warfare, report finds', *The Observer* (15 June 2003).
5 Shane Harris and Matthew M. Aid, 'Exclusive: CIA Files Prove America Helped Saddam as He Gassed Iran'. *Foreign Policy* (26 August 2013).
6 Benjamin S. Lambeth, 'AirLand Reversal', *Air & Space Forces* (1 February 2014).
7 Tim Ripley, *Operation Telic: The British Campaign in Iraq 2003–2009* (2014).
8 Ibid.

Chapter 2

1 Lt Col Orpen-Smellie, 'Mobilisation', *British Army Journal* (2004).
2 Nicholas Pettit, *Modern Day Hero* (2007).

Chapter 3

1 Ritchie, Dr Sebastian, 'The RAF in Operation Telic: Offensive Air Power, March–April 2003', *Air Power Review* (Winter 2015).
2 Lt Col J. Storr, *The Command of British Land Forces in Iraq 2003*, Army Doctrine Paper (2003).
3 Ibid.
4 Captain Coates RRF, 'The infantryman', *British Army Journal* (2003).
5 Pettit, *Modern Day Hero*.
6 Brigadier A. Gregory CRA, *Journal of the Royal Artillery* (2004).
7 MOD Military Aircraft, Board of Inquiry accident summary RAF Tornado Mk4 ZG710 (2004) www.GOV.UK.
8 Damien Lewis, *Zero Six Bravo* (2013).

Chapter 4

1 Mike Rossiter, *Target Basra* (2004).

Chapter 5

1 Coates, *British Army Journal* (2003).
2 Lt Olly Campbell, '1RRF BG breach into Iraq – A Platoon perspective', *British Army Journal* (2003).
3 Lt Thomas Orde-Powlett, 'Iraq 2003 – A Platoon Commander's perspective', *British Army Journal* (2003).
4 Pettit, *Modern Day Hero.*
5 Ibid.

Chapter 6

1 Mick Flynn, *Bullet Magnet* (2010).
2 Sgt D. Clarke, 'Operation Telic, I R Irish BG, A NCO's experience', *Journal of the British Army* (2004).
3 Flynn, *Bullet Magnet.*

Chapter 7

1 Fiona Wingett, 'I saw Cherie weep for her son going to university. I've given my lovely twins to a war I can't believe in', *The Mail on Sunday* (30 March 2003).
2 Niall Edworthy, *Main Battle Tank* (2010).
3 Ibid.

Chapter 8

1 The Royal Regiment of Fusiliers, *Hackles Raised: The Story of the First Fusiliers Battlegroup's Battle for Basra 2003* (Gateway, Cambridge 2003).
2 S/Sgt Shepherd, AAC 662 Squadron: After action report (2004).

Chapter 9

1 Edworthy, *Main Battle Tank.*

Chapter 10

1 Tim Ripley, *Operation Telic: The British Campaign in Iraq 2003–2009.*
2 Sgt Maj J. Tymon, AAC 662 Squadron: report (2004).
3 Ibid.
4 The Royal Regiment of Fusiliers, *Hackles Raised.*

Chapter 11

1 Ministry of Defence, UK Government Website, www.gov.uk/government/fields-of-operations-iraq
2 Tim Ripley, *Operation Telic: The British Campaign in Iraq 2003–2009.*
3 Ben Barry, *Blood, Metal and Dust: How Victory Turned into Defeat in Afghanistan and Iraq* (2020).

Sources

First-Hand Accounts

I wish to acknowledge my debt to all the following, without whose valuable assistance this book could never have been written.

Company Sergeant Major Andy Abbott, Royal Engineers
Staff Sergeant Bertie Banfield, Army Air Corps
Marine Barney Barnett, Royal Marines
Sergeant Major Jon Bell, Royal Army Medical Corps
Corporal Scott Blaney, Royal Electrical and Mechanical Engineers
Major Tim Brown, Royal Scots Dragoon Guards
Corporal Paul Burton, Royal Electrical and Mechanical Engineers (Attached Black Watch Regiment)
Lieutenant Sarah Chapman-Trim, Royal Australian Navy Psychologist
Colour Sergeant Dom Collins, Royal Marines
Major John Cotterill, Worcester and Sherwood Foresters (Attached Irish Guards)
Lieutenant Ian Cross, Royal Tank Regiment
Major Ben Curry, Royal Marines
Major Gareth Davies, Royal Tank Regiment
Sergeant Gary Edwards, RAF Police
Sergeant Rey Fadil, Royal Engineers
Major Ben Farrell, Irish Guards
Lieutenant Zoe Ferry, Royal Logistics Corps
Sergeant Robert Giles, Irish Guards
Staff Sergeant Mark Goldsmith, Royal Engineers
Lieutenant Mick Garraway, Royal Australian Army (Attached Irish Guards)
Major David Green, Royal Army Medical Corps
Flight Lieutenant Andy Johnson, RAF
Corporal Steve Johnstone, Royal Electrical and Mechanical Engineers
Corporal Freddie Kruyer, Parachute Regiment
Major Duncan McSporran, Royal Regiment of Fusiliers
Captain Jonathan Milner, Royal Engineers
Lance Corporal Steve Penney, Royal Marines
Lieutenant Commander Jon Pentreath, Royal Naval Air Service
Captain Mike Peters, Army Air Corps
Lieutenant Ed Pugh, Royal Regiment of Fusiliers
Lieutenant Chris Rees-Gay, Royal Regiment of Fusiliers
Band Sergeant Major Leigh Sharpe, attached Royal Army Medical Corps
Chief Petty Officer Peter Skyrme, Royal Navy
Colonel Jim Tanner, Staffordshire Regiment (attached 1 (UK) Armoured Div HQ)
Major Stuart Taylor, Royal Marines

Lieutenant Colonel Jeremy Tuck, Royal Army Medical Corps
Squadron Leader Andy White, RAF
Marine Engineer Mechanic Anthony Williams, Royal Navy
Major Neil Wraith, Royal Marines

Books

Barry, Ben, *Blood, Metal and Dust: How Victory Turned into Defeat in Afghanistan and Iraq* (Osprey Publishing, 2020).
Edworthy, Niall, *Main Battle Tank* (Penguin, 2010).
Flynn, Mick, *Bullet Magnet* (Weidenfeld & Nicolson, 2010).
Lewis, Damien, *Zero Six Bravo* (Quercus, 2013).
Meyer, Christopher, *DC Confidential* (Phoenix, 2005).
Pettit, Nicholas, *Modern Day Hero* (Pegasus Elliot Mackenzie Publishers, 2007).
Ripley, Tim, *Operation Telic: The British Campaign in Iraq 2003–2009* (Telic-Herrick Publications, 2014).
RRF, *Hackles Raised, The Story of the First Fusiliers Battlegroup's battle for Basra,* Gateway, Cambridge (2003)
Rossiter, Mike, *Target Basra* (Corgi, 2004).
Salmon, Paul M., *Human Factors, Methods and Accident Analysis: Practical Guidance and Case Studies* (CRC Press, 2005).

Official Reports

Chilcot, Sir John (chairman): *The Report of the Iraq Inquiry,* 2016.
MOD Military Aircraft accident report, Board of Inquiry, 2004.
Shepherd, S/Sgt, AAC 662 Squadron: After action report, 2004.
Tymon, Sgt Maj J., AAC 662 Squadron: Report 2004.

Articles

Beaumont, Peter, Antony Barnett and Gaby Hinsliff, 'Iraqi mobile labs nothing to do with germ warfare, report finds', *The Observer* (15 June 2003).
Campbell, Lt Olly, RRF, '1RFF BG breach into Iraq – A platoon perspective', *British Army Journal* (2003).
Coates, Capt, RRF, 'Breach into Iraq', *British Army Journal* (2003).
Harris, Shane and Matthew M. Aid, 'Exclusive: CIA Files Prove America Helped Saddam as He Gassed Iran'. *Foreign Policy* (26 August 2013).
Lambeth, Benjamin S., 'AirLand Reversal', *Air & Space Forces Magazine* (1 February 2014).
Orde-Powlett MC, Lt The Hon Thomas, IG, 'Iraq 2003 – A Platoon Commander's perspective', *British Army Journal* (2003)
Ritchie, Dr Sebastian, 'The RAF in Operation Telic: Offensive Air Power, March–April 2003', *Air Power Review* (Winter 2015).
Sargent, Captain N., RA, 29 Commando Regiment 'Warfighting in Iraq', *Journal of the Royal Artillery,* Vol 131, 2004.
Storr, Lt Col J., *The Command of British Land Forces in Iraq 2003,* Army Doctrine Paper (2003).
Wingett, Fiona, 'I saw Cherie weep for her son going to university. I've given my lovely twins to a war I can't believe in', *The Mail on Sunday* (30 March 2003).

Websites

Ministry of Defence, UK Government Website, gov.uk

Index